FOUNDATIONS
of Social Work Practice
in the Field of **Aging**

A Competency-Based Approach

2nd Edition

Colleen M. Galambos
Roberta R. Greene
Nancy P. Kropf
Harriet L. Cohen

NASW PRESS

National Association of Social Workers
Washington, DC

Kathryn Conley Wehrmann, PhD, LCSW, President
Angelo McClain, PhD, LICSW, Chief Executive Officer

Cheryl Y. Bradley, *Publisher*
Stella Donovan, *Acquisitions Editor*
Julie Gutin, *Managing Editor*
Sarah Lowman, *Project Manager*
Julie Palmer-Hoffman, *Copyeditor*
Sue Harris, *Proofreader*
Bernice Eisen, *Indexer*

Cover by Diane Guy, Blue Azure Design
Interior design, composition, and eBook conversions by Xcel Graphic Services
Printed and bound by Sheridan

First impression: March 2018

Library of Congress Cataloging-in-Publication Data

Names: Galambos, Colleen, author. | Greene, Roberta R. (Roberta Rubin), 1940-
Title: Foundations of social work practice in the field of aging : a
    competency-based approach / Colleen M. Galambos, Roberta R. Greene, Nancy
    P. Kropf, and Harriet L. Cohen.
Description: Second Edition. | Washington, DC : NASW Press, [2018] | Includes
    bibliographical references and index. | Revised edition of Foundations of
    social work practice in the field of aging, c2007.
Identifiers: LCCN 2017056586| ISBN 9780871015242 (pbk.) |
    ISBN 9780871015259 (e-book)
Subjects: LCSH: Social work with older people—United States. | Gerontology.
    | Older people.
Classification: LCC HV1451 .F68 2018 | DDC 362.6/7532–dc23
LC record available at https://lccn.loc.gov/2017056586

Printed in the United States of America

Contents

About the Authors   v

Acknowledgments   vii

1   Context and Philosophy of Practice   1

2   Incorporation of Values and Ethics in Practice with Older Adults   25

3   Diversity, Difference, and Redress   45

4   A Human Rights and Social Justice Approach to Older Adults   65

5   Theory and Concepts Underpinning Assessment in Practice   81

6   Engagement and Assessment of Older Adults, Their Families, and Their Social Supports   103

7   Interventions   121

8   Group Work: Addressing Issues of Later Adulthood   139

9   Shift in Organizational Practice: Meeting the Needs of an Increasingly Aging Society   163

10   Building Community Capacity   183

11   Policy Practice: Advocating for Older Adults   205

12   Geriatric Case Management: Assembling a Broad Repertoire of Practice Skills   225

References   243

Index   277

About the Authors

Colleen M. Galambos, PhD, ACSW, LCSW, LCSW-C, FGSA, is the Helen Bader endowed chair in gerontology at the University of Wisconsin–Milwaukee. An NASW Pioneer, she has over 30 years of experience in quality improvement, aging in place, gerontological practice, and working to improve health and long-term care systems of delivery. She has held many local, state, and national leadership positions, such as with the John A. Hartford Faculty Development Institute Project and the Council on Social Work Education, and was a member of the Joint Commission on Accreditation of Health Care Organization's Professional and Technical Advisory Committee on Long-Term Care. She has extensive experience developing services and practice models for older adults, advocating for policies and programs that enhance the well-being of older adults, and teaching and conducting research. A fellow of the Gerontological Society of America, she has published extensively, including several books, journal articles, and book chapters.

Roberta R. Greene, PhD, LCSW, professor emerita, was the Louis and Ann Wolens Centennial Chair in Gerontology and Social Welfare at the University of Texas at Austin. She has a wide range of practice experience, including clinical practice, policy, administrative, and research expertise. She is an NASW Pioneer, known for her advocacy work on nursing home reform. She was the 2015 recipient of the Knee/Whitman Outstanding Achievement Award, which recognizes those who have made a significant impact on national health, public policy, or professional standards. A fellow of the Gerontological Society of America, she has conducted significant research on resilience among Holocaust survivors. A prolific author, she has written numerous books, including *A Handbook of Human*

Behavior in the Social Environment (Aldine Transaction Press, 2017), Social Work with the Aged and Their Families (Transaction Press, 2016), *Caregiving and Care Sharing: A Life Course Perspective* (NASW Press, 2014), and *Resiliency Theory: An Integrated Framework for Practice, Research, and Policy* (NASW Press, 2012).

Nancy P. Kropf, PhD, is dean and professor at the Byrdine F. Lewis School of Nursing and Health Professions, Georgia State University. A former John A. Hartford Foundation scholar, she has authored and coauthored numerous publications and books, including *Evidence-Based Treatment with Older Adults* (Oxford University Press, 2017), *Caregiving and Care Sharing: A Life Course Perspective* (NASW Press, 2014), and *Competence: Theoretical Frameworks* (Transaction Press, 2011). A national authority on caregiving, she served on the National Advisory Board to the Rosalynn Carter Institute on Caregiving. She is a fellow of the Gerontological Society of America and served as the association's treasurer in 2009.

Harriet L. Cohen, PhD, MSW, is associate professor emerita in the Department of Social Work, Texas Christian University. A former John A. Hartford Foundation scholar, her social work practice experience spans over 35 years in a variety of nonprofit organizations to build community and organizational capacity to serve older adults and their families. Her research and publication interests include forgiveness and older Holocaust survivors, spirituality in midlife, and older adults and older lesbian and gay men issues.

Acknowledgments

We would like to thank our families, friends, and colleagues for all their support while writing this book. Special thanks to Ms. Joann Ferguson, who provided editorial and organizational expertise, and to Dr. Dale Fitch, director of the University of Missouri School of Social Work, for his support. The assistance of these two individuals was critical to the success of this book.

We would also like to recognize the important work of Dr. Nancy Hooyman, National Work Group Members, and National Task Force Participants, who developed the *Specialized Practice Curricular Guide for Gero Social Work Practice*.

1

Context and Philosophy of Practice

RATIONALE: Social work practice is guided by an ever evolving person-in-environment perspective. Practice is carried out within multiple contexts—social, cultural, political, and historical—that affect the lives of clients and constituencies and the design of social services delivery systems. The demographic imperative—a rapidly expanding aging population—suggests that all social workers need to be prepared to serve older adults and their families.

COMPETENCY: "Competency-based education is an outcomes-oriented approach to curriculum design. . . . The goal of the outcomes approach is to ensure that students are able to demonstrate the integration and application of the competencies in practice" (Council on Social Work Education [CSWE], 2015, p. 6).

"The demonstration of competence is informed by knowledge, values, skills, and cognitive and affective processes that include the social worker's critical thinking, affective reactions, and exercise of judgment in regard to unique practice situations" (CSWE, 2015, p. 6).

SPECIALIZED PRACTICE: Specialized practice builds on generalist practice and extends "the Social Work Competencies for practice with a specific population, problem area, method of intervention, perspective, or approach to practice. Specialized practice augments and extends social work knowledge, values, and skills to engage, assess, intervene, and evaluate within an area of specialization" (CSWE, 2017, p. xviii).

Gerontology, the multidisciplinary study of aging, encompasses biology, sociology, and psychology. Gerontologists study the physical, mental, and social changes associated with the aging process and provide an understanding of the life course, that is, how a client has functioned over time, the timing of family life events, and the historical and cultural changes associated with those events (Greene, 1986/2000; T. K. Hareven, 1996; Sugar, Rieckse, Holstege, & Faber, 2014). Geriatric social workers also may address clients' spiritual concerns. They combine this body of knowledge with social work values and skills to practice with and deliver services to their clients.

To appreciate the context of geriatric social work practice in the 21st century, it is important to consider the factors shaping the society in which people age and to recognize movements within the behavioral health and social sciences that emphasize effective functioning in old age. Societal changes in the past quarter century have brought about a significant shift in the challenges confronting social workers and other practitioners serving the older population (Wilson, 2014). "Not since more than half a century ago have the political, economic, cultural, and ideological views of the time so dramatically affected how social work practice is defined" (Greene, 2005b, p. 37).

Sociocultural changes have been accompanied by an interest in strengths-based human behavior theory and positive psychological frameworks (see chapter 5 for further discussion of theoretical concepts). As the result of societal influences and decades of research, a "new gerontology" has emerged: Instead of viewing old age as solely a time of deterioration and decline, it examines how people can and do experience a healthy and engaged old age (Holstein & Minkler, 2003; Kiyak & Hooyman, 1999; Peluso, Watts, & Parsons, 2013; Rowe & Kahn, 1998; Scharlach & Kaye, 1997; Sugar et al., 2014).

The new gerontology provides an exciting view of older adults in expanded roles and increased opportunities. It also is only as effective as a practitioner's commitment to a strengths-based resiliency orientation: It is all too easy for a social worker interviewing a frail older adult to ignore that client's abilities. But as Kivnick and Murray (2001) have pointed out, social workers who wish to keep older people as "independent" or "in the community" as long as possible must learn about each client's personal values and lifelong commitments and how the client wants to live out his or her life. Conversely, many older adults of racial or ethnic minority groups may live in extended family households. In each case, practitioners must focus on the life strengths that allow the client to remain engaged in the world. Social work students should evaluate their own commitment to strengths-based assessment (see chapter 6 for assessment information).

DEMOGRAPHIC IMPERATIVE

The need for social workers who are prepared to serve older adults is escalating. Why has there been a rise in career opportunities in geriatric social work? A "longevity revolution" is under way (see Figure 1.1). In the United States, life expectancy at birth is now 76.3 years for men and 81.3 years for women, and it is anticipated that life expectancy for both genders will continue to increase. By 2040, the population of those age 65 years and older is projected to be over twice as large as in 2000—or about 82.3 million older people—and will represent nearly 22 percent of the total U.S. population. The number of people 85 and

Figure 1.1: Longevity Projections
Number of Persons Age 65 and Older: 1900–2060 (numbers in millions)

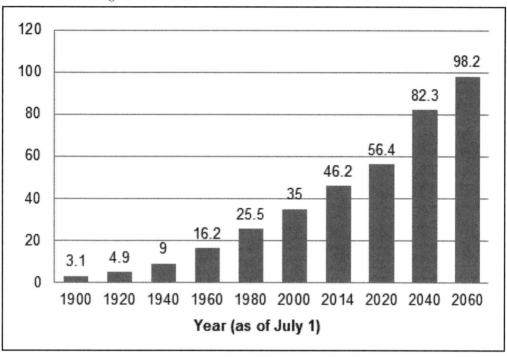

Note: Increments in years are uneven.
Sources: U.S. Census Bureau, Population Division, Annual Estimates of the Resident Population for Selected Age Groups by Sex for the United States, States, Counties, and Puerto Rico Commonwealth and Municipios: April 1, 2010 to July 1, 2014, Release Date: June 2015; Intercensal Estimates of the Resident Population by Sex and Age for the United States: April 1, 2000 to July 1, 2010, Release Date: September 2011; Intercensal Estimates of the White Alone Resident Population by Sex and Age for the United States: April 1, 2000 to July 1, 2010; 2014 National Population Projections: Summary Tables, Table 3; Projections of the Population by Sex and Selected Age Groups for the United States: 2015 to 2060, released December 10, 2014; and NP2014_D1: Projected Population by Single Year of Age, Sex, Race, and Hispanic Origin for the United States: 2014 to 2060.

older is expected to triple to 14.6 million in 2040 (U.S. Department of Health and Human Services, Administration on Aging, Administration for Community Living [HHS, AoA, ACL], 2016).

With the swelling numbers will come an increasingly ethnically diverse elderly population, adding to the complexity of service needs (HHS, AoA, ACL, 2016). The United States has experienced an increase in racial and ethnic minority older adults from 6.5 million in 2004 to 10 million in 2014. This number is expected to increase to 21.1 million in 2030 (HHS, AoA, ACL, 2016). These older adults will have differing social, cultural, and political experiences as well as general worldviews. Clearly, social workers have a demographic imperative to attend to the old and very old (85 years and older), some of whom may be frail or may suffer from chronic health and cognitive impairments. A practitioner's ability to understand—and respect—the differences in a client's meaning and perception of old age will be paramount.

AGEISM

To successfully work in the field of aging, practitioners must first explore, identify, and resolve their own biases, myths, and stereotypes about older adults and the aging process. Thinking in negative ways about older adults and considering them poor candidates for various forms of psychosocial treatments are biases that have long permeated the helping professions. Freud's belief that older adults were poor candidates for psychotherapy was adopted by most mental health professionals of his era and continued well into the 1980s. In addition, human behavior theories (such as Piaget's) addressed only childhood learning. Moreover, some physicians still attribute forgetfulness to natural processes of old age without critically exploring possible causative factors (Centers for Disease Control and Prevention, 2013b; Greene, 2008b).

Robert Butler, the first director of the National Institute on Aging, coined the term *ageism* to refer to the blatant prejudice underlying stereotyping older adults as helpless and nonproductive. Ageism, he said, is a process of systematic stereotyping of and discrimination against people because they are old. Ageism allows younger generations to see older people as different from themselves. Thus, they subtly cease to identify with their elders as human beings (R. N. Butler, 1975).

The following myths of aging checklist of common old-age stereotypes (Harrigan & Farmer, 2000) can be completed to gauge what myths a person may believe about older adults.

Biological myths

- Getting older means a life fraught with physical complaints and illness.
- Older people are not attractive people. They smell, have no teeth, can hardly see or hear, and are underweight.
- Older people should not exert themselves; they may have a heart attack or fall and break a bone.
- Older people sleep all the time.
- Sex ends at age 60.

Psychological myths

- Most older adults are set in their ways and unable to change.
- Old age is a time of relative peace and tranquility.
- Older adults are unresponsive to psychological interventions.
- Senility is inevitable in old age.
- Older people cannot learn anything new; intelligence declines with advancing age.
- Memory loss in old age is inevitable.

- Older people can't solve day-to-day problems.
- Older people are asexual, have no interest in sex, and are unable to function as sexual beings.
- Older people are dependent and need someone to take care of them.

Social myths

- Older people inevitably withdraw from the mainstream of society as they grow older.
- Older people become preoccupied with religion as they age.
- Older adults are dependent but socially isolated and neglected by their families.
- Social services provided to older people by organizations usurp the family's traditional care and interpersonal functions.
- Most older adults are abused and neglected.
- Generation gaps lead to alienation of older adults.
- Old age is a time of relative peace and tranquility when people can relax and enjoy the fruits of their labor after the stresses of life have passed.
- Older adults are unable to work or do not want to work. Older people are poor people.
- Older adults desire to be left alone and spend most of their time watching television.

Ageism, like other forms of prejudice, carries with it the risk of spreading and becoming institutionalized. When this form of discrimination becomes widespread, it can influence practitioners' attitudes about the employment of older adults and their rights to health care. Indeed, some social workers may internalize societal misconceptions and hence view older adults negatively (Greene, 2008b). Their personal views and ageist attitudes thus may interfere with the range and types of choices they present to older adults.

To avoid falling into the ageism trap, social workers should analyze older clients' views of their own aging process. In addition, older adults' perceptions of the aging process influence expectations about their future health (Sarkisian, Steers, Hays, & Mangione, 2005).

ETHICS AND THE AGING POPULATION

Historical Overview

Ethical dilemmas permeate our society. They may occur at multiple systems levels in the social work or biomedical communities, legal system, social policy arena, or broader societal contexts. At the broadest societal level, tensions that exist between the powers of the state and an individual's rights contribute to public policy debates about ethical issues, such as the right to die or decision to forgo life-sustaining treatment. In the 1970s and 1980s, two federal groups, the National Commission for the Protection of Human Subjects of Biomedical and Behavioral Research (henceforth the National Commission) and the President's Commission for the Study of Ethical Problems in Medicine and Biomedical and Behavioral Research (henceforth the President's Commission), considered many issues that social workers still encounter today. Those commissions issued a series of reports and proposed state statutes to guide professionals' ethical decision making.

Especially important to geriatrics was the first issue examined by the President's Commission: whether the law ought to recognize a new means for officially establishing that death has occurred. In studying the definition of death, the commission was struck by the "depth of public concern about life-sustaining treatment of patients who are dying or permanently unconscious" (President's Commission, 1983b, p. 31). As the President's Commission became aware that "conflicting values between physicians and patients, between patients and their families, or among family members are not uncommon," it decided it was necessary to "clarify the rights, duties, and liabilities of all concerned" (p. 32). Furthermore, it decided to clarify the nature of death because medical technology enables an individual's heart and lungs to function when the patient's brain may not. Such technology poses a dilemma in that sometimes it is difficult to distinguish between patients who are clinically dead and those who are dying or severely injured.

The President's Commission (1983b) concluded that developments in medical treatment necessitated a restatement of traditionally recognized standards for determining death. The commission decided that the standards ought to be uniform across all 50 states, thereby proposing the following statute:

> An individual who has sustained either (1) irreversible cessation of circulatory and respiratory function, or (2) irreversible cessation of all functions of the entire brain, including the brain stem, is dead. A determination of death must be made in accordance with accepted medical standards. (President's Commission, 1983b, p. 16)

The commission also concluded that defining death should be a matter for each state legislature; a state's health and judiciary subcommittees would be responsible for coordinating that task.

The National Commission and the President's Commission studied another issue important to geriatric social workers: when and how patients and their families might forgo life-sustaining treatment. Of the people who die in the United States, the vast majority will have been treated by health care professionals who possess, through advanced medical technology, a powerful means to forestall death. Sometimes, though, that objective may so dominate care that the therapy or treatment those professionals provide may not be consistent with the patient's own goals and values. Therefore, attempts to postpone death should, at times, yield to other, more important patient goals. Overall, the following themes flowed through the final reports of the two commissions:

- Respect the choice of competent individuals who decide to forgo life-sustaining treatment.
- Provide mechanisms and guidelines for decision making on behalf of patients so that they may make their own decisions.
- Maintain a presumption in favor of sustained life.
- Improve the medical options available to dying patients.
- Provide respectful, responsive, and supportive care to patients for whom no further medical therapies are available or elected.
- Encourage health care institutions to take responsibility for ensuring that adequate procedures for decision making are available for all patients. (President's Commission, 1983a)

Professionals debate ethical issues at the societal and biomedical community levels, and ethical topics are the focus of debate among members of the social work community who may hold differing values about client care. Ethical dilemmas typically surface during the client–social worker encounter, where issues such as autonomy and how to treat client self-determination may arise. For example, should a client who appears to be unsafe be allowed to continue to live alone, or should the social worker attempt to have the client protected? Or when a social worker and the client's family differ in their views about the right to reject heroic life-saving interventions, how shall the parties involved resolve this matter? The frameworks presented in chapter 2 are intended to facilitate the deliberation of such ethical dilemmas and their possible resolution.

Ethics and Values

According to the *Code of Ethics of the National Association of Social Workers* (National Association of Social Workers [NASW], 2017), ethics and professional values guide professional conduct; that is, social worker integrity and self-understanding are essential for practitioners to act in the best interest of their clients or client system. An ethical social worker tolerates ambiguity, respects divergent opinions, and recognizes a client's right to self-determination.

Skills, the behaviors that bring knowledge and values together and put them into action, may also be thought of as knowledge in action (Schon, 1983). Within the larger sociopolitical context, professional social work practitioners use the skills of interpreting complex situations and reflecting on how to conduct their practice (Laird, 1993). To enhance their skills, practitioners have traditionally imparted client-centered, relationship-building qualities, including empathy, the ability to deal sensitively and accurately with client feelings; nonpossessive warmth, acceptance of the client as an individual; and genuineness, or authenticity (CSWE, 2015; Rogers & Dymond, 1957). These process-oriented skills are necessary for client or system engagement, assessment, intervention, and evaluation.

EMBRACING DIVERSITY

Competencies are not just knowledge, attitude, and skills for student practitioners to master. Rather, the work of applying content in our chosen field of practice begins before the social worker sees the client. That is, the intake interview begins before the participants meet (Greene, 1986/2000). Social workers need to be cognizant of the diverse demographics of an aging population. There has been an increase in the numbers and types of ethnic and racial groups because of changes in population level, fertility, longevity, and migration (Whitfield & Baker, 2014). Social workers working with a diverse aging population must be mindful of the impact of health disparities, economic disadvantages, and issues related to immigration during the assessment and intervention phases of practice (see chapters 6 and 7; Whitfield & Baker, 2014).

Practitioners must also be mindful of the fact that the lesbian, gay, bisexual, and transgender (LGBT) population is expected to grow to 6 million by 2030 (Fredericksen-Goldsen et al., 2011). As a result of their marginalization and invisibility, health and service disparities exist for this population. Social workers should be mindful of the challenges faced by this population of older adults. Older women also face income inequities in later life because of cumulative discrimination in the workplace that affects lifetime earnings and retirement. Women are more likely to be institutionalized, have reduced incomes, and live in poverty (Sugar et al., 2014). Given the marginalization of women in our society, social workers should consider how cumulative challenges affect older women's quality of life.

VARIATIONS IN HELP-SEEKING BEHAVIORS

Clients bring to the social worker–client relationship expectations about the helping process that are based on their own and their family's beliefs and norms (Greene, 1986/2000). Moreover, they frequently will describe their requests and needs in terms used within their own cultural milieu. The events these clients have experienced throughout their lifetimes will have shaped their thoughts about specific services and acceptable solutions. They also will express their own unique views about the world at large.

For the social worker to "begin where the client is," the practitioner must use critical and reflective thinking and cognitive and affective processes to gain an awareness of his or her own personal biases before being able to act on a client's concerns (CSWE, 2015). Furthermore, the practitioner must have knowledge of the client's aging process within his or her particular historical and sociocultural contexts. Having an awareness of clients' help-seeking behaviors—one way of embracing their diversity—helps to remove barriers to a client-centered relationship. Practitioners might also use the following strategies to ensure that services are client centered:

- Maintain a positive and affirmative attitude toward the client.
- Engage in active listening—listen to discern client concerns and realize client possibilities for a positive future.
- Conduct client meetings in environments familiar to them.
- Talk candidly about behaviors and activities.
- Remain nonjudgmental.
- Express a willingness to assist.
- Initiate the helping process according to client directions. (Tice & Perkins, 1996)

When the social worker asks about the client's conception of a better tomorrow, the client is motivated to think about his or her future, and the helping relationship is on its way.

CHANGES IN FAMILY STRUCTURE

When working with an older adult, the social worker must decide who the client is. Although the social worker may address an older adult's particular concern, family members may be relevant to the problem and its solution. An important part of this assessment is determining who in the client's family or social support system is the most active and available to the client (chapter 6 further describes the tools used in making an assessment). The practitioner, however, needs to be aware that family structures have taken on different shapes owing to the longevity of the population, decreased fertility rates, and higher divorce rates (Peluso et al., 2013). Demographic factors and changing societal norms have changed family membership. These changes have occurred within and across generations and have led to the development of different family structures. For instance, marital patterns have changed, including increased cohabitation, multiple partner childbearing, increased rates of divorce and remarriage, later life marriages, and older adults increasingly living alone (Blieszner & Bedford, 2012). This changing family structure means there is less potential for intrafamily support and caregiving (Moody & Sasser, 2015; Peluso et al., 2013).

However, because of cultural and socioeconomic differences, the extent to which families and friends provide help to older adults varies across racial and ethnic groups. The social worker may observe cultural differences between clients' household and living arrangements. In fact, households of Pacific Islanders at 10 percent and Hispanics, African Americans, and Native Americans each at 8 percent have the largest percentage of grandparents living with grandchildren (Peluso et al., 2013). Also, the nuclear family no longer is the predominant family type. There are a number of ways in which family caregiving is provided in our society. For instance, members of the LGBT community serve as caregivers for their loved ones (Whitten & Eyler, 2012). Because the effects a family's structure has on family members' ability to care for older adults remain unclear (Greene, 2005a), social workers, during their assessment of the client and family system, must determine how families carry out various role demands (Tennstedt, 1999; see also chapter 7 for a discussion of interventions).

ESSENTIAL ELEMENTS OF PRACTICE

Informed and effective action with individuals, families, groups, organizations, and communities is required for competent social work practice. Social work competence is composed of "knowledge, attitudes, skills, and cognitive and affective processes" (CSWE, 2015, p. 2).

The following essential elements of the curriculum proposed for the new CSWE (2015) Educational Policy and Accreditation Standards should inform practice. Social workers should be able to do the following:

Competency 1: Demonstrate Ethical and Professional Behavior

- Make ethical decisions by applying the standards of the NASW *Code of Ethics*, relevant laws and regulations, models for ethical decision making, ethical conduct of research, and additional codes of ethics as appropriate to context.
- Use reflection and self-regulation to manage personal values and maintain professionalism in practice situations.
- Demonstrate professional demeanor in behavior; appearance; and oral, written, and electronic communication.
- Use technology ethically and appropriately to facilitate practice outcomes.
- Use supervision and consultation to guide professional judgment and behavior.

Specialized Practice Competency Description. Practitioners in aging respect the worth, dignity, and integrity of all older people and advocate for their self-determination, access to services, and ethical application of technology. They recognize ethical issues in practice and distinguish frameworks for decision making that support older adults' needs and rights. To ensure ethical practice, they use self-reflection, self-regulation, and supervision, consultation, and life-long learning to address how their attitudes and biases about aging and older adults may influence their personal and professional values and behaviors. Gero social workers recognize the dynamics of self-determination and the continuum of decision-making support. Practitioners in aging serve as leaders to ensure ethical practice with older adults and their care networks.

Competency Behaviors. Practitioners in aging with, and on behalf of, older adults and their constituencies should

- demonstrate awareness of aging-related personal and professional values through self-reflection and self-regulation.
- select and incorporate ethical decision-making frameworks that integrate social work values.
- practice in a culturally competent manner that demonstrates recognition of and ability to use the principles included in the NASW *Code of Ethics*, evidence-based knowledge, and relevant legal and policy-related information.
- recognizing social structural inequities, advocate within the health and social service communities and as members of interprofessional teams on behalf of older adults and their families. (CSWE, 2017, pp. 1–2)

Competency 2: Engage Diversity and Difference in Practice

- Apply and communicate understanding of the importance of diversity and difference in shaping life experiences in practice at the micro, meso, and macro levels.
- Present themselves as learners and engage clients and constituencies as experts of their own experiences.
- Apply self-awareness and self-regulation to manage the influence of personal biases and values in working with diverse clients and constituencies.

Specialized Practice Competency Description. Practitioners in aging understand the impact of discrimination and oppression on older adults and their caregivers and identify the intersectionality of age with multiple characteristics of diversity and structural inequities throughout the life course. Gero social workers practice cultural humility and effectively work with diverse, older adults and their caregivers, groups, and communities.

Competency Behaviors. Practitioners in aging with, and on behalf of, older adults and their constituencies should

- appraise their own values related to diversity in aging.
- analyze how diversity and oppression affect older adults and families.
- address the cultural and spiritual histories, values, and beliefs of older adults and their families.
- defend the impact of structural inequalities and the value of diversity among older adults as part of their roles on interprofessional teams and in organizations and communities. (CSWE, 2017, p. 13)

Competency 3: Advance Human Rights and Social, Economic, and Environmental Justice

- Apply their understanding of social, economic, and environmental justice to advocate for human rights at the individual and system levels.
- Engage in practices that advance social, economic, and environmental justice.

Specialized Practice Competency Description. Practitioners in aging work to advance human rights and social and economic justice for older adults and their caregivers. They incorporate the historical context and the physical and social environment, including experiences of trauma and microaggressions, which may create barriers to social, economic, and environmental justice for older adults. Practitioners in aging critically and objectively analyze how policies and programs promote or inhibit justice and use story and narrative to effect change at the micro, meso, and macro levels. As members of interprofessional teams, they engage other disciplines to recognize such contextual and environmental barriers and ensure that older adults are aware of their rights. Aware of ageism and other institutionalized biases, they practice cultural humility and address discriminatory policies, practices, and language by utilizing culturally and linguistically appropriate measures and evidence-informed services and interventions.

Competency Behaviors. Practitioners in aging with, and on behalf of, older adults and their constituencies should

- engage older adults, their caregivers, and other constituencies to become aware of their rights to available resources and how these relate to social, economic, and environmental inequities.
- participate in system changes at all levels to promote well-being for and among older adults.
- empower individuals and groups within local communities, including older adults themselves, to advocate for social, economic, and environmental justice for all older adults and their caregivers.

Competency 4: Engage in Practice-Informed Research and Research-Informed Practice

- Use practice experience and theory to inform scientific inquiry and research.
- Apply critical thinking to engage in analysis of quantitative and qualitative research methods and research findings.
- Use and translate research evidence to inform and improve practice, policy, and service delivery.

Specialized Practice Competency Description. Practitioners in aging value their essential role in building knowledge and evaluating research. They identify critical gaps and promote the adoption of evidence-informed practice in organizations working with, and on behalf of, older adults and their caregivers. They integrate social–behavioral approaches to aging research with knowledge from their practice. Gero social workers recognize factors that affect the inclusion of older adults' participation in research and understand how evaluation processes within organizations can contribute to broader knowledge building within social work and aging.

Competency Behaviors. Practitioners in aging with, and on behalf of, older adults and their constituencies should

- understand and build knowledge central to maximizing the well-being of older adults and their caregivers.
- adopt, modify, and translate evidence-informed practices that are most appropriate to particular aging-focused practice settings and populations. (CSWE, 2017, p. 40)

Competency 5: Engage in Policy Practice

- Identify social policy at the local, state, and federal level that affects well-being, service delivery, and access to social services.
- Assess how social welfare and economic policies affect the delivery of and access to social services.
- Apply critical thinking to analyze, formulate, and advocate for policies that advance human rights and social, economic, and environmental justice.

Specialized Practice Competency Description. Practitioners in aging understand how a vast array of policies at the local, state, national, and global levels influences the design and delivery of services for older adults and caregivers, as well as how policy shapes the extent to which environments are supportive and inclusive of diverse subgroups of older adults and caregivers. They apply critical thinking to analyze the effects of social policy on interconnected domains of well-being in later life, with special attention to older adults from marginalized groups and those facing cumulative disadvantages. Practitioners in aging value the profession's role in enhancing the capacity of individuals, families, and organizations to expand access to the intended benefits of social policies. Practitioners in aging are skilled at formulating arguments in support of evidence-informed policy making to optimize the health and well-being of all older adults and caregivers, and they know how to engage with coalitions addressing key policy issues that affect older adults and caregivers.

Competency Behaviors. Practitioners in aging with, and on behalf of, older adults and their constituencies should

- educate key stakeholders on how policy for an aging society relates to human rights and social, economic, and environmental justice, from the local to the international level.

- advocate for policies across all levels to enhance service delivery to promote well-being among all older adults and constituencies. (CSWE, 2017)

Competency 6: Engage with Individuals, Families, Groups, Organizations, and Communities

- Apply knowledge of human behavior and the social environment, person-in-environment, and other multidisciplinary theoretical frameworks to engage with clients and constituencies.
- Use empathy, reflection, and interpersonal skills to effectively engage diverse clients and constituencies.

Specialized Practice Competency Description. Practitioners in aging engage older adults, caregivers, and related systems by understanding and applying a range of appropriate theories. To foster this engagement, gero social workers interpret the diverse life courses (including resilience, contributions, and strengths) of older adults and consider the cohorts and contexts in which they have lived. They also recognize how their own life trajectory influences their engagement with diverse older adults and their constituents.

Competency Behaviors. Practitioners in aging with, and on behalf of, older adults and their constituencies should

- establish and maintain strong relationships with older adults and their constituencies for the purpose of working toward mutually agreed-on goals.
- plan engagement strategies and interventions based on understanding of older adults' diverse life courses, strengths, challenges, and contexts. (CSWE, 2017, p. 65)

Competency 7: Assess Individuals, Families, Groups, Organizations, and Communities

- Collect and organize data, and apply critical thinking to interpret information from clients and constituencies.
- Apply knowledge of human behavior and the social environment, person-in-environment, and other multidisciplinary theoretical frameworks in the analysis of assessment data from clients and constituencies.
- Develop mutually agreed-on intervention goals and objectives based on the critical assessment of strengths, needs, and challenges within clients and constituencies.
- Select appropriate intervention strategies based on the assessment, research knowledge, and values and preferences of clients and constituencies.

Specialized Practice Competency Description. Practitioners in aging use ecological systems theory, a strengths-based and person- and family-centered framework, to conduct assessments that value the resilience of diverse older adults, families, and caregivers. They select appropriate assessment tools, methods, and technology and evaluate, adapt, and modify them, as needed, to enhance their validity in working with diverse, vulnerable, and at-risk groups. The comprehensive biopsychosocial assessment takes into account the multiple factors of physical, mental, and social well-being needed for treatment planning for older adults and their families. Practitioners develop skills in interprofessional assessment and communication with key constituencies to choose the most effective practice strategies. Gero social workers understand how their own experiences and affective reactions about aging, quality of life, loss, and grief may affect their assessment and resultant decision making.

Competency Behaviors. Practitioners in aging with, and on behalf of, older adults and their constituencies should

- conduct assessments that incorporate a strengths-based perspective, person- and family-centered focus, and resilience while recognizing aging-related risk.
- develop, select, and adapt assessment methods and tools that optimize practice with older adults, their families, caregivers, and communities.
- use and integrate multiple domains and sources of assessment information and communicate with other professionals to inform a comprehensive plan for intervention. (CSWE, 2017, pp. 89–90)

Competency 8: Intervene with Individuals, Families, Groups, Organizations, and Communities

- Critically choose and implement interventions to achieve practice goals and enhance capacities of clients and constituencies.
- Apply knowledge of human behavior and the social environment, person-in-environment, and other multidisciplinary theoretical frameworks in interventions with clients and constituencies.
- Use interprofessional collaboration as appropriate to achieve beneficial practice outcomes.
- Negotiate, mediate, and advocate with and on behalf of diverse clients and constituencies.
- Facilitate effective transitions and endings that advance mutually agreed-on goals.

Specialized Practice Competency Description. Practitioners in aging aim to promote wellness, build aging-friendly communities, empower older adults to manage their chronic conditions, optimize elders' productive contributions to families and communities, and ensure their quality of life, including reducing social isolation, suicide, and elder mistreatment. Gero social workers address ageism and discrimination at the individual, group, community, and policy levels and aim to reduce inequality based on lifelong disparities. Practitioners in aging build on comprehensive biopsychosocial assessments to plan and implement effective and culturally appropriate interventions, including peer support. They are knowledgeable about, critically analyze, and apply evidence-informed interventions as well as emerging practices. Gero social workers value and draw on strengths-based and person- and family-centered approaches to ensure that interventions are consistent with mutually agreed-on goals at the individual, family, group, organizational, and community levels. They use technological resources, where appropriate, to improve quality of care. Practitioners in aging advocate to improve access, coordination, and quality across a continuum of medical, community, and social services.

Competency Behaviors. Practitioners in aging with, and on behalf of, older adults and their constituencies should

- promote older adults' social support systems and engagement in families, groups, and communities.
- provide person-centered and family-directed interventions that take account of life course disparities and are targeted to diverse populations, groups, organizations, and communities.
- assess for quality and access a range of services, supports, and care options, including groups and technology, for older adults and families to ensure optimal interdependence.
- monitor and modify interventions as needed to respond to individual, family, and environmental challenges. (CSWE, 2017, pp. 90–100)

Competency 9: Evaluate Practice with Individuals, Families, Groups, Organizations, and Communities

- Select and use appropriate methods for evaluation of outcomes.
- Apply knowledge of human behavior and the social environment, person-in-environment, and other multidisciplinary theoretical frameworks in the evaluation of outcomes.
- Critically analyze, monitor, and evaluate intervention and program processes and outcomes.
- Apply evaluation findings to improve practice effectiveness at the micro, meso, and macro levels. (CSWE, 2015, pp. 7–9)

Specialized Practice Competency Description. Practitioners in aging integrate sources of knowledge—including gerontological and social work theories and research, input from constituencies, and awareness of broader societal trends—within evaluation processes. They value the role of older adults and their caregivers as contributors to evaluation and adapt research designs and measurement tools to fully include them across diverse practice settings. Practitioners in aging communicate evaluation findings and implications for improvement for example, financial, operational) across micro, meso, and macro levels of aging-focused practice and policy.

Competency Behaviors. Practitioners in aging with and on behalf of older adults and their constituencies should

- plan and conduct evaluations to continuously improve programs, policies, and practice affecting older adults and their caregivers.
- use and translate evaluation outcomes to enhance the effectiveness and sustainability of programs, policies, and practice for an aging society. (CSWE, 2017, p. 109)

A list of skills recognized by gerontological social workers as key to working with an older adult population was developed initially from projects conducted by CSWE as part of the Strengthening Aging and Gerontological Education in Social Work Initiative and the Practice Partnership Scale, a project funded by the John A. Hartford Foundation. These competencies have been further refined with participation from the Social Work Leadership Institute. Programs may build and apply these competencies in an area of concentration, such as aging. The Gero-Ed Center and the Hartford Partnership Program in Aging Education partnered to ensure consistency of one set of gero competencies for all the Gerontology Education in Social Work Initiative programs. A scale was developed that can be used to gauge progress in the development of these key skills or competencies. This scale, Geriatric Social Work Competency Scale II with Life-long Leadership Skills: Social Work Practice Behaviors in the Field of Aging, can be located at the following Web site: https://www.cswe.org/getattachment/Centers-Initiatives/CSWE-Gero-Ed-Center/Teaching-Tools/Gero-Competencies/Guidelines-and-Scales/GeriatricSocialWorkCompetencyScaleII-LifelongLeadershipSkills.pdf.aspx.

PRACTICE DEMOGRAPHICS

To prepare themselves to serve older adults effectively, students must learn about the changing nature of the aging population. For example, some older adults have access to private pensions, but access to these private pensions has been affected by gender, race, and income, and more employers are opting to reduce these plans (Blieszner & Bedford, 2012). Others will not have access to those resources because of a lifetime of economic hardships and discrimination. As social workers contemplate new designs for social services and health care systems, we must address this two-tiered nature of opportunity (Greene, 2005a; see also chapter 11 for a discussion of policy practice).

SHIFTING HEALTH AND HUMAN SERVICES DELIVERY SYSTEMS

The demographic shifts in the aging population combined with dramatic changes in the shape, delivery, and financing of health and human services are influencing both the skills that social workers must bring to practice and their ability to provide quality care to older adults (Blieszner & Bedford, 2012). For example, privatization, the use of technology, especially in health care delivery, and a greater focus on quality, cost-effectiveness, and outcome measures are significant factors affecting health and human services delivery systems. The need for medical and psychosocial care providers to work closer together and align goals of care is another consideration (Greene & Kropf, 2017).

Although some of these factors may have resulted in improved care, practitioners must be aware that particular changes, such as cost containment, have led to skewed access to and distribution of health care and other services (Sugar et al., 2014; Wilson, 2014). Because clients may have had a difficult time accessing and receiving help from various service systems, social workers may want to ask clients what other agencies they have used. Frequently, the practitioner acts as case manager—advocating for and coordinating the delivery of services (for more on competencies for case management practice, see chapter 12). However, a key intervention for the practitioner is to empower clients to traverse delivery systems on their own.

USING CONCEPTUAL THINKING AND ANALYTICAL REASONING

An essential element of the social work curriculum that informs practice is the use of both conceptual thinking, in which the practitioner identifies underlying issues in a complex problem; and analytical reasoning, in which the social worker purposefully, systematically, and logically examines the problem to determine its implications and identifies strategies for resolving the problem. This is a cognitive and affective process that enables social workers to carry out a learning stance in their assessment of a client's situation.

USING SCIENCE

In addition to learning about a client's views on aging, practitioners must acquire knowledge of current social concerns. For example, recent scientific research provides findings about diseases and treatments that involve older clients. Technological advances have revolutionized home health care, with families assuming more medical follow-up at home after hospitalization. The ability to integrate and apply science, technology, and empirically based innovations into practice is a characteristic of contemporary social work.

Social workers use critical thinking to synthesize research findings and to develop a deeper understanding of social issues. In assessing a client's situation and to gain a deeper understanding of how recent scientific information may affect the client, practitioners may ask several questions (Gibbs & Gambrill, 1996):

- How do I know a claim is true?
- Who said the claim was accurate? What could their motivation be? How reliable are these sources?
- Are the presented facts correct?
- Have any facts been omitted?
- Have there been any critical tests of this claim? Have any experimental results been replicated? Were these studies relatively free of bias? What samples were used? How representative were they? Was random assignment used?
- Are there other plausible explanations?
- If correlations are presented, how strong are they?
- What weak appeals are used (for example, to emotion or special interest)?

In short, social workers understand that evidence informs practice (CSWE, 2015).

COMPETENCY-BASED EDUCATION

Competency-based education is outcomes oriented. It is informed by knowledge, values, and skills. This text presents an array of issues and practice areas needed for competent practice with older adults and their families and support systems. This content allows students to "actualize through its quest for social and economic justice, the prevention of conditions that limit human rights, the elimination of poverty, and the enhancement of the quality of life for all persons" (CSWE, 2015, p. 5).

In addition, the attention to both person and environment has been a continuing and unifying theme in the historical development of social work and is fundamental to geriatric practice. This multisystemic approach, also known as the ecological perspective, focuses on enhancing social functioning and creating the strongest mutually beneficial interaction between people and their environments (Bronfenbrenner, 1989; Cournoyer, 2000; Greene & Barnes, 1998). The ecological perspective also acts as a guide for social workers in the helping process, suggesting practitioners address issues involving individuals, families, groups, organizations, communities, and society.

AGING-RELATED COMPETENCIES

Gerontological social workers have long struggled to ensure that competencies for geriatric practice would find a place in the social work curriculum, and their efforts have paid off. The strengths-based social work movement emphasizes client assets and capabilities (Saleebey, 1997, 2004). In the strengths-based, positive approach, organizing constructs center around a philosophy that emphasizes resilience and how the social worker can help older clients to negotiate life transitions competently (H. L. Cohen & Greene, 2006; Diehl, 1998; Fraser, Richman, & Galinsky, 1999; Saul, 2003; Willis, 1991). This philosophy builds on the body of literature underscoring that a successful treatment outcome is the product of a client's own strengths and resources (Duncan & Miller, 2000; Miller, Duncan, & Hubble, 1997) and his or her worldview, culture, and life experiences (Ronch & Goldfield, 2003).

ECOLOGICAL PERSPECTIVE

The underlying theoretical foundation of this book is the ecological perspective. This perspective views the person as directly connected to and influenced by the environment (see Figure 1.2 for a pictorial representation of the ecological perspective).

The environment is composed of concentric layers that involve increasingly larger spheres of influence. This text focuses on assessment and intervention at

Figure 1.2:   Theoretical Model Based on the Ecological Perspective

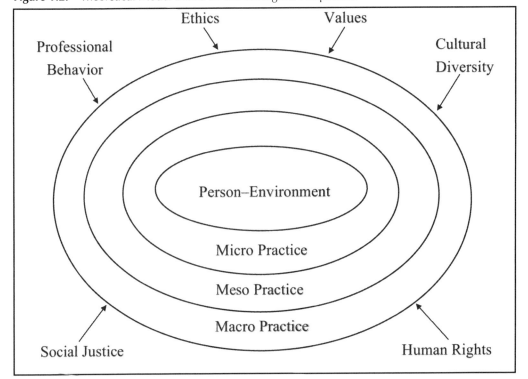

the micro or individual practice level; the meso or family and group practice level; and the macro or organization, community, and policy practice level. These practice levels are affected by ethics, values, professional behavior, cultural diversity, human rights, and social justice. Within this book, the levels of practice and other factors are integrated with the CSWE competencies discussed in this chapter.

Case Study: The Stanley Family as an Example of Custodial Grandparenting

To highlight content of the textbook, each chapter will integrate chapter content with the case example of Mrs. Stanley and her family. Eva Stanley is a 68-year-old African American woman who was widowed at age 47, when her husband died from cancer. Mrs. Stanley has three adult children, ages 35 to 45 years. Mrs. Stanley also has seven grandchildren, and she is the custodial grandparent of two of her son John's children. John was incarcerated five years ago for drug-related offenses. The mother of the two children, Loverne, has addiction problems and lost custody because of severe abuse and neglect. Loverne's family lives in another state and has never met either of these children. Almost four years ago, Mrs. Stanley assumed primary custody so that the children would not have to enter the foster care system.

The two grandchildren in Mrs. Stanley's care are 11-year-old Jasmine and seven-year-old Terrell. Both children have special needs. Jasmine has been delayed in school for a year and has impulse control issues, along with defiant, oppositional behavior. Terrell is a shy boy who suffers from health-related issues, including asthma and a seizure disorder. Jasmine has memories of her years living with her two parents and often describes the experience of being physically abused, left alone, and going without food. Terrell does not have many memories of either of his parents and the time that they lived together.

The Stanley family lives in a large southern city in a neighborhood that has a higher than average crime rate for the area. Mrs. Stanley and her husband moved into that house when they had their first child and raised their children there. Although there is enough room for the children, the household is in need of several repairs that are beyond the financial ability of Mrs. Stanley. Over the decades, the community has experienced decreased property values, higher uninhabited vacancy rates, and declining school performance. Despite these disadvantages, the families who continue to live in the neighborhood share close ties, and the church is the focus of the community for many of the older adults who live here.

To move in with Mrs. Stanley, Jasmine and Terrell had to move from a different neighborhood and transfer schools. Mrs. Stanley and her grandchildren collectively have experienced a number of significant transitions over recent years. The process of coming together as a family unit has entailed challenging aspects for everyone involved.

Throughout the rest of the book, the case of the Stanley family will be explored through the context of each chapter topic. As this chapter described, family life has created additional roles during older adulthood. The rate of custodial grandparenting has increased over the past two decades (Ellis & Simmons, 2014). The additional responsibilities of caregiving intersect with the experience of growing older for the care provider. Through a discussion of case material on the Stanley family, practice, policy, and research issues will be anchored in the situation of a family in later life.

WHAT WE LEARNED IN THIS CHAPTER

- There have been many sociocultural changes that affect older adults.
- There has been a new paradigm in gerontology that emphasizes positive and productive aging.
- The need for social workers trained in gerontology is high.
- Ageism is the stereotyping of older adults as helpless and unproductive.
- Ethical dilemmas specific to the practice and treatment of older adults present challenges for the practitioner. Professional values and the NASW *Code of Ethics* can help aid resolution of these issues.
- Changing demographics, cultural diversity, and changes in family structure affect practice approaches and work with older adults.
- The new CSWE Educational Policy and Accreditation Standards should inform practice.

SUGGESTED EXERCISES TO EVALUATE STUDENT COMPETENCY

1. Have students take the Geriatric Social Work Competency Scale II with Life-long Leadership Skills: Social Work Practice Behaviors in the Field of Aging scale to assess their present gero skill level. At the end of the course, have them take it again and discuss the differences in scores between the two tests.
2. Review the Myths of Aging checklist. Using this checklist, have students reflect on their own biases.

ADDITIONAL RESOURCES

AARP is a nonprofit, nonpartisan, social welfare organization that provides information and resources on a variety of topics important to older adults.

The organization also offers advocacy and policy resources. Visit http://
www.aarp.org/.

The Association of Gerontology Education in Social Work provides leadership
in the areas of gerontological social work education, research, and policy.
Networking, mentoring, and training opportunities are available at http://
www.agesocialwork.org/.

The Association of Gerontology in Higher Education provides leadership and
support of geriatrics and gerontology education at institutions of higher
education. Faculty and student support is also provided at https://www
.aghe.org/.

The Association of Gerontology in Higher Education's competency guide provides guidance on developing competency-based gerontology education at
various levels of educational programming and can be found at https://
www.aghe.org/images/aghe/competencies/gerontology_competencies
.pdf.

The Council on Social Work Education's *Specialized Practice Curricular Guide for
Gero Social Work Practice* is a resource designed to help programs conceptualize specialized practice in aging and infuse aging into their curricula and
can be found at https://www.cswe.org/CSWE/media/GeroEdResources/
Gero_Guide_WEB_final_NewSite.pdf.

The National Association of Social Workers' *Code of Ethics* provides ethical standards and guidelines for professional practice and can be found at https://
www.socialworkers.org/pubs/code/default.asp.

The National Council on Aging provides access to resources on a number of
topics and issues that affect older adults. Visit https://www.ncoa.org/.

2

Incorporation of Values and Ethics in Practice with Older Adults

RATIONALE: "Practitioners in aging respect the worth, dignity, and integrity of all older people and advocate for their self-determination, access to services, and ethical application of technology." When ethical dilemmas occur, social workers use "frameworks for decision-making that support older adults' needs and rights" (CSWE, 2017, p. 1). Social workers understand frameworks of ethical decision making and how to apply principles of critical thinking to those frameworks in practice, research, and policy arenas (CSWE, 2015, p. 3).

COMPETENCY: Practitioners will

- demonstrate awareness of aging-related personal and professional values through self-reflection and self-regulation.
- select and incorporate ethical decision-making frameworks that integrate social work values.
- practice in a culturally competent manner that demonstrates recognition of and ability to utilize the principles included in the NASW *Code of Ethics* evidence-based knowledge and relevant legal and policy-related information.
- recognizing social structural social inequities, advocate within the health and social service communities and as members of interprofessional teams on behalf of older adults and their families. (CSWE, 2017, pp. 1–2)

WHAT ARE THE CORE VALUES AND ETHICAL STANDARDS AND PRINCIPLES?

The social work profession is built on a set of values that influence and direct practice. As professionals, social workers are responsible for working within the parameters of ethics set forth by their profession. This chapter describes the specific values, knowledge, and skills—or competencies—required of practitioners to effectively apply ethical standards and principles in their work with older adults that guide and underpin interventions with the client population. In their seminal work on social work practice, Pincus and Minahan (1973) defined *values* as

> beliefs, preferences, or assumptions about what is desirable or good. An example is the belief that society has an obligation to help each individual realize his fullest potential. They are not assertions about how the world is and what we know about it, but how the world should be. As such, value statements cannot be subjected to scientific investigation; they must be accepted on faith. Thus, we can speak of a value as being right or wrong, only in relation to the particular belief system or ethical code being used as a standard. (p. 38)

Values influence and structure social workers' responses to, and interventions with, older adults. According to Levy (1973), social workers, agencies, and professional associations must have a set of values on which to base their choices and decisions related to client interventions or their deliberations with regard to institutions and society. In earlier work on ethics, Levy (1984) developed a framework with four core values—societal, organizational and institutional, professional, and human services practice—and pointed out the importance of the profession adopting a set of outcomes with the goal of achieving standards for practice. Levy's values framework may be applied to any of the practice levels: micro, meso, or macro.

The *Code of Ethics of the National Association of Social Workers* (NASW, 2017) identifies the following key values of the profession:

- service—service to others takes precedence over self-interest;
- social justice—advocate for the rights of clients, particularly the most vulnerable in society, and pursue social change when indicated;
- dignity and worth of the person—treat people courteously and in a caring manner and respect individual differences as well as cultural and ethnic diversity;
- importance of human relationships—hold relationships among people in the highest regard and recognize that those relationships may be catalysts for change;
- integrity—be mindful of the profession's mission, values, ethical principles, and standards, and apply them in practice;
- competence—obligation to increase professional knowledge and skills and use them in practice.

NASW points out that this group of core values distinguishes the profession of social work from other disciplines. These values should be considered within the context of the human experience.

Although values play a central role in social work practice, professional ethics, according to Dolgoff, Harrington, and Loewenberg (2012), guide social workers to transform professional values into practice activities. Values relate to what is good and desirable, whereas ethics pertain to what is right and correct.

Social workers must be mindful of professional values and ethics when working with older adults. For example, when facing circumstances in which it appears clients may be a danger to themselves, practitioners may find it challenging to remain objective. Their objectivity may be further tested if they perceive that clients are not making the best decisions to further their own well-being or are being exploited by family members or neighbors. To remain objective, it is essential that practitioners use tools such as those presented in this chapter to help them in clarifying the dynamics and factors involved in each client's particular situation.

RESOURCES FOR ETHICAL PRACTICE

Assessment Tools

A number of tools are available to practitioners working with older adults. Dolgoff and colleagues (2012) designed a decision-making model to help social workers engage in a rational planning process that emphasizes planned, ethical decision making. This tool is designed to assist gerontological social workers in the intervention phase. In addition to taking these steps, social workers should ask whether there are any cultural considerations that may affect the ethical issue. There are seven assessment steps in the decision-making model:

Step 1: Identify the problem and the people, institutions, clients, professionals, support systems, victims, and others involved in this problem.

Step 2: Determine who should be involved in decision making.

Step 3: Identify the relevant values held by those identified in Step 1, including the client and worker.

Step 4: Identify the goals and objectives whose attainment you believe may resolve (or reduce) the problem.

Step 5: Identify alternative intervention strategies and targets, and assess the effectiveness and efficiency of each alternative in terms of the identified goals.

Step 6: Select and implement the most appropriate strategy.

Step 7: Monitor the implementation, paying particular attention to unanticipated consequences; evaluate the results and identify additional problems, opportunities, and options.

In using this model, consider, for example, the case of an 80-year-old woman who lives alone in an apartment building for older adults. It is her choice to live independently; however, her cognitive functioning has declined over the years. One day, unaware that she has not turned off the stove, she places a tea towel on the stovetop, resulting in a kitchen fire. By using the decision-making model, the practitioner can weigh the importance of honoring the client's independence and autonomy against the need to protect the safety and well-being of the other residents.

Another aid for ethical decision making is Kitchener's (1984) critical evaluation model. Four ethical principles form the basis of this model:

1. Autonomy: the promotion of self-determination or the freedom to make choices for oneself
2. Beneficence: the promotion of goodness, kindness, or charity and the prevention or removal of harm
3. Nonmaleficence: the act of doing no harm
4. Justice: the provision of equal treatment to all

When applying this model to practice, the social worker factors into the assessment personal and environmental influences affecting the client's situation. For instance, certain cultures may emphasize family decision making over individual decision making. Within such a cultural dynamic, autonomy is less important for the older adult than the other three principles.

A model designed by G. Corey, Corey, and Callanan (2011) allows practitioners to assess those factors that may affect the older adult's situation in a thorough and systematic manner. Using their model, practitioners would follow these eight steps:

1. Identify the problem or dilemma: The practitioner gathers information about the older adult's situation. Is the conflict an ethical, legal, or moral one?
2. Identify the issues: What are the critical issues that pertain to the situation? What are the rights, responsibilities, and welfare of all concerned? Are there competing factors that embody the moral principles of autonomy, beneficence, nonmaleficence, and justice?
3. Review relevant ethical guidelines: What are the relevant aspects of professional codes of ethics that would apply in the particular situation?
4. Know laws and regulations: What are the applicable state and federal laws? How do they provide guidance on the ethical dilemma?
5. Obtain consultation: Acquire a different perspective on the situation by conferring with colleagues.
6. Consider possible or probable courses of action. List them.
7. Enumerate the consequences of various decisions. Ask: What are the implications of each course of action for the older adult? For the family? For the community? For the social worker? Use the principles of

autonomy, beneficence, nonmaleficence, and justice as a framework for evaluation.

8. Decide on the best course of action. Assess the information obtained in steps 1–6 and come to a decision. (G. Corey et al., 2011, pp. 24–27)

G. Corey et al.'s (2011) model encourages practitioners to include existing codes of ethics and colleagues' opinions in the assessment process. The use of codes of ethics provides clear guidelines and outlines considerations to be made in the decision-making process with older adults and their families.

A model developed by Congress (1999) specifically helps social workers to resolve ethical dilemmas. This five-step model, which can be applied in practice situations that involve older adults, is called ETHIC:

1. Examine relevant personal, societal, agency, client, and professional values.

2. Think about what ethical standard of the code of ethics (NASW, 2017) applies to the situation, and consider relevant laws and case decisions.

3. Hypothesize about possible consequences of different decisions.

4. Identify who will benefit and who will be harmed in view of social work's commitment to the most vulnerable people.

5. Consult with one's supervisor and colleagues about the most ethical choice. (Congress, 1999, pp. 31–33)

This model encourages social workers to methodically examine all values that may influence their decision making and to review the available options systematically. One advantage in using ETHIC is that it includes input from the code of ethics and colleagues before the practitioner reaches a conclusion on the best course of action to take in working with the older adult.

As society copes with a growing aging population, gerontological social workers will need to balance the rights of older adults against those of others. Issues requiring attention include how to allow older clients as much autonomy as possible while protecting them and others from harm. As older adults lose physical and cognitive capacity, such ethical decision making becomes more complicated.

Codes of Ethics

Many professional organizations have established codes of ethics, which usually include standards and principles to guide practice. For example, the NASW *Code of Ethics* (NASW, 2017) serves six purposes, as follows:

1. Identifies core values on which social work's mission is based.

2. Summarizes broad ethical principles that reflect the profession's core values and establishes a set of specific ethical standards that should be used to guide social work practice.

3. Is designed to help social workers identify relevant considerations when professional obligations conflict or ethical uncertainties arise.
4. Provides ethical standards to which the general public can hold the social work profession accountable.
5. Socializes practitioners new to the field to social work's mission, values, ethical principles, and ethical standards.
6. Articulates standards that the social work profession itself can use to assess whether social workers have engaged in unethical conduct. NASW has formal procedures to adjudicate ethics complaints filed against its members. In subscribing to this code, social workers are required to cooperate in its implementation, participate in NASW adjudication proceedings, and abide by any NASW disciplinary rulings or sanctions. (Dolgoff et al., 2012, p. 257)

The values, principles, and standards in the code of ethics guide practitioners' decision making and conduct. When social workers apply the code to practice, however, they must consider the context of a situation and any conflicts between the code and the practice situation. For example, the code of ethics cannot resolve all ethical issues. An important component of the ethical decision-making process is the social worker's informed judgment. In addition, social workers may avail themselves of various tools to help them with their ethical decision making. Such tools include ethical theory or state regulations, laws, and other professional codes that might provide additional guidance on working through a dilemma.

Dolgoff and colleagues (2012) have developed two tools to help practitioners presented with an ethical dilemma to prioritize the elements of that conflict. The first tool is an ethical rules screen (see Figure 2.1). This screen helps social workers determine whether the code of ethics applies to a situation and whether it provides sufficient guidance to resolve the dilemma (Dolgoff et al., 2012).

If a social worker is unsuccessful in applying the code of ethics to a practice situation, he or she may use the ethical principles screen (Dolgoff et al., 2012) to rank order principles (see Figure 2.2). Using this tool, the social worker decides which principle applies to the case and the location of that principle on the screen. Fulfilling a higher-order principle takes precedence over fulfilling a lower-order one.

Because the code of ethics is not a blueprint for professional conduct, practitioners must be prepared to engage actively in ethical decision making when working with older adults. Particular challenges gerontological social workers may face include allowing older adults as much autonomy in the decision-making process as possible while promoting the best approach that avoids harm, advocating for fair and equitable treatment of older adults, and encouraging interventions that promote the most good. To respect autonomy is to recognize people as self-determining agents who are entitled to decide their own destiny. It is to recognize that people have the right to their own opinions and to act on them. It is to acknowledge that people have the right to their own judgments.

Figure 2.1:   Ethical Rules Screen

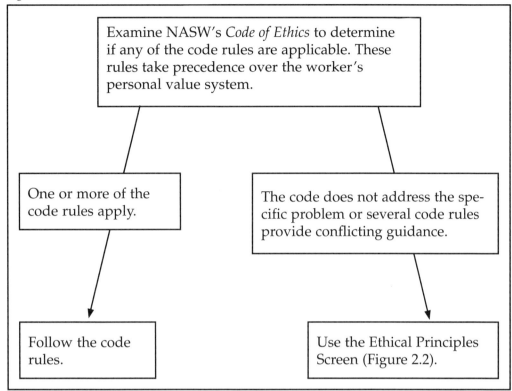

Source: Dolgoff, R., Harrington, D., & Loewenberg, F. M. (2012). *Ethical decisions for social work practice* (9th ed., p. 79). Belmont, CA: Brooks/Cole. Adapted with permission from South-Western College Publishing, a division of Cengage Learning.

People who are autonomous are free from external constraints and can handle their own affairs (Beauchamp, Walters, Kahn, & Mastroianni, 2014).

Liberty-Limiting Principles

Although practitioners ought to respect autonomous decision making whenever possible, sometimes it is necessary to restrict an individual's freedoms to protect the older person and others affected by the individual's behavior. Beauchamp et al. (2014) identified four liberty-limiting principles that justify such action:

1. The principle of paternalism: A person's liberty is justifiably restricted to prevent the individual from harming self.
2. The harm principle: A person's liberty is justifiably restricted to prevent harm to others caused by that person.
3. The principle of legal moralism: A person's liberty is justifiably restricted to prevent that person's immoral behavior.

4. The offense principle: A person's liberty is justifiably restricted to prevent offense caused by that person to others (p. 33).

The first two liberty-limiting principles are the ones most often applied to practice with older adults. Ethical conflicts occur when an older adult has compromised internal capacities for self-governance—for instance, when the individual has dementia, temporary memory loss, or a developmental disability. In such situations, the principle of beneficence applies, directing social workers to prevent or remove possible harm to the individual. These encounters may lead to application of the liberty-limiting principle of paternalism, one form of

Figure 2.2:   Ethical Principles Screen

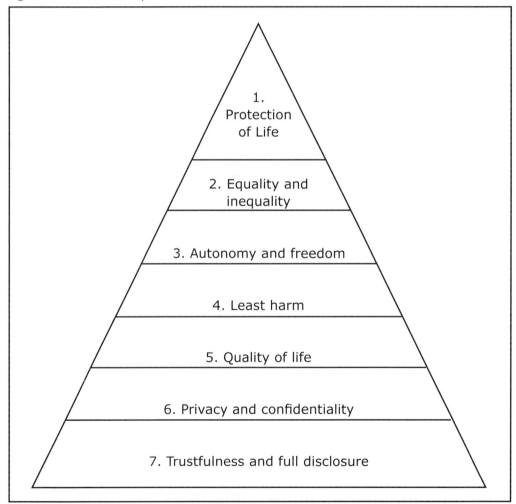

Source: Dolgoff, R., Harrington, D., & Loewenberg, F. M. (2012). *Ethical decisions for social work practice* (9th ed., p. 80). Belmont, CA: Brooks/Cole. Reprinted with permission from South-Western College Publishing, a division of Cengage Learning.

beneficence. Often, in such situations, the practitioner is intervening "for the good of the person" or to protect the older adult from potential risk or harm to self.

Another liberty-limiting principle social workers may encounter in their work with older adults is the harm principle, which addresses life-safety issues. A practitioner might apply this principle, for example, in the case of an older male adult who has a diagnosis of schizophrenia and has threatened the safety of another person because the voices in his head have directed him to harm that person. Using the ethical principles screen outlined in Figure 2.2, the social worker could examine whether the protection of life is a more compelling principle than autonomy and freedom. Therefore, both that tool and the liberty-limiting principle might direct the practitioner to intervene in the older adult's autonomous decision making because another person's life might be at stake.

Sometimes the issue of whether an older adult is capable of self-governance arises, thus leading to a question of legal competence. By definition, a person who is legally incompetent performs below a minimum level of cognitive ability. To make an initial evaluation of the cognitive functional capacity of an older adult, the social worker might ask several assessment questions, adapted from Herr and Weber (1999), Kapp (1998), and Linzer (2002):

- Can the older adult make and communicate by spoken words (or by other means) his or her decisions or choices?
- Can he or she provide reasons why these choices were made?
- Are the reasons underlying the choices rational?
- Is the individual able to understand the implications or the risks and benefits of the choices he or she has made?
- Are the choices consistent with the older adult's values and preferences?

The answers to these questions will reveal a sense of the client's legal competence. If the older adult appears able to articulate and understand the reasons for selecting a course of action, and no obvious harm or safety issues are present, then the social worker ought to respect the individual's autonomy even if the choices conflict with the practitioner's own expectations or social expectations.

To further protect an older adult's right to autonomous decision making, social workers and other practitioners should apply informed consent procedures to every intervention or treatment decision. Informed consent enables the older adult to accept or refuse treatment. Informed consent involves three elements (Herr & Weber, 1999):

1. Competency: The individual or surrogate decision maker must be legally capable of giving consent.
2. Knowledge: The social worker needs to furnish adequate information so that the individual can evaluate and understand the benefits and risks of an intervention. The social worker also needs to provide an opportunity for the client to ask questions and receive understandable answers.

3. Voluntariness: The individual should not be coerced to make a decision one way or another. He or she ought to have the option to abstain from the intervention.

Informed consent must occur prior to the intervention. Informed consent requires practitioners to explain each intervention and procedure thoroughly so that clients will understand the risks and benefits and will be in a position to make informed decisions. Health care or social work practitioners may convey the following information to older adults (Herr & Weber, 1999, p. 48):

- diagnosis
- nature and purpose of the intervention
- risks or consequences of the intervention
- prognosis or probability of success
- alternatives to the intervention
- possible outcomes if procedure is not done
- provider limitations, if any
- professional advice or recommendations

If the three elements—competency, knowledge, and voluntariness—are present and the social worker or health care practitioner has provided a reasonable amount of information to the older adult, then informed consent has been achieved.

Obtaining informed consent from an older adult whose cognitive functioning fluctuates may be difficult. In such cases, the practitioner should wait for a good day—when cognitive functioning is optimal—to provide that client with information. Again, it is important to note that informed consent must occur before an intervention. It also is recommended that a trusted family member, friend, or designated health care proxy observe the informed consent session and lend support to the older adult.

As Congress (1999) has pointed out, "Ethical social work with older persons begins with the client" (p. 97). Thus, in all situations, social workers need to maximize older adults' participation in decision making to the fullest extent possible.

THOROUGH DECISION MAKING

It is important for professional social workers to gather as much information as possible about a client's situation, using that information to conduct a thorough assessment. In cases involving ethical conflicts or dilemmas with older adults, this step in the assessment process is key to the deliberations that must occur before deciding on the right course of action. It is essential that social workers facilitate the decision-making process in a thoughtful and inclusive manner, especially when older adults and their families are considering whether to pursue life-sustaining treatment or to relinquish decision-making responsibilities.

A Decision-Making Model

Dolgoff and colleagues (2012) proposed the general decision-making model to serve as a practice guide. One intent of their model is to keep social workers mindful that the input of several people, including family members, neighbors, and health care workers, can be useful before rendering a decision about the best intervention approach for the older adult. Practitioners may apply Dolgoff et al.'s model (2012) to any practice situation, even one that does not involve an ethical problem.

Each person in the decision-making process has the potential to present new information, suggest options, and provide or withdraw support, all of which can alter or refine decision making. Because ethical decision making is a complex process, practitioners must remain flexible and thoughtful, often using more than one problem-solving approach.

Consultation with Committees and Teams

The most prominent use of ethics committees is within hospital settings, and such committees are now appearing in long-term care facilities (Agich, 1993; Beaulieu, 2012; Moeller et al., 2012). When medical and treatment decisions are at hand, social workers may seek opinions from an ethics committee or ethics consultation group to ensure the thoroughness of the decision-making process. Ethics committees serve a number of purposes. They can provide education, develop institutional policies and guidelines, or offer consultation services. The last function often involves cases concerning the withholding, withdrawing, or continuation of life-sustaining medical care (Weiss, Berman, Howe, & Fleming, 2012). A typical ethics committee is composed of a physician, a nurse, a social worker, an attorney, hospital administrators, clergy, a community member, an advocate for the aged population, and a medical ethicist. Some committees include the client and family in their membership (Beaulieu, 2012).

In the social services agency setting, practitioners may use peer review and services planning committees to oversee delivery of services (Galambos, 1999). Such committees monitor client services and handle ethical conflicts as they emerge within an agency. They determine whether the services provided are reasonable, too few, or too costly or whether the social worker's use of services is reasonable to meet a client's needs. In essence, this process is a form of ethical consideration in the delivery of services (Galambos, 1997). Research has shown that peer review and interdisciplinary collaboration have positive effects on service delivery (Netting & Williams, 1995).

Administrative teams composed of administrators and service providers also may assist with ethical deliberations. These teams meet periodically to discuss issues and practices related to quality of care, consumer choice, and service delivery. This type of interdisciplinary dialogue raises awareness about the constraints, problems, and successes of client services provided within an agency (Galambos, 1999).

PRINCIPLES OF AUTONOMY AND PATERNALISM

Trying to balance an older adult's right to autonomy and the professional's responsibility to intervene in situations potentially harmful to the older adult and others—and responding effectively to everyone's needs—may lead to an ethical conflict, that is, a clash between opposing obligations (Galambos, 1997) or an ethical dilemma. Ethical dilemmas typically occur when the social worker chooses between two or more relevant but contradictory ethical directives, or when every alternative results in an undesirable outcome for one or more people. Each party to an ethical disagreement may put forth moral principles to support his or her competing conclusions.

In matters of client self-determination, guardianship, and end-of-life decision making, the ethical conflict is that of autonomy versus paternalism. Autonomy supports an older adult's independence in terms of decision making and living arrangements, and it encourages respect of an older adult's preferences. Paternalism obligates the practitioner to help others and to prevent harm or ameliorate harmful situations. A paternalistic approach deprives an older person of his or her own free choice; rather, others make decisions out of concern for the individual's own good. Following the principle of paternalism, the social worker's concept of what constitutes benefits and harm prevails over the client's view, which may differ. For example, on learning that a senior client with a history of chronic depression has admitted to having a concrete suicide plan, the social worker would arrange for the client's psychiatric hospitalization.

Autonomy–paternalism conflicts occur when practitioners must judge whether an older adult is competent to make independent decisions about, for instance, living in a community with limited resources or in an unsafe or unhealthy environment, or whether to comply with medical treatment. One risk in making such a judgment is that the social worker may discount a person's competency as a decision maker if the older adult's viewpoint differs from his or her own (Kane, 1992).

Furthermore, autonomy–paternalism conflicts may be exacerbated by boundary issues, that is, when "human service professionals encounter actual or potential conflicts between their professional duties and their social, sexual, religious, or business relationships" (Reamer, 2001, p. 1). A particular challenge in maintaining boundaries is protecting the client's right to confidentiality and privacy. A social worker has an ethical obligation to maintain confidences; therefore, sharing information with anyone without the client's consent is a boundary violation (Galambos, Watt, Anderson, & Danis, 2005). In their guidelines for protecting client confidentiality, Galambos and colleagues (2005) have recommended that practitioners use informed consent procedures, discuss potential boundary issues during the assessment process, and explain how they will handle confidentiality. They should periodically assess whether they are treating confidentiality in a manner that is acceptable to their clients.

Sometimes a care provider's and an older adult client's autonomies compete (Kane, 1992). For example a frail older adult may choose to return home after a hospitalization, yet that community placement may create hardships—increased care and support and increased financial responsibilities—for the care provider. In such circumstances, the social worker must delicately balance the needs of the care provider with those of the older person. In considering the family unit as a whole, while being mindful of any boundary issues, the social worker might decide that paternalism should take precedence over the client's autonomy. It is essential, however, that the parties involved clearly communicate with each other about the issues and options available to the older adult and that they ensure that the older adult has an equal voice in the decision making.

Involving Clients in the Care Plan

Practitioners may use several techniques to increase a senior client's autonomy. One is to encourage the client's active participation in the development of the care plan and to ensure that participation continues throughout the goal planning, implementation, and monitoring processes (Galambos, 1997). Practitioners encourage independent decision making by soliciting client input.

Atchley and Barusch's (2004) concept of negotiated risk is gaining popularity within assisted living facilities and home care programs as a means of preserving client autonomy. In this model, the social worker gives the older adult an opportunity to state what risks he or she is willing to assume as a condition of providing less strict procedures and close monitoring of the client's situation.

Following Informed Consent Procedures

Another technique for encouraging client autonomy is to use informed consent procedures. Informed consent assists clients in understanding available options, thereby enabling them to weigh the pros and cons of a decision. It also provides social workers with a structured form for dissemination of information.

The informed consent process is ongoing and "includes the systematic disclosure of information to a client over time, along with an opportunity to engage in dialogue with the client about forthcoming treatment and service" (Reamer, 1987, p. 428; see also, Price, Bereknyei, Kuby, Levinson, & Braddock, 2012). Informed consent allows social workers to offer continuing information about the type of services recommended to functionally and legally competent clients and provides an opportunity for clients to refuse services (Price et al., 2012; Reamer, 1987, 1990). In cases in which an elder has been legally declared incompetent, informed consent procedures may be extended to legal guardians or surrogates (Reamer, 1990).

Shared decision making is an increasingly acceptable approach to providing care to older adults in health and mental health care environments. It is regarded as the model for patient–provider communication. Shared decision making emphasizes collaborative communication and joint decision making between health care providers and clients. In doing so, the elements of informed consent are emphasized in the process. Increasingly, palliative care and hospice programs are adopting this type of approach to their work with older adults (Romo, Walhagen, & Smith, 2016).

Including Clients and Others in the Care Planning Process

Another approach to protecting the rights of all people involved in a case is to include all relevant parties in deliberations. Whenever possible, the social worker should involve family members and care providers in the assessment process and in the development of treatment or care plans. When a senior client's care needs have increased or in cases in which functional and cognitive functioning has decreased, it is particularly important to include care providers in the planning process.

Considering Guardianship

Practitioners who have determined through mental status exams and medical testing that an older adult is marginally competent may pursue "guardianship," a legal mechanism by which a person is invested with the power and responsibility to assume control and decision-making responsibility over another person adjudicated to be unable or incompetent to manage his or her own affairs (W. G. Bell, Schmidt, & Miller, 1981; Falk & Hoffman, 2014; Gibson, 2011). There are two types of guardianship: (a) property, in which the guardian controls financial and property affairs; and (b) person, in which the guardian makes personal decisions for the client about, for example, medical care and social services (Falk & Hoffman, 2014). Guardianship may be beneficial in situations in which a frail older adult requires protection and is unable to manage his or her own affairs—for example, in situations in which there is suspected abuse, neglect, or exploitation; in other situations in which the older adult is vulnerable, unsafe, and unprotected; or in situations in which the individual is under undue influence by another. Guardians may be family, friends, or professionals, or they may be appointed by the courts. For the practitioner, guardianship presents an ethical dilemma between the competing principles of autonomy and beneficence.

Some forms of personal guardianship protect the older adult's rights more than others. A "limited" guardianship allows for increased autonomy; it supports independence and self-control; and it provides the elder with an opportunity to participate in the decision-making process (Falk & Hoffman, 2014). A "full" guardianship, in contrast, severely limits a person's autonomy, and social workers should pursue this legal status judiciously. Because full guardianship reduces the legal status of the elder to that of a minor, social workers ought to seek this legal status only as a last resort. Under full guardianship status, older adults may lose control over their property and are unable to act independently. Furthermore, guardianship removes an older adult's right to vote or to refuse medical treatment, manage his or her finances, drive a car, or make other independent decisions, including treatment decisions (W. G. Bell et al., 1981; Gibson, 2011). For these reasons, limited guardianships are the least restrictive option given that the older adult retains some rights and recognized capacities and the guardian's duties and powers are limited (Falk & Hoffman, 2014).

In situations in which guardianship is being considered, it is important to ensure that proper assessments are conducted to determine the capacity of an older adult. These evaluations should incorporate multiple sources of data and focus on functional abilities (Falk & Hoffman, 2014). The purpose of these evaluations is to determine areas of challenges and declining abilities and also preserved areas of ability and strengths. Medical records should be reviewed; clinical interviews conducted; and screening, assessment, and evaluation tools incorporated in the interview process. Collateral information should be collected with individuals who have a significant relationship with the older adult. Capacity assessments are often, and ideally, interdisciplinary in nature. Capacity assessments may lead to a clinical diagnosis, but the purpose of the evaluation is to identify functional strengths and weaknesses. Gibson suggests that one key question to ask throughout the process is, "Why is guardianship needed now?" (Gibson, 2011, p. 813). Determining functional ability and environmental supports and barriers is the most important purpose of capacity assessments. This ensures that alternatives to guardianship can be considered. These alternatives can capitalize on an individual's strengths while both putting into place a plan that addresses the challenge areas and still supporting the least restrictive choice that offers the highest degree of independence possible.

Discussing Advance Directives

An inclusive alternative to decision making about medical care is an approach that supports client autonomy—the enactment of *advance directives,* or written instructions, "such as a living will or durable power of attorney for health care recognized under State law and relating to the provision of such care when the individual is incapacitated" (Osman & Perlin, 1994, p. 246). When appropriate, social workers can encourage elderly clients to discuss and assist in executing advance directives. These documents will aid in decision making on medical issues if the client has a terminal illness or is in a persistent and vegetative state and is consequently unable to communicate his or her wishes (Galambos, 1998; Kapp, 1998).

Advance directives fall into two categories: (1) an instruction directive, written by the principal, that details the life-sustaining treatments the person desires under certain types of clinical situations; and (2) a proxy directive, by which the principal appoints an individual to make health care decisions for him or her in the event of incapacitation. The proxy decision maker is obligated to make the same decision that the incapacitated elder would make, thus preserving some autonomy. The proxy approach works well in situations in which an older adult's wishes are known and when the proxy selected honors those wishes.

Because older adults sometimes defer end-of-life decision making to family members, social workers can support their clients' autonomy by offering information on end-of-life options. In addition, research has indicated that the provision of educational programs on advance directives to older adults and their family members increases the frequency and intensity of discussions about end-of-life decision making (Bailey & DePoy, 1995). Social workers are in an excellent position to coordinate such programs (Galambos, Starr, Rantz, & Petroski, 2016). A variety of tools and resources are available to help with this type of education. See the Additional Resources section at the end of this chapter for information on relevant Web sites that contain important content and tools.

Increasingly, situations occur in which individuals who lack decision-making capacity and whose important medical decisions must be made for them have no designated surrogates or proxies to help with those decisions. In these cases, professionals will use enacted advance directives, ethics committees, or health care providers such as physicians to guide recommendations about next steps for care. Sometimes family members are consulted about treatment options, and families are often willing to step in to provide support in these situations even if they are not the legally appointed proxy. However, for older adults without family or friends who can act in this capacity, the situation becomes more complicated. Guardianship can be attained for these individuals, but it is not a timely process. The concept of health fiduciaries as a new type of professional who would be certified to act as a surrogate decision maker has been proposed as a solution to such situations (Weiss et al., 2012). The health fiduciary enables individuals without close family or friends whom they can appoint as proxies to find a trained individual to act as a surrogate for them (Weiss et al., 2012).

CONCLUSION

In today's practice world, ethical challenges are becoming more prevalent as people live longer and medical advances create new and different treatment approaches. As society faces declining resources and simultaneously confronts an increasing demand for services, social workers will find themselves involved in ethical dilemmas requiring their thoughtful responses, so that they may resolve conflicts in practice situations.

When applied consistently, the models and tools presented in this chapter can assist practitioners in working through competing ethical principles, at the same time ensuring a fair process for their older adult clients. Mastery of the ethics competencies highlighted in this book will help social workers develop the skills necessary to work effectively with an aging population.

Case Study: Ethical Issues in the Stanley Family

The Stanley family case example includes several ethical issues. One is competence, as grandparents' ability to raise grandchildren can be questioned for several reasons. Because many custodial grandparents are beyond the usual time of caregiving, they may be viewed as physically unfit to take on child care responsibilities. This is a type of ageism where they are evaluated on their chronological age instead of their skills and abilities. In addition, grandparents are sometimes questioned because their own sons or daughters are unable to raise their children. In this case, John's drug addiction and criminal activity may be viewed by others as a failure in Mrs. Stanley's parenting, and her ability to raise her grandchildren may be questioned.

However, a corollary is when there is a reason that a grandparent is unable to provide adequate care or the situation endangers the grandparent's health and well-being. The do-no-harm principle or nonmaleficence can be difficult to evaluate in cases where a grandparent's own health or functioning may suffer as a result of the caregiving role. With increasing age, there is a probability that the custodial grandparents may be experiencing their own health-related changes that can compromise their ability to provide care. In these situations, the needs of the grandparent and grandchildren should be balanced and evaluated to determine an appropriate course of action.

Custodial grandparents like Mrs. Stanley also struggle with decision making around the future of the grandchildren. The majority of grandparents provide care informally; that is, they do not seek legal custody of their grandchildren (Urban Institute, 2003). This situation can create ethical challenges, such as a situation when a grandparent needs to render legal decisions for a grandchild. This situation arose within the Stanley family when Terrell needed emergency medical treatment for his asthma. Although he was living with his grandmother, she did not have any insurance information for him and was not his legal guardian. Some grandparents do seek legal guardianship, and others move forward with adopting their grandchildren. Although these options provide a legal pathway for decision making, some grandparents are reluctant or unwilling to pursue these options. This stance may partially reflect a feeling that terminating parental rights is a sign that they are giving up on their own child—that the father or mother will never become competent enough to regain the parenting role. That is the case for Mrs. Stanley, who has a hope that John will be released from prison and will be able to take care of his two children. Realistic or not, the divided loyalties that custodial grandparents experience can be a significant source of stress for them (Goodman, 2007).

WHAT WE LEARNED IN THIS CHAPTER

- There are values, ethical standards and principles, and practice regulations that influence and direct practice approaches.
- There are a variety of ethical decision-making tools available to help in determining the best plan of action to resolve an ethical dilemma or conflict.
- Liberty-limiting principles help to determine situations in which an older adult's freedom might be restricted.
- Social workers, whenever possible, should protect an older person's right to autonomous decision making.
- Apply informed consent procedures and involve the client in care planning as pro forma procedures.

- When guardianship is necessary, consider the least restrictive form, such as limited guardianship.
- To preserve autonomous decision making, reinforce the enactment of an advance directive.
- When ethical dilemmas cannot be resolved, consult with ethics committees or teams.

SUGGESTED EXERCISES TO EVALUATE STUDENT COMPETENCY

Students will use Dolgoff et al.'s (2012) general decision-making model to evaluate a case involving ethical practice issues. Answer the following questions:

1. What can you do to minimize conflicts among your personal, societal, and professional values?
2. What can you do to minimize conflicts among your clients', others', and society's rights and interests?

ADDITIONAL RESOURCES

The mission of the Association of Social Work Boards is to strengthen consumer protection and advance competent and ethical social work practice through the provision of support to the social work regulatory community. Visit https://www.aswb.org/.

The Conversation Project provides information and tools that can be used to help people make decisions about end-of-life care: http://theconversation-project.org/.

The Hastings Center addresses ethical issues in the areas of health, health care, life sciences research, and the environment as they affect individuals, the community, and the environment. Visit http://www.thehastingscenter.org/.

The Markkula Center for Applied Ethics offers a framework for ethical decision making, including an ethical decision-making app at https://www.scu.edu/ethics/ethics-resources/ethical-decision-making/a-framework-for-ethical-decision-making/.

The National Health Care Decisions Day's mission is to help people understand the value of advance care planning. A variety of helpful tools and resources may be found at http://www.nhdd.org/.

The National Hospice and Palliative Care Organization is committed to improving end of life care and expanding access to hospice care with the goal of profoundly enhancing quality of life for people dying in America. Practice and educational tools can be located at http://www.nhpco.org/.

The National Association of Social Workers' *Code of Ethics* provides ethical standards and guidelines for professional practice and can be found at https://www.socialworkers.org/pubs/code/default.asp.

The National Association of Social Workers' perspective about advance care planning may be accessed at http://www.socialworkers.org/practice/practice_tools/reexamining_advance_care_planning.asp.

Social work roles and opportunities in advance directives and health care decision making may be accessed at http://www.socialworkers.org/practice/aging/advdirct.

The Social Work Hospice and Palliative Care Network is a national network of psychosocial care professionals that provides the latest in information, resources, policy, and education and research at http://www.swhpn.org/.

3

Diversity, Difference, and Redress

RATIONALE: Social workers should "understand how diversity and difference characterize and shape the human experience and are critical to the formation of identity" (CSWE, 2015, p. 7). "The dimensions of diversity are understood as the intersectionality of multiple factors including but not limited to age, class, color, culture, disability and ability, ethnicity, gender, gender identity and expression, immigration status, marital status, political ideology, race, religion/spirituality, sex, sexual orientation, and tribal sovereign status" (CSWE, 2015, p. 7). "Practitioners in aging understand the impact of discrimination and oppression on older adults and their caregivers, and identify the intersectionality of age with multiple characteristics of diversity and structural inequities throughout the life course" (CSWE, 2017, p. 13).

COMPETENCY: "Practitioners in aging, with or on behalf of older adults and their constituencies

- appraise their own values related to diversity in aging.
- analyze how diversity and oppression impact older adults and families.
- address the cultural and spiritual histories, values, and beliefs of older adults and their families.
- defend the impact of structural inequalities and the value of diversity among older adults as part of their roles on interprofessional teams and in organizations and communities." (CSWE, 2017, p. 13)

You are beginning your social work career at a time when the United States is increasingly multicultural. Immigrants and people of color continue to make up an increasingly greater percentage of the population in this country (Federal

---

*Youjung Lee and Olivia Lopez contributed to this chapter.

Interagency Forum on Aging-Related Statistics [FIFARS], 2016). Furthermore, older adults are becoming more ethnically diverse (FIFARS, 2016). By 2050, the population of Asians 65 years of age and older will have grown by approximately 720 percent; Hispanic elders by 553 percent; black elders by 262 percent; and white elders by 116.7 percent (FIFARS, 2016). Today's geriatric social workers will also need to address how clients' lives are influenced by the intersectionality of many factors. As Hooyman (1996, p. 20) so aptly put it, a social worker's mandate is "to promote the full humanity of all voices which have been marginalized in our society."

Older adults of racial and ethnic minority groups encounter more barriers to health and human services than their white counterparts (Whitfield & Baker, 2014). Cultural barriers and differences in attitude about accessing health and mental health services include older adults' feelings of shame and stigma, their fear and mistrust of the treatment system, and their limited financial and transportation resources (Whitfield & Baker, 2014). Moreover, models of community health based on a person-in-environment perspective continue to document that health outcomes are disproportionately unfavorable among older adults in minority groups, frequently bringing about a more rapid decline in their functional status compared with white older adults (Whitfield & Baker, 2014). High blood pressure, for example, affects a disproportionate number of black American older adults relative to their white counterparts, putting them at greater risk of other health complications (Whitfield & Baker, 2014).

Yet, an ethnic minority family's resilience may be enhanced by cultural values and the provision of mutual psychological support (Whitfield & Baker, 2014). Evidence increasingly suggests that the capacity to transcend the risks of oppressive environments can be enhanced by strengthening a family's unique cultural protective factors (Greene, 2002; Whitfield & Baker, 2014). For example, religiosity, particularly among elders of racial and ethnic minority groups, can be a mediating factor in reducing caregiver stress (Chadiha & Fisher, 2002; Morano & King, 2005; Whitfield & Baker, 2014).

The new multicultural aging population requires that social workers rethink the complex nature of diversity (Whitfield & Baker, 2014). Cultural competence is a major challenge that each new social worker will face in his or her career (Whitfield & Baker, 2014). This chapter outlines a culturally sensitive approach to social work practice that can help the new practitioner begin that process.

ON THE ROAD TO CULTURAL COMPETENCE

Cultural diversity, according to Fong (2001), "embraces the multiple dimensions of human identity, biculturalism, and culturally defined social behaviors. In the broadest sense, it encompasses people of color, women, the aged, gays and lesbians, physically and emotionally challenged, the poor and homeless, and a host of other disenfranchised groups" (p. 1). *Cultural competence*, conversely, is the ability to "provide services, conduct assessments, and implement interventions that are reflective of the clients' cultural values and norms, congruent with their natural help-seeking behaviors, and inclusive of existing indigenous solutions" (Fong, 2001, p. 1). In effective cross-cultural practice, then, social workers recognize that they and their clients are from different cultures, and therefore culturally specific information must be infused into the helping process (Greene, 2008b).

What these definitions mean for geriatric social workers is that they will need to craft their assessments to gain a better understanding of an older client's worldview and work together with the client to select culturally appropriate interventions. Services will also have to be provided with cultural humility (NASW, 2016b). The delivery of social services should take into consideration cultural elements and be provided in such a way that ethnic minority group participation and power is enhanced and respected (Greene, 2008b).

PREPARATION FOR COMPETENT PRACTICE

Social workers who strive to be culturally competent have to undergo a life-long process of acquiring the requisite knowledge, attitudes, and skills. Even before seeing their first client, practitioners can begin to gain knowledge associated with culturally competent practice—that is, information they will need to develop an informed understanding of the client's life experiences. Social workers should ask themselves: What do I already know about my client's culture? What more can I learn more about my client's community? What symbols and rituals must I know? How will I apply a learning stance? Can I be self-aware and self-regulated? (CSWE, 2015, p. 4).

As the practitioner listens to clients' life stories, he or she begins to learn how those clients' personal, political, and economic factors influence their lives. Other knowledge gained may include an understanding of clients' cultural norms, religion and spirituality, place in the life cycle, finances, and medical needs. Because such knowledge is individualized, it is used differentially with each client. This knowledge-seeking process will stretch the practitioner's ability to be more inclusive of the different people who will enter his or her practice. Moreover, practitioners must see their "clients and constituencies as experts in their own experiences" (CSWE, 2015, p. 4).

The attitudinal dimension of culturally competent practice requires that practitioners be open-minded and learn to appreciate other cultures (Okayama, Furuto, & Edmondson, 2001). A social worker who is proficient in diversity practice recognizes that older clients and social workers may have different attitudes about autonomy, self-determination, and choice. Furthermore, each client has a different comfort level when it comes to disclosing personal information. Moreover, the broader societal attitudes clients have encountered will influence their developmental path to resilience in later years: Practitioners must consider, for instance, whether an older client has faced discrimination and oppression. Because U.S. mainstream values or beliefs may clash with those of other cultures—for example, how clients approach death and dying—the geriatric social worker must create an atmosphere of acceptance and learn about the client's worldview on such matters (Whitfield & Baker, 2014). Most theorists agree that knowledge of a repertoire of skills is essential to reinforce cultural values and support appropriate interventions (Fong, 2001), as practitioners use culturally competent skills along each step of the social services delivery process (Okay-ama et al., 2001).

EXPLORATION OF CULTURAL INFLUENCES ON SELF AND CLIENT

NASW (2016b) has mandated that all social workers strive to be culturally competent. Cultural competence requires self-awareness and an acknowledgment of how culture shapes a client's life experiences.

Self-Awareness

Most professionals today, including social workers, are white, English speaking, and middle class (Green, 1999). A larger percentage of licensed social workers are non-Hispanic white than in the U.S. population. Yet social workers increasingly serve diverse constituencies. To work effectively across cultures, social workers must possess a heightened sense of self-awareness, the ability to reflect on one's own thoughts and actions. Self-regulation is a process that involves taking stock of "white privilege," a term sometimes used to describe the advantages granted to the white, middle-class population, including freedom of movement in housing, jobs, and recreation and access to resources such as education and health care. Furthermore, self-awareness entails conducting a self-inventory to determine how we as practitioners perceive other cultures. It also requires self-examination to see whether we believe in the power of family and culture as protective factors that can buffer people from adverse events and thus heighten resilience.

Acknowledgment of Cultural Influences

Culture is "a way of life of a society and comprises institutions, language, artistic expression, and patterns of social and interpersonal relationships" (Greene, 2008a, p. 28). It encompasses the values and beliefs that people learn are important, appropriate, and desirable. Because of the important role culture plays in affecting people's life experiences, social work educators have advocated for "ever-expanding parameters related to cultural diversity" (Tully, 1994, p. 235). For example, Green (1999) recommended that social workers take a broad view and consider culture as a community of interest that includes communities not explicitly racial or ethnic, such as a school for deaf people, a drug house, or street people. Culture, he added, is not a specific value, physical appearance, or something that people have; rather, it is people's shared cognitive map, their discourse, and how they go about their lives. Diversity and difference shape people's life perspective (CSWE, 2015, p. 4).

As people grow up in families, they become socialized into cultural norms and behavioral expectations. Such teachings will have also influenced older clients. Culture, for example, may affect caregiving of family members with dementia: It may shape how a family designates a primary caregiver, uses outside help, makes decisions about placement in a nursing home, and heals through the bereavement process.

MEANING MAKING

An important aspect of culture is that it sets the general parameters of how group members structure behavior and guides the meaning they ascribe to life events. Cultures differ in their worldview and in their "concept of the essential nature of the human condition" (Devore & Schlesinger, 1996, p. 9). For example, a Western (mainstream) orientation to the view of the self is that people should aspire to be autonomous or independent. However, some black Americans, Asian older adults, and members of tribal nations may be more comfortable with a relational world-view model—a world in which people strive for a unified community and collective responsibility such as those expressed in the symbolism of Kwanza (Daly, Jennings, Beckett, & Leashore, 1995; see http://officialkwanzaawebsite.org). Discerning how a client thinks about his or her independence is a key feature in geriatric assessment. Does he or she expect to live independently or with extended family?

HELP-SEEKING MODELS

Help-seeking models are used to understand how an older adult's culture has influenced his or her patterns of asking for help. These models also shed light on the meaning attributed to using social work services. Meaning making takes a personal and communal course. As individuals process life events, they develop a sense of direction and purpose (Krause, 2004). They also create a life story that embodies a larger cultural and historical context, and they bring their stories with them when seeking help.

   Help-seeking models were originally designed to account for cultural differences in describing and understanding illness. How do differing cultural views of sickness and treatment affect communication among an older client, family, and professionals? Are there culturally specific and universal characteristics of the healing process? These models suggest that various cultures have their own ideas about the nature of illnesses, treatments, and types of healers. Such models also portray health care systems as culturally based systems with their own symbolic meanings, particular patterns of social interactions, and institutional arrangements. Because helping systems are an outgrowth of culture, they are governed by cultural rules that shape beliefs and behaviors. People's awareness of their cultural life becomes more relevant or heightened when they contrast their culture with another by crossing a social boundary, such as class, education, religious affiliation, ethnicity, occupation, or social network (Kleinman, 1978, 1992). This contrast in culture can present conflicts for older adults and their families as they work their way through bureaucratic requirements in health care settings. It is often the social worker who can help negotiate these transactions.

KLEINMAN'S HELP-SEEKING MODEL

Kleinman's (1980) work on the meaning of illness focuses on the cognitive and belief systems of different cultures. This model has been defined by various social sciences, such as anthropology, and used in various helping professions. The primary characteristic of this model is that it emphasizes understanding the experience of illness from the subjective culturally based view of the client (McSweeney, 1990). This approach to understanding the meaning of illness is holistic, focusing on cultural belief systems.

Help-seeking models suggest that episodes of sickness and their treatment are tied to systems of knowledge and values. Such models are, however, characterized by vagueness, multiple meanings, frequent changes, and lack of sharp boundaries. They are unconsciously formed; tend to change over time; and are influenced by environment, ethnicity, individual interpretation, familial illness experience, exposure to Western medical practices, and tacit knowledge (Luyas, 1990; McSweeney, 1990).

Because such models incorporate the personal beliefs people use to recognize, interpret, and respond to a particular illness, social workers will have to learn how older adults perceive their medical diagnosis. People construct these models through interaction with the sociocultural environment, creating a commonsense understanding of body function (McSweeney, Alan, & Mayo, 1997; Schoenberg, Amey, & Coward, 1998). This accounts for why the meaning of an illness among patients and health practitioners may often differ or conflict.

For example, when farm-working women interact with a social work professional, they bring with them medical "philosophies" related to cultural beliefs and practices based on long-standing traditions and notions about sickness and treatment (Lopez, 2007; C. D. Thompson & Wiggins, 2002). This cultural system of health and healing often differs from the more accepted and recognized Western medical model (Kleinman, 1980). For these women, the meaning of illness rests on the interpretation of symptoms and an understanding of diagnosis based on a cultural understanding of illness, experiences of family members, and social networks.

It is important for social workers to explore clients' cultural interpretations of illness and treatment in a respectful manner to gain an understanding of their orientation toward and acceptance of Western medical practices. For example, Holland and Courtney (1998) reported that many Mexican Americans do not think of their cultural health beliefs and practices as "folk" medicine. Rather than asking patients whether they use folk medicine, social workers can ask how a particular illness is treated in their home community. This may demonstrate cultural sensitivity and help create a positive partnership between patients and practitioners. Social workers must also explore how Western health systems relate to local folk meanings. It will be at these intersections that patients and Western medical practitioners can help move toward a more unified health care plan.

Multigenerational legacies and stories often shape a family's beliefs and responses to illness and treatment. Furthermore, they convey beliefs about illness and treatment patterns across generations (Scollan-Koliopoulos, O'Connell, &

Walker, 2005). Thus, family expectations become another very important component of health-seeking models and cultural health systems. It is likely that a patient has expectations about illness, treatment, and caregiving linked to familial history. It is also likely that a patient has provided care to a parent or grandparent and has clear ideas about caregiving. As a result, this patient may have expectations about who should provide care for him or her as well. Therefore, social workers will need to address this area during the preliminary evaluation of care and pay careful attention to the client's familial experience of illness, treatment, and the suitability of any care plan.

The notion that the helping process is imbued with cultural elements of both clients and professionals has been applied to social services (Green, 1999). A client's culture is in direct contrast with that of the professional subculture. For instance, when an older adult of a racial or ethnic minority group meets with a social work professional, both parties are communicating across cultural boundaries. This cultural incongruence may also be present when members of the LGBT community interact with the medical community. The client brings a distinct set of assumptions about his or her own difficulties, such as beliefs about the cause of a problem. The professional has his or her own perceptions and interpretations. The greater the cultural distance between social worker and client, the more important is the need to build a relationship based on good communication and trust.

RELATIONAL WORLDVIEW

The relational worldview model offers another perspective of health found among indigenous peoples and other cultural minority groups—that is, the model illustrates how Native American clients may view "dis-ease" and health (Cross, 1998) (see Figure 3.1). The model depicts culture as a circle resembling a medicine wheel consisting of four factors: (1) context, including family, culture, and history; (2) mind, embodying intellect, emotion, and memory; (3) spirit, encompassing dreams, symbols, and stories; and (4) body, involving genetics, condition, and age. Native Americans believe that when a person keeps all four parts in balance, he or she experiences harmony or health. But a person has a sense of imbalance when he or she feels disharmony or dis-ease. Learning about such cultural meanings related to well-being is central to the helping process with older adults and their families.

CULTURAL DETERMINANTS OF HELP SEEKING

Saint Arnault (2009) developed the cultural determinants of help seeking model, which stipulates that perception, meaning interpretation, and resource exchange are filtered through models of wellness and distress that are defined culturally. Perceptions of wellness or distress are identified and labeled as important, optimal, or abnormal. These perceptions are interpreted and evaluated in terms of causal interpretations, social significance, resource availability, and

Figure 3.1:   A Relational Worldview Model

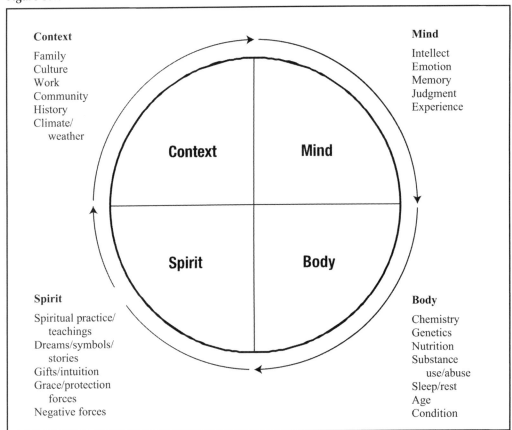

Context
Family
Culture
Work
Community
History
Climate/
   weather

Mind
Intellect
Emotion
Memory
Judgment
Experience

Spirit
Spiritual practice/
   teachings
Dreams/symbols/
   stories
Gifts/intuition
Grace/protection
   forces
Negative forces

Body
Chemistry
Genetics
Nutrition
Substance
   use/abuse
Sleep/rest
Age
Condition

Notes: The items listed are examples only. All of life and existence is included in the circle. Balance among all four parts brings harmony, and harmony equals health. Nothing in the circle can change without every other thing in the circle changing as well. The circle is constantly changing because of the cycles of the days, weeks, and seasons and because of development and different experiences. Individuals are considered ill if the circle becomes out of balance. Lack of balance causes "disease." In this view of health and mental health, healing may come from any or all of the four parts of the circle.
Source: Cross. T. L. (1998). Understanding family resiliency from a relational world view. In H. I. McCubbin, E. A. Thompson, A. I. Thompson, & J. E. Fromer (Eds.), *Resiliency in Native American and immigrant families* (pp.143–158). Thousand Oaks, CA: Sage Publications. Adapted with permission.

reciprocity rules. All of these factors are considered within a dynamic process before a person engages in help-seeking behavior. In some cultures, such as within East Asian families, the interpretation of values, social resources, and social exchange are to foster group harmony through the use of family as the primary source of support. This same group harmony value may discourage open displays of emotion, particularly negative emotions, and encourage self-reliance, using available resources sparingly and only when absolutely necessary (Saint Arnault, 2009).

PRACTICE WITHIN A CULTURAL CONTEXT

Relationship

One of the most challenging aspects of forming a helping relationship with clients from cultures other than one's own is the perceived power differential (Pinderhughes, 1983, 1989). Pinderhughes has suggested that both clients and practitioners bring feelings and behaviors to the helping encounter that are related to social markers of power, including social class, age, race, and ethnicity. Empathy, she argued, is the key ingredient to neutralizing the client's feelings of powerlessness within the client–social worker relationship.

Kadushin (1992) advised that practitioners working across cultures be ready to listen and be open to correction. Social workers should be prepared to accept that they will be scrutinized by clients who are different from themselves. They might ask themselves: Am I being perceived as genuine? Will I demonstrate a nonjudgmental attitude? Do I use the relationship to address issues of stigma and privilege?

Interview

The social work interview is a vehicle for learning about cultural differences. A successful interview involves suspending habitual judgments and engaging in dialogue that explores differences. For most practitioners, this process involves taking risks during the interaction, especially when asking for clarification or when admitting ignorance (Okayama et al., 2001). Conducting a skillful interview with diverse populations requires the selective and differential use of human behavior theory and practice methods (Greene, 2008a). For example, can practitioners be empathetic if they share few of the client's life experiences (Kadushin, 1992)? Can social workers protect a client's right to self-determination and informed consent in situations such as working with Korean American families who believe they must shield their elderly parents from difficult events and "unseemly" information (Fong, 2001)?

Narrative

An increasingly popular way of obtaining client information, particularly people's recollection of memories, is through narrative. In "narrative gerontology," a postmodern approach to helping, the focus is on eliciting a story or an account of critical life events as told by an older adult in his or her specific sociocultural context (Diehl, 1999; Kenyon & Randall, 2001). This approach offers several benefits: An individual's story, told in his or her own words, can "uncover how life reflects cultural themes of the society, personal themes, institutional themes, and social histories" (Creswell, 1998, p. 49). Personal stories are a link to one's personal past and to collective historical events (Andersen, Reznik, & Chen, 1997). Moreover, a narrative provides a means of understanding an individual's life course through the unfolding of critical life events, such as unemployment, an accident, or experiences with discrimination and its associated risks (Cohen & Greene, 2006). Critical life events—changes in a person's health, for instance—may also affect the person's sense of control and self-efficacy.

Most important, the narrative can be a means of helping members of a stigmatized group to get on the path to resilience. In this instance, the client can explore how negative societal themes can contribute to harmful images of the self. The practitioner assists in reframing these negative images, thus empowering the client.

CROSS-CULTURAL MODELS AND CONCEPTS

An assumption common among cross-cultural models of social work practice is that social workers cannot possibly have detailed and comprehensive knowledge about every diverse group or client. Rather, these models offer an overarching framework for learning about a specific client's concerns. Models do not put clients into categories or describe a list of traits that characterize people of a certain culture, but they do provide methods that enable practitioners to clarify the client's help-seeking behaviors.

When learning about unfamiliar people and places, every social worker should take the following steps in cross-cultural learning (Green, 1999, p. 94):

- read ethnographic descriptions
- prepare a social map
- act as a participant and observer
- plan community contacts
- meet key respondents
- conduct formal interviews
- identify specific culturally competent skills for the particular community

In the social services, according to Green (1999, p. 133), "We do not want or need to know everything about the cultural background of every client. What is needed is cultural data bearing on the presenting issue." When working with an older family, determine the family's expectations for care. For example, the practitioner may learn that for Asian or Latino families, *familism*—"the perceived strength of family bonds and sense of loyalty to family"—is of primary importance (Luna et al., 1996, p. 267) (for more on familism, see the section Work with Families later in this chapter). This brings with it the expectation that the extended family will care for an older relative or that the family will consult specially trained folk healers for advice. As described by Green (1999), to successfully engage in cross-cultural social work, practitioners must have the following five competencies:

1. Ethnic competence as awareness of one's own cultural limitations
2. Ethnic competence as openness to cultural differences

3. Ethnic competence as a client-oriented, systematic learning style
4. Ethnic competence as using cultural resources
5. Ethnic competence as acknowledging cultural integrity

DUAL PERSPECTIVE

As practitioners cross social boundaries, cultural differences become more apparent. Norton (1976) has provided a tool to help practitioners learn about these differences: This is the dual perspective, a "conscious and systematic process of perceiving, understanding, and comparing simultaneously the larger societal system with those of the client's immediate family and community system (p. 3)." According to Norton's model, people are a part of two systems: (a) the dominant or sustaining (mainstream) system, which is the source of power and economic resources; and (b) the nurturing (racial and ethnic group) system, which is the immediate social environment of the family and community. Individuals first learn about their immediate culture in the nurturing family system. They later encounter the mainstream, sustaining cultural system as they interact with the institutions, such as schools and health and human services agencies, that control the provision of goods and services.

From the dual perspective, evaluation involves assessing two disparate systems to determine the source of the client's major stressors (Norton, 1976). Social work practice often focuses on the risks—that is, the tensions and conflicts—that a client experiences because of the dissonance between the client's sustaining and nurturing systems. That focus, however, must factor in culture. Culture can serve as an insulator, offering comfort and affirmation. For example, elderly Latino clients often feel a sense of belonging, purpose, and pride in their *comunidad* (community). They develop a "blueprint for their behavior" within this immediate environment (Applewhite, 1998). Because a client may describe his or her difficulties in terms familiar in that person's nurturing culture, the practitioner will want to learn more about the client's meanings, symbols, and rituals.

The dual perspective is particularly important when working with immigrants. A culturally competent social worker will more effectively engage a family by using a *culturagram,* an instrument that allows the practitioner to examine a family's culture in a nonjudgmental manner (Congress, 1994). This tool enables practitioners to better understand culturally diverse families by gathering information from them on such factors as reasons for immigration, contact with cultural institutions, and language spoken at home and in the community. Social workers usually discover that there are intergenerational differences in families that sometimes can cause conflict when grandparents are far less acculturated than their grandchildren. Refer to the additional resources section of this chapter and the Web site the Social Work Podcast. This Web site contains a visual interpretation of the culturagram and an interview by its creator, Elaine Congress.

COMPETENCE IN AN OPPRESSIVE ENVIRONMENT

Competence is the ability to remain effective in one's environment over the life course. A critical issue in examining personal competence is how people living in hostile environments—characterized by "social injustice, societal inconsistency, and personal impotence" (Chestang, 1972, p. 105)—are able to cope. Environments that limit personal opportunity—that may be directed toward minority groups or people who are gay or lesbian—have the potential to inhibit development and impede the fulfillment of human potential. At the same time, minority cultures can promote adaptive strategies and foster resilience. Therefore, practitioners must consider what resources and coping strategies clients have developed for surviving hostile environments (Greene, 1999b, 2002).

Some research suggests that institutional homophobia, the irrational fear and hatred of those who love and sexually desire someone of the same sex, may not necessarily lead to negative coping. Researchers have found that older lesbians and gay men have developed affirming and positive images of themselves as they have deconstructed negative stereotypes from the past. The term "crisis competence" is used to describe how older lesbians and gay men restructured homosexuality from something negative to something positive in their lives (Kimmel, 1978). In fact, because there are resilient LGBT communities that engage in mutual support, they may be better prepared to handle a crisis and more able to deal with losses associated with the aging process (Barranti & Cohen, 2000; H. L. Cohen & Greene, 2006).

ACCULTURATION

Acculturation is the process of acquiring the language, customs, values, and so forth of a dominant or alternative culture (Skinner, 2002). It constitutes "phenomena which result when groups of individuals having different cultures come into continuous first-hand contact, with subsequent changes in the original cultural patterns of either or both groups" (Redfield, Linton, & Herskovits, 1936, p. 149).

To assess the extent to which an older client is acculturated, the practitioner must find answers to several questions: Does the client have a degree of acceptance of mainstream culture? Does that person feel loss for certain aspects of his or her original cultural heritage? Has the client adapted, thus combining mainstream and ethnic cultures? Has he or she had a negative reaction to mainstream culture? There often is a generational effect when considering the degree to which an older client is acculturated, with some older clients preferring to keep traditional cultural patterns more easily given up by their grandchildren.

BICULTURALISM

Biculturalism is the ability to conduct oneself in two different cultures. The ability to move between two different cultures differs from person to person (Greene, 2008a). Some may feel a high sense of success entering the mainstream culture, whereas others might experience discomfort. Usually, members of the younger generation are more bicultural and able to reach out and participate in mainstream culture.

WORK WITH FAMILIES

Contemporary social workers will find themselves practicing with a family unit that no longer is the "traditional" nuclear unit comprising blood relatives. Today's families may differ in structure, form, and culture (Greene & Schriver, 2016). Racial and ethnic minority group households may consist of multiple generations. Or a practitioner might work with a "blended family," in which a woman with children marries a man with children (resulting in two sets of grandparents). Social workers might also serve aging gay men and lesbian couples. These self-defined families are bound together by the same emotional relationships, interdependence, and loyalty that characterize traditional families. With states increasingly recognizing same-sex marriages, gay men and lesbian couples have had more freedom to legally marry, and social workers will increasingly work with married gay and lesbian couples.

INTERDEPENDENCE

Family-focused social work is based on the premise that over time each family develops a network of relationships with discernible structural and communication patterns (Greene & Schriver, 2016). How members interact and relate is reflected in observable structures and is influenced by the standards of what is considered acceptable in that family's culture. How interdependent is the family? When difficulties arise, how does the family expect to come up with solutions? What conflicts persist?

FAMILISM

Familism is a protective factor that buffers the effects of risk and enhances adaptation commonly experienced by racial and ethnic minority groups in the United States (Bullock, Crawford, & Tennstedt, 2003; Hinton, Guo, & Hillygus, 2000). As an abstract term, it incorporates several cultural aspects of family dynamics. In a review of familism among Latino family caregivers, Magana (2006) identified three such dynamics: (1) support from family members, (2) obligations to family, and (3) family members as referents. She found that the informal support network of Latino family caregivers consisted primarily of family members. Those informal caregivers made an exceptional commitment to their ill family members—besides the principal caregiver, the rest of the family was obliged to care for ill relatives. Furthermore, Latino family members tended to seek advice from other family members rather than from outside sources. Magana argued that although more similarities than differences exist across Latino family cultures, diversity within this ethnic group was apparent because families have varying countries of origin, primary language, and religion.

Familism guides families in racial and ethnic minority cultures in their decision making about whether to seek assistance from social workers. Frequently, families decide to reject outside help because they do not wish to disclose sensitive issues. Such decisions are influenced by a widely held cultural value that families are the first, and possibly the only, source of help (Hicks & Lam, 1999; Whitfield & Baker, 2014). For example, some Asian American families may choose to keep an ill parent or spouse home despite burdensome caregiving tasks because of the strength of their philosophy. Researchers have found that, in the caregiving process, caregivers from racial and ethnic minority groups prefer to rely on extended family networks rather than on formal services (Bullock et al., 2003; Dilworth-Anderson, Williams, & Gibson, 2002; Whitfield & Baker, 2014). Thus, many Asian American family caregivers limit the handling of issues to within the family network until the need for professional assistance is inescapable (Moon, Lubben, & Villa, 1998; Watari & Gatz, 2004; Whitfield & Baker, 2014).

The family unit has protected many immigrant families from racial discrimination in mainstream U.S. culture and has provided families with the strength to survive. Familism has allowed those families to celebrate their lives and to think positively about themselves in a foreign country. They may perceive that discussions about a family member's health problems with outsiders would tarnish the family's image in the community. That perception and cultural barriers to the use of health care systems influence many families of racial and ethnic minority groups to decide not to replace informal care with outside services (Bullock et al., 2003; Whitfield & Baker, 2014).

FILIAL PIETY

Filial piety is a social value that deeply affects the parent–child relationship of much of the East Asian population (Sung, 1997; Whitfield & Baker, 2014). Like familism, this cultural factor now shapes the dynamics of Asian American families. It is a core idea in Confucian ethics (Hwang, 1999; Yeh & Bedford, 2003). Confucianism is "the tradition and doctrine of *literati/* scholars. In fact, [Confucianism] is more than the values of a group of people. It contains a socio-political programme, an ethical system, and a religious tradition" (Yao, 2000, p. 31). From a Confucianistic perspective, humans are "part of the natural order and the natural state . . . one of harmony, not discord" (Ihara, 2004, p. 23). This tradition, in which family cohesion and continuity are the most important components for sustaining the community and the state, has strongly influenced China and other Asian countries (I. Park & Cho, 1995).

Originally, the philosophy of filial piety was that children have responsibilities to their parents; that is, offspring will respect and care for their aging parents (Yeh & Bedford, 2003). Modern filial piety continues this tradition, although in a modified form because of the cultural exchange with the West. In a study of 1,227 Korean adults and preadults, Sung (1997) identified two dimensions of modern filial piety: *behaviorally oriented filial piety*, which involves sacrifice, responsibility, and repayment; and *emotionally oriented filial piety*, which is characterized by family harmony, love or affection, and respect. Yeh and Bedford (2003) proposed a dual model that distinguishes *reciprocal filial piety*, when a child emotionally and spiritually attends to a parent, from *authoritarian filial piety*, when a child suppresses his or her own wishes and follows the parents' requests.

Knowledge about familism and filial piety will assist those social workers who are members of mainstream culture to be aware of how these philosophies may influence family dynamics, such as the emergence of a proxy decision maker or the selection of primary caregivers. For example, in mainstream culture, a spouse is more likely to be the primary caregiver for his or her partner (Janevic & Connell, 2001), but in East Asian culture, in observance of Confucian values, the eldest son and his wife typically provide care to parents (Brown & Browne, 1998). Even when the first son and his wife do not reside with the older adult client, they are assumed to be the main caregivers (Youn, Knight, Jeong, & Benton, 1999). In contrast, daughters in Latino and African American cultures play a larger role as alternative decision makers (Hornung et al., 1998) and main caregivers. Research has suggested that those caregiving patterns may account for lower caregiving burden because family roles are clear (Lee & Sung, 1998).

When the family and social worker mutually decide to arrange for outside services, the practitioner should attempt to complement the informal family assistance. The social worker should begin the assessment of client families by asking about their perceptions and expectations of familism and filial piety in their culture. For example, an Asian American family might report that they expect their oldest child or daughters-in-law to be major care providers for a parent with dementia. Even though such expectations may be modified in today's society, some caregivers may still hold to more traditional beliefs. During assessment, the practitioner must respect heterogeneity within a racial or ethnic minority group by attending to factors such as a caregiver's country of origin, reason for immigration to the United States, socioeconomic status, and educational attainment. An immigrant family's level of acculturation is a significant factor contributing to that family's adjusted norm and lifestyle in a foreign country. Because acculturation is a process rather than a product (Berry, 1997; Skinner, 2002), the practitioner must conduct a multidimensional assessment for the acculturation level of families of racial and ethnic minority groups. That assessment needs to include socioeconomic factors, education in the United States, income, and other factors that may strongly influence the family's level of acculturation.

END-OF-LIFE DECISIONS

Asian culture usually considers death to be a part of life and a time of family decision making. Therefore, Asian families might feel uncomfortable in planning procedures related to death. Research has suggested that familism and filial piety are particularly powerful influences on end-of-life decision making, such as the knowledge and use of advance directives (Kwak & Haley, 2005). When a family in a racial and ethnic minority group faces end-of-life decisions, the social work staff must be sensitive to the family's cultural and linguistic concerns. For example, in some cultures, an adult child translating a parent's concern to an English-speaking social worker may be perceived by the parent as a form of disrespect. Thus, the social worker must pay special attention to building trust and establishing a connection with families of racial and ethnic minority groups to overcome language and cultural barriers.

PERSONAL AND INSTITUTIONAL OPPRESSION

Power differentials continue to exist between the mainstream population and members of racial and ethnic minority groups as well as members of the LGBT community. On a personal level, power is related to the goodness of fit between person and environment. Thus, a social worker should assess an older adult's environment to determine whether it is sufficiently nutritive, providing the necessary resources, security, and support to enhance the client's well-being (Greene, 2008a; Solomon, 1976). Unfortunately, many older clients with limited political power may have experienced a lifetime of discrimination and have lived in marginalized neighborhoods (Lum, 1999).

On entering a field placement or new place of employment, it is advisable for the social worker to strive to understand the ecological context in which he or she will practice. The practitioner may want to complete a mental ecomap (see chapter 6) for, or needs assessment of, the community (see chapter 10), and ask himself or herself: Can I imagine my older client's environment? What ethnic and cultural groups exist in my service community? Social classes? What family types? The practitioner will need to seek information to determine whether a client is experiencing

- inequality in social resources, social position, or political and cultural influences
- inequality in opportunities to make use of existing resources
- inequality in the division of rights and duties
- inequality in implicit or explicit standards of judgment that often lead to differential treatment in law, the labor market, educational practices, and so forth
- inequality in cultural representations, that is, devaluation of the powerless group, stereotyping, or references to the nature (or biological essence) of the less powerful
- inequality in psychological consequences, that is, a "psychology of inferiority" (such as insecurity, "double-bind" experiences, and sometimes identification with the dominant group) versus a "psychology of superiority" (such as arrogance or an inability to abandon the dominant perspective)

- social and cultural tendency to minimize or deny power inequality such that potential conflict is represented as consensus and one views power inequality as "normal." (Davis, Leijenaar, & Oldersma, 1991, p. 52)

CONCLUSION

A critical task when examining personal competence is to discover how people who live in hostile environments are able to cope. Environments limiting personal opportunity may potentially inhibit development and impede the fulfillment of human potential. Therefore, practitioners must consider what resources and coping strategies clients have developed for surviving under such hostile conditions (Greene, 2002).

Case Study: The Many Forms of Diversity in the Stanley Family

The Stanley family includes several types of diversity, including the family form itself. These intergenerational families, sometimes called "skipped generation families," represent the diversity across family forms in contemporary society. Although once prominent, the nuclear (or heterosexual, two-parent) family has now become only one form of families—with others including same-sex, blended, single-parent, interracial, and multiethnic families.

Issues of race and gender are also part of the Stanleys' experience. Although the greatest number of custodial grandparents are white, African American and Latino/Latina families are disproportionately represented (Goyer, 2010). This situation is coupled with the health and financial disparities that exist, with older individuals of these racial and ethnic minority backgrounds having less favorable outcomes in later life. Similarly, this type of care provision is similar to other forms, as the majority of custodial grandparents are women. In Mrs. Stanley's situation, she is also parenting without the benefit of a partner. Taken together, this circumstance indicates that many ethnic minority custodial grandparents assume the responsibility and costs of raising grandchildren with poorer health and economic foundations than their white counterparts.

For Mrs. Stanley, her faith and the church are extremely important. Beyond serving as a spiritual center of the community, the church provides a focus for culture and welfare. Often, the pastor is the first individual consulted when an individual or family needs guidance or counseling. In addition, the church provides a refuge for custodial grandparents, as several members are in this role. The "kinkeeping" aspect of African American family life is very vibrant in this community, with the custodial grandparents sharing the strong belief of keeping their grandchildren in the spiritual and cultural center of their life. When asked whom she turns to for support in her caregiving role, Mrs. Stanley replies in this order: God, her pastor, other grandparents in the church.

Sadly, oppression also factors into the Stanley family situation. African American communities experience disproportionate incarceration rates, as African American men are imprisoned at six times the rate of white men (NAACP, 2016). This condition affects the Stanley family, as prison and addiction are the major causes that led Mrs. Stanley to assume primary care of Jasmine and Terrell.

WHAT WE LEARNED IN THIS CHAPTER

- tips to strengthen culturally competent practice skills
- tools and resources that will help social workers move toward cultural competence
- the influences of culture on behavior and practice
- help-seeking models as tools to understand how culture influences patterns of asking for help
- the impact of oppressive environments on aging and client well-being

SUGGESTED EXERCISE TO EVALUATE STUDENT COMPETENCY

Students will conduct research to increase their knowledge of a culture other than their own. They will

- use empirical research to understand and give a presentation on disparities in health care, possibly relying on the following sources: the Institute of Medicine, the Administration of Aging, the Federal Interagency Forum on Aging, or the National Council on Aging
- research the cultural end-of-life beliefs among an ethnic minority population and write a paper reflecting on how these beliefs may differ from their own
- write an agency plan on adapting organizational policies, procedures, and resources to facilitate the provision of services to diverse older adults and their family caregivers

ADDITIONAL RESOURCES

The Centers for Disease Control and Prevention hosts a government site dedicated to increasing the health security of America, addressing diseases, and providing resources to aid in prevention. A plethora of resources on race and ethnic minority populations, minority health, LGBT issues, mental health, and older adults can be found at https://www.cdc.gov.

The Latino Social Work Organization supports the recruitment and retention of Latino social workers through training educational programming, workshops, and mentoring. Visit http://lswo.org/.

The National Association of Black Social Workers advocates for social change, justice, and human development of African people. Conferences, and other educational offerings, publications, and a code of ethics can be found at http://nabsw.org/.

The National Association of Puerto Rican/Hispanic Social Workers organizes social workers and other human services professionals to strengthen, develop, and improve resources and services that meet the needs of Puerto Rican and Hispanic families. Visit http://www.naprhsw.org/.

The National Association of Social Workers has published standards and indicators of cultural competence. These standards may be accessed at https://www.socialworkers.org/practice/standards/NASWCulturalStandards.pdf.

The National Council on Aging provides a wealth of information and resources for professionals, older adults, and advocates, available at http://www.ncoa.org/.

The publication *Older Americans 2016: Key Indicators of Well-Being* can be accessed at https://agingstats.gov/docs/LatestReport/Older-Americans-2016-Key-Indicators-of-WellBeing.pdf.

The Social Work Podcast provides valuable information on the culturagram, including tips on how to use this tool in practice: http://socialworkpodcast.blogspot.com/2008/12/visual-assessment-tools-culturagram.html.

The U.S. Census Bureau is a government agency that provides data about the nation's people and economy as well as publications and working papers at http://www.census.gov.

4

A Human Rights and Social Justice Approach to Older Adults

RATIONALE: "Social workers understand that every person regardless of position in society has fundamental human rights such as freedom, safety, privacy, an adequate standard of living, health care, and education" (CSWE, 2015, p. 7). "Practitioners in aging work to advance human rights and social and economic justice for older adults and their caregivers. They incorporate the historical context and the physical and social environment, including experiences of trauma and micro aggressions, which may create barriers to social, economic, and environmental justice for older adults. Practitioners in aging critically and objectively analyze how policies and programs promote or inhibit justice and use story and narrative to impact change at the micro, mezzo, and macro levels." (CSWE, 2017, p. 27)

COMPETENCY: "Practitioners in aging with, and on behalf of, older adults and their constituencies

- engage older adults, their caregivers, and other constituencies to become aware of their rights to available resources and how they relate to social, economic, and environmental inequities.
- participate in system changes at all levels to promote well-being for and among older adults.
- empower individuals and groups within local communities, including older adults themselves, to advocate for social, economic, and environmental justice for all older adults and their caregivers." (CSWE, 2017, pp. 27–28)

Human rights advocacy and the social work profession appear to be natural partners, as suggested by the mission of social work "to enhance human well-being and help meet the basic human needs of all people with particular attention to the needs and empowerment of people who are vulnerable, oppressed, and living in poverty" (NASW, 2008, p. 1). The two largest social work organizations, the National Association of Social Workers (NASW) and the Council on Social Work Education (CSWE), have identified their responsibilities to educate social work students and professionals about human rights. The social work core values articulated in the NASW *Code of Ethics*, the right to self-determination and the inherent dignity and worth of the individual, stress the interconnections between social work and human rights. They emphasize the social worker's ethical responsibility to help people in need, to address social problems, to challenge social injustice, and to respect the inherent dignity and worth of the person (NASW, 2017). Ife (2008) referred to social workers as "human rights workers" because social workers seek to ameliorate social problems not only by securing access to services, such as appropriate mental and physical health care, better standards of living, and an improved quality of life for individuals, families, and communities, but also by working as policy analysts and advocates for change. The International Federation of Social Workers (IFSW) refers to human rights as the heart of the social work profession (IFSW, 2012).

CSWE, an organization that serves as the accrediting body for schools of social work, developed competency-based student learning outcomes for social work programs to use in assessing students' readiness to practice. The 2015 Educational Policy and Accreditation Standards have identified a separate social work competency, requiring that social work programs prepare students for generalist social work practice with the knowledge, skills, and values needed to effectively "advance human rights and social, economic, and environmental justice" (CSWE, 2015, p. 7). Social work students are challenged with the responsibility to advocate for and engage in practices that advance political, civic, social, cultural, economic, and environmental human rights (CSWE, 2015, pp. 7–8). The gerontological social work competencies specify that practitioners in aging work with, and on behalf of, older adults and their constituencies to advocate for and engage in change strategies to promote older adult well-being and social, economic, and environmental justice for all older adults and their caregivers (CSWE, 2017). These essential social, economic, and environmental rights are defined in the Universal Declaration of Human Rights (United Nations, 1948) discussed below. The United Nations manual for schools of social work (United Nations, 1994, p. 6) described the relationship and responsibility between social work and human rights as follows:

> Social workers have a role to play in strengthening such solidarity [with international consciousness] and ensuring that the principles enshrined in the texts of human rights instruments are gradually translated into reality, paving the way for a world in which people's most urgent and legitimate needs are satisfied.

This chapter examines the relationship between social work practice, human rights, and older adults. The global population is aging, creating individual and societal opportunities; however, ageism and lack of policies and services to support the aging population prevent older adults from living with dignity and security. Neither mainstream aging nor health care systems are prepared to support the advancing health and well-being of older adults. Older adults have the same rights as others, as established in the United Nations Declaration of Human Rights and later conventions. Human rights are universal rights and are based on principles of dignity, fairness, respect, autonomy, and equality, regardless of age, gender, religion, language, nationality, or any other characteristic. Although these values may sound like social work values, human rights are global, are legally mandated, and require accountability. Social workers are well positioned to work with older adults and to create age-friendly policies and programs that reflect a human rights approach, delivered in a supportive environment that offers person-centered, consumer-driven care and services that are fiscally responsive and accountable to the older adult client (Australian Human Rights Commission, 2012). Social workers can promote the well-being of older adults and strengthen human rights for older adults by working to ensure older adults' full integration into society, including those with physical, mental, and psychological challenges; promoting age-friendly policies, programs, and culturally competent aging and health care workers; and eliminating discriminatory practices and socioeconomic health disparities that limit older adults' participation. Social workers can also advocate for passage of an international human rights mechanism that prohibits age discrimination and ageism and protects and respects the rights of older adults (IFSW, 2012).

WHAT ARE HUMAN RIGHTS?

Because of the atrocities of the Holocaust and World War II, the international community developed the Universal Declaration of Human Rights (UDHR). In 1948, under the leadership of First Lady Eleanor Roosevelt and representatives from other member states, the General Assembly of the United Nations adopted Resolution 217(lll)A, known as the Universal Declaration of Human Rights, describing the fundamental human rights and freedoms that must be protected by countries and governments for every child and adult throughout the world. The UDHR expressed the world's collective horror at the atrocities committed against other human beings with total disregard for their human rights and conveyed the hope that such an agreement would prevent future horrific events (Witkin, 1998). It has served as the human rights template and foundation for all other human rights efforts (NASW, 2008).

Human rights are defined as those universally accepted and indivisible rights that one enjoys because of being human. The UDHR has identified 30 rights or freedoms, which establish the highest quality of life for all persons, communities, and societies by honoring the inherent worth and dignity of all people, regardless of ethnicity, nationality, or religion. Human rights are based on shared ideas about what it means to be human and the nature of humanity that transcends physical boundaries and artificial boundaries, such as differences in culture or ethnicity, age, gender, race, class, sexual orientation, gender identity, and (dis)ability (Ife, 2008). Human rights differ from civil rights. Whereas human rights are available to everyone, civil rights are the legally protected rights and privileges that one receives based on citizenship. In the United States, civil rights are granted by the U.S. Constitution and its amendments (NASW, 2016a). As a society, the concept of a socially just world was promoted by Martin Luther King, Jr. (Wronka, 2016). The concept of human rights is not new for social work; it has been a part of social work history, as the profession has continued to advocate and promote public policies that expand rights for all people (Reichert, 2007).

The UDHR contains five core ideas about human rights. They include the right to human dignity (Article 1), the right to live free of discrimination and stigma (Article 2), and civil and political rights (Articles 3–21). These civil and political rights include the right to vote, freedom of speech, the right to a fair trial, freedom from torture and abuse, and freedom of religion and voting rights. The fourth critical area (Articles 22–27) calls on the government to allocate resources to meet the economic, social, and cultural rights of its people, including the right to education, housing, health, employment, an adequate income, and social security (Witkin, 1998; Wronka, 2016). The fifth theme expressed in the document and found in Articles 28–30 is sometimes called the collective rights or community development rights and includes environmental and personal or spiritual development rights within a community context—that is, the right to clean air, water, and an environment that helps individuals, families, and communities to realize their highest potential (Ife, 2008; Wronka, 2008b). These rights to a better quality of life at the macro level are clearly within the scope of the social work profession (D. Flynn, 2008; Ife, 2005; Wronka, 2008a).

The U.S. Constitution and the Bill of Rights are two important documents that contain many of the same civil and political rights and privileges spelled out in the UDHR. The Advocates for Human Rights has linked 14 of the 30 articles from the UDHR with 12 amendments to the U.S. Constitution. Table 4.1 demonstrates the relationship between the human rights articulated in the UDHR and corresponding amendments to the U.S. Constitution.

In addition to the rights indicated above that are included in the United States Constitution, several human rights are not included in the U.S. Constitution: for example, Article 1, the right to equality and dignity; Articles 13–16, identified as civil and political rights; and Articles 22–30, known as the economic, cultural, and social rights. Although the United States ratified the UDHR in 1948, because it is not a legally binding document, any violations are not enforceable by international monitoring (Advocates for Human Rights, n.d.; Ife, 2008).

Between 1965 and 2006, the United Nations created two covenants about human rights and seven that address the rights of specific groups. These covenants reflect the ongoing human rights discourse and struggle while recognizing the obligations of countries and governments around the world to ensure that everyone has the right to be treated with the highest respect and dignity

Table 4.1: Relationship between the Universal Declaration of Human Rights (UDHR) and the U.S. Constitution

Rights	UDHR	Amendments to U.S. Constitution
Freedom from discrimination	Article 2	14th Amendment
Right to life, liberty, and security	Article 3	14th Amendment
Freedom from slavery	Article 4	13th Amendment
Freedom from cruel and unusual punishment	Article 5	8th Amendment
Right to equal protection under the law	Article 6	14th Amendment
Right to equal protection against discrimination	Article 7	14th Amendment
Freedom from arbitrary arrest	Article 9	5th Amendment
Right to a fair trial	Article 10	6th Amendment
Right to protection and privacy of home, family, and honor	Article 12	4th Amendment
Right to own property	Article 17	5th Amendment
Freedom of religion	Article 18	1st Amendment
Freedom of speech	Article 19	1st Amendment
Freedom of association	Article 20	1st Amendment
Right to vote	Article 21	15th, 19th, 23rd, 24th, and 26th Amendments

and has access to a minimum standard of living. The United States took an early leadership role in writing the UDHR; however, most of the major human rights treaties have not been ratified by the United States. The nine conventions and treaties and their ratification status by the United States are as follows:

- International Convention on the Elimination of All Forms of Racial Discrimination 1965 (CERD): ratified by the United States
- International Covenant on Civil and Political Rights 1966: ratified by the United States
- International Covenant on Economic, Social and Cultural Rights 1966 (ICESCR): not ratified
- Convention on the Elimination of All Forms of Discrimination against Women 1979 (CEDAW): the United States is the only industrialized country that has not ratified

- Convention against Torture and Other Cruel, Inhuman or Degrading Treatment or Punishment 1984: the United States claims limitations based on the U.S. Constitution
- Convention on the Rights of the Child 1989: signed by President Clinton but not ratified
- International Convention on the Protection of the Rights of All Migrant Workers and Members of Their Families 1990: not signed
- International Convention for the Protection of All Persons from Enforced Disappearance 2006: not signed
- Convention on the Rights of Persons with Disabilities 2006 (CRPD): signed by President Obama but not ratified.

The economic, social, and cultural human rights for women, children, people with disabilities, and so forth mentioned earlier in the CSWE Social Work and Gerontological Social Work Human Rights Competencies, such as the right to education, housing, an adequate standard of living, and participation in the community, are not considered human rights in the United States. Although these international treaties protect the rights of children, racial and ethnic minorities, people with disabilities, women, and other groups, older adults are at high risk of human rights abuse and are not protected by any of the human rights conventions (AgeUK, 2011; Ife, 2008). In some countries, older women or older adults with disabilities or older people of color may be able to file complaints with the United Nations Human Rights Office of the High Commissioner because of ratification in those countries of CEDAW, CRPD, or ICESCR; however, in the United States, women, people of color, and people with disabilities are not protected by these international treaties, and most international human rights treaties lack explicit reference to older adults (International Labour Organization, Office of the United Nations, 2015). The United States' failure to guarantee an adequate standard of living and the right to live with dignity (Articles 22–27) significantly affects the quality of life and well-being for all its citizens, including older adults (D. Flynn, 2005; Ife, 2008). Sadly, there is not even a centralized human rights database in which to gather statistics about the extent of human rights abuse in the United States. In fact, the only U.S. federal law that specifically protects older adults is the Age Discrimination in Employment Act of 1967, which protects people 40 years and older from employment discrimination based on age in hiring, firing, promotion, training, compensation, or assignments (AARP, 2014).

HUMAN RIGHTS AND OLDER ADULTS

Because the United States has not signed or ratified many of the aforementioned conventions and no international UN treaty for the protection of older adults has been developed, an older African American woman with a disability (CEDAW, CERD, CRPD) is neither protected from discrimination nor guaranteed access to health care that is affordable, available, acceptable, and adequate (Advocates for Human Rights, 2013, p. 155). The following are not protected by ICESCR: an older white male who faces caregiving responsibilities for his gay partner, which prevents him from getting to work on time; a gay, lesbian, or transgender older adult who is afraid to go to the hospital or to access needed home or community-based services for fear of discrimination; an older Latina female who lacks transportation to shop for food or medicine and has no safe walking areas in her neighborhood; and an older person whose son and daughter-in-law have moved into his home to help care for him but instead experiences emotional abuse and financial exploitation by his own children. These are just a few examples of why human rights protections are needed for older adults.

From 1982 to 2002, aging moved from an isolated issue to an international concern in developed and developing countries. The projected growth of the over-60 population from now until 2050 means that aging will have a significant impact on most facets of life, not only within individuals and families but within the national and international communities as well. Recognizing the increasing number and diversity of older adults throughout the world and the limitations of existing human rights protections, in 1991 the United Nations articulated 18 rights in the "United Nations Principles for Older Persons." Although this document does not carry the same weight as a UN human rights convention, it serves to encourage countries throughout the world to incorporate these principles into their national policies whenever possible. The principles are divided into five critical aspects that directly affect the quality of life of older adults: independence, participation, care, self-fulfillment, and dignity (United Nations Human Rights Office of the High Commissioner, 1991). Although there is no specific international convention that protects the rights of older adults, the "right to freedom, equality and dignity does not change in old age" (HelpAge International, 2009). Table 4.2 summarizes the United Nations Principles for Older Persons, demonstrates the connection between the UDHR and UN principles, and identifies examples of human rights violations faced by older people.

The United Nations Principles for Older Persons (United Nations Human Rights Office of the High Commissioner, 1991) reminds us that human rights are not just about older people being frail and vulnerable. Human rights and creating a human rights culture is also about promoting greater understanding and respect among all people. It is about human beings receiving the support they need to realize their highest potential.

The first World Assembly for Ageing met in 1982; 20 years later, the Second World Assembly of Ageing met and developed the Madrid International Plan of Action on Ageing, which identified three areas that needed immediate international attention: older adults and development, advancing health and well-being into older adulthood, and building and sustaining supportive communities for older adults (Ageing in the 21st Century). This was the first time that governments and countries connected the challenges of older adults with other important work on human rights and social and economic development (United Nations Madrid).

In December 2010, the UN General Assembly created the Open-Ended Working Group on Ageing to identify weaknesses and solutions in the current human rights protections for older adults and strategies to address these gaps. Ban Ki-Moon, UN secretary-general, explained, "Existing human rights mechanisms have lacked a systematic and comprehensive approach to the specific circumstances of older men and women" (International Labour Organization, Office of the United Nations, 2015). The 2011 report to the United Nations secretary-general identified four human rights challenges affecting older adults that will require concerted effect by the international community. They include the elimination of age discrimination, poverty, violence, and abuse and the lack of needed resources and services to care for older adults in their own homes and in residential settings (United Nations Human Rights Office of the High Commissioner, 2010; United Nations Population Fund & HelpAge International, 2012).

Globally, the world is aging; older people's rights are human rights (HelpAge International, 2009), and the current human rights mechanisms do not protect the rights of older adults (Sleap, 2012). Older people face discrimination, violence, invisibility, ageism, abuse, and lack of access to services. The Madrid International Plan of Action on Ageing listed demographic indicators and outcome and instrumental indicators for the three priority areas—older persons and development, advancing health and well-being into old age, and building supportive communities. However, age discrimination has never been included when existing treaties are monitored, and governments across the globe have failed to challenge age discrimination national policies, laws, and practices (HelpAge International, 2009; United Nations Population Fund & HelpAge International, 2012). The need for an international convention to protect the rights of older people is desperately needed. Without it, human rights violations against older people will continue to rise dramatically as the older adult population grows exponentially.

HUMAN RIGHTS AND GRAND CHALLENGES OF SOCIAL WORK

Although a strong relationship between human rights and social work is obvious, D. Flynn (2005) argued that the traditional model of human rights is inherently individualistic. Flynn's model of human rights includes the notion of collective responsibilities, along with individual rights, because the "developmental model of rights and responsibilities is one way of conceptualizing the integration of the micro and macro forces that come into existence whenever individuals form communities" (D. Flynn, 2005, p. 254). He challenged the notion that marginalized groups receive special human rights by explaining that human rights are universal. Society has a collective responsibility to provide additional resources to help vulnerable populations to overcome oppressive structures and previous human rights exploitation or degradation. The concept of collective responsibility, consistent with the NASW *Code of Ethics*, is particularly helpful when discussing the relationship between human rights and older adults. By framing social work as a human rights profession, the goals and value inherent in social and economic justice are situated in a global, rather than national, conversation

Table 4.2: United Nations (UN) Principles for Older Persons:
A Comparison

UN Principles for Older Persons	Universal Declaration of Human Rights	Human Rights Challenges Faced by Older Adults
Independence Principles		
Right to standard of living, including adequate food, clean water, housing, clothing, and health care	Article 25	Neighborhoods that are no longer safe; lack of health care because of cost, language barriers, or transportation
Opportunity for meaningful work with fair and safe working conditions	Article 23	Workplace discrimination, including hiring, promotion, and retention issues
Live in environments that are safe and adaptable to personal preferences and changes in ability to care for self	Article 22	Physical, emotional, psychological, and financial abuse
Participation Principles		
Right to contribute to the development of policies affecting older persons' quality of life	Article 21	Policies are developed without input from older adults, which devalues the potential contribution of older adults
Opportunities for meaningful civic engagement and cultural life of community	Article 27	Barriers to participation in community life because of ageism, lack of transportation, or lack of safe areas to walk
Care Principles		
Access to mental and physical health to support functioning at the most optimal level of physical, mental, and emotional well-being	Article 25	Lack of access to affordable preventative or rehabilitative care; ageism, racism, sexism, transphobia, and homophobia that affect quality of care; poverty
Care provided by family and community without interference	Article 12	Family members balancing care for older family members with work; homelessness
Availability of appropriate residential and community services provided with compassion and respect	Article 28	Elder abuse or neglect; degrading treatment provided to vulnerable older adults; staff turnover

(Continued)

Table 4.2: United Nations Principles for Older Persons: A Comparison (*Continued*)

UN Principles for Older Persons	Universal Declaration of Human Rights	Human Rights Challenges Faced by Older Adults
Self-fulfillment Principles		
Access to cultural, spiritual, educational, and leisure resources that promote full development of one's potential	Articles 26–28	Transportation barriers; services not visually, auditory, or literacy friendly to some older adults
Dignity Principles		
Ability to live with dignity and respect, free of abuse and exploitation, regardless of age, sexual orientation, gender identity, racial or ethnic identity, class, disability, or diagnosis	Articles 1–2	Age discrimination in the popular culture, from Hallmark cards to lack of older adults in key roles on TV and in movies, reinforcing negative stereotypes about older adults; separating couples because one needs different level of care than the other

about the nature of "our shared humanity that transcends culture, race, gender, age, class" (Ife, 2008, p. 129). The concept of collective responsibility is reflected in the Grand Challenges for Social Work initiative, launched in early 2016 by the American Academy of Social Work and Social Welfare. The Grand Challenges initiative articulates an agenda to create evidence-based solutions to the top 12 social problems in society during the next decade to "build a more cohesive society that fights exclusion and marginalization, creates a sense of belonging, promotes trust, and offers pathways for social and economic mobility for everyone" (American Academy of Social Work and Social Welfare, 2016). Social work is a human rights profession, because human rights belong to everyone, regardless of where people live or work (Reichert, 2003). An example of human rights that belong to everyone, but is especially important to the growing older adult populations and is reflected in the Grand Challenges, is the right to health care access. The goal for social work is to close the health care gap and ensure access to basic health care while reducing health disparities, such as poverty, discrimination, and toxic environments, which lead to higher rates of chronic and often preventable illnesses. The right to health care can be found in UDHR Article 25; it is included in the second generation of human rights, which prohibits the government of any country from denying access to economic, social, and cultural rights and charges them with the obligation and responsibility to take measures to improve overall social conditions. The *right to health* was defined by the ICESCR (1966) as "the right of everyone to the enjoyment of the highest attainable standard of physical and mental health" (United Nations Human Rights Office of the High Commissioner, 2017).

The World Health Organization (WHO), established in 1946, 20 years prior to ICESCR, included the right to health care in its constitution, in which it defined its mission to achieve "the highest attainable standard of health" as a "fundamental right of every human being" (WHO, 1946). The WHO constitution was the first international mechanism to promote a human rights approach to the right to health; however, in some countries, this right still is unaffordable or unavailable to older people, or health care workers may refuse to treat older adults (HelpAge International, 2009).

WHO projects that between 2015 and 2050, the world population of those 60 years old and older will increase from 12 percent to 22 percent. In actual numbers, this will be an increase from 900 million people to 2 billion people over 60 years of age. By the year 2020, the number of older adults above 60 years old will be greater than the number of children who are younger than five years old. John Beard, director of Ageing and Life Course at WHO, projects that to ensure healthy aging to the rapidly increasing older adult population, "deep and fundamental reforms of health and social care systems will be required. . . . But we must be careful that these reforms do not reinforce the inequities that drive much of the poor health and functional limitation we see in older age" (WHO, 2014). Although about 20 percent of older adults will be living in high-income countries throughout the world, about 80 percent of the world's population will be living in low- and middle-income countries. Throughout the world, people are living longer; however, this does not mean that they are living healthier lives. WHO (2014) warned that if significant strategies are not implemented soon, the long-term burden of increasing numbers of older adults living with chronic illness and reduced well-being will become a global public health challenge for older adults, their families and caregivers, health care and social service systems, and, in some countries, the economy. Attention must focus on how to address healthy aging for all.

Healthy aging, a term used by WHO, is "the process of developing and maintaining the functional ability that enables well-being in older age" (WHO, 2016b); it demands both universal and local strategies to achieve. Internationally and nationally, the human rights–based planning approach recognizes the benefits and contributions of older adults who are active, healthy, and productive in their own lives and as members of a community. This approach should be integrated in discussions and action plans concerning older adults. Needs-based strategies that seek to address the costs associated with aging are also important components of these discussions (WHO, 2014, 2016a, 2016c).

Human Rights, the Right to Health Care, and Older Adults

Until recently, a human rights approach to the health care, health disparities, and other structural, social, and legal barriers to health care and other human rights for older adults has received limited attention (Baer, Bhushan, Taleb, Vasquez, & Thomas, 2016; Gostin, Hodge, Valentine, & Nygren-Krug, 2003;

Osborne & Furlong, 2009). Gostin et al. (2003) addressed the intersection of health and human rights in examining how health care systems' "responsiveness" can contribute to people's well-being even though there may not be a corresponding improvement in physical health. The concept of responsiveness was operationalized to include eight factors: dignity and respect for the person, autonomy in making health care decisions, privacy and confidentiality, acceptable quality of care, accessibility to care, clear communication, access to social support networks (family and community), and options in accessing health care providers. A human rights approach to health and the domains of responsiveness, like the mission of social work, share a common goal—that is, to improve the process (whether people's rights are respected when accessing the health care system) and the outcome of the health care system (whether people's health improves; Gostin et al., 2003). This responsiveness framework reflects a human rights approach to health care; however, without research there is no mechanism for accountability to ensure that the quality of the relationship between patients, their families, and health care systems is met.

Baer et al. (2016) addressed the intersection of health, aging, and human rights, recommending the need to gather and analyze data about the extent to which older adults experience the right to health and other related human rights, to monitor progress to ensure access to services for older adults, and to establish criteria for accountability. The report also encourages stronger collaboration among communities, with global discussions on health and aging and on the creation of an international human rights convention on the rights of older people (AgeUK 2011; Australian Human Rights Commission, 2016; Baer et al., 2016; HelpAge International, 2009). The *Multisectional Action for a Life Course Approach to Healthy Ageing: Global Strategy and Action Plan on Ageing and Health* was adopted by the World Health Assembly in May 2016. The *Global Strategy and Action Plan on Ageing and Health (2016–2020): A Framework for Coordinated Global Action by the World Health Organization, Member States, and Partners across the Sustainable Development Goals* envisions a world where all older people can live long and healthy lives (WHO, 2016b), where the right to health is available, accessible, acceptable, affordable, and of good quality for all (Baer et al., 2016). The plan identifies two strategic goals and five strategic objectives to move member states toward its world vision with progressive realization. Progressive realization recognizes the complexity, urgency, and challenges inherent in providing the highest possible standard of health while addressing the health disparities and structural barriers that influence the quality of health and well-being of older adults.

The two goals include gathering five years of evidence-based action, which will maximize individual functional ability, and, by 2020, creating evidence and collaborations necessary to sustain a "Decade of Healthy Aging" from 2020 to 2030. The strategies include (a) requesting a commitment from every country to begin acting on approaches to healthy aging, creating age-friendly environments and communities that foster autonomy, promote health, and provide support and safety for people who have experienced physical, social, or emotional losses; (b) aligning health care and related systems to promote person-centered, integrated care that centers on the rights and needs of older adults and developing home-and community-based long-term care services delivery systems that are person-centered, sustainable, and offer options; and (c) improving measurement and research approaches to better understand healthy aging (WHO, 2016c). Building health care and social service systems and challenging negative stereotypes about older adults "will be a sound investment in a future where older people have the freedom to be and do what they value" (WHO, 2016c, p. 1).

WHO (2106a, 2016b, 2016c) has identified four care strategies to help countries prepare for the increase of older adults: (1) training health care and social service professionals to care for older adults; (2) preventing and managing chronic conditions, including cognitive, mental, and substance abuse disorders; (3) implementing policies and procedures related to long-term and palliative care; and (4) developing age-friendly communities and settings in which healthy aging strategies and living environments that support well-being for all of its residents are promoted (see chapter 10 for discussion about age-friendly communities).

Developing a Human Rights Approach to Older Adults

As social workers, "we need to do a better job of using human rights to inform our practice, scholarship, and teaching" (Witkin, 1998, p. 198). From a practice perspective, we can evaluate the success of a program by using a human rights approach to measure the positive change in people's lives. The four human rights indicators—safety and security, nondiscrimination, accountability, and participation—will indicate progress toward human rights. For example, we might ask: Did working on an interdisciplinary team with the older adult in the hospital help to increase the sense of dignity, justice, peace, or freedom in the life of the older adult and his or her family members? Does the change in policies and practices at the long-term care facility, requiring all staff and volunteers to be trained in culturally compassionate care, allow LGBT older residents to feel more secure and to reduce the fear of discrimination and stigma? How can we help transform current neighborhoods into age-friendly communities? How can we help communities to change to support human rights so that people feel safe from violence and can enjoy the right to an adequate standard of living, participate in the cultural life of the community, and have access to different ways to contribute to the life of their community through engagement in decision making and leadership roles (Advocates for Human Rights, 2013)?

Although social work and human rights have many areas of overlap, it has been demonstrated throughout this chapter that there is a lack of national and international commitment to the well-being of older adults. A human rights approach to social work and social welfare goes beyond social work's concern for meeting basic human needs, respecting diversity, and understanding the person in his or her environment. Social work with older adults builds on the social work foundation of the strengths perspective, social work values and ethics, recognition of life course understanding of the person in the environment, and micro- to macro-level intervention; however, a human rights approach shifts the context of understanding issues from psychological to human rights (Steen & Mathieson, 2005). By shifting the focus to human rights, the definition and interventions shift as well. Human rights are internationally recognized and accepted. Universal human rights imply not only individual rights but collective responsibility by society because these rights are legally binding (Gostin et al., 2003). This approach will require transformation in societal and organizational cultures so that older Americans are treated with respect and dignity; services and programs are person-centered; and care is consumer directed, integrated, and delivered without discrimination or judgment. As mentioned earlier, systems of delivery should be responsive and include service standards that are accessible, available, and acceptable to all cultures, ethnicities, gender identities, and races. These services should be medically appropriate, suitably monitored, and held accountable to governments and organizations (Australian Human Rights Commission, 2012; Witkin, 1998).

The United Nations Programme on Ageing and the International Association of Gerontology and Geriatrics developed the Research Agenda for Ageing in the 21st Century to support the Madrid International Plan on Ageing (United Nations Population Fund & HelpAge International, 2012). Research priorities were developed for specific countries. Examples of the common research priorities include Priority 1—poverty, intergenerational support, urban–rural differences; Priority II—health and well-being and quality of life; and Priority III—family caregiving, age-friendly communities, age discrimination and stereotypes, and violence (United Nations Population Fund & HelpAge International, 2012). These research areas overlap with the 12 Grand Challenges for Social Work and present opportunities for social work educators, researchers, and practitioners to adopt the human rights approach, making significant and sustainable changes in how we "view [older] people not as oppressed and disadvantaged populations, but as beings worthy of rights that the world has not yet respected" (Steen & Mathieson, 2005, p. 155). With this approach, social work will help to make human rights a reality in the lives of older adults in the 21st century (American Academy of Social Work and Social Welfare, 2016; Sleap, 2012).

Case Study: The Stanley Family and Limited Human Rights Protection

Because the United States has not ratified or signed many of the UN conventions, the Universal Declaration of Human Rights and the UN Principles for Older Persons do not apply to the Stanleys. So, Eva Stanley is not guaranteed access to health care that is affordable, available, acceptable, and adequate. As the surrounding neighborhood continues to deteriorate, access to health care may prove to be an issue for Mrs. Stanley, creating hardships for her to receive adequate care for her ongoing medical condition of hypertension. The fact that she is parenting two grandchildren and coping with stressors brought on by her adult children places her at risk for additional health problems (Blieszner & Bedford, 2012; National

Alliance for Caregiving, 2015). There are no guarantees that she will receive the health care that she will need in the future or that she will have access to preventive health care. If Mrs. Stanley's health deteriorates, her grand-children are at risk for placement in foster care. Although Mrs. Stanley is covered under Medicare health insurance, her fixed income on Social Security provides limited means for her to pay out-of-pocket expenses or co-pays. Limitations in coverage affect any financial resources that she has, creating financial problems for her. It is sometimes difficult for Mrs. Stanley to have enough food in the house to feed everyone adequately until the next Social Security check arrives. Also, any changes to Medicare have the potential to put Mrs. Stanley at further risk for declining health care access and affordability.

WHAT WE LEARNED IN THIS CHAPTER

- why human rights are important and how they developed internationally
- the components of the UDHR
- how the U.S. Constitution and Bill of Rights compares with the UDHR
- the components of the UN Principles for Older Persons
- the intersection between the Grand Challenges for Social Work and human rights

SUGGESTED EXERCISES TO EVALUATE STUDENT COMPETENCY

1. Take one core idea from the UDHR and assess how well this idea protects older adults under the U.S. Constitution and Bill of Rights.
2. Research human rights violations against older adults that have occurred in the United States.
3. Using the four human rights indicators of safety and security, nondiscrimination, accountability, and participation, develop a plan for how these rights can be advanced in the United States.

ADDITIONAL RESOURCES

The Grand Challenges for Social Work Initiative is a call to action for social workers to work together to solve some of social work's most challenging problems. More information on these 12 Grand Challenges can be found at http://aaswsw.org/.

The mission of the International Federation of Social Workers is the promotion of social work, best practice models, and the facilitation of international cooperation to address social justice, human rights, and social development. Visit http://ifsw.org/.

The mission of the Open Society Foundation is to build tolerant democracies whose governments are accountable and to encourage the participation of all peoples. Visit https://www.opensocietyfoundations.org/.

The Social Welfare Action Alliance, formerly the Bertha Capen Reynolds Society, is a national organization of progressive workers in human services who promote social justice, peace, and coalition building. Information on educational and publishing opportunities can be found at http://www.socialwelfareactionalliance.org/.

The goal of the World Health Organization is to build a healthier future for people across the globe. Health data, tools and resources, and information on political initiatives can be found at http://www.who.int.

The United Nations' main focus is the maintenance of international peace and security, the protection of human rights, delivering humanitarian aid, promoting sustainable development, and upholding international law. For resources, documents, and policies, go to http://www.un.org.

The United Nations Population Fund and HelpAge is a global network of organizations whose mission is to promote the rights of all older people to lead dignified, healthy, and secure lives. For resources, practice tools, and publications, go to http://www.helpage.org/.

5

Theory and Concepts Underpinning Assessment in Practice

RATIONALE: Social workers will "understand theories of human behavior and the social environment and critically evaluate and apply this knowledge in the assessment of diverse clients and constituencies, including individuals, families, groups, organizations, and communities" (CSWE, 2015, p. 9).

COMPETENCY: "Practitioners in aging engage older adults, caregivers, and related systems by understanding and applying a range of appropriate theories" (CSWE, 2017, p. 65).

Social work educators have debated how to use theories in social work practice. Some have contended (Laird, 1993; Saleebey, 2004) that theories offer social workers perspectives—not truth—and hence contribute narratives and interpretive devices. For example, Dennis Saleebey (2004), a pioneer in the strengths-based approach to social work practice, has characterized theories as follows:

- Theories are associated with power and the dominant culture. The origins of theories of human behavior are sociocultural, political, and relational.

- Theories offer multiple, not singular, views. Practitioners must consider theories in light of the uniqueness of individuals and cultures.

- Theories best address individuals as social phenomena. Theories need to address people as interdependent beings or as persons in environments.

- Theories reflect language and intersubjectivity. Language is the basis for the exchange and creation of meanings. Theories imply or reflect values.

Conversely, educators have argued that theories ought to organize practitioners' observations logically and bind facts and data together to provide explanatory power (Newman & Newman, 2005). That is, there should be empirical support for major assumptions. Throughout this book, we have suggested a working knowledge of theory, following the definition that a theory is a "framework to structure professional activities, to guide the practitioner through the social work processes of conducting assessments and selecting intervention strategies, and creating new meanings through discourse" (Greene, 2008a, p. 2).

As conceptual frameworks from various theories are understood and adopted, competencies will be developed that comprise the building blocks of a resilience-enhancing practice. The first consideration is whether the adopted concept will be effective with older adults. For example, combining an understanding of the ecological perspective with the idea that the risks faced by older clients may be in their immediate or more distant environment provides a broader view. Also, the life course perspective suggests that clients face and overcome many life challenges before entering their later years. This positive perspective may lead to an adoption of resilience-enhancing interventions that help tap into clients' current strengths.

KNOWLEDGE

Ecological Perspective

Ecological theory views human behavior in a person-in-environment context—that is, the mutual accommodation of an active, growing human (in this specific situation, the older adult) to his or her environment (Bronfenbrenner, 1979). The person-in-environment orientation that guides practice is highly compatible with social work's long-standing concern for individual well-being and improved societal or environmental conditions locally and globally. An ecological viewpoint expands social workers' worldview so that they may better understand their clients' psychological concerns, material needs, and economic and social conditions (Greene & Watkins, 1998). Approaching assessment of client systems from an ecological standpoint is congruent with resilience-enhancing social work practice and advantageous to practitioners in the field of aging for a number of reasons. The principles of an ecological assessment, as adapted from Greene and Barnes (1998), are as follows:

- Assessment requires identification of a focal system to receive primary attention—the person, housing complex, or neighborhood.
- Practitioners need to comprehend clients' stress levels and ability to cope with stress and the imbalance between demands and the use of resources.
- Social workers need to assess client efficacy or confidence to act on the environment.

- Assessment encompasses how clients engage with people and their natural environment—that is, the extent and quality of their relationships and social and emotional ties.
- Key to the assessment process is determining the goodness of fit between the older adult and the older adult's family and their environment and whether the client family is in a position to exercise their life choices.
- Agency assessment should address the climate for services for diverse client populations and whether agency services are culturally sensitive.
- Assessment at the macro level should explore the large-scale societal context and how the client's family is affected by legal regulations or policies.

The ecological perspective is the theoretical foundation for this textbook.

Multisystemic View

One important advantage of the ecological perspective is that it enables practitioners to delineate clearly not only who the case or the client is, but also what the systemic boundaries are:

> The case may be defined as a person, a family, a hospital ward, a housing complex, a particular neighborhood, a school population, a group with particular problems and needs, or a community with common concerns. . . . The drawing of a systemic boundary rather than a linear one provides for the true psychosocial perception of a case, because it includes the significant inputs into the lives of the individuals involved. (Meyer, 1973, p. 50)

The ecological perspective emphasizes the connections between the older adult and the various systems levels with which he or she interacts (Bronfenbrenner, 1979) (see Figure 5.1). From this perspective, multilevel client assessments allow geriatric social workers to gain an understanding of how older clients function within their total environment and to plan a range of helpful interventions that promote continued competence (see chapters 6 and 7).

When deciding on which system to focus, practitioners may ask: What are the older adult's risks? Where do his or her solutions lie? Because the ecological perspective is a multisystemic approach, social workers may apply it to their work with small-scale *microsystems*, which involve face-to-face relationships (for example, in families and peer groups); *mesosystems*, which are the connections between systems (for example, the linkages between the family and senior centers); *exosystems*, which encompass the connections between systems—at least one of which does not directly involve the developing person (for example, the Area Agency on Aging or the adult child's workplace); and *macrosystems*, which are overarching large-scale systems (for example, the legal and political systems that enact and administer policies affecting client systems).

Figure 5.1:   Clinical Application of the Ecological Perspective

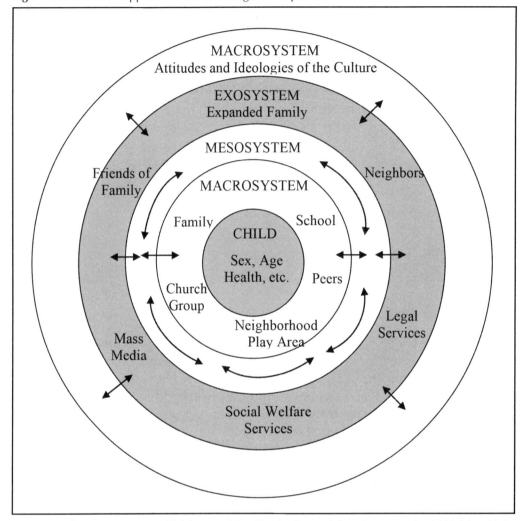

Source: Garbarino, J. (1982). *Children and families in the social environment* (p. 648). New York: Aldine. Reprinted with permission from Taylor & Francis.

From this perspective, practitioners are able to better understand the multiple forces affecting an older adult's concerns and opportunities. For example, an older adult may have interpersonal issues that are exacerbated by the political environment, or the political environment may contribute to a lack of social support. How does the older adult work to improve her or his environment?

What are the relative risks and protective factors? Using an ecological approach as reflected in resilience-enhancing practice, practitioners learn how each system functions so that they may target a particular system or systems for intervention. They may need to engage in "boundary-spanning practice" in which they secure resources for an older client from several different systems to maintain his or her well-being.

In addition to deciding to which system or systems they will devote their primary attention, practitioners must determine, on the one hand, how to best use their skills. Will they engage in face-to-face dialogue with their older clients? Will they engage with and attempt to change other client systems? Will they plan programs on behalf of their client or advocate for policy changes that might improve access to services? On the other hand, social workers may carry out any or all of these roles and functions.

During the assessment and intervention process with older adults, their families, and support systems, social workers typically follow six steps (Longres, 1990, pp. 47–48) by identifying

1. the client system to be assessed
2. the condition in the client system that the practitioner needs to understand
3. factors about the client system itself that contribute to the condition
4. factors in the social context of the client system that contribute to, or assist with, the condition
5. resources available to the client system that exist within the system itself
6. resources that exist within the environment of the particular system.

Life Course Perspective

Another useful feature of ecological theory is that it assumes people will experience growth throughout the life course. The life course concept provides a way for social workers to view and appreciate a client's key life events. This approach reveals the experiences that the client has shared with his or her cohort, or group of people born in the same era. Was he or she shaped by the Great Depression, wars, or the civil rights movement? The life course concept is a useful approach for working with older adults and their families because it considers individual life transitions within family and social contexts (T. L. Hareven, 1982). It also helps to explain the critical events people faced during their lifetime (see Figure 5.2). This information about coping can enlighten the practitioner as he or she plans the present intervention.

The life course concept does not just look at events chronologically. Rather, it considers a person's life within multiple contexts, including gender, race, ethnicity, and sexual orientation. The life course contrasts with the "life stage approach" in which social workers gather a detailed social history to determine whether a person has successfully negotiated the developmental tasks or milestones associated with life transitions (Masten, 1994). Some theorists (Germain, 1991; T. L. Hareven, 1982) adopt a more universal approach in which the practitioner explores a client's life story to discover the timing of personal and family life events and the historical and cultural changes associated with them.

Figure 5.2:   Example of a Time Line

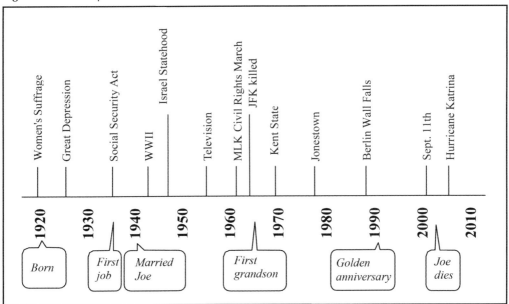

Source: Frank, C., Kurland, J., & Goldman, B. (1978). *Tips for getting the best from the rest* (p. 13). Baltimore: Jewish Community Services. Reprinted with permission.

The time line provided in Figure 5.2 can be adapted to examine critical events in a client's life history.

STRESS AND ADAPTATION TO PROBLEMS IN LIVING

The ecological perspective calls attention to how older adults, their families, and their communities deal with the stressful events of life. Carter and McGoldrick (1999) have provided a schema to represent two dimensions of stress, including the developmental path of the individual, family, and society and the multiple systems levels along which development takes place. See the Expanded Family Life Cycle Web site located in the Additional Resources section at the end of the chapter for a visual representation of this model. Once the PDF is located, turn to page 6. What are the many obstacles in life that resilient older adults and their social support systems have had to overcome?

In this visual representation, the vertical axis of systems levels reflects the individual's biological and genetic makeup. The horizontal axis defines the individual's emotional, cognitive, interpersonal, and physical development over the life course, taking into account the person's sociohistorical context. At the family level, the vertical axis depicts the family history and intergenerational patterns of relating. The horizontal axis or time line refers to family changes over time as members move through family life transitions. At the sociocultural level, the vertical axis relates cultural and societal history, stereotypes, power, privileges, and oppression (see chapter 3). The horizontal axis encompasses community connections, current events, and social policy.

A resilience-enhancing model can be used to explain the sources of an older client's stressors and how to alleviate them (Greene, 2007). When does stress occur? What precipitates it? According to Germain and Gitterman (1995), people will meet natural stressors at any time over the life course. These include

- difficult life transitions and developmental or social changes, such as retirement or widowhood
- traumatic life events, including grave losses (such as those experienced by survivors of Hurricane Katrina) or illness (for example, people who live with cancer or HIV)
- environmental pressures, such as poverty and violence.

As ecological approaches emerged in the 1970s and 1980s, social workers began to emphasize healthy, realistic adaptation to such life challenges (Kirschner, 1986). A clear benefit of the ecological perspective as a building block in a resilience-enhancing approach is that it directs the social worker's attention to the way in which older adults meet everyday life tasks and the support they receive from and provide to their social support systems (Germain & Gitterman, 1995). A successful contemporary practitioner is one who understands how older clients handle the stressors imposed daily by their environments and the steps they take to remain competent.

RELATEDNESS

A successful assessment involves examining not only how the older adult adapts to stress, but also how he or she forms relationships and continues to connect with others. Social workers who practice with intergenerational families need to learn about how issues such as loyalty obligations and indebtedness to family members influence or affect family dynamics (Boszormenyi-Nagy & Spark, 1973). This perspective is helpful to social workers in the field of aging because it recognizes that relationships can positively influence the development of resilience. Clearly, the bonding of infants and children with their parents is an important developmental task. However, bonding continues to be important as the family develops and as the individual ages and participates in social networks (E. Brody, 1985).

Practitioners will also want to learn more about the older client's (and family's) connection to other social systems. An ecomap, shown in chapter 6, can facilitate the discussion of these connections. As people age and their contemporaries die, support networks often diminish. These losses can precipitate difficulties, particularly depression. Therefore, knowledge about the people available to the client (and family) is important to the assessment process.

GENERAL SYSTEMS THEORY

Practitioners often use general systems theory, a set of abstract assumptions—adopted from cell biology—about how systems work, to understand and assess older adults within family systems. The word "families" is understood to encompass multiple forms, including blended families, single-parent families, and partners (Greene & Schriver, 2016). From the systemic point of view, the social worker sees that the whole is more than the sum of its parts. According to Buckley (1967), a pioneer in the development of systems thinking, the "more than" points to the fact of organization, which imparts to the aggregate characteristics that are not only different from but not found in the components alone; and the "sum of the parts" must be taken to mean not only their numerical addition, but also their unorganized aggregation (p. 42). General systems theory suggests, then, that to understand a family, it is necessary to examine the relationships among family members, and any one individual's behavior should be considered to be a consequence of the total social situation. This phenomenon can clearly be seen in caregiving families and whether they work together effectively.

The following are other theoretical assumptions:

- Each family (of later years) has a unique, discernible "structure," or a pattern of stable relationships, among family system members that is based on the functions that each person carries out.
- The nature of family relationships is reflected in its "organization," or the groupings or working arrangements of the system members.
- All social systems have two interrelated systems of roles: the "instrumental," dealing with socioeconomic tasks; and the "expressive," dealing with emotions. Family members may play different roles at different times in the life of the family. The caretaking role, for example, may be fulfilled by the parent for a child or by an adult child for a parent.
- "Complementarity" of family roles, which refers to the fit of role relationships and the growth and creative adaptability of the family group, is of major importance to family functioning. To achieve complementarity of roles, one member of the family system acts to provide something that is needed by another. When there is failure in role complementarity, stress is placed on the family system.
- Throughout the life cycle, family members must be able to negotiate required changes, shifting and altering their relationships to meet the needs of all. This movement through the life cycle is called "family development" (see Greene, 2008a).
- As family systems develop, they can be resilient in their own right. Their resilience is dependent on the meaning that the collective attributes to life events.

Such abstract assumptions can enable practitioners to better understand how the family group behaves as an organized social system and whether the group is meeting the needs of family members (Greene, 2008a).

COLLECTIVE IDENTITY

A social system is an organization of people united in some form of regular interaction and interdependence. As practitioners conduct a family assessment, it is important that they remain mindful of the collective identity of individuals who are members of the social system. According to the systems model, to comprehend collective behavior, social workers must examine the relationship among and between members and focus on the social system's properties in its own right (Greene, 2008a; Greene, Galambos, Cohen, & Greene, 2016). How does the adult child perceive his or her aging parent? How does the aging parent perceive his or her child? Are they able to communicate effectively?

In many instances, particularly when communication is less than effective, the practitioner might decide that the family system itself is the client. The practitioner will understand the family as a social system consisting of individuals who influence one another. Thus, individuals and their roles are interdependent. Family rules develop over time, such as who is in charge of certain functions. To fully understand the caregiving provided within a family, the social worker must appreciate the development of the family as a group of interacting, interdependent individuals (Klein & White, 1996).

FUNCTIONAL-AGE MODEL OF INTERGENERATIONAL FAMILY TREATMENT

The functional-age model of intergenerational family treatment developed by Greene et al. (2016) allows social workers to assess and intervene with older adults and their families in caregiving situations. In this model, the social worker views the family as a mutually interdependent unit with a shared past and future. During assessment, the social worker explores the functional capacity of the person needing care. The family is assessed as a social system with an emphasis on how members carry out their roles and deal with life transitions. When these general systems theory assumptions are joined with resilience-enhancing principles, they direct the practitioners' attention to "the adaptive qualities of families as they encounter stress" (Hawley & DeHaan, 1996, p. 284).

Theorists interested in family resilience will also focus on the family's natural resources, patterns of functioning, and capabilities that enable the family to meet challenges and even thrive in the face of crisis. A family is not only a social system, but also a boundary-maintaining system—that is, it is open to societal or environmental resources and demands. Can a family link with other social systems and adapt to changing situations? What external forces has a family faced over time? Has it obtained needed resources?

Using family systems theory, as outlined above, practitioners may begin to observe and understand how family structure may be changed through planned interventions (Greene, 2008a). Systems theory guides social workers in their assessment of a family by

- working with the family to define its membership
- learning about the family's culture
- assuming that each family is a unique structure with its own communication patterns
- observing how the family is organized and what roles each family member carries out
- assessing how the family deals with stress
- determining how the family uses its internal resources and what resources it needs to acquire from other social systems
- ascertaining what are mutually acceptable interventions.

FAMILY MEANINGS AND STRESS

Families can be understood by addressing family meanings that have developed over time. Families share collective meanings that are distinct from individual meanings.

Family meanings are collective constructs created through the life experiences of family members as they interact over time. Patterson and Garwick (1998) have suggested that there are two levels of meaning: (1) situational meaning, involving the individual's and family's perceptions of their daily demands and capabilities; and (2) global meaning, encompassing a transcendent set of beliefs about the relationships of family members and the family to the community. The social worker can learn about a family's global beliefs as she or he explores the family's sense of common purpose. Do members accept that they are part of a collective? Are they able to view their situation optimistically? How do they perceive demands? Do they share control and trust each other?

FAMILY TRANSITIONS

An important aspect of a family assessment is learning how members have functioned as a group over time. Families may go through normative (usual and expected) transitions, such as births, marriages, and deaths, or they may have to handle unexpected events, such as the death of a child. The more difficult transitions families in Western culture face are dying, death, and bereavement. Social workers must have the appropriate preparation and skills to work with families in such difficult times.

CAREGIVING

The family continues to be the primary caregiver to older adults with disabilities or other conditions that affect functional ability (Blieszner & Bedford, 2012).

Caregiving is a normative task that represents a major family transition, experienced by many families, and can be difficult and time consuming, particularly when an older relative has advance-stage dementia or is incontinent. Family members who care for an impaired relative may develop physical or psychological difficulties of their own. For example, they may become depressed or experience deterioration in their own health. This is referred to as "caregiver burden." Therefore, assessing family stress and exploring how to lessen caregiver burden are central social work functions in dealing with the family of later years (Greene & Kropf, 2014).

One means of helping caregivers reduce their burden is to share the possible rewards of caregiving. Recent research has shed light on the fact that caregiving can increase psychological well-being and resiliency (J. Riley, 2007). The literature indicates that caregiving has five positive aspects:

1. caregiver satisfaction—caregiving experiences that provide a positive feeling about life

2. uplift of caregiving—daily events that can make the caregiver feel good

3. caregiver esteem—the confidence caregivers can gain as a direct result of their caregiving

4. any positive return—any return caregivers receive because of the experience

5. ability to find or make meaning of positive appraisal—which transforms the meaning of the caregiving experience (Hunt, 2003)

In addition to offering the social worker a slightly different view of the personal rewards of caregiving, each of these rewards also provides an avenue to pursue during assessment interviews (Gaugler, Kane, & Newcomer, 2007; see chapter 6 for discussion of assessment strategies).

END-OF-LIFE ISSUES

One of the most difficult challenges geriatric social workers face is helping a family make end-of-life decisions, face the death of a loved one, or go through the bereavement process. Social workers will often help families make ethical decisions involving advance directives—that is, documents signed by a competent person giving direction to health care providers about treatment choices in certain circumstances—or help families determine what type of care to pursue, such as hospice care (see chapter 2 for a discussion of ethical issues).

Practitioners must recognize that end-of-life decision making—another major family transition—may vary given a client family's culture (see chapter 3 for a review of how cultural differences influence end-of-life decisions). For example, how an older adult and his or her family perceive the meaning of dying may differ depending on how members have been socialized to think about death. Are they fearful, or do they consider death to be a natural part of life? Furthermore, family members may have varying reactions to the loss of a loved one who has died after a prolonged illness or peacefully during sleep. Also, cultural differences will influence the type of funeral or memorial that is selected. These decisions are affected by social, cultural, and religious norms (Sugar et al., 2014).

BEREAVEMENT

A universal response to the loss of a loved one, bereavement is the ability to sustain, integrate, and recover from loss. Although bereavement is a natural part of growth and development throughout life, affective or emotional reactions may range from sadness and restraint to anger. The acceptance of various expressions of grief requires social workers to view mourning responses as resilient acts of healing (Greene, 2002; Sugar et al., 2014).

SOCIAL SUPPORT NETWORKS

In assessment, geriatric practitioners will want to include information about the structure and content of their clients' social support networks or potential "consultants"—that is, biological and extended family members, friends, partners, and others who have established relationships with the individual or family. This information may indicate how people's attachments and support systems contribute to resilience. The structure of support systems refers to the number, types, and interconnectedness of ties, and content includes information about the type of assistance a person has received. When people need help, they may turn to neighbors and friends for counseling or emotional support (Farris, 2006). Such social support has been found to be related to well-being. For example, social integration may positively affect physical or mental health; furthermore, it provides a buffer against damages a person may suffer because of a major life crisis (Thoits, 1995).

In the future, some older clients' social support networks will include fewer adult children who are available to care for them. Today, an estimated one-fifth of Americans 65 years of age and older have no children, and one-third of the baby boomer generation will have no children. To some degree, we are living in a "small-family society." Consequently, this "thinning of the caregiving cohort" among mainstream families places a greater reliance on other members of one's social support networks for the well-being and care of older adults (Gironda, Lubben, & Atchison, 1999). Social workers will want to consider how these data affect their client families.

GERONTOLOGICAL KNOWLEDGE

Many older adults prefer to age in place—that is, in their own homes. They desire to grow old in a familiar environment, a place they have established over time and to which they have developed a psychological and physical attachment. Such familiarity may assist an older adult in overcoming the limitations posed by his or her physiological and sensory conditions. Our homes are often an expression of who we are. Home may be in a neighborhood that is linked to one's personal history and life events. This may explain why some older adults are reluctant to relocate (Rowles, 1993). For geriatric social workers to better assess the feasibility of an older adult's desire to age in place and that adult's readiness to remain competent in his or her home environment, they must first understand the concept of *environmental press*, an environmental context that places a demand on the older adult.

ENVIRONMENTAL PRESS COMPETENCE MODEL

Like social work theoretical approaches, an ecological model of aging examines behavior as the function of a person and the environment. The person is viewed in terms of a set of competencies, and the environment is defined in terms of demands. Thus, the fit between the two involves the interaction between an older individual and his or her environment.

Environment

Just as Bronfenbrenner (1979) classified environmental systems by their size and linkages to the individual, environments may be characterized by their influences on behavior. Will the risks in an older adult's environment be *proximal*, those closer to the individual, or *distal*, those situated further away, such as the political climate of the day? *Personal environments* consist of significant others, such as family or friends, who engage in a one-to-one personal relationship with the older adult. Does the older adult maintain friendships? *Suprapersonal environments* are the modal characteristics of all the people in physical proximity to an older person, including his or her neighbors or ethnic group (Lawton, 1982). Is the older adult living close to his or her cultural group? *Social environments* comprise the norms or values (such as the wish to live independently or not) and institutions operating in the individual's subgroup, society, or culture. Do the norms of the social environment promote independence or interdependence? *Physical environments* refer to the nonpersonal, nonsocial aspects of the environment, such as space, noise, and pollution. Does the older adult, for example, live in a neglected neighborhood? When using this model, the social worker's assessment is based on the client's positive behavioral outcome, exploring whether the older adult is able to balance capabilities with the demands—or press—of his or her environment (Lawton & Nahemow, 1973).

Competence

How does the social worker decide that a client appears competent in his or her environment? Historically, competence has been defined by an individual's "attributes associated with a white middle-class type of success in school or society . . . commonly involving the performance of a culturally specified task"

(Ogbu, 1981, p. 414). From the perspective of environmental press, *competence* is defined as "the theoretical upper limit of capacity of the individual to function in the areas of biological health, sensation–perception, motoric behavior, and cognition" (Lawton, 1982, p. 38). When social workers examine the upper limit of an individual's capacity to function in the environment, they are exploring the least restrictive environment in which the person wants to function. If a client prefers to stay in his or her home, can he or she remain there? Does the client need or want additional help?

Factors the geriatric social worker will examine to assess client competence include

- biological health—absence of disease states that prohibit functioning in the home
- sensory–perceptual capacity—processes of vision, auditory function, olfaction, gestation, somesthesis (bodily perception), and kinesthesis (the ability to sense the position, orientation, and movement of one's body parts) that, when not functioning properly, can make movement in the home extremely difficult
- motor skills—muscular strength and complex coordination that are necessary to perform on one's own
- cognitive capacity—ability to comprehend, process, and cope with the external world required to live alone
- ego strength—internal psychological strength that enhances independence. (Lawton, 1982)

In relativistic models, competencies are carried out within the context of a particular culture. Social workers are concerned with the person-in-environment fit, that is, how well a client is able to function within his or her home environment. *Goodness of fit* refers to an appropriately supportive environment (see chapter 3 to review how discrimination and oppression affect goodness of fit). From this viewpoint, geriatric social workers recognize that competence is not static but is subject to interventions that improve functional capacity. Thus, in an assessment of the person-in-environment fit, the practitioner examines the older adult's functional limitations, such as severe loss of sight or loss of upper extremity skills, and environmental barriers, such as inaccessible bathrooms or bedrooms or unsafe stairways. The practitioner and client then develop a plan of care that includes the interventions that will be taken (see chapter 6).

BIOPSYCHOSOCIAL AND SPIRITUAL FUNCTION

Another way of assessing the person-in-environment fit is to explore an older client's biopsychosocial and spiritual functioning. "Functional-age assessment," which provides indications of a person's competence, resilience, or both, involves understanding the biopsychosocial and spiritual behaviors that affect a person's ability or competence to perform behaviors central to everyday life (Greene,

2014). The geriatric social worker must examine the client's biological factors, or functional capacity, including health, physical capacity, or vital life-limiting organ systems. Psychological factors also come into play during assessment; they encompass an older adult's affective state or mood, cognitive or mental status, and behavioral dimensions. Sociocultural aspects to consider are the cultural, political, and economic aspects of life events (Greene et al., 2016). Spiritual factors may include a person's relationship with his or her faith or religious community or an inner system of beliefs. The importance of spiritual functioning is that it contributes to a person's ability to transcend the immediate situation and to discover meaning in seemingly meaningless events.

From a systems standpoint, social workers will consider an older adult's biopsychosocial and spiritual functioning as intertwined (Greene et al., 2016). The outcome of the holistic assessment when viewed from the vantage point of ecological press will allow the practitioner to help the older adult (and his or her family) come to a decision about resources and services that may be required for the older adult to remain living in his or her home. They will also indicate how well a client system has overcome difficulties in past and current functioning that may positively affect resilience.

KNOWLEDGE: THE RESILIENCE PERSPECTIVE

Resilience as Competence in One's Environment

Risk and resilience theory explains why some people better withstand adversity or high levels of stress than others. Risk and resilience theory has its roots in a public health model that explored risk factors for heart and lung disease. For example, in the Framingham Heart Study, which started in the 1950s, risk was defined as the statistical probability that smoking behavior would likely increase the development of a problem condition, namely, heart disease. Researchers informed participants in the study of the risks resulting from inactivity, smoking, and a high-fat diet. The study outcome was that many smokers would develop heart disease. The question was why. Investigations of how people have overcome adversity have influenced theories of human development (Fraser et al., 1999; Greene, 2002, 2007). What protective factors provided a defense against the risks or reduced them altogether? What allowed a person to successfully negotiate these risks? The research suggests that people who are able to overcome adverse or stressful events have protective factors that defend them, such as a supportive family member (Garmezy, 1991; Masten, 1994). People who readily overcome adversity are called resilient.

The most important aspect of resilience-based practice models is that they view older adults as advocating for themselves, directing their own care, and working hand in hand with the social worker to explore the options available in their environment or community. Consumer-directed care allows older adults to exercise their choices and preferences in the services they have requested and received. Practitioners who are considering using this care approach, however, must be mindful that some family cultures may prefer more family-centered decision-making processes rather than individual decision making. For example, the head of the family may be the designated person to contact the physician. Knowing what to expect in caregiving situations will better prepare the practitioner in assisting caregivers as consumers.

In addition, resiliency is often attributed to family and other support systems in which cultural groups experience strong communal and spiritual ties (Cross, 1998) (see chapter 3 for further discussion). Knowledge of how people successfully adapt despite stressful experiences can help practitioners better work with older adults. Such asset-focused research has led social workers in the field of aging to understand how an increase in the number or quality of resources may improve an older adult's quality of life. Resilience-enhancing strategies that have emerged from this theory base have provided practitioners with a set of practice skills that address how they can better maintain and enhance client competence within the client's environment (Cohen & Greene, 2006; Greene et al., 2016).

Risk and resilience theory represents a shift in thinking about human behavior in the social environment to positive aspects of human development across the life course. This book incorporates this emerging theory as a wellness approach to highlight the older adult's adaptability and capacity to meet life challenges, giving attention to culturally specific personal stories. The risk and resilience perspective adds to the gerontological stock of knowledge because it is based on an ecological metaphor, helping geriatric practitioners understand the network of influences—family, peer group, school, neighborhood, and society—on an older adult's sources of strength (Brooks, Nomura, & Cohen, 1989). By comprehending these influences, practitioners may recognize the social context in which individual resilience is embedded, that is, the larger social systems that act "as nested contexts for social competence" (Walsh, 1998, p. 12).

Defining Risk and Resilience

Fraser and colleagues (1999) have argued that the social work profession should reserve the term *resilience* for "unpredicted or markedly successful adaptations to negative life events, trauma, stress, and other forms of risk" (p. 136). They contend that if "we can understand what helps some people to function well in the context of high adversity, we may be able to incorporate this knowledge into new practice strategies" (p. 136). Definitions of resilience vary, as can be seen from the following:

- "Resilience is concerned with individual variations in response to risk. Resilience refers to the positive role of individual differences in people's response to stress and adversity, as well as hope and optimism in the face of adversity" (Rutter, 1987, pp. 316–317).
- "Resilience is not defined in terms of the absence of pathology or heroics. Rather, it is an ability to cope with adversity, stress, and deprivation" (Begun, 1993, pp. 28–29).

- "Resilience is the ability to maintain continuity of one's personal narrative and a coherent sense of self following traumatic events" (Borden, 1992, p. 125).
- "Resilience is normal development under difficult conditions" (Fonagy, Steele, Steele, Higgitt, & Target, 1994, p. 233).

Although definitions differ, associating resilience with risk—the probability that a problem may emerge—can be useful in the assessment of older adults when safety issues are of concern.

In her research, Masten (1994) focused on the protective factors or circumstances that moderate the effects of risks and enhance adaptation. This approach, originally used with children, is also useful to geriatric social workers because it gives us a way to think about what critical events or traumas an older adult may have overcome over his or her life course. For example, a client who lived through the Great Depression or World War II may have developed various coping strategies that he or she can tap in old age. Furthermore, life review and other storytelling techniques, such as narrative therapy, frequently used as interventions with older adults, are particularly applicable in working with older adults because they reveal their resilience—clients' ability to maintain the continuity of their personal story (Borden, 1992) (see chapter 7 for more information on interventions).

Philosophy

An interest in risk and resilience theory can be traced to several social science movements, including the positive psychology movement (based on positive emotions such as hope, humor, and joy) and the demand for evidence-based practice (based on research findings and protocols) and prevention (based on interventions that attempt to avert a problem) (H. L. Cohen & Greene, 2006). The positive psychology movement is "a science based on the idea that if . . . people are taught resilience, hope, and optimism, they will be less susceptible to depression and will lead happier, more productive lives" (Seligman, 2002, p. 3). Positive psychology refocuses practitioners' attention to assess clients' adaptive functioning—how people maintain well-being despite stumbling blocks or trauma.

The health and wellness movement invites social workers to promote health and well-being among their clients. This may be accomplished by using positive thinking techniques (Ryff & Singer, 2002). Combining this philosophy with other theoretical information about normal functioning of older adults may enable the social worker to be more likely to see the client from a strengths-based perspective (see chapter 7 for interventions that follow a resilience-enhancing philosophy).

Resilience-Enhancing Model of Social Work Practice

These shifts in beliefs and scientific understanding about human development contribute to a different kind of understanding of clients and to a changed view of social work practice. This alternative type of practice is proposed by the resilience-enhancing model (REM), which centers on promoting and maintaining client competence or self-efficacy. According to Greene (2007),

> REM embodies a philosophy of hope, instilling positive expectations for the future. It is based on the belief that people have an innate capacity to lead productive lives, and offers practitioners the means of fostering health-promoting behaviors across the life course. As a model that centers on a client's assets and propensity to grow and heal, it generally avoids problem-saturated client descriptions. (p. 70)

Although the model suggests that practitioners pay attention to client loss, vulnerability, and stress, it also emphasizes that they help clients take as much control over their life decisions as possible. In addition to ensuring that older clients have basic life necessities, the social worker uses various techniques—for instance, listening for the signs of positive emotions, such as humor and hope—to mobilize clients. In some cases, practitioners using REM enable their clients to make meaning of negative events so that they are better able to transcend the difficulties of the immediate situation.

Many of the intervention strategies in REM are derived from social construction theory, which suggests that one's views of social reality grow out of one's interactions and discourse in daily life experiences (Gergen, 1985). Accordingly, REM focuses on how people retain a sense of competence as they age. In large measure, this ability is attributed to a client's facility at making meaning of critical life events—that is, the older adult has "a sense of direction, a sense of order, and a reason for existence, a clear sense of personal identity, a greater sense of social conscious" (Reker, 1997, p. 710).

When an adverse event first occurs, a client may feel that the world is meaningless. However, as time passes, an older adult may begin to understand the meaning and significance of the event, depending on his or her appraisal of the event (Janoff-Bulman & Berger, 2000). Thus, an important social work role is to interview the client to help that individual appraise his or her life story to determine whether the event is a loss or a challenge (Lazarus & Folkman, 1984). This interviewing process is described further in chapter 6.

THEORY CRITIQUE

The preceding key theoretical concepts delineate the knowledge a successful social worker will need to conduct assessments of older adults, their families, and their social support networks effectively. However, when using these theories, one should assume a critical stance (Laird, 1993). During assessment, it is important to evaluate theories to determine how well they apply to a particular client situation. When a social worker critiques a theory, it will help the practitioner gain confidence in his or her knowledge about a theory and the interweaving of its components.

To evaluate a model or theory fully, the practitioner needs to examine first the model or theory author's background, credentials, and demographic characteristics (Meyer, 1983). The social worker must then ask the following questions about the model or theory:

- When was it developed? What prompted the author to develop it? What important social, cultural, or historical events surrounded its development?

- Are the ideological biases of it articulated? If so, what are they (for example, a differential emphasis on person and the environment or use of a particular knowledge base)? On what psychological or social sciences theory or theories does it draw?

- What is the purpose of it?

- What is the real value system of it? What consideration does it give to the role of race or ethnicity, gender, sexual orientation, age, physical or mental challenge, or socioeconomic class?

- What are the client characteristics (for example, demographics, skills, knowledge, or personality type) thought to be necessary for appropriate use of it?

- What unit or units of attention are addressed by it?

- How does it define problems?

- What causes psychological or interpersonal problems according to it?

- How is assessment defined and conducted within it?

- What interventions are described within it? What skills are required by the practitioner?

- What is the role of the practitioner and that of the client? How is the professional relationship defined and described?

- What are the desirable outcomes or goals of it?

- How is time structured within it?

- Are there any personnel exclusions stated or implied by it?

- Is it consistent with collaboration and referral to other agencies or practitioners?

- To what extent can it be evaluated for effectiveness? What research has been done to evaluate it?

- How is it similar to or different from social work's person-in-situation paradigm?

- How is it consistent or inconsistent with the NASW *Code of Ethics* (NASW, 2017)?

By addressing such questions, social workers can come to "understand how their personal experiences and affective reactions may affect their assessment and decision-making" (CSWE, 2015, p. 7).

CONCLUSION

Finally, a theory should help the social worker to configure or put together the various factors involved in a client's situation. What are the challenges? What are the opportunities? Has the theoretical information used in assessment helped you and your client make meaning of the situation? Do you understand your client's situation and mutually agree on a future direction? (See chapter 6 for more assessment information.) Have you embarked on a path that uses theory in the strengths tradition of social work practice?

Case Study: Assessment of the Stanley Family's Functioning

The models of assessment in this chapter provide various frameworks to understand the individual and collective functioning of the Stanley family. Using the ecological perspective, a social work practitioner would assess individuals within the family—Mrs. Stanley, Jasmine, and Terrell—from a biopsychosocial and spiritual perspective. However, the "missing members" need to be understood as well, including John (in prison), Loverne (residence unknown), and Mrs. Stanley's other two children and their families. At the meso level, the relationship between the family and other systems in the environment would be assessed, including the children's schools, their church, their friendships, and the neighborhood context. In addition, macrosystem aspects of the family situation, such as laws, policies, and regulations that affect family life, need to be included.

Life course and developmental issues are also crucial to understand. Mrs. Stanley is parenting beyond the normative time frame for this role. It may be difficult for her to understand and relate to the norms, mores, and customs of children; it may even be challenging for her to keep up with their use of technology. A source of stress within the family is Jasmine's preference for hip hop music, which Mrs. Stanley does not tolerate and considers offensive and obscene. In addition, developmental issues of the grandchildren are important, such as Jasmine's entry into puberty and increased interest in boys. Terrell's behavior also needs to be understood developmentally, as he is very shy, has no friends, and clings to his grandmother.

Attachments are also important aspects of assessment in this case example. Jasmine and Terrell experienced insufficient nurturing during their formative years, with their needs for safety and connection not met by their parents. The behaviors exhibited by both (defiance and opposi-tional behavior from Jasmine; clinging and reclusiveness by Terrell) indicate insecure attachments. Relatedly, assessment of Mrs. Stanley's connection to her other children and grandchildren needs to be considered. Does she have any relationship with these members of her family? How do these members view her relationship with John, Jasmine, and Terrell? All of these aspects are important to assess.

Despite these challenges, the family demonstrates resilience. They continue to function, using social resources in the environment, such as their relationship to the church and other families in the neighborhood, to keep going. Because of the trauma her grandchildren experienced, however, Mrs. Stanley may need help discerning risk situations. What is normal teenage behavior in establishing independence, and what are risks that provide evidence that she needs additional help and support? The teenage years can be difficult regardless of circumstance, but the early life trauma experienced by these children may create situations in which maladaptive behavior is more likely to occur.

WHAT WE LEARNED IN THIS CHAPTER

- How to use theories, such as ecological perspective, general systems theory, and resilience theory, to shape the social work assessment process for older adults
- How to critique a theory or model to determine whether it applies to a client situation
- Tools developed from the theoretical models that can be used in the assessment process

SUGGESTED EXERCISE TO EVALUATE STUDENT COMPETENCY

Students will critique a theory by using a conceptual framework, considering whether a theory has a balance between

- pathology and health (Do concepts focus on deficits or on well-being?)
- practitioner and client control (Does the theory allow for mutual or shared control?)
- personal and societal impact (Does the theory see the client difficulty as client based or societal?)
- internal and external change (Does the theory emphasize personal or societal change?)
- rigidity and flexibility (Does the theory allow for adjustments for diverse clients?) (summarized from Trader, 1977)

ADDITIONAL RESOURCES

The Center of Design for an Aging Society is an organization that provides solutions to modify living environments that help older adults maximize their abilities to maintain independence and dignity. Design information and resources can be found at http://www.centerofdesign.org.

The Children of Aging Parents Web site provides information on caregiver support groups, home care services, and other social services information. For information on these services, visit http://www.caps4caregivers.org.

Help Guide is a Web site that focuses on tools and articles to help individuals deal with behavioral and social health challenges. The Coping with Grief and Loss section provides a discussion of grief and tips on how to deal with the grieving process. For resources, go to http://www.helpguide.org.

The Expanded Family Life Cycle presents the stages of the family life cycle and diagrams the flow of stress through the family. For a detailed discussion on this topic, visit http://sw2.haifa.ac.il/images/stories/Field_studies/family_1.pdf.

The Family Caregiver Alliance provides services, education, and resources for families and friends providing long-term care for loved ones at home. For more information, go to http://www.caregiver.org.

The Gerontological Society of America is an interdisciplinary organization that promotes research, education, and practice in the field of aging. For resource and educational materials, visit http://www.geron.org.

Therapist Aid: Genograms for Psychotherapy provides information and examples of genograms and how to use them in practice. Go to http://www.therapistaid.com/therapy-guide/genograms.

6

Engagement and Assessment of Older Adults, Their Families, and Their Social Supports

ENGAGEMENT

RATIONALE: "Social workers understand that engagement is an ongoing component of the dynamic and interactive process of social work practice with, and on behalf of, diverse individuals, families, groups, organizations, and communities. Social workers understand strategies to engage diverse clients and constituencies to advance practice effectiveness" (CSWE, 2015, p. 8). To foster this engagement, gero social workers interpret the diverse life course (including resilience, contributions, and strengths) of older adults and consider the cohorts and contexts in which they have lived.

Practitioners in aging engage older adults, caregivers, and related systems by understanding and applying a range of appropriate theories. To foster this engagement, "gero social workers interpret older adults' diverse life courses (including resilience, contributions, and strengths) and take account of the cohorts and contexts in which they have lived" (CSWE, 2017, p. 65).

COMPETENCY: Practitioners in aging with, and on behalf of, older adults and their constituencies

- establish and maintain strong relationships with older adults and their constituencies for the purpose of working toward mutually agreed upon goals.
- plan engagement strategies and interventions based on understanding of older adults' diverse life courses, strengths, challenges, and contexts (CSWE, 2017, p. 65).

ASSESSMENT

RATIONALE: "Social workers understand that assessment is an ongoing component of the dynamic and interactive process of social work practice with, and on behalf of, diverse individuals, families, groups, organizations, and communities. Social workers understand methods of assessment with diverse clients and constituencies to advance practice effectiveness. Social workers recognize the implications of the larger practice context in the assessment process and value the importance of interprofessional collaboration in this process" (CSWE, 2015, p. 9). "The comprehensive biopsychosocial assessment takes into account the multiple factors of physical, mental, and social well-being needed for treatment planning for older adults and their families" (CSWE, 2017, p. 89).

COMPETENCY: Practitioners in aging

- conduct assessments that incorporate a strengths-based perspective, person/family-centered focus, and resilience while recognizing aging-related risks.
- develop, select, and adapt assessment methods and tools that optimize practice with older adults, their families, caregivers, and communities.
- use and integrate multiple domains and sources of assessment information and communicate with other professionals to inform a comprehensive plan for intervention. (CSWE, 2017, pp. 89–90)

This chapter focuses on the engagement of older adults in the helping process. It then outlines initial assessment interviews for working with older clients. Special techniques are described that can make interviews more comfortable for older clients. This chapter also presents tools and instruments commonly used in geriatric assessment. These tools can be used selectively to ascertain a client's functional capacity. The use of the interview as shaped by various schools of intervention is discussed in depth in chapter 7, as are accompanying intervention strategies.

HELPING PROCESS

The helping process starts with a preparatory process in which the practitioner becomes well grounded in the theory necessary for geriatric social work practice (see chapter 5). This period is called *engagement* but is "an ongoing component of the dynamic and interactive process of social work practice" (CSWE, 2015, p. 6). After gathering potential information and knowledge about client situations in engagement, social work practice generally goes through other stages, including assessment, intervention, and evaluation. These stages overlap. For example, a client's request for help may be characterized as a form of self-change or intervention.

ENGAGING CLIENT AND CLIENT SYSTEM

Practitioner–Client Relationship

The practitioner–client relationship is the key to effective engagement that leads to social work assessment and intervention (Kirst-Ashman & Hull, 1999). The client-centered social work tradition suggests that practitioners can develop relationships and foster an older client's constructive personal growth by imparting *empathy,* or the ability to deal sensitively and accurately with client feelings; *nonpossessive warmth,* or acceptance of the older client as an individual; and *genuineness,* that is, authenticity (Rogers & Dymond, 1957).

When older clients perceive that the social worker is supporting them, they develop a sense of trust, and their natural ability to change is set in motion. Research findings suggest that interventions are more successful when practitioners believe that their clients have the strength and the resources necessary to solve their problems (Asay & Lambert, 1999; Hubble, Duncan, & Miller, 1999). Tallman and Bohart (1999) contended that a client's capacity to heal is the most potent common factor in any kind of intervention, the very "engine" that makes practice work.

Here is an exercise to prepare for an initial interview:

Close your eyes and imagine yourself as 80 years old. Then, answer the following questions:

- Where do you live? Describe your home. With whom do you live? Do you have friends or family nearby? How often do you see family?
- What do you look like? How changed are you from your younger years? Are you attractive to others?
- In what activities do you engage? Do you cook for yourself? Do you read, watch TV, or garden? Do you exercise? How often do you get out? Where do you go? What form of transportation do you use? Do you have many friends?
- How is your physical and mental health? Do you have any illnesses or disease? Are you on medication? Are you mobile?
- Do you often feel depressed?
- How will you celebrate your birthday? What foods do you eat? Who will be with you?
- What are the general customs of a birthday?
- Have you aged successfully? Why or why not?

Other questions to ask include those that picture yourself in need of care:

- When will you need care? How old are you?

- Why do you need care?
- What form will that care take?
- How mobile are you?
- Do you need help bathing?
- Do you receive Meals-on-Wheels? A friendly visitor? Are you on a ventilator?
- Can you change your bed linens?
- How will you go about making the arrangements for your care?
- Who is giving you the care?
- Is the care formal or informal? Is there more than one person involved?
- Where are you living?
- What do you most enjoy in life?
- How do you feel about receiving help?

This exercise helps the practitioner identify crucial questions to ask an older adult that will enable collection of important information.

Initial Interviews

Initial social work interviews with older clients set the stage for the unfolding of a mutual helping process. It is important that, when appropriate, the social worker involve significant family members, partners, and friends at this time (Greene, 2008b). If an older client has an impairment that affects communication, it may be necessary to modify the interview. For example, if a client wears a hearing aid, the practitioner will need to determine that the device is working, make sure to face the client directly, and speak at a normal conversational volume. A client who has had a stroke may have totally or partially lost the power to use and understand words. Therefore, the social worker must allow that client plenty of time to communicate and to complete his or her thoughts. The best environment for an interview with clients having Alzheimer's disease is a quiet space without distractions. Use a low-pitched voice and ask one question at a time (http://www.ec.online.net/Knowledge/Articles/communication .html). First meetings are important for both client and social worker. How does the practitioner begin, and what should he or she say? Important issues to cover include the following (see Shulman, 2006):

- Clarify the social worker's purpose and role. Offer a simple statement of the reason for the encounter and the services provided by the social worker's agency.
- Reach for client feedback; that is, make an effort to understand the client's perceptions of his or her needs.
- Partialize or separate into segments the client's concerns—help him or her break down sometimes overwhelming difficulties into manageable parts.

- Deal with issues of authority by striving to establish mutuality in the working relationship.

Assessing the Client System

Assessment of older adults is the process of gathering information about their everyday functioning to select appropriate interventions to enhance client (system) well-being. This process includes appraising the client's current biological, psychological, and social attributes and spiritual well-being and how effectively they have functioned over time. Many times an assessment will also include the family system and an evaluation of a client's support network (Greene, 1986/2000). An important feature of the assessment is gaining an understanding of the resources available to the client and learning whether the older adult engages effectively with other social systems, such as health care or recreational programs.

Assessment Teams

Assessments may be conducted by the social worker alone or by a team of geriatric specialists. In collaborative exchanges, the social worker will work with team members from different disciplines, for example, medicine, nursing, occupational therapy, nutritional counseling, and physical therapy. The team will collectively set goals and share responsibilities and resources (Merck & Co., 2005). Geriatric social workers "value the importance of interprofessional teamwork" (CSWE, 2015, p. 8) and may encounter blurring of professional boundaries and training across disciplines, requiring them to learn more about the roles of allied health professionals.

Geriatric Assessment

Geriatric assessment varies from an assessment with other age groups. Lichtenberg (2000) recommended four assessment principles for evaluating an older adult:

1. The first principle is that chronological age alone does not necessarily reflect *functional age*, or a person's capacity to live effectively in his or her environment. Recognizing this ability is central to the geriatric assessment process (Greene, 1986/2000). This person-in-environment perspective, which takes into account environmental press, allows for a dynamic picture of the older adult's functioning as he or she adjusts to changes in the environment. From this perspective, the social worker gains information about how the individual responds and adjusts to changes in social setting (family and community) and the process of aging (physical and mental well-being) that influence functioning (Lawton, 1989; Lawton & Nahemow, 1973; Parmelee & Lawton, 1990).

2. The second principle is that practitioners should use brief assessment instruments to supplement the traditional interview and thus reduce the time it takes to evaluate older adults. Lichtenberg (2000) pointed out that research demonstrates the reliability and validity of many of these assessment instruments.

3. Assessment, according to the third principle, must result in a delineation of strengths and weaknesses (or risks and resilience). Knowledge of a client's unique characteristics and capacities can inform both the care planning process and treatment recommendations.

4. The fourth principle is that social workers need to use multiple assessment methods to improve the quality of information.

Because assessment instruments have rarely been validated with minority populations, geriatric social workers should use caution when adopting them (Tran, Ngo, & Conway, 2003) (see chapter 3 for further discussion of diversity).

Theory-Based Interview

Assessments not only relate to the aging population, they incorporate theory-based principles. The use of a particular theory will allow the practitioner to interpret and organize the interview. However, the social worker can ask general questions to better understand how the older client is functioning within his or her environment:

- Is the older adult able to meet the demands presented, or is he or she overwhelmed?
- What is the nature of the stress that precipitated contact with the social worker's agency?
- What biopsychosocial or spiritual factors stand in the way of effective functioning?
- What resources may permit the client to function better?
- What are alternative explanations for the perceived difficulties?
- What solutions have been tried?
- What actions have been successful so far?
- Does the client agree with the practitioner's perceptions of the older adult's situation?

Strengths-Based Assessment

A general principle that guides social work assessment is that it should be strengths based. The strengths-based movement rests on a philosophy of helping in which "all [clients] must be understood and assessed in the light of their capabilities, competencies, knowledge, survival skills, visions, possibilities, and hopes" (Saleebey, 1997, p. 17). Social workers make a conscious decision to pay attention primarily to those factors of people's lives that can contribute to their growth and well-being. A strengths-based assessment requires that practitioners get to know their older clients and how they currently function and have functioned over time. Each client is unique, having his or her own psychosocial profile (Kivnick, 1993; Kivnick & Murray, 2001). Therefore, it is necessary to listen for each person's strengths and capacities, as well as client risks and constraints. When used in an assessment, the following 10 questions will provide a comprehensive strengths-based assessment:

1. What makes a day a good day for you? What do you hope for at the start of a new day?

2. What are the things you do, each day or each week, because you really want to—not because you have to—when you get totally absorbed, forget about everything else, and the time seems to fly?

3. What are you good at? What kinds of things did you used to be good at? What about yourself has always given you confidence or made you proud?

4. What kinds of exercise do you do regularly? What kinds could you do to help you feel better?

5. What kinds of help, service, or assistance do you give? To whom? What help or service would you like to give?

6. When you get out, what do you like to do? Where do you like to go? What would you like to do? Where would you like to go?

7. What lessons have you learned about how to cope with life from day to day? Are there ways you wish you could cope better?

8. Who are the people especially important to you these days? Tell me about these relationships.

9. What physical things or objects do you have that are most precious to you? What things do you save? Or take special care of? If you had to relocate, what few things would you take with you?

10. To interviewer: What additional strengths, values, commitments, skills, or assets do you know (from whatever source) that this person has?

In addition to REM, presented throughout the text, there are several models used to foster client strengths. For example, Graybeal (2001) argued that the traditional problem-based assessment used in the medical model conflicts with the alternative strengths-based assessment, which explores a person's skill, capacities, and resilience. Consequently, he coined the acronym ROPES to guide practitioners' strengths-based interviews so that they will pay close attention to

Resources: personal, family, social environment, organizational, and community.

Options: present focus, with an emphasis on choice. What can be accessed now? What is available and hasn't been tried or used?

Possibilities: future focus, imagination, creativity, one's vision of the future, play. What have you thought of trying but haven't yet?

Exceptions: When is the problem not happening? When is the problem different? When will part of the hypothetical future solution occur? How have you survived, endured, or thrived?

Solutions: Focus on constructing solutions rather than solving problems. What is currently working? What are your successes? What are you doing that you would like to continue doing? What if a miracle happened? What can you do now to create a piece of the miracle? (Graybeal, 2001, p. 237)

The Interview: An Assessment Tool

As an assessment tool, the interview is a means for setting the helping process in motion. It is a "conversation with a deliberate purpose that the participants accept. . . . [It involves] both verbal and nonverbal communication between people during which they exchange ideas, attitudes, and feelings" (Kadushin & Kadushin, 1997, p. 4). Hepworth, Rooney, and Larsen (1997) suggested that the purpose of the interview is to shed light on and to solve problems while promoting client growth and improving quality of life. Assessment interviews also may be thought of as a way of "individualizing the person–situation configuration" (Northen, 1982).

Interpretations of Client Answers

An effective social worker must possess good communication skills to interpret the client's responses to interview questions accurately. Practitioners need to send a specifically chosen message verbally and engage in "active listening," both of which require that they understand the client's story clearly. For example, on some occasions the social worker may hear only a noncommittal response. The message the older client might be conveying is that he or she is still processing the information imparted, hence the client's hesitancy. Do not rush the client. Instead, a practitioner could indicate that he or she is unsure of the client's response. Client and social worker then might decide together whether they should discuss the issue further.

It might be helpful for the practitioner to acknowledge that the situation is difficult. Older adults may be sensitive to certain topics, such as their sexuality or finances, so it may be best to bring these up later in the helping process. The practitioner should remember that he or she is often younger than the client, who will have made many decisions and choices during his or her lifetime. Therefore, the social worker and client need to be collaborators in the helping process.

ASSESSMENT COMPONENTS

Determination of Normal Aging

Aging is a process of gradual and spontaneous changes that result in maturation through childhood, puberty, and young adulthood. Then, certain bodily functions begin to ebb (Merck & Co., 2005). Variations in physical and mental status increase as people age because individuals age at different rates. Even within one person, the signs of aging of organs and organ systems vary. Scientists believe that aging is a complex phenomenon arising from a combination of genes, lifestyle, and disease. All older adults must navigate a decline in bodily functions that tend to cause frailty. Normal changes due to aging (Poinier & Herman, 2014) include the following:

- The heart grows slightly larger, and oxygen consumption during exercise declines.
- Arteries stiffen with age, and fatty deposits build up.
- Lungs decline in terms of breathing capacity.
- The brain loses some cells and some may become damaged; the number of connections between cells may regrow.
- The kidneys become less efficient; if urinary incontinence occurs, it may be managed through exercise and behavioral techniques.
- Muscles may decline without exercise.
- Skin becomes less elastic and more lined and wrinkled.
- Hair turns grayer and thins.
- One's height declines slowly by as much as two inches by 80 years of age.
- One's eyesight declines, with loss of peripheral vision and decreased ability to judge depth.
- Taste decreases, sensitivity to touch lessens, and ability to smell declines.
- Hearing lessens, with loss of acuity.
- Personality is maintained, and stability is expected.

Many of the changes that accompany aging, such as wrinkles and thinning and graying of hair, may seem to be cosmetic. But the social worker will need to learn from each client the particular meaning that the person attaches to physical and social changes that accompany the aging process. Does the client seem to "go with the flow" and have vitality and grit? Does he or she seem sluggish or depressed? The great majority of people 65 years and older are healthy, happy, and fully independent. Some older adults will have made positive lifestyle choices, such as engaging in exercise. Others, though, may have problems of living severe enough to require the assistance of a geriatric practitioner. A comprehensive biopsychosocial and spiritual assessment is required to enable the social worker and client to make intervention decisions. Approaching the client system from a biopsychosocial–spiritual standpoint involves examining the client's physical and psychological functioning, economic and political factors affecting the client's life, and his or her spiritual health and looking at the risk and protective factors influencing each of these areas.

Biopsychosocial and Spiritual Assessment

A *functional-age assessment* enables geriatric social workers to understand the biopsychosocial–spiritual factors affecting a person's ability or competence to perform behaviors central to everyday life. Although many scientists continue to see older adults as going through a period of declining health and function, there is remarkable variability among individuals (Seeman & Chen, 2002). A functional-age assessment helps distinguish normal age-related changes from those requiring intervention by allowing the social worker to identify risk and protective factors for each area of functioning.

   Biological factors are related to functional capacity and include health, physical capacity, or vital life-limiting organ systems; *psychological* factors encompass an individual's affective state or mood, cognitive or mental status, and the person's behavioral dimensions. *Sociocultural* aspects are the cultural, political, and economic components of life events (Greene et al., 2016). In addition, *spiritual* factors may include a person's relationship with his or her faith or religious community or an inner system of beliefs. Spiritual functioning is important because spirituality contributes to a person's ability to transcend the immediate situation and to discover meaning in seemingly meaningless events.

Biological Functioning

Although physicians generally diagnose a person's biological functioning, the social worker, through an assessment of the client's independence in activities of daily living (ADLs), can address many physical attributes affecting everyday life. Particularly in the client's home environment, the practitioner can quickly get a clear picture of the older adult's abilities and the risks involved in navigating that environment. Always take health complaints seriously. Note the medications a client has on hand. Are those medications current, and is the client using them properly?

ADLs

The holistic assessment on how well an older adult fits with his or her home environment is measured by evaluating a client's capacity to perform ADLs (Iwarsson, 2005), which include feeding, toileting, dressing, bathing, cooking, shopping, cleaning, transferring (for example, from bed to chair), and using transportation.

Psychological Functioning

Older adults may be at risk for mental disorders: One in every five people 55 years and older experiences mental health concerns that are not part of the normal aging process. In addition, the suicide rate for people 65 years and older, especially among men, is higher than in any other age group (Gonyea, Hudson, & Curley, 2004). An assessment of psychological functioning involves examining, among other factors, the client's life satisfaction. For example, social workers might use the life history, a methodological tool, to explore an older adult's perceived identity.

Depression

Practitioners also will want to assess their client's coping abilities, mood or affect, and past or current mental health problems. In particular, depression, or feelings of sadness or feeling "down," affects 6.1 percent of adults 55 years of age and older (Sugar et al., 2014). Older adults with depression have more health care visits, including trips to the emergency room, and use more medication. Left untreated, depression can lead to the onset of physical, cognitive, and social impairments as well as increased health care use, delayed recovery from medical illness and surgery, and suicide. People over the age of 65 account for 15.6 percent of all suicides (Sugar et al., 2014). However, depression is treatable, and most people recover from it.

Contrary to popular belief, depression is not a natural part of aging; it is often reversible with prompt and appropriate treatment. It is essential, then, that practitioners learn whether a client has had a history of depression. Is the client depressed by perceived "damage"—such as surgery or a heart attack—to his or her body image? Is the depression associated with chronic or severe pain? Is the client suffering from a side effect of a medication? Geriatric social workers will want to assess what environmental factors, such as a diminishing social support system, may be playing a role in depression. They must be aware, however, that various cultural groups may conceptualize or describe depression differently. Clients who exhibit prolonged symptoms, for example, a lack of attention to personal care and feelings of discouragement or hopelessness, should be seen by a specialist who can administer medical tests and make a differential diagnosis.

Neurocognitive Disorders

In their geriatric practice, social workers may encounter many different types of neurocognitive disorders among their clients. The risk of developing neurocognitive disorders increases with old age, and families are affected and challenged by such diagnoses. Alzheimer's disease, the most widely known form of neurocognitive disorder, is a process of degeneration of brain tissue that results in loss of intellectual reasoning and cognitive function. It is generally found in people 65 years of age and older. The causes of this degeneration of brain tissue are unknown but are thought to be a combination of genes and environmental factors.

The social worker may be the first professional to suspect that a client has a neurocognitive disorder, based on the older adult's answers to questions about his or her mental status (see Additional Resources at the end of this chapter). In such cases, the practitioner should discuss his or her concerns with the client and perhaps with the client's family. A referral to a qualified specialist must be made.

The social worker's suspicion of early Alzheimer's disease may lead to an improvement in the older adult's situation and that of his or her family. Direct benefits to the older adult include a more definitive diagnosis of other potentially reversible causes of neurocognitive disorders. Furthermore, Alzheimer's disease sometimes is confused with depression and anxiety, both of which may be treated with pharmacological interventions. Family members also may benefit from early detection, which may provide them with more time to adjust to the diagnosis and plan for the future and create an opportunity to obtain other family members' input into decisions about advance directives and other care preferences while that person is still at a mild stage of the illness (see also chapter 2 for a discussion of the social worker's role in ethical decision making).

Sociocultural Functioning

A client's social age comprises the roles and social habits that person performs in the family and other social structures. All cultures use age as a factor to prescribe role-appropriate behaviors: Deciding to retire and acting as a grandparent are both examples of age-appropriate behaviors and one's timing of life events (Greene et al., 2016). As people age, the meaning of various roles they play intensifies or becomes greater in importance (Krause, 2004). Given certain circumstances, such as insufficient income, some older adults may or may not find new meaningful roles in old age (for example, older adults may be concerned whether they can still afford to give presents to their grandchildren after retiring).

Because having positive social supports and remaining connected to those support networks are protective factors to help buffer stress and contribute to older adults' well-being, learning how successful a client feels about fulfilling personal and social obligations is an important assessment task. As the geriatric social worker evaluates how much social support a client has, he or she will want to use a social network scale to explore the structure and content of the older adult's social relationships. Structure refers to the number, types, and interconnectedness of ties, and content describes the kind of assistance a person gives and receives (for example, whether the client babysits or performs volunteer work).

Spiritual Well-Being

In an effort to address the person in environment, the helping professions are increasingly recognizing religion and spirituality as components of the helping process (Canda & Furman, 1999). Spirituality, or a person's quest "to transcend the self and discover meaning" (Conrad, 1999, p. 63), is an important protective factor and "serves as a modifiable resource that can be drawn upon during times of personal crises" (Angell, Dennis, & Dumain, 1998, p. 616). Hodge (2001) developed a broad-based anthropological questionnaire to help geriatric social workers better understand their clients' spiritual lives (see the Additional Resources section for more information about spiritual assessments).

Home Environment Assessment

Assessing older adults at home allows practitioners to observe firsthand clients' mobility and physical functioning in their own setting, plus any safety concerns. However, conducting a home-based assessment presents both challenges and opportunities (Naleppa & Hash, 2001). When entering a client's home, one challenge is helping the client to maintain boundaries, that is, to be cognizant that the social worker is in the client's home as a professional, not as a friend. Practitioners frequently wonder whether they should accept food, drink, or small gifts from a client in that person's home. The decision regarding whether to take these items hinges on the context of the situation (Naleppa & Hash, 2001). Is accepting a cup of tea important in the client's culture? Distractions, such as a television running or an unexpected visitor, are other potential obstacles social workers face during home visits. And, occasionally, social workers may arrive at a client's home during an emergency and find themselves calling emergency personnel.

Yet, interviewing an older adult in his or her own home provides an opportunity for the client to feel more comfortable. Even though the state adult protection agency may conduct a complete evaluation of home safety, a home-based visit will allow the geriatric practitioner to survey the home for safety issues. For a home safety checklist, see the Additional Resources section at the end of this chapter.

Assessment of Client Competence in Handling Environmental Issues

The ecological model of aging proposes that the older adult's ability to function with competence is an outcome of how that person meets environmental demands (Lawton, 1989). However, a biopsychosocial and spiritual assessment alone will not provide a complete picture of client competence. Rather, the social worker needs to determine the client's appraisal of critical life events. *Appraisal* has a special meaning referring to whether the older adult has perceived a demand as a threat, loss, or challenge, and whether he or she views a demand as controllable (Lazarus & Folkman, 1984). How a client appraises an event varies depending on his or her culture, role demands or conflicts, and belief systems or personal values. According to Janoff-Bulman and Berger (2000), the appraisal process, particularly following adverse events in the older adult's life, may produce several outcomes, including a greater appreciation of life, taking little for granted, or being motivated to live life differently.

Assessment of Client Resiliency

During one's lifetime, a person appraises and attaches meaning to critical events. In fact, meaning making may be a natural process people undergo to counter stress and strive for health (Antonovsky & Sourani, 1988). They want their worlds to be comprehensible, manageable, and meaningful. A time line is an assessment tool that allows the practitioner and the client to review the important events in the client's life. As older individuals reminisce about their lives, they decide whether their lives were "acceptable." Erikson (1959/1980) was one of the first theorists to argue that old age is a time of increased meaning making. He contended that in the last stage of life, people struggle with integrity: "how to grow old with integrity in the face of death" (Erikson, 1959/1980, p. 104). *Integrity* means having few regrets and coping well with failures as well as with successes. In the final step in the assessment process, the practitioner learns how the client perceives his or her own life course. The practitioner will have examined how the client has appraised his or her life events. Has the older adult come to terms with those events? By listening to a client recount life events, the social worker will discover the client's degree of resiliency:

> What we call resilience is turning out to be an interactive and systemic phenomenon, the product of complex relationship of inner strengths and outer help throughout a person's life span. Resilience is not only an individual matter. It is the outward and visible sign of a web of relationships and experiences that teach people mastery, doggedness, love, moral courage and hope. (K. Butler, 1997, p. 26)

Assessment of the Family of Later Years and Caregivers

Understanding how the older client's needs and capacities fit within a family context requires that the social worker conduct a family assessment. Initially, the practitioner needs to learn about the family. The genogram will help the social worker visualize the family structure, and the ecomap will enable the social worker to assess the relationship among family members and their social network visually. See the Additional Resources section at the end of this chapter for more information.

To determine how changes in an older adult's functional capacity influence the family unit, the geriatric social worker may use the functional-age model of intergenerational treatment (Greene et al., 2016). The practitioner will assess the family as (a) *a social system*—that is, how group members interact with and influence each other; (b) *a set of reciprocal roles*—that is, what members' behavioral expectations are for each other; and (c) *a developmental unit*—that is, how the family as a whole faces life transitions. The practitioner tries to determine the following during this assessment:

- Are family communication patterns viable enough for the family to make decisions?
- Is the family role structure sufficiently flexible to meet new demands?
- Is the family's shared history positive enough to face transitions? A crisis?

During a family assessment, it is also important to determine the caregiver's needs and level of stress. Typically, a primary caregiver provides "direct care" by doing the personal-care tasks, such as bathing the older family member, giving medications, or checking and monitoring the older adult's behavior. A caregiver may also perform "indirect care" involving care management tasks, such as coordinating the use of services, and household tasks, such as shopping or bill paying. The caregiving role may be rewarding. However, caregiving tasks have the potential to adversely affect the caregiver's mental and physical well-being, be disruptive to marital or family relationships, or cause problems in meeting work and other social responsibilities. These conflicting responsibilities may result in caregiver burden (Pearlin, Aneshensel, & Leblanc, 1997; J. Riley, 2007).

Caregiver burden is a product of the financial, physical, psychological, and social demands of caregiving (George & Gwyther, 1986). It may be an "objective burden," those events and activities that are associated with a negative caregiving experience, or a "subjective burden," leading to emotional reactions, including worry, anxiety, frustration, and fatigue (Pinquart & Sorensen, 2003). To help reveal the caregiver's attitudes toward his or her experience, the geriatric practitioner may wish to use assessment tools available to gauge caregiver attitudes about their responsibilities (see Additional Resources section). Caregiving may also provide rewards that benefit the caregiver. These rewards should be assessed and include the intrinsic rewards experienced by the caregiver.

CONCLUSION: SERVICES PLANS AND EVALUATION OF CLIENT GOALS

The final step in the assessment of older adults, their families, and their social supports is to develop clear, timely, and appropriate services or care plans with measurable objectives. The client and social worker develop the plans together. They should take into account a client's functional status, life goals, symptom management, and financial and social supports and address financial, legal, housing, medical, and social needs. Following the implementation of services or care plans, the geriatric social worker must be prepared to reevaluate, adjust, and "improve practice effectiveness" on a continuing basis (CSWE, 2015).

Case Study: Developing a Relationship with the Members of the Stanley Family

Evidence exists that custodial grandparents benefit from interventions that provide support and resources to increase their effectiveness as caregivers for grandchildren (cf. Kolomer, 2009). However, there are often relationship issues that need to be considered when a social worker works with these families. Because of the pathways into this caregiving arrangement, there are often circumstances that can create feelings of mistrust on the part of the grandparent. For example, Mrs. Stanley was initially reluctant to seek help from a program for grandparents that was offered through social services. Because both parents of her grandchildren engaged in criminal behavior and had drug problems, Mrs. Stanley worried that her grandchildren would be taken away from her and placed in custody of the foster care system. Professionals need to engage in relationship development with these grandparents, with particular attention to building trust and security between themselves and their clients.

However, getting grandparents linked to resources is often a crucial component of helping these families remain together. For example, Mrs. Stanley became involved with a multidisciplinary program for custodial grandparents that includes social support, case management, and health care services. Because she was prioritizing her time and finances for her grandchildren, Mrs. Stanley was neglecting her own health. As part of a team-based assessment, a nurse determined that Mrs. Stanley had untreated hypertension that was in a critical range. The social worker was able to help Mrs. Stanley locate a physician to treat this condition and get assistance to afford medication that was needed.

Part of the assessment process is a thorough biopsychosocial–spiritual assessment of the individuals within the family. Several needs of the family members were identified, including respite for Mrs. Stanley during times when the children were not in school; activities and social outlets for the children; help in managing Terrell's asthma and seizures; and counseling for Jasmine to deal with her experiences of abuse, neglect, and abandonment. In addition, the home environment also required some upkeep, such as fixing parts of the home that were in disrepair.

Part of the assessment addressed the difficulty Mrs. Stanley had with setting boundaries and enforcing rules with Jasmine, which created a power imbalance. As a result, her granddaughter was establishing the rules within the household, such as playing music as loudly as she wanted and staying out later than her curfew. All of these different areas provided the social worker with a clearer picture of the family, their environment, and relationships.

WHAT WE LEARNED IN THIS CHAPTER

- how to effectively engage older adults in the helping process
- how to conduct a theory-based interview
- how to use assessment tools and approaches
- how to develop service plans and client goals from the assessment process

SUGGESTED EXERCISE TO EVALUATE STUDENT COMPETENCE

Students will demonstrate their practice effectiveness when they

- role-play the opening interview for the professor to evaluate
- read the case history of the Gray family below and answer the questions posed at the conclusion of the study

Mrs. Gray is a 77-year-old widow who has been living alone for the past 10 years. Recently, she began to exhibit signs of dementia, such as wandering outside her home at odd hours (for example, the middle of the night) and forgetting things on the stove. Her son and daughter-in-law became very concerned about her functioning and had her move into their home across town. Mrs. Gray has been living with them for about six months.

In that time, Mrs. Gray's condition has worsened. She is very disoriented, and on a few occasions she has been confused in the household; for example, she urinated in a chair insisting it was the toilet, and she stores inappropriate items in the refrigerator (clothes, her purse, and so forth). Her 12-year-old granddaughter was moved to a sleeper sofa in the basement to give Mrs. Gray her own bedroom. The granddaughter has been quite vocal about her disappointment about leaving her bedroom.

The move of Mrs. Gray into the household has also had an impact on family activities. A planned vacation was canceled because the family could not afford to hire someone to stay with Mrs. Gray during the time they were away. Currently, the daughter-in-law is considering decreasing her hours of work or quitting her job altogether because they are concerned about Mrs. Gray staying by herself all day. The family worries that a crisis may be "waiting to happen."

The impact on the family has been quite profound. They are trying to decide how to handle this situation—whether Mrs. Gray can continue to live with them or whether they need to investigate a nursing home for her.

Questions

- Care provision for an older family member often involves multiple stresses. Identify and discuss three sources of stress that are evident in the Gray family.
- What tools provided in this chapter would assist you in your assessment? Why?

ADDITIONAL RESOURCES

The American Psychological Association's Depression and Suicide in Older Adults Resource Guide offers access to state-of-the-art research and publications on depression and suicide in older adults at http://www.apa.org/pi/aging/resources/guides/depression.aspx.

Information on the components of an eco-map and how to construct one can be found at http://www.dhs.state.mn.us/main/groups/children/documents/pub/dhs16_178770.pdf.

A video that explains eco-maps and how to construct one can be found at https://www.youtube.com/watch?v=dpV-Y-2-yHE.

"Factors Associated with Caregiver Readiness to Use Nonpharmacologic Strategies to Manage Dementia-Related Behavioral Symptoms" is a research article by Gitlin and Rose (2014) that discusses an evidence-based study on nonpharmacological interventions to use with dementia. Go to https://www.ncbi.nlm.nih.gov/pmc/articles/PMC3989482/

The Geriatric Depression Scale is a tool to measure depression that has been tested and used extensively with the older adult population. A copy of this tool can be found at https://consultgeri.org/try-this/general-assessment/issue-4.pdf.

The Geriatric Mental Health Foundation offers a variety of information on resources and programs to help older adults and families coping with a mental illness at http://www.gmhfonline.org.

The Helping Attitudes Scale measures a person's beliefs, feelings, and attitudes about helping and can be used in the assessment process with caregivers. The scale can be located at http://fetzer.org/sites/default/files/images/stories/pdf/selfmeasures/HELPING_OTHERS-HelpingAttitudesScale.pdf.

The Home Safety Checklist, developed by the Centers for Disease Control and Prevention, is a home fall prevention checklist for older adults and can be found at https://www.cdc.gov/homeandrecreationalsafety/pubs/english/booklet_eng_desktop-a.pdf.

Information about the Lubben Social Network Scale used to measure the strength of social ties can be found at http://www.bc.edu/schools/gssw/lubben.html.

The Lubben Social Network Scale and scoring instructions is located at http://www.bc.edu/schools/gssw/lubben/downloads.html.

The Merck Manual of Geriatrics provides information on diseases and health conditions affecting older adults: http://www.merckmanuals.com/~/link.aspx?_id=697ADA1B49B540E6B75B799094EE9062&_z=z

The Mini Mental State Exam is used to measure cognitive impairment. A copy of the test and scoring instructions can be found at http://www.dementia-today.com/wp-content/uploads/2012/06/MiniMentalStateExamination.pdf.

The Mini-Cog Exam is a screening test for cognitive impairment. The instrument and instructions for administering and scoring it can be found at https://www.alz.org/documents_custom/minicog.pdf.

The Preparedness for Caregiving Scale measures how well prepared caregivers perceive they are for caregiving responsibilities and can be used in caregiver assessments. Go to https://consultgeri.org/try-this/general-assessment/issue-28.pdf.

The SAMHSA-HRSA Center for Integrated Health Solutions offers screening and assessment tools, information on evidence-based practices, and other resource information for behavioral health issues affecting older adults: http://www.integration.samhsa.gov/integrated-care-models/older-adults.

"Spiritual Assessment: A Review of Complementary Assessment Models" (Hodge & Holtrop, 2002) provides information on spiritual assessment models useful in the assessment process with older adults: http://www.nacsw.org/Download/CSW/SpiritualAssess.pdf.

Therapist Aid provides information on how to create a genogram and how to use genograms in social work practice: http://www.therapistaid.com/therapy-guide/genograms.

7

Interventions

RATIONALE: Social workers understand that intervention is an ongoing component of the dynamic and interactive process of social work practice with, and on behalf of, diverse individuals, families, groups, organizations, and communities. Social workers understand methods of identifying, analyzing, and implementing evidence-informed interventions to achieve client and constituency goals (CSWE, 2015). "Practitioners in aging build on comprehensive biopsychosocial assessments to plan and implement effective and culturally appropriate interventions, including peer support. They are knowledgeable about, critically analyze, and apply evidence-informed interventions as well as emerging practices" (CSWE, 2017, p. 99).

COMPETENCY: "Practitioners in aging with, and on behalf of, older adults and their constituencies

- promote older adults' social support systems and engagement in families, groups, and communities.
- provide person-centered and family-directed interventions that take into account life course disparities and are targeted to diverse populations, groups, organizations, and communities.
- monitor and modify interventions as needed to respond to individual, family, and environmental challenges. (CSWE, 2017, pp. 99–100)

CONTINUUM OF CARE

This chapter discusses interventions and services for individuals and families. It explores intervention strategies derived from various theories and schools of thought. Community-based services are discussed further in chapter 10. Services to older adults may be informal, those provided by family and friends; or formal, those provided by community-based agencies. The total delivery system for services to frail older adults who have some limits on biopsychosocial functional capacity that interfere with their autonomous functioning is generally termed *long-term care*.

Needs, services, and interventions form five continua:

1. a continuum of client need, or how independent or dependent an older adult is
2. a continuum of services, that is, services suggested by need
3. a continuum of services settings, or the degree of support for living the client requires
4. a continuum of service providers, that is, whether a person can manage without outside care, can conduct self-care, or requires professional care
5. a continuum of professional collaboration, that is, whether the client requires help from more than one discipline. (Hooyman, Hooyman, & Kethley, 1981) (see Table 7.1)

These continua help geriatric social workers visualize how to match a client with needed services and care along a full continuum of care. This encompasses a range of activities—from those with the most capacity to those with the least (Vourlekis & Greene, 1992). It also allows for practitioners to think about services that are least restrictive or those environments that permit the most independent functioning.

To arrive at a holistic picture of the older adult's functioning and an intervention plan that is acceptable to the older client (and the client's family), the social worker must synthesize the various elements of the assessment and integrate them into a plan. Questions to ask include the following:

- What do the biopsychosocial and spiritual assessments indicate?
- Are the demands of the client's environment putting the person at risk?
- What protective factors, such as a rich support network, exist?
- Has the client overcome many hurdles or adversities in his or her life?
- Would you think of the client as resilient?
- What services and interventions does the client (and his or her family) appear to need?
- Is there general agreement on a plan of action?
- Are these services available in the client's community?
- Does the client need a day care program, a homemaker, or congregate meals?
- What interventions and services would promote client competence?

Table 7.1: Continuum of Care

1. Continuum of Need

Independent (Little or no need)	Moderately Dependent	Dependent (Multiple Needs)

2. Continuum of Services

Health promotion/ disease prevention	Screening and early detection	Diagnosis and pretreatment evaluation	Treatment	Rehabilitation: skilled nursing services	Continuing care and hospice

3. Continuum of Service Settings

Own home, apartment, etc.	Friend or relative's home, apartment, etc.	Congregate living situation	Subacute care facility (e.g., day hospital)	Acute-care facility (e.g., hospital)	Skilled long-term care facility (e.g., nursing home)	Continuing care and hospice

4. Continuum of Service Providers

Nonservice	Self-care	Family friends (support network)	Paraprofessionals	Professionals

5. Continuum of Professional Collaboration

Single discipline	Multidisciplinary	Interdisciplinary

Source: Hooyman, N., Hooyman, G., & Kethley, A. (1981, March). *The role of gerontological social work in interdisciplinary care.* Paper presented at the annual program meeting of the Council on Social Work Education, Louisville, KY. Reprinted with permission from Nancy Hooyman.

Addressing these types of questions will provide the necessary information for a comprehensive intervention plan.

HEALTH EDUCATION

A continuum of care should encompass health education that includes the goals of prevention. Prevention programs serve a number of purposes: they aim to reduce a person's likelihood of becoming ill or disabled and promote a healthy lifestyle by improving eating habits, exercise, and health screenings (Sugar et al., 2014). Public campaigns about the signs of depression and associated hotlines that connect the caller with help and information, healthy eating education programs, and immunization education programs are good examples of wellness programs and preventive services. Some programs have implemented Educating About and Screening Elders for Depression, which includes mental health education, depression screening, and treatment linkages (Berman & Furst, 2011).

Such programs may conduct outreach to older people in need and are designed to inform community organizations, religious groups, senior centers, and local businesses about the issues older adults face and where to seek help. Prevention and health promotion require that practitioners rethink how they conduct assessment and intervention so that they follow the principle of basing the level of care on the individual's functional capacity—from the person who is most independent to the person who is least independent (Vourlekis & Greene, 1992). Greene (2005b) has proposed that practitioners evaluate care needs using *client triage,* a process by which the most frail or physically and mentally challenged clients receive the most intense service. Triage allows the practitioner to meet the challenges of those most in need. This process must be accompanied by an understanding that clients may reverse their frailty and regain strength. Also, because caregivers often bear heavy responsibilities and frequently do not take care of themselves—for example, failing to take a break or eat properly, according to the National Alliance for Caregiving (2015)—geriatric practitioners should also assess whether caregivers are at risk for burnout and identify prevention programs for them.

ADULT PROTECTIVE SERVICES

Adult protective services are at the other end of the care continuum from preventive services. These state agencies are mandated to ensure the safety and well-being of older adults and adults with disabilities, who may be in danger of being mistreated or neglected and are unable to care for themselves, are unable to protect themselves from harm, or have no one to assist them (Sijuwade, 1995). As with child protective services, social workers are mandated to report elder abuse. The following definitions describe the various types of adult abuse and neglect a gerontological social worker is likely to encounter:

- *Neglect,* the most common form of abuse, involves failure to provide essential physical or mental care for an older person. Neglect may be unintentional or intentional (withholding food, water, or medication).
- *Physical neglect* includes withholding food or water, failing to provide proper hygiene, or neglecting to offer physical aids or safety precautions.
- *Physical violence* involves actions that may result in pain, injury, impairment, or disease. Pushing, striking, slapping, pinching, force-feeding, or improperly using physical restraints or medications are examples of physical violence.
- *Psychological abuse* is any action by the caregiver that causes fear, isolation, confusion, or disorientation in an older person. These acts are intended to harm and may include verbal aggression using words that humiliate and infantilize.
- *Financial exploitation* is the misuse of an older person's income or resources for another's personal gain.

- *Violation of rights* is when the older adult is deprived of legal rights and personal liberties.

- *Domestic abuse* refers to several forms of maltreatment of an older person in his or her home by someone who has a special relationship (often the caregiver) with that elder.

- *Self-neglect*, in which the elder does not take care of himself or herself, is more often found among very old and cognitively impaired older adults, whereas physical and emotional abuse is often carried out by perpetrators with problems.

- *Institutional abuse* occurs in nursing homes and other long-term care settings. The perpetrator can be a staff member or family or friend.

Because self-neglect is the most prevalent type of abuse, it is important during an assessment of an older adult for the social worker to determine whether the person has "the capacity to make an acceptable choice with respect to a specific decision" (Weisstub, 1990, p. 68). If the practitioner finds that the older adult is not mentally competent or tends to make faulty judgments, the practitioner should then collaborate with state and local protective agencies to develop a plan to ensure the adult's safety in the home. Confidentiality may be difficult under such circumstances, presenting ethical dilemmas.

EVIDENCE-BASED PRACTICE IN GERIATRIC MENTAL HEALTH CARE

Twenty-five percent of older adults age 65 and older have some type of mental health problem (Substance Abuse and Mental Health Services Administration [SAMHSA], 2016). Consequently, during the past decade, research on treatments for mental illnesses experienced by people in their later years has grown dramatically (CDC, 2016c). A number of evidence-based practice models are available that can be used by the mental health practitioner, such as the "Treatment of Older Adults Evidence-Based Practice Kit" (SAMHSA, 2016). Because social workers are often on the front lines, working directly with older adults and their families, they must keep abreast of the latest assessment instruments and research supporting the effectiveness of pharmacological and psychosocial interventions, particularly for clients with depression or dementia (Institute of Medicine, 2001). Distinguishing between evidence-based practice techniques and those that are less "proven" may be beneficial to clients' well-being.

Geriatric social workers must make use of evidence-based practice or knowledge procured from literature reviews of aggregate meta-analyses of relevant randomized controlled trials. This approach includes being aware of relevant consensus statements and consensus reviews. Both the CDC and SAMHSA offer information and resources on proven evidence-based practice models for treating mental health disorders in the elderly. Another helpful resource for treatment of neurocognitive disorders is the Alzheimer's Association.

TRADITIONAL PSYCHOSOCIAL INTERVENTIONS AND NEW INTERVENTION PARADIGMS

Social workers were among the first professionals to engage in psychosocial interventions to enhance the coping capacity of older clients (Lowy, 1991). As they adopted new theoretical concepts and practice strategies, the way in which coping was conceived also evolved, providing a rich repertoire of treatment strategies (Greene & Cohen, 2005). The practitioner may choose from a variety of treatment strategies, choosing from contemporary models or traditional models as described below.

TRADITIONAL INTERVENTIONS

Early in this evolution, caseworkers simply provided material or concrete services such as financial aid. However, during the 1950s and 1960s, the works of psychodynamic theorists such as Sigmund Freud and Erik Erikson came to the fore. Practitioners began to evaluate ego functioning and ego strengths, and they provided techniques for ego support. Although Freudian interventions were never widely used with older adults, Erikson's (1959/1980) theory about coping style in old age—the resolution of the conflict between integrity versus despair—was and remains popular today.

Life Review

The idea that it is natural and possibly curative for older adults to talk about their past was first brought to light by Robert Butler, a geriatric psychiatrist who coined the term *life review* in 1963. He espoused a form of reminiscence therapy based on an Eriksonian psychodynamic perspective in which recall of the past was said to allow for the resolution and integration of past conflicts (Greene, 1986/2000). Butler argued that older adults who were better adapted and able to deal with personal, social, and medical adversities experienced an improved resolution of life cycle stages. The fundamental issue involved in helping older adults was to set in motion a process of coping with death and loss (Greene et al., 2016).

Butler (1968) was optimistic that autobiographic processes could help people maintain self-identity and tranquility. Butler's words embody social work practice with older adults, thus foreshadowing a resilience approach:

> Psychotherapeutic work with older people involves the management of small deaths and intimations of mortality. Put succinctly, the psychotherapy of old age is the psychotherapy of grief and of accommodation, restitution, and resolution. "Coming to terms with," "bearing witness," reconciliation, atonement, construction and reconstruction, integration, transcendence, creativity, realistic insight with modifications and

substitutions, the introduction of meaning and of meaningful, useful, and contributory efforts: these are the terms that are pertinent to therapy with older people. (R. N. Butler, 1968, p. 237)

According to Erikson's theory of human development, at each of eight stages of life, people struggle to resolve a psychosocial crisis pertaining to how they see themselves and the world at large. Integrity versus despair, the eighth psychosocial crisis, takes place during old age, when the psychosocial crisis is "how to grow old with integrity in the face of death" (Erikson, 1959/1980, p. 104).

Integrity is realized by older adults who have few regrets, have lived fruitful lives, and cope equally well with failures as with successes. The person who has achieved a sense of integrity appreciates the continuity of past, present, and future experiences. He or she also comes to accept the life cycle, cooperate with the inevitabilities of life, and experience a sense of being complete (Greene, 2007). In contrast, despair is found in those who fear death and wish life would give them another chance. The older adult who has a strong sense of despair believes that life has been too short and finds little meaning in human existence. That person has lost faith in himself or herself, as well as in others. The person in whom despair dominates has little sense of world order or spiritual wholeness (Greene, 2007). An older adult can engage in life review in many ways, such as through oral recitation of memories, bibliotherapy, journaling, memory books, and time capsules (Caldwell, 2005). Drawing pictures of important life events or tapping naturally occurring memories are examples of artistic life-review methods. Social workers frequently use creative techniques to engage their clients—for instance, suggesting that clients write poetry or attend antique fairs to help them remember past events (Malekoff, 2004).

The oral traditions of a people often guide life review. For example, social workers encouraged Hispanic people living in northern New Mexico to reminisce in a way that embodied their oral traditions. Practitioners used theatrical settings, food, drink, and proverbs to stimulate verbal accounts of historical events (Andrada & Korte, 1993).

To obtain older adults' complete life history, the social worker must ask them to describe what kind of person they think they are, the circumstances under which they have lived, and their relationships with significant others (these topics may also be addressed in the assessment process). Clients' responses may result in further discussion of what changes might lead to enhanced functioning. The efficacy of life-review interventions has been well documented. Rennemark and Hagberg (1997) found that positive self-evaluations of Erikson's life stages were generally important for well-being, particularly when life events were understood within a context of significant others.

Ecological Systems Thinking

Subsequent to psychodynamic approaches, family systems theory and its companion, the ecological perspective, have been used to better understand how older adults interact with others and with various social systems. When bringing families of later years together, geriatric social workers generally use systems theory to improve communication and organization related to caregiving. These theories afford an understanding of an older adult's resource needs and form the basis for family-focused interventions.

Cognitive–Behavioral Approach

A scientific basis exists for conducting one-on-one psychotherapeutic-type interviews with older adults: A review of the literature documents that cognitive and behavioral interventions are efficacious for treating depressed older adults (Teri, Logsdon, Uomoto, & McCurry, 1997).

Cognitive interventions help a client recognize distorted thinking and learn to replace those thoughts with more realistic substitutes. For example, following a heart attack, an older adult may feel that he or she has lost all meaning in life. The social worker would then reinforce that the client still has choices and would explore those possibilities with the client. Interventions with depressed people might require social workers to explain the nature of the disorder, so that clients do not view themselves as crazy or weak. Because some older adults may expect their practitioners to be paternalistic, social workers must guide those clients to learn how to become active participants in their own care.

Interviews as part of the cognitive intervention process may cover fewer points, but the practitioner could enhance those points by using visual or memory aids. He or she could adapt interventions to address older adults' context, or their social–environmental setting; cohort differences, that is, the specific historical period in which they lived; maturity, or their emotional complexity and wealth of experience; and their specific challenges, including chronic medical conditions and neurological disorders (Knight, 1999).

Despite these adjustments, the greatest barrier to effective treatment of older adults with mental illnesses such as depression is inadequate recognition of the disease by individuals themselves or by their families or physicians (CDC, 2016c; Karel & Hinrichsen, 2000). Behavioral interventions, which focus on modifying negative behaviors or helping clients to unlearn them rather than exploring the underlying causes of those behaviors, have proven efficacious in working with older adults, including those with mental illness. The primary purpose is to deal with immediate and specific problems and reward positive changes. Techniques include biofeedback, relaxation training, and disease self-management (CDC, 2016a).

Advantages of the behavioral approach include avoiding ageism—the belief that aging is equated with inevitable decline. Because behavioral interventions focus on how to improve functional-age challenges, they offer an optimistic orientation to solving problems (such as urinary incontinence or paying attention to personal grooming). Behavioral techniques are particularly successful in nursing homes when the staff works together to develop and evaluate plans to modify disruptive behaviors (Dupree & Schonfeld, 1998; Geriatric Mental Health Foundation, 2016). Behavioral approaches are also useful for training caregivers in the principles of management of troublesome behaviors at home (Gallagher-Thompson, Coon, Rivera, Powers, & Zeiss, 1998).

PARADIGM SHIFT

Constructionist Therapy

Psychosocial interventions from the social-constructionist school are intended to help clients appraise stressful life encounters by having them assign meaning to the stressors at hand and then help them cope with those encounters. The client and social worker come to understand stressful life encounters within the context of an individual's life purposes and goals (Park & Folkman, 1997).

Meaning systems orient, motivate, and guide people in actions they expect to take throughout the life course. When people encounter a specific stressful event, they measure that event against their expectations. The level of distress is determined by the degree of discrepancy between the meaning of the specific event and one's meaning system. For example, an older adult may be severely troubled about the death of an adult child, because the elder's expectations were that he or she would die before the child. Therefore, such a critical event would be highly stressful and particularly difficult to resolve (Blieszner & Bedford, 2012; Greene, 1986/2000).

Grief Counseling

The death of a significant person in an older client's life poses a tremendous challenge to his or her ability to adapt or cope. Social workers use a process called *normalizing* to help bereaved clients learn that the feelings of loss that they are experiencing, such as anger, guilt, anxiety, helplessness, and sadness, are typical. Normalizing also means that each individual must go on to see his or her life without the deceased person. Practitioners must remember, however, that people may normalize the grieving process differently.

Grieving individuals struggle with how to affirm or reconstruct personal meaning in the face of loss (Blieszner & Bedford, 2012; Neimeyer, 2001). Therefore, an effective intervention following the death of a loved one is a social-constructionist conceptualization of grief resolution, which pays significant attention to the ever-present human ability to organize experience in narrative form and make sense of troubling events.

Narrative Gerontology

Narrative therapy, a psychotherapeutic approach in which an older adult recalls his or her life experiences (sometimes in writing), is another means for clients to make sense of their life events. This approach might be useful in both assessment and intervention. Increasingly, researchers are finding that maintaining a coherent narrative—one that makes sense to the client—is important to a person's well-being (McAdams, Diamond, Mansfield, & de St. Aubin, 1997).

Narrative therapy is closely aligned with constructionist therapy. Both approaches help clients reconstruct what is important to them, to provide them with more choices for action. The time the social worker and client spend together is used to explore the client's meaning of life experiences. The practitioner attempts to see the world through the client's eyes, and when issues are perceived, alternatives or reinterpretations are sought (Viney, Benjamin, & Preston, 1988). Narratives benefit the client and practitioner alike because they help

- communicate hope
- build rapport
- establish connections
- inspire and encourage
- preserve cultural identity
- clarify emotions
- help clients cope with death, illness, and tragedy.

Narratives contain an individual's story as well as macro-level or larger stories that reflect a client's "shared history, values, beliefs, expectations, and myths" (Webster, 2002, p. 143). Therefore, life histories provided through client narratives enable geriatric social workers to learn about their clients' critical life events (Greene & Cohen, 2005)—personal, interpersonal, sociocultural, and societal episodes.

RESILIENCE-ENHANCING MODEL

As practitioners listen to and analyze critical life events, they will find opportunities to intervene and elaborate on the information provided. Social workers often learn how resilient a client is and what previous successes he or she has had. For example, Patricia J tells her social worker that religion has helped her cope with life. That information may prompt an acceptable intervention tailored for Patricia J. Maybe she has not gone to church recently because she is in a wheelchair and lacks transportation. Can she imagine what it would be like to return to her congregation? Can she see herself taking a specialized van? Social-constructionist models of change support intuitive client thinking and use positive emotions to promote resilience (Wartel, 2003). Such models also encourage an older client to see aging "as part of a new season, a journey one takes" (Ronen & Dowd 1998, p. 83).

The resilience-enhancing model and other strengths-based approaches do not deny clients' problems and concerns. Rather, such interventions are carried out in an atmosphere in which clients can examine problems "from a perspective of enhanced dignity and sense of agency . . . highlighting aspects of their lives that are going well" (Saul, 2003, p. 300). In putting together a resilience-enhancing practice model, the social worker

- considers the practice context—that is, the societal cultural milieu and historical time

- subscribes to the purposes of the profession
- bears in mind governmental policy
- applies human behavior theories
- draws from various schools of thought
- respects client diversity and spirituality
- struggles with ethical dilemmas
- uses evidence-based practice protocols
- identifies and applies research findings
- calls on best practices or state-of-the-art interventions.

FAMILY INTERVENTION

Functional-Age Model of Intergenerational Therapy

Historically, interventions with older adults and their families have been based on systems theory and thus have addressed matters of intergenerational connectedness. What are expressions of family loyalty? Can the family resolve "old debts" (Boszormenyi-Nagy & Spark, 1973)? Can they continue to act as a system of mutual aid? Indebtedness varies by family, and in some instances family members may deny gratitude or recognition or may angrily express that another is indebted to them because of past "wrongs." Other families may foster loyalty through the cultural norms involving familism. One intergenerational intervention model that helps older adults and their families to resolve past or current issues is the functional-age model of intergenerational treatment (see Figure 7.1). The functional-age model allows the geriatric social worker to do the following:

- Observe the structure and communication patterns within the family. Who is the contact person for the older adult? Who has primary caretaking responsibilities? Does each family member communicate his or her needs? Does the older adult participate? As these patterns are revealed, the practitioner clarifies, reframes, and redirects communications. He or she encourages family members to direct their remarks to one another. When an apparent "failure" exists in mobilizing the family on behalf of the older adult, the social worker addresses the issue with the family explicitly.

- Develop a picture of how the family has functioned over time. Has it been able to meet crises before? If so, how? If it is currently experiencing difficulties, what are they? Does the family have ideas about how they will face these challenges?

- Learn about role responsibilities within the family. How does the family carry out caregiving roles and responsibilities? What is the division of

Figure 7.1:   Functional-Age Model of Intergenerational Treatment

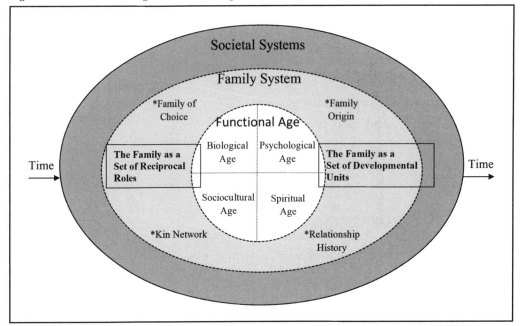

Source: Greene, R., Galambos, C., Cohen, H. L., & Greene, N. (2016). *Social work with the aged and their families* (4th ed., p. 2). New Brunswick, NJ: Transaction Publishers. Reprinted with permission.

labor? Is one family member overburdened? Does the primary caregiver have conflicts with work, child care, and adult caregiving responsibilities?

- Examine how the family deals with stress. How is caregiving proceeding? Who does what? Is there time for respite? Do family members experience any rewards?

Family Resilience

Walsh (1998) has promoted family well-being through interventions that "identify and fortify key interactional processes that enable families to withstand and rebound from disruptive life challenges" (p. 3). According to Walsh, the family unit has the potential to meet crises through self-repair and growth. Practitioners examine and reframe "family belief systems," the values and attitudes that form a family's ideas about how to act, and organizational and communication patterns. "Family organizational patterns," which are based on behavioral expectations, reflect how the family is structured to carry out tasks, such as having the ability to rally together to cope with stress. "Communication patterns" point to the relationships in a family and how those relationships influence the exchange of information within that family.

Family-centered models call for social workers to take an active role in modifying and enhancing the way in which families perform their caregiving function. Practitioners typically carry out this role through family decision-making meetings, or semistructured gatherings of extended family members intended to open communications and facilitate services provider and family collaborations (Brodie & Gadling-Cole, 2003).

CAREGIVER INTERVENTION

Caregivers' attitudes and feelings about the caregiving process and the recipients of their care influence their caregiving experience. Is the caregiver able to find rewards in the experience? Is he or she gaining something from the experience that promotes coping and resilience? Because it is essential that caregivers maintain their emotional and physical health, an important role of the geriatric social worker is to assess the situation and subsequently discuss the range of interventions available to a caregiver. Is the caregiver taking care of himself or herself, or is the person at risk for depression or physical ills?

Traditional interventions for caregivers include support groups, individual and family counseling, case management, online support and resources, respite services, skills training, or a combination of those strategies (Bourgeois, Schulz, & Burgio 1996; National Alliance for Caregiving, 2015). Nontraditional caregiving interventions include tapping positive emotions, exploring spirituality, and discovering the benefits of caregiving (Riley, 2007). For example, a social worker and client may foster the following six rewards of caregiving:

1. The caregiver feels useful and needed and that he or she is doing something meaningful.
2. The caregiver has a sense of competence and mastery.
3. The caregiver has an opportunity to share feelings of love and empathy with the care recipient.
4. The caregiver feels satisfied with being there for someone who took care of the caregiver in the past.
5. The caregiver feels appreciated by other family members and friends for what the caregiver is doing.
6. The caregiver has feelings of altruism and self-respect as a result of doing—without being asked—what needs to be done. (Toseland & Smith, 2001)

A recurrent theme in interviews with caregivers is that they use religious faith and prayer to find meaning in, and to cope with, the caregiving experience (Riley, 2007). Consequently, social workers need to understand how faith and faith-based practices contribute to client resilience. For instance, they may ask clients to describe their cultural practices and perceptions of how those practices have influenced their life experiences.

PUTTING THE RESILIENCE-ENHANCING MODEL INTO ACTION

The following is a case study showing how REM can guide a social worker in intervening with an older adult (Greene, 2007). In this case, the social worker meets with her client Jim in the hospital. Jim had suffered a heart attack three days earlier.

Case Study: Jim

The practitioner first acknowledges the client's loss, vulnerability, and future: She helps Jim move from "this could not happen to me" to "I must face this challenge." She makes an alliance with his hopes, vision, and values. The social worker assumes that now that Jim's condition has stabilized, he will feel a heightened sense of vulnerability. She avoids saying phrases such as "I know everything will be all right." She lets him talk about how frightening it was to recognize that he was having symptoms of a heart attack. She acknowledges that he has lost a sense of security—"I am no longer physically well." Once Jim's loss is acknowledged, she guides him to a discussion of the future. Can he still picture playing with his grandson? Taking a trip?

The social worker identifies the client's source of stress: She discovers what about the event made it most troubling. She wants to know how Jim experienced the event. He would like to do those things in the future, but he is worried about another heart attack. This is his major source of stress.

The practitioner recognizes client stress: She accepts Jim's source of distress. The social worker wants Jim to know that she has heard his "complaint." The social worker recognizes that his concern about having another heart attack can be a worry. She wonders aloud about other family member concerns.

The social worker stabilizes or normalizes the situation: She helps Jim understand that it is okay to feel a general tension. She wants to impart empathy and affirmation. The social worker explains that almost all the patients she sees following a heart attack have similar concerns. Jim talks about picturing himself in a helpless situation when in public.

The practitioner helps the client take control: She suggests that Jim is capable of carrying out his role responsibilities. The social worker wants to empower him to take control. The social worker asks whether Jim has been to the patient education group. She explains the type of information available from the nurse educator. She also asks whether Jim has talked with his doctor about the severity of his attack and his prognosis.

The social worker provides resources for change: She assures Jim that resources are at hand to support his physical and psychological safety. Her goal is for Jim to use the available resources. At his bedside, the social worker leaves a number of pamphlets that discuss a patient's recovery following a heart attack. She says she will return the next day.

The social worker promotes client self-efficacy: She communicates to Jim that he can manage his own affairs. She wants to reinforce the idea that he can solve his difficulty. The next day Jim says he has asked his doctor about his recovery. He tells the social worker that he was relieved to learn about the extent of the damage to his heart and that it was not as serious as he had thought.

The practitioner collaborates in client self-change: She sets in motion a self-motivating process. She wants Jim to know that he can take charge of himself. The social worker wanted to know what else he has done. Jim says he has signed up for the nurse educator lecture that afternoon.

The social worker strengthens the client's problem-solving abilities: She brings the client into the problem-solving relationship with her. The practitioner wants Jim to know that they are collaborators. The social worker asks Jim what his major questions are. She asks him, "What do you hope to learn?" Jim replies that he wants to know how much he can still roughhouse with his grandson.

The practitioner addresses positive emotions: She helps Jim escape from harsh realities to images of pleasure. She wants to reframe events so that Jim can be hopeful. The social worker says Jim's grandson sounds like a rascal.

The social worker listens to the client's stories and uses humor: She realizes that the story of the event contains a mixture of pain and joy. She wants to help Jim put the problem outside of him. Jim and the social worker laugh about a story of Jim's grandson and how he got into trouble trampling his grandmother's rose bush.

The practitioner achieves creativity: She discovers new ways for the client to meet his goal. The social worker hopes Jim will find creative ways to live with his illness. The social worker asks Jim what activities he does with his grandson. Jim realizes that he and his grandson often sit and read. He suggests that he might have to "resort to" computer games.

The social worker makes meaning of the client's critical events: She appraises the critical event with new eyes. The social worker hopes the appraisal process will lead to positive outcomes, such as a greater appreciation of life. Jim says, "I know one thing: I'll be playing with him every chance I get!"

The practitioner helps the client to discern the benefits of adverse events: She guides him to resolving a negative event by finding a positive meaning. "I have learned one thing," Jim says. "I will never say I can't babysit!"

The social worker attends to the client's spirituality and transcends the immediate situation: She determines whether spirituality can be a personal strength. The social worker anticipates that the client will look for "greater" opportunities. "God willing," says Jim, "I will be at [his grandson's] high school graduation!"

CONCLUSION

Social work professionals are increasingly using risk and resilience theory to define and augment their practice because they consider this theory to be effective in alleviating distress and promoting well-being at the individual, family, and community levels. Their practice with various client systems is based on the belief that people possess a natural ability for self-change and self-correcting behaviors (Greene, 2007). Therefore, social workers begin the helping process with an assessment of client system strengths and challenges. Their intervention choices emphasize client self-determination (see chapter 2), explore client resources, adopt a collaborative client–helper relationship, build on healthy tendencies, and take on an anti-ageist perspective (Ronch & Goldfield, 2003).

An important consideration for practitioners is the increasing shift in practice toward the use of interventions with a demonstrated level of effectiveness (Kropf & Cummings, 2017). Evidence-based practice must take into consideration the best available clinical research and consider issues of treatment fidelity. Did the intervention result in clinically significant outcomes, and is the intervention consistent each time it is used in a clinical context (Kropf & Cummings, 2017)? Thoughtful deliberations about intervention approaches that take into account client and environmental considerations and whether these approaches are having the intended outcomes are critical to the intervention process.

Case Study: Constructing an Intervention Plan with the Stanley Family

Using client data from the assessment phase, social workers collaborate with clients to develop intervention plans to address the challenges and strengthen the aspects that are functioning well. For Mrs. Stanley, it was clear that she needed help in managing aspects of her own health and mental well-being. Raising two children as a single parent involves challenges, and both of her grandchildren have special needs that require attention. Part of the intervention plan was getting the children linked to professionals who could be helpful—Jasmine was matched with a counselor at the mental health center, and Terrell was referred to a pediatrician with expertise in seizure disorders.

However, the intervention approach also addresses Mrs. Stanley's health and well-being. In addition to treating her hypertension with medication, her stress level also had to be addressed. A case manager helped Mrs. Stanley construct a daily schedule to include two positive things a day that benefited her—for example, spending time reading her Bible, visiting a neighbor for a chat, or watching her favorite game show on television. She also agreed to join a grandparent support group that was run out of the local Area Agency on Aging. Through this affiliation, she became more engaged with other grandparents who could share knowledge, information, and stories of their experiences. In this way, all the grandparents felt less alone in their caregiving role.

It was also clear that the children needed outside activities. The social worker was able to arrange transportation to the local Boys and Girls Club for both Jasmine and Terrell. There they could interact with other children in positive experiences such as taking field trips around the city and volunteering. For Jasmine, this was a very positive experience as her natural leadership talents began to emerge in a constructive way. She started being less obstinate at home and was very engaged with many of the projects at the Boys and Girls Club. Terrell became interested in some of the activities that were run through the organization, including learning how to play chess. In particular, this club also helped during times of school vacations as there were extended programs to provide Mrs. Stanley with respite from her caregiving duties.

WHAT WE LEARNED IN THIS CHAPTER

- The continuum of care for needs, services, and interventions was explained, and practical explanations for its use were provided.
- Evidence-based practice was defined, and models were discussed. Links to further discussion of these models are listed in the Additional Resources for this chapter.
- Traditional psychosocial intervention models were reviewed, including family intervention.
- The resilience-enhancing model was explained, and application to a practice case further explained its components.

SUGGESTED EXERCISE TO EVALUATE STUDENT COMPETENCY

Using the case study in chapter 6, students will develop a (mutually acceptable) care plan that includes an evaluation component.

ADDITIONAL RESOURCES

The Alzheimer's Association provides educational and resource material related to dementia. Support group information can also be accessed at http://alz.org/.

The Centers for Disease Control and Prevention is dedicated to increasing the health security of America, addressing diseases, and providing resources to aid in prevention. Information on behavioral health screening and treatment can be found at https://www.cdc.gov/.

The Community Guide provides information on evidence-based practices on mental health and mental illnesses in clinical work with older adults: https://www.thecommunityguide.org.

Evidence-Based Behavioral Practice provides training resources and information for evidence-based behavioral practice across disciplines at http://www.ebbp.org.

The Legacy Project provides practical information on how to conduct life reviews, an intervention technique that can be used with older adults. For more information, visit http://www.legacyproject.org/guides/lifeinttips.html.

The National Alliance for Caregiving is a nonprofit coalition of national organizations that focus on providing support to family caregivers and raising awareness of family caregiver issues. Resource information to use when working with family caregivers can be accessed at http://www.caregiving.org.

The National Center on Elder Abuse provides tools, approaches, and national resources to aid in the delivery of direct services: https://ncea.acl.gov/.

The National Network to Eliminate Disparities in Behavioral Health addresses disparities in behavioral health care through information sharing, training, and technical assistance: http://nned.net/.

For additional reading, the Social Work Policy Institute provides additional references on resiliency in practice: http://www.socialworkpolicy.org/research/resiliency.html.

The Substance Abuse and Mental Health Services Administration National Registry of Evidence-Based Programs and Practices is a searchable database of interventions for the prevention and treatment of mental and substance use disorders: https://www.samhsa.gov/nrepp.

8

Group Work: Addressing Issues of Later Adulthood

RATIONALE: "Social workers understand that intervention is an ongoing component of the dynamic and interactive process of social work practice with, and on behalf of, diverse individuals, families, groups, organizations, and communities. Social workers are knowledgeable about evidence-informed interventions to achieve the goals of clients and constituencies including individuals, families, groups, organizations, and communities" (CSWE, 2015, p. 9).

COMPETENCY: "Practitioners in aging with and on behalf of older adults and their constituencies

- promote older adults' social support systems and engagement in families, groups, and communities.
- provide person-centered and family-directed interventions that take account of life course disparities and are targeted to diverse populations, groups, organizations, and communities.
- assess for quality and access a range of services, supports, and care options including groups and technology, for older adults and families to assure optimal interdependence." (CSWE, 2017, pp. 99–100)

Students will be able to prepare, engage, assess, intervene, and evaluate their work with groups.

Social workers often practice with clients in group settings. Indeed, the process of bringing individuals together in a group format has been a part of social work since the early days of the profession. A historical perspective on the importance of group work within the profession of social work will provide a context for understanding how a group intervention can benefit older adults in current times. In a classic group process text, Zastrow (2001) traced the roots of social group work that took hold in the early 1800s in the Young Men's Christian Association and Young Women's Christian Association, Boy Scouts and Girl Scouts, and Jewish Community Centers. Programs delivered in group formats provided opportunities for education, social interaction, recreation, and collective social action. Group participation promoted the development of social skills, helped members create a social network, and provided an opportunity to work with others to change the social environment (for example, to advocate for additional community resources).

How are groups used with older clients as part of social work practice? Why are groups effective intervention approaches during later life? One reason is that a group is the basic social unit within society's social structure. An infant's first group affiliation is his or her family as membership begins during the prenatal period. Even before a baby is born, she or he is part of a family by transmission of genetic material, exposure to cultural family practices (for example, food the mother eats), and other factors that begin to shape the child physically and emotionally. Typically, after birth, a baby joins a family social system (for example, birth family, adoptive family, or foster family). Although family social structures vary considerably, most have multiple members, including parents, grandparents, siblings, cousins, and other kinship relations. Throughout life, children make other social connections by establishing friendship groups; joining sports or activity groups (such as Boy Scouts, debate club, choir, or band); and perhaps even joining gangs. Into adulthood, people add to their group affiliations through other memberships at work (for example, being part of a managerial or treatment team), in civic life (for instance, by serving on a board of directors), or in family life (such as marrying into a partner's family group or participating in a group for parents of children with disabilities). As these examples illustrate, both naturally and purposefully formed group affiliations exist across the life course.

What is the difference, though, between membership in these various social groups and participation in a group as part of a social work intervention? Gisela Konopka (1983), one of the founders of group work, defined that form of practice as "a method of social work which helps individuals to enhance their social functioning through purposeful group experiences, and to cope more effectively with their personal, group or community problems" (p. 18).

Adding to that definition is Lowy (1982), a pioneer in advancing aging issues within social work, who said that group work is "one method of social work which places emphasis on maximizing group process so that the group may become the instrument in which and through which the participating members may benefit, their interpersonal relationships may improve, and the participants may collaborate[,] improving conditions in their environment" (p. 22). The power of group interventions is evident in the description of group work offered by M. S. Corey and Corey (1997, p. 5):

> Groups provide a natural laboratory that demonstrates to people that they are not alone and that there is hope for creating a different life. . . . Groups are powerful because they allow participants to experience some

of their long-term problems being played out in the group sessions with opportunities to do something different from what they have been doing.

During later life, group interventions often target conditions that result from loss, isolation, or disengagement. For example, a systematic review of interventions to decrease loneliness in older adults found that the majority of effective interventions were conducted in group formats (Hagan, Manktelow, Taylor, & Mallett, 2014). Guided by theories of human functioning, practitioners need to select evidence-based practice approaches in work with clients. For this reason, social workers should be aware of those interventions that are most effectively delivered within a group format with the older population.

GROUP PROCESS AND OUTCOME

In groups that function well, individuals have the opportunity to share similar life experiences and explore their uniqueness in a secure and accepting atmosphere. There are many benefits of participating in groups, especially during later adulthood. These include

- Fostering affiliation and connection among members. These aspects are especially important for those who are experiencing or are at risk for social isolation. An example is individuals who have recently become single through divorce or widowhood.

- Mirroring thoughts, feelings, and experiences among members. An example is a group of older gay and lesbian individuals who lived much of their early developmental period in an oppressive and nonaccepting social and cultural environment.

- Providing emotional and informational support. For example, in groups for care providers of individuals with dementia, members may exchange experiences and knowledge about care provision.

- Building capacity and skill development. A nutrition and cooking class for newly diagnosed diabetics is an example.

- Providing an opportunity for enjoyment and social engagement. A book club at a senior center is an example of purposefully coming together for engagement and pleasure.

As demonstrated in the examples above, groups can take numerous forms and provide opportunities for engagement, relationship development, and affiliation. Older adults can also benefit from therapeutic groups as they deal with some of the challenges of later life.

As Greene (2008b) has indicated, group participation can potentially offer older adults an opportunity to facilitate continued personal growth, provide support through crises or difficult challenges, provide rehabilitation, and positively affect mental health. Although group work is beneficial for older clients, practitioners must consider some unique aspects of group interventions with this population:

- Be aware of the physical environment. Is the setting conducive to interaction among members? This includes noise level and physical structure.
- Consider privacy issues. Does the setting promote privacy for group members? Is the area free from intrusion and interference? Consider spaces like hospitals or nursing homes where other patients and residents can create disruptions in the setting.
- Determine most effective delivery methods. In groups where skill development is the goal, consider multiple ways to deliver content, such as orally and in written form.
- Be sensitive to the experience of the group members. In older cohorts, there is less familiarity with the psychotherapeutic process. Be aware that some older adults may feel uncomfortable sharing feelings and personal issues.
- Assess physical issues that may be present for group members. Group experiences that may be appropriate for younger adults may tax older adults who have less stamina or lower functioning levels. Modifications in the group format may be necessary (compare Lenze et al., 2014; Moss et al., 2015).

As a result, group facilitators need to complete a thorough assessment of the group structure. Before the group begins, the following questions need to be addressed:

- Is the physical environment appropriate for the older group participants?
- Do the group members have any conditions that will limit their participation or the experiences of others?
- How well does the group protocol fit with the functioning and experiences of the group members? Are modifications necessary?

An evaluation of these and related questions provides an important beginning to consider group work with older adults.

RESILIENCE-ENHANCING MODEL APPROACH TO FACILITATING GROUPS OF OLDER ADULTS

The resilience-enhancing model (Greene, 2007) for social work practitioners who work with older adults is an effective method for increasing resiliency in group interventions. The principles of REM are organized into the skill development areas of engagement, assessment, intervention, and evaluation. From a group work perspective, the skills of engagement are those required to convene the group. They include developing a group structure, assessing environmental issues, and determining the type of leadership style that will best facilitate the particular intervention group, such as a social support, psychoeducational, or activity group. The competencies related to assessment include paying attention to relationship development and determining what influences multicultural issues have on group members. When applying REM in group practice with older adults, practitioners must be aware that interventions will vary by type of group. In their evaluations of group interventions, social workers will look not only at a group's progress toward goals but also at how effective group interventions are in fostering resilience, coping, and functioning among group members.

Assembling the Group

Because the environment sets the context for a group's process and dynamics, selection of a meeting place is critical. Practitioners must consider physical space: Where will the group meet? How will participants feel about that meeting space? Is it conducive for recruiting all potential members of the group, for example, or does it send a message that might inhibit involvement? Is the environment welcoming to all potential members? Other factors, adapted from Pritchard (2004, p. 34), that social workers need to take into account when selecting a meeting room for older adults are

- Privacy: Is there a glass door or window into the room?
- Room size: Taking into account that personal space may be very important, and depending on the emotional content being discussed, is there enough space? Consider the needs of members who may wish to speak privately about a topic with the group leader.
- Chairs: Is there room for people who might be in wheelchairs or who use some other type of assistive device? Are the chairs hard or soft? Do they have arms? What is the height? Are group members able to easily get up and sit down?
- Tables: Are adequate tables available on which to rest drinks or food? Are larger tables handy so members may work in pairs?
- Noise: How noisy is the heating or air conditioning unit? Listen to the traffic and noise from hallways to determine whether they may be disruptive.
- Amenities: Is the meeting location along a mass transportation line? Is parking convenient? Are restrooms nearby?

The following example emphasizes how important it is for social workers to be sensitive to the feelings, views, and perceptions of potential members about the context for group meetings:

A local aging services provider sponsored a support group for caregivers. The agency advertised that the meeting was open to any caregiver within the community and that the group would meet in a hall located in a local church building. Despite the open invitation, some potential members perceived that the group was affiliated with that particular faith organization and thus felt uncomfortable participating in a church that was outside their own faith experience. Because the aging agency did not provide enough explanatory information or use more personal recruiting techniques, potential members were reluctant to join the group.

A practical factor to consider when choosing an appropriate physical environment for a group meeting is transportation, a major issue for many aging individuals. Some people may no longer drive or may have driving restrictions, such as being unable to negotiate difficult traffic patterns (that is, driving on freeways or high-volume roads), to drive in poor weather conditions, or to drive after dark. Group facilitators need to investigate alternative transportation methods, including locating the meeting place on a public transportation route; securing transportation services for participants, for example, using a community agency van; or arranging for shared transportation among members.

As residential models for older adults expand, there are opportunities to create group experiences that are conveniently located for participants. For example, as Scharlach, Davitt, Lehning, Greenfield, and Graham (2014) noted, villages are untapped resources for offering programs and resources that can benefit the health, functioning, and mental health of older adults. Group programs and options can be part of what is offered for residents. Because the sessions can be offered or promoted within the community of older adult residents, this model can overcome some of the barriers to participation.

Challenges to participation do exist, however, and group workers must address the particular issues that might prevent people from affiliating with a group. For example, when facilitating a group of grandparents raising grandchildren, a group leader might hold meetings during school hours or select a space where child care is available on-site. A suitable meeting place for a support group for people with health impairments would be one that participants could easily and conveniently access, with parking close by, wheelchair ramps, and handicap-accessible restrooms.

In addition to environmental issues, social workers need to think about leadership within a group. In certain types of groups, such as a psychoeducational one that offers a curriculum, the practitioner might retain a more formal leadership role. That is, the social worker could provide some of the content by delivering lectures or structuring role-playing or other activities. In other types of groups, such as support or mutual aid groups, participants should assume a greater proportion of leadership responsibility. In support groups, for example, the members who have had the most experience with a particular issue (for instance, those who have been caregivers for several years) might assume the role of a veteran member. Others who are beginning in their caregiving role would look to the veterans for information, assurance, or hope.

How leadership dynamics potentially unfold is a process social workers ought to consider before a group first meets. Leadership, like listening and empathizing skills, is a learned behavior (Kottler, 2001). If the social worker wishes to function as group leader (such as in a psychoeducational group), he or she needs to incorporate ways to share power, authority, and decision making with group members. The social worker might, for instance, ask the group about how to structure various sessions, perhaps by using outside speakers or by integrating readings. If part of the group process involves developing leadership within the group, the social worker should strategize about identifying potential leaders and encouraging members to assume leadership roles. Practitioners will need to determine the group structure in the early stages of the group's development. Several aspects of group structure are related to the type of group offered (Reed, Ortega, & Garvin, 2009). One is the group's composition, including the heterogeneity or homogeneity of group members. In a caregiver support group, for example, social workers might ask themselves whether it is appropriate to restrict the group to addressing one form of caregiving, such as family members caring for older family members or grandparents caring for grandchildren.

Even within caregiver categories, there are subpopulations that would benefit from a group that could focus specifically on its unique issues. McCallion, Janicki, Grant-Griffin, & Kolomer, (2000) have described an intervention approach specifically designed for grandparents who are raising grandchildren with disabilities. Although these caregivers have similar experiences as other grandparents who are rearing grandchildren, they face other challenges related to their grandchildren's disabilities, such as finding educational options and connecting with services delivery networks involving developmental disabilities or mental health. This type of group illustrates that social workers need to consider carefully how broadly or narrowly they need to define membership composition.

Heterogeneity of members may be a desirable characteristic in some groups, however. Cusicanqui and Salmon (2004) detailed the development of an intergenerational singing group that brought together residents of a senior living facility with children in the community. This activity group had the dual goals of helping the residents feel more integrated into their community and providing the children with an opportunity for interaction with older adults. The groups rehearsed separately but gathered together periodically to meet and sing. In addition, the groups performed a program together at the end of the school year. Although the older adults and the children could have easily established independent singing groups, the intergenerational aspect provided each age cohort with greater opportunities for social interactions.

Other aspects of group structure worthy of examination by social workers in the early stages of group development include

- Optimal size for group: If the group is too large, limited interaction among members will occur. If it is too small, any attrition will significantly affect the group's numbers.
- Duration of group session: How long will each session last? Participants who have limited functional abilities may not have the stamina for lengthy sessions ranging from two to three hours. Sessions that are too short, however, will limit the content or conversation that may develop.

- Number of sessions: Will there be a fixed number (for example, 10 total), or will the group be ongoing?
- Membership structure: Groups tend to be open or closed. With open groups, members can join throughout the life of the group as other members leave. This structure allows for a more consistent level of membership—that is, if two people leave, the group leader can invite two people to join. In contrast, members of closed groups generally remain until the group finishes. A closed group allows for a different type of dynamic among the members because relationships can potentially develop in greater depth than in open groups.

With the increasing ease of using technology, computer-based groups have been implemented. This type of intervention provides an additional level of accessibility as members are able to participate within their own environment. In addition, research on the outcomes of technology-based groups indicates that these interventions can be successfully implemented with older adults and care providers (compare C. A. Thompson et al., 2007). As other technological innovations emerge, there will be additional ways to provide access and membership that can benefit the older population and others who experience challenges in attending group sessions.

Relationship Building

As group members begin to meet, the social worker needs to assess various dimensions and dynamics. Within some groups, such as those in long-term care facilities, the members hold preexisting relationships. In other groups, relationships are established, and it is hoped that trusting and positive relationships will form. Important to the development of relationships within groups is the social worker's assessment of the dynamics that emerge among the group members and the social worker's awareness of multicultural characteristics within the group. As REM principles state, the assessment process should include an understanding of the older adults' risk situations, resilience, functioning across the life course, and factors that promote or inhibit well-being.

To begin this assessment process, the social worker may structure pregroup meetings with the individuals expected to participate in the group (M. S. Corey & Corey, 1997). During these sessions, the practitioner could provide information about the group and evaluate the optimal fit among group members. At this initial session, the social worker could also prepare each member for the group experience and address members' questions. He or she may query the members about their perceptions, expectations, and goals related to the group experience. Pregroup meetings might also help the practitioner to begin to assess how members' personalities and experiences may combine to shape the "group personality" as the members begin to develop relationships.

During the assessment process, social workers will also need to determine how to integrate multicultural characteristics and experiences into the group dynamic. Experiences might be quite different for group members from diverse backgrounds and thus may affect the participants' behavior. Cultural and religious practices (for example, praying prior to a meal, serving tea instead of coffee for refreshments) may seem like minor details but may be very important to participants. At the time when the practitioner is establishing group identity and relationships, these issues can promote (or inhibit) feelings of connection and affiliation for members.

In addition, practitioners must strive to understand the language used in a group within a multicultural context. The following examples illustrate how language can create feelings of exclusion, alienation, or marginalization:

- An end-of-the-year party is called the "group Christmas party" by some members. Consider the effect on members who are of other faiths or religious communities that do not celebrate Christmas.

- Use noninclusive language when discussing intimate relationships. Now that same-sex marriage is legal in the United States, "spouse" can be used instead of "husband" or "wife." In addition, older adults may be in committed relationships without being married, so including "partnered" as a relationship status is advisable.

- Discussion of later life sources of income, such as pensions, home equity, and investment accounts. Consider how individuals from lower socioeconomic strata feel about their own financial conditions.

Instead of integrating differences in an exclusionary way, social workers should seek opportunities to enhance members' experiences with one another by stressing inclusion. They ought to use language to encompass the breadth of and diversity among group members. For instance, instead of a "Christmas party," the social worker could take the lead by reclassifying the event as the "holiday" or "end-of-the-year party." Within the group, members might brainstorm about an appropriate theme, integrating experiences from the cultural and spiritual traditions represented within the group to create a new type of celebration.

In the exclusionary language example, the social worker should strive to use inclusive relationship language by, for instance, describing committed relationships as "husbands, wives, partners, and significant others." Although a bit more cumbersome, that phrasing will likely have a positive outcome: People in committed, nonmarried relationships will feel included.

The income example illustrates how important it is for social workers to be sensitive to issues of socioeconomic status. Because of longer life expectancies, lower wage structures, and a more sporadic labor force pattern, some older women may have fewer economic resources than older men, especially in later life. Because economic vulnerability is real for many older adults, social workers must avoid framing later-life economic matters from a middle-income perspective.

TYPES OF GROUPS

From a resilience perspective, interventions should help individuals deal with life transitions and events to promote functioning and make meaning of their situation. Regardless of the type of group offered, social workers need to be well grounded in theoretical frameworks for working with older members (see chapter 5). This section highlights several types of groups commonly used with older adults and provides examples of the issues they address.

Support Groups

Social workers frequently use support groups to assist older clients with transitions and changes related to the aging process. A support group is "attentive to the emotional needs of the membership as they pertain to a particular life event or challenge" (Ruffin & Kaye, 2006, p. 532). This type of group characteristically includes a great deal of interaction between members, a shared sense that members are dealing with a life situation that is not well understood by others outside the group, and a high level of self-disclosure among the group's participants (Toseland, 1995). Practitioners who lead support groups work to facilitate an atmosphere of trust and openness and help establish interaction patterns that include all group members.

Caregiver support groups typically strive to help relieve caregiver stress. Care provision is a significant role: For example, about 10 million adult children are care providers for aging parents, with the proportion of care providers having more than tripled over the past 15 years (MetLife Mature Market Institute, 2011). For female caregivers, in particular, the costs of care provision are very high (MetLife Mature Market Institute, 2011). The combined costs of lost wages and impact on retirement and social security is about $324,000 for one care provider. In addition, these caregivers often have other responsibilities, such as providing support for their own children or grandparents. Support groups provide caregivers with a forum to meet others in this role, as well as process the stresses of caregiving.

In addition to assisting care providers, support groups also assist older adults during transitions and periods of change. For example, support groups might be available for older adults who are dealing with non-age-specific challenges, such as addictions or domestic violence. Evidence indicates that older adults facing these particular challenges are more responsive and have positive experiences when participating in a group specifically for their age cohort (Blow, Walton, Chermack, Mudd, & Brower, 2000; Brandl, Hebert, Rozwadowski, & Spangler, 2003; Brownell & Heiser, 2006; Lemke & Moos, 2002; Wolf, 2001). Salient factors for older adults include the primacy of isolation, feelings of depression, and health or functional declines that are associated with the addiction or abuse. Victims of violence or people with addictions may feel accepted and more comfortable discussing these and other related issues with a group of similarly aged peers.

The integration of technology into the structures of support groups is an exciting development. Because many older adults have transportation or mobility issues, support groups have begun to use computers or telephones to help establish membership. For example, one intergenerational support program brought together by computers consisted of a group of older adults ages 80 to 86 and school-age children as pen pals (Marx, Cohen, Renaudat, Libin, & Thein, 2005). The program promoted exchanges between different age groups and provided a social outlet for each of those groups. When it began including face-to-face visits, 88 percent of the adult members rated the program favorably.

The following example highlights some positive outcomes of participation in a support group.

Case Study: YA

After serving as a care provider for her husband, YA was widowed. As a result of her experience in a bereavement group, the social support available to her increased, she learned more about the normal process of grief and loss, and she was able to provide encouragement to others.

After the death of her husband of 42 years, YA felt like a part of her own body was missing. During the previous four years, she had been the primary caregiver for her husband, Ira, as he battled cancer and emphysema. Because he had received his diagnoses shortly after they had moved from their home in the Northeast to Florida, there was little time to make new friends and become integrated into their new community. Now with all of her family still living in the Northeast, YA was confused about whether she should stay in Florida or move back to be closer to her children.

The hospice social worker encouraged YA to join a support group to help her deal with grief and bereavement issues, as well as to connect with others who had gone through similar experiences. A group offered through a local hospital was specifically for older adults who had undergone the loss of a spouse. Although reluctant initially, YA regularly attended the group. She was amazed at how helpful it was to hear other members' experiences and to be able to share her stories about "her Ira." Many of the widows and widowers had also been in long-term marriages and were experiencing very similar adjustment issues. The social worker who led the group normalized YA's grief reactions—such as when she experienced hearing Ira's voice or would break into tears at unexpected moments.

Now YA says she feels supported and is helped by others in the group sharing their own similar experiences about the grief process. Most important, YA reports that she feels she has found a place where she can hold onto the memories of her husband, share the laughter and the tears of her experience, and offer others in the group support and caring during their time of loss. Through her involvement in the group, YA has discerned that she does not want to permanently move back north and has discovered she has additional support in her community.

Mutual Aid and Empowerment Groups

Mutual aid and empowerment groups are discussed together because they share some similar characteristics; for example, both emphasize the shared use of skills, knowledge, and talents of the group members. In a group context, the terms "self-help" and "mutual aid," often used synonymously, underline the reciprocal assistance provided among the members (B. H. Gottlieb, 2000). Mutual aid groups can be especially transforming for older adults because they are "an important substitute for lost social support, provide a vehicle for coping with a [sometimes] devastating life transition, restore diminished self-concept, prompt life review, and maximize strengths while promoting health and mental health" (Kelly, 2004, p. 114).

An empowerment group stresses the collaboration and shared resources that individuals bring to the group and highlights the fit between individuals and their environments. E. O. Cox and Parsons (1996) have described the philosophy of empowerment as "emphasiz[ing] the importance of collaborative problem definition and decision-making, collective action, client strengths, education, *mutual aid and self-help activities,* and resource access" [italics added] (p. 130). Within this conceptualization, the mutual assistance provided among group members promotes empowerment because it leads to an increase in participants' experiences of social action and collaborative change.

Like support groups, mutual aid and empowerment groups appear across a broad spectrum of issues. For example, residents in long-term care can experience feelings of disempowerment, meaningless, and isolation. A mutual aid group intervention was evaluated within a residential setting that included both discussion (sharing stories and experiences) and activities (singing). Outcomes indicated that positive outcomes such as pleasure, engagement, and meaning were experienced as a result of this group intervention (Theurer, Wister, Sixsmith, Chaudhury, & Lovegreen, 2012).

Mutual aid groups also may assist with emotional issues involved in end-of-life care. Goelitz (2004) described how the ending of a time-limited group for caregivers of terminally ill family members provided a normative pathway into the more difficult topics of death, loss, and grief. As they discussed the upcoming ending of the group, care providers achieved greater insight into members' feelings about the impending death of a family member. Through extended discussions, they arrived at ways to commemorate the collective meaning of the group. In that way, each group member shared his or her own story, which was woven into a mosaic of shared experiences and emotions about their lives and losses.

The following example of an empowerment group demonstrates how the members provided each other with emotional, instrumental, and tangible support. The group, which consisted of 10 grandmothers who were raising their grandchildren, also focused on how members could work to change the social environment.

Case Study: Grand Group

The grandparent group, called the Grand Group, met monthly at a local social services agency in a small city. Typically, the all-women group started a session—the beginning time—by singing a hymn, saying a prayer, or reading a devotional passage. Group members decided which one to do; spirituality was often a theme discussed within the group. The agency supplied coffee and the grandmothers shared the responsibility of bringing in additional light refreshments.

During the beginning time, the members checked in with each other to find out what had happened in their lives and families since the previous meeting.

The Grand Group had been meeting for about two years and had an open membership structure so grandmothers could join and leave over time. An ongoing goal of the group was to assist the grandmothers to feel a greater sense of empowerment as caregivers and community members. Through sharing their stories, they made several decisions that effected changes within their communities and benefited themselves and their families. Those decisions included

- holding a celebration at the end of each school year so that their grandchildren could interact with others who had similar family structures
- developing a clothes co-op, which involved grandparents bringing in outgrown clothes from their grandchildren to share with each other
- inviting a local elected official to one of their group meetings to hear stories about life as a custodial grandparent and to discuss family needs and support issues

The social work group facilitator assumed an active role in helping the group move from "storying" to "social action." She encouraged the Grand Group members to share their resources in an action-oriented approach and offered suggestions for doing so. Because of those and similar initiatives, the group members reported a greater sense of agency within their families and communities.

Psychoeducational Groups

Psychoeducational groups function as both emotional and informational support systems for members. They combine educational and psychosocial processes within an intervention to enhance knowledge or skill attainment (Schneider & Cook, 2005). Typically, this type of group has a greater degree of structure than a support group and may follow a specific curriculum. Because of issues people experience in later life, psychoeducational groups can be important interventions to enhance functioning.

Psychoeducational groups are often framed within the context of a particular theoretical perspective that is integrated into the group content and process. Hébert and colleagues (2003) described a psychoeducational group for caregivers of people with dementia that was based on the stress and coping model (Folkman et al., 1991; Lazarus & Folkman, 1984). Within that theoretical perspective, a stressor is conceptualized as either a modifiable or nonmodifiable behavior or event. The group intervention began with group members' identification of those caregiving aspects that they found stressful; the members proceeded to determine whether the particular aspects were modifiable or nonmodifiable. The objective of the second part of the intervention was to help care providers learn adaptive coping mechanisms. For modifiable events, the caregivers built solution-focused coping strategies. They developed more emotion-focused coping (for example, reframing) for events they could not modify. Each group session was two hours long, and the group ran for 15 weeks.

During the initial four meetings, caregivers examined their stressors, and their understandings shifted from global to specific stressors. In this particular example, a caregiver might have started the group by stating, "I always feel stressed" but later shifted to identifying specific stressful events related to caring for her mother. Specific stressful experiences might have been as follows: "I feel most stressed when my mother and my children require my attention at the same time" or "I feel stressed when my mother asks me the same question several times in a row." In the remaining sessions of the group, the caregivers determined which stressors were modifiable—one could be feeling simultaneously overwhelmed by one's children and the care recipient.

Through problem-focused solution coping, members worked collectively to entertain possible strategies to relieve their stress. For example, the caregiver who felt stressed juggling responsibilities involved in caring for both her mother and her children might have decided to put out cereal so that the children could fix their own breakfast while the caregiver attended to her mother. In a nonmodifiable situation—for instance, when the older care recipient repeated the same question to her daughter—the social work group facilitator and other group members could help the caregiver rethink her responses. The group might help the caregiver reframe the annoying situation of repeated questioning by reminding her that her mother's behavior is not malicious but is the result of a disease process in the brain; by giving the caregiver permission to provide the same answer to her mother each time; and by helping the care provider seek support from other family members who might provide a respite from that behavior. This particular psychoeducational caregiver group helped participants learn new ways of understanding and handling the multiple and stressful experiences of caregiving for someone with dementia.

An example of an alternative intervention is a group for older women with cognitive complaints. Within this intervention, a sample of 50 women was randomized into either the treatment or a control group (Hoogenhout, de Groot, van der Elst, & Jolles, 2012). The intervention consisted of four weeks of 1.5-hour sessions that assisted these women with understanding normal age-related aging processes and offering information about cognitive aging. Additional group discussions addressed societal and personal beliefs about aging, as well as disputing negative aging stereotypes. Outcomes indicated that those participants in the treatment group had fewer negative emotional reactions toward cognitive functioning in later life as compared with the control group. As a result, the participants were less likely to ascribe normal age-related changes to pathologies or problem conditions.

Psychoeducational interventions can assist older adults and their care providers to enhance their functional status, as illustrated in the following case study. In addition, this type of group may have a wellness and preventive focus, as revealed in the story about GB, who enrolled in a cardiac wellness group after a checkup with his doctor:

Case Study: GB

GB is a 67-year-old man who is in overall good health. Although he has had no heart problems, his father and brother died of heart-related conditions when they were both in their fifties. After his last exam, GB continued to be bothered by fears and worries about his health even though his doctor found no major medical problems. Through a story in the newspaper, GB learned about a psychoeducational group called Me and My Heart offered through the local chapter of the American Heart Association. He decided to join the two-month-long program. Although it was not promoted as a program for older adults, GB was relieved to learn that most of the participants were in his age range. Just this aspect of participation helped normalize his feelings about wanting to learn more about his health and take care of himself in the best way possible.

During the first meeting, GB learned more about the heart and how it functions. In discussions with other members, he also felt validated because several other people were attending because of familial heart conditions. He learned basic information about cardiac issues, but he also felt normalized in his desire to take better care of his cardiac functioning. In addition, the facilitators discussed various reasons older adults are at risk for cardiac conditions. A large part of the session was teaching participants to be proactive in taking care of themselves prior to the onset of cardiac problems.

The group covered several topics in subsequent sessions: cardiac risk factors, including hereditary and lifestyle ones; a "heart-healthy" diet; the positive impacts of exercise; sexuality and cardiac functioning; ways to handle stress; and basic cardiopulmonary resuscitation techniques. Each session included delivery of content, through a lecture, film, or panel presentation, and an activity or discussion. After the eight-week course, GB reported that he had learned information about his health and was able to clear up some of his questions with health care professionals who were guest speakers. In addition, he said that he had learned some techniques to take better nutritional care of himself as well as deal with stressful situations in his life.

Activity Groups

Toseland (1995) has described *activity groups* as "social, recreational, and educational groups [to] provide members with an opportunity to become actively engaged with peers in activities that enhance enjoyment" (p. 184). From a resilience perspective, opportunities for older adults to have satisfying social relationships, continue to learn and discover new ideas and skills, and remain actively involved in their communities are important components in preventing several physical, social, and emotional problems of later life.

This type of group is highly structured and typically is organized around a program or activity. The social worker involved with the group may assume a large portion of planning, such as dealing with logistics (getting transportation set up for an outing and the like); making contingency plans (for example, finding out how to handle an outdoor activity if it rains); and addressing cost issues (for instance, paying for activities). Such behind-the-scenes work may not feel like "real" social work practice, yet the outcome for the group is often quite powerful and reaches far beyond the completed project or program (Toseland, 1995). Activity groups appeal to a variety of older adults, and topics of interest to them vary but may include exercise, music, games, health and legal issues, aging or memory problems, and movies (J. F. Cohen, Parpura, Campbell, Vass, & Rosenberg, 2005). A number of agencies or organizations may host activity groups: senior centers, faith-based organizations, senior living facilities, and others. Quite often, a social worker does not administer the activity or program; rather, someone with particular expertise in a topical area undertakes that effort.

Exercise programs provide positive health outcomes for older adults and an opportunity for social connection. In a randomized controlled trial, community-based older adults who were at risk of falling engaged in group exercise (Barnett, Smith, Lord, Williams, & Baumand, 2003). For one year, the treatment group attended a weekly exercise program to improve individual strength and balance. At the end of the intervention, those participants in the activity group had 40 percent fewer falls and demonstrated better balance than a control group who did not participate in the activity group.

Social workers can structure activity groups so that they preserve functioning, even in situations in which members have significant impairments. In long-term care settings, for example, residents can participate in structured activities that could help them preserve their cognitive functioning and enhance their integration and engagement with others. Offering activity groups to people with cognitive impairments requires additional considerations, however (Griffin, 2005). The group facilitator needs to keep the group size small, with fewer than eight members; steer away from activities that promote winning or losing;

discourage interruptions by staff or others during the activity; be sensitive to participants' physical and cognitive capabilities; have enough staff assistance to help deliver the program; and distract or remove participants who disrupt the group.

Activity groups offer a way to integrate learning, socialization, and enjoyment. In addition, such groups may capitalize on the strengths and resources found in the community. The following is an example of a program on a university campus:

> The Life-Long Learning Group (the "Triple Ls") was a lively bunch of senior adults who lived in a small university town. A social worker led the group, and the group elected an executive board that decided which programs and activities would be undertaken. Often, interesting topics emerged from events that were happening within the community. During the previous year, the university baseball team had a strong season and went to the college world series. That event sparked a great deal of interest among the group members.
>
> During the following spring, the executive board capitalized on the group's excitement about baseball. The Triple Ls organized a program for learning about the sport and supporting the university's team. During one session, a history professor with expertise in sports gave a lecture on the history of baseball. At another session, a physical education professor talked about the strategy of the game. The third week, the group went on a behind-the-scenes tour of the dugout and field and met the coaches and players. During the final week of the program, the group attended a baseball game. The group members enjoyed the program. It struck the right balance of learning, enjoyment, and socialization. Because the university was a focal point of the town, the program provided an avenue for older adults in the community to feel connected to campus life.

LIFE REVIEW AND REMINISCENCE

For the most part, people like to tell stories about their past. It is natural to recall the "good old days" at high-school reunions, on birthdays or anniversaries, or during retirement parties. Within Erikson's (1959/1980) theory of human development, older adulthood involves the psychosocial stage of integrity versus despair; that stage focuses on the integration of life stories and experiences from the past into a current understanding of self. From a narrative gerontological perspective, those life stories go beyond synthesizing parts of people's own narratives to situating them in the community of others. As Randall (1995) has put it,

> Not only might we be a story . . . but we might be many stories as well—of many kinds, on many levels, with many subplots and versions. Also, given [an] emphasis on the stories that we are, it points beyond the individual dimension of our existence to the communal one. It reminds us

that, in the end, none of us is an island whose saga can be separated from the story of a particular family, from the stories of colleagues and friends, from the countless larger stories of which our world is constructed or indeed from history as a whole. (p. 10)

As part of the life review, we share and blend our past with our present and future and blend our narratives with those around us. From Randall's (1995) perspective, using review and reminiscence in a group format also blends life histories into a more collective whole. In fact, meta-analyses and systematic reviews on the effectiveness of life review and reminiscence indicate that most of these interventions are delivered in a group, instead of an individual-based format (Bohlmeijer, Roemer, Cuijpers, & Smit, 2007; Lin, Dai, & Hwang, 2003; Pinquart & Forstmeier, 2012; Woods, Spector, Jones, Orrell, & Davies, 2005).

Life review is a positive part of group experiences for older adults. It involves reminiscence, yet is a professionally facilitated intervention that aims to reduce group members' unfinished issues, affirm their histories, and ultimately achieve integration (Molinari, 2002). To determine which participants might benefit best from this type of intervention, social workers need to assess group members for their level of motivation, ego functioning, and personality variables, such as openness to entertaining difference and change. In general, though, participation in reminiscence groups aids older adults. Indeed, the incorporation of reminiscing and reflecting can assist older group members to recount positive accomplishments throughout their lives and support their current ability to function despite losses and functional changes (Toseland & Rizzo, 2004). Consider the example of a therapy group that focused on mild to moderate depression (Preschl et al., 2012). The six-week intervention was half face-to-face contact, with the remaining half conducted online. The group format was structured around periods within the life course (for example, childhood, adolescence). In addition to group reminiscence, individual questions were put online for participants to delve more deeply into positive life experiences that were unique to them. Group facilitators worked with participants to elicit positive memories and experiences. After the conclusion of the intervention, participants had lowered depression scores that continued to decrease over a three-month postintervention time frame.

Social work group facilitators may also structure the sharing of life stories around important cultural or social contexts. They might use relevant events to examine self-histories within a group format. In the following case study, a social work intern led a reminiscence group to engage male participants at a senior center.

Case Study: LM

LM, a second-year intern in a master of social work program, was completing her practicum at a senior center. One of the internship goals was to deliver culturally and gender-sensitive interventions to her client population. With her supervisor and field liaison, she observed that male participants were less integrated into the center's programs. Because so many more women participated, men had few activities or programs that seemed to attract their interest. LM set this as her goal: offering an intervention with particular relevance to male participants.

During LM's practicum, the center was completing a history of its new building, an old railway station. This subject seemed to spark an interest in the men at the center. They sat in clusters and talked about the old train station, thus giving LM an idea for a reminiscence group.

LM did her homework about the station's history and implemented a group that centered on that subject. For two months, the men came together to reminisce about various related issues. Some of the topics elicited deep emotion, such as the men's stories of themselves as young soldiers who were leaving on the train to go to war. During one very emotional session, a black American man related his experience waiting in the "colored section" of the station, which prompted members to launch into a discussion about living in the segregated South.

Some lighter sessions included stories about playing with toy train sets with their fathers and grandfathers and the brotherhood of fixing machinery. Although LM could not always add knowledge to the content (she reported that she was not mechanically inclined), she helped illuminate the themes of history, community, and relationships that the men shared. In the end, some of their stories were included in the monograph of the center's history.

GROUP EFFECTIVENESS

Although evaluation often refers to the outcome of a group, different types of evaluation may occur throughout a group's life. Social workers conduct a *formative*, or *process, evaluation* when a group is ongoing. Zastrow (2001) defined another type as the *group process evaluation*, which is "an assessment, generally by group members, of the aspects of the group that were useful or detrimental. Feedback about techniques and incidents that blocked or enhanced process is of immense value to the group leader" (p. 533). Using the information derived from such evaluations, social workers can decide which techniques or processes will be most helpful to the members, refine their group work skills, and learn about group dynamics through members' perceptions.

Group facilitators may integrate process evaluations into a group in various ways. Certain sessions devote some time to member check-ins, in which participants share their impressions of the group. During the discussion time, members discuss their experiences in the group and identify both helpful and problematic aspects. A different strategy is a "peer evaluation," in which one peer or more (typically other than the group leader) provides feedback on what is occurring within the group. Sometimes the peer evaluates the group through a one-way mirror or by participating in a group session. A similar strategy involves audio-taping or videotaping part of a session, followed by a review of the tapes by someone with expertise in running groups. Of course, the social worker would need to inform participants that nonmembers would be viewing the group process and then request their consent to the use of this strategy.

Practitioners may also use quantitative measures in the formative evaluation process. An example is the Groupwork Engagement Measure (GEM), a 37-item measure of engagement across multiple dimensions (Macgowan, 1997, 2003). Macgowan developed GEM by drawing on the social work literature on groups and designed the instrument for closed membership groups. The social worker administers GEM after the third or fourth session of a group. Macgowan's (2003, p. 7) particular measurement strategy determines members' participation and integration across the following seven dimensions:

1. attending: "member arrives at or before start time"
2. contributing: "member contributes his or her share of talk time"
3. relating to worker: "member supports work that the worker is doing with other members"
4. relating to other members: "member helps other group members to maintain good relationships with others"
5. contracting: "member expresses continued disapproval about what the group members are doing together"
6. working on own issues: "member makes an effort to achieve his or her particular goals"
7. working on others' issues: "member talks with others in ways that help them focus on their issues"

Each group member receives an overall score and subscores on various dimensions. Using the data, the social worker can determine strategies to increase participants' engagement in very individualized ways.

At the end of the group, the social worker performs a *summative,* or *outcome, evaluation,* which typically determines whether the group had a positive effect on group members' functioning. It can also examine whether the group achieved anticipated outcomes, such as reducing depression, increasing coping, increasing social support, and decreasing isolation. Cummings and Kropf (2008) have compiled evidence-based treatments for older adults, including groups that deal with health, mental health, cognitive status, and social role functioning.

Group evaluation could comprise several designs ranging from a single subject to a randomized clinical trial. In single-subject designs, the group worker compares the baseline scores for each member of the group to scores at various points throughout and after the intervention. In the example of YA, the worker would hypothesize that grief and depression scores would decrease as a result of YA's participation in the support group. Another research design would involve comparing the aggregate score of a group participating in a group intervention with that of a group of nonparticipants, such as people on the waiting list. The hypothesis would be that group participants would have significantly better scores than the control group. With GB, for example, the group that participated in the Me and My Heart group would be predicted to have significantly higher scores on cardiac health measures than a waiting group of individuals who had not yet participated.

The gold standard of research is the randomized clinical trial; however, the costs and level of control needed may prohibit a social worker from implementing such a research design within social services programs. In clinical trials, the researcher randomly assigns participants to two or more groups, one of which receives a particular group intervention. (In the section describing activity groups, the community-based exercise program described is a randomized clinical trial.) The random assignment provides a way to distribute differences among individuals to the groups before the intervention. Thus, researchers have higher confidence that any differences after group treatment are a result of the group experience rather than because of other rival hypotheses (for example, differences in the two groups before intervention that might have accounted for the differences). When reviewing evaluation studies about groups, social work group workers should keep in mind that randomized control designs, when available, typically provide the strongest outcome evidence.

FROM ROOTS TO FUTURE: IMPORTANCE OF GROUP WORK

This group work clearly has been an enduring method of social work intervention throughout the history of professional practice. The method is particularly relevant in contemporary practice with older adults facing issues of later adulthood. Group work gives social workers an approach to increase older adults' social support, provide them with information and skill enhancement, offer members opportunities for new learning and shared enjoyment with peers, and introduce ways in which group participants may share resources and wisdom. For these and other reasons, many practitioners who work with older adults will facilitate one or more of the types of groups discussed in this chapter. Although group work is a method of intervention that has been part of professional practice from social work's beginnings, it continues to hold promise for current and future generations of older adults. The relationships between group members are powerful and provide curative and therapeutic qualities from the interactions. With age, individuals may have limited opportunity to enhance social networks through naturally occurring means (for example, the workplace, clubs). Group membership provides a method to be in relationship with others who have similar interests, needs, or experiences.

CONCLUSION

This chapter has presented an array of various types of groups that have particular utility with the older population. To introduce effective group strategies to promote physical, emotional, and social functioning of older adults, we presented content to help beginning practitioners prepare to launch a group, recruit members, and structure group formats to deal with germane issues (for example, bereavement, transitions, staying connected). In addition, a typology of group structures was presented: support, mutual aid and empowerment, psychoeducational, activity, and reminiscence groups. For each one, we provided examples to illustrate how various groups would run and the type of activities or content that would be included.

It is critical for the next generation of social workers to have skills in working with groups of older adults. Even nontraditional settings (for example, schools, prisons) are being transformed by the population explosion of older adults. Clearly, social work's roots in group work are deep and will continue to have a hold on the profession.

Case Study: Group-Work Interventions with the Stanley Family

As mentioned in the previous chapter summary of the Stanley case, part of the intervention plan for Mrs. Stanley was a support group. Initially, she resisted the idea as she stated that there were several custodial grandparents in her church. After additional discussion with the social worker, Mrs. Stanley decided to attend. It was more than she imagined.

First, the group facilitator was a social worker from the local Area Agency on Aging where the group was held. There was transportation to the group meeting, so the participants did not have to worry how they would get to the group. In addition, there were always refreshments, such as coffee, tea, juice, cookies, and sometimes homemade treats by one of the members. Although this might seem insignificant, it was one of the only times in the month that the grandparents had someone do something special for them. The group had a little ritual that they would not start "business" until everyone had a beverage and treat.

This open-ended group was truly supportive in nature, as the grandparents constructed the content for discussion. On occasion, someone would ask for something specific, such as one time when the grandparents wanted to talk with a local elected official about their experiences. For this type of request, the social worker helped arrange the meeting. But for the discussion, the grandparents brought up topics that were salient and pertinent to them at that point.

The group also provided mutual aid to each other during difficult times. For example, one session was about dealing with children's parents who came back into the home for short amounts of time, such as during periods of sobriety. Several grandparents shared their stories about when this happened—how the parent would promise to stay but leave again, the confusion of the children when the parent is present, and the reabandonment when the parent left again. The grandparents helped each other get through these times and offered their wisdom and experience to others in the group.

The group also included elements of mutual aid for needed resources. At the change of seasons, for example, the grandparents would swap clothes that no longer fit their grandchildren that they could share with others. In this way, grandparents also were able to develop sustaining bonds and offer support to each other.

WHAT WE LEARNED IN THIS CHAPTER

- How to plan a group specifically for older adults
- How to apply the resilience-enhancing model in social work group intervention
- The importance of relationship building in effective group practice
- The types of groups used in working with older adults, including the issues they address
- How to evaluate group effectiveness

SUGGESTED EXERCISES TO EVALUATE STUDENT COMPETENCE

Activity 1

Students will demonstrate their ability to develop a plan for leading a group in a nursing home. The plan will address

- Physical space: Where will the group meet? How will participants feel about that meeting space? Is the locale conducive to recruiting potential members of the group? For example, does it send a message that might inhibit involvement, or is the environment welcoming to potential members?
- Optimal size: Is the group too large or too small? Why?
- Length of the session: How long will each session last? Will there be a fixed number of sessions, or will the group be ongoing?
- Membership structure: Will the group be open or closed?

Activity 2

Students will demonstrate their ability to work in small work groups. Students will divide into small groups, and then each group will select a subpopulation of older adults that it believes will benefit from participation in a group experience. This group can be based on life experiences that are shared (such as older gay men or lesbians, Holocaust survivors, or older Korean Americans) or particular problems or challenges that are encountered (for example, older adults struggling with alcoholism, those recently diagnosed with diabetes, or black American caregivers).

After selecting the subpopulation, address the following questions to determine how the group experience can be beneficial:

- What type of group would be most beneficial for the population you selected? Why did you select this type of group?

- What type of setting (for example, hospital, senior center, gay or lesbian center) would you use for this group? Why do you think this setting would be most conducive to formation of the group?

- How would you recruit for this type of group? What might be some recruitment challenges?

- How would you structure the group?

- What are some of the goals the group can accomplish?

- How would you evaluate the success of the group?

ADDITIONAL RESOURCES

Evidence-Based Group Work provides links to research-based evidence about group work: http://www.evidencebasedgroupwork.com/.

The International Association for Social Work with Groups is a professional association for social workers and other mental health professionals committed to promoting excellence in group work practice. Standards, strategies, educational opportunities, and other resources can be accessed at http://www.iaswg.org.

The National Association of Social Workers offers tools and standards for professional practice in 14 topic areas, including aging, health, and hospice and palliative care: https://www.socialworkers.org/practice/practice_tools/index.asp.

The New Social Worker features several practice-related articles on group work. Visit www.socialworker.com, http://www.socialworker.com/feature-articles/practice/A_Good_Group_Runs_Itself,_and_Other_Myths/, and http://www.socialworker.com/feature-articles/practice/Running_An_Effective_Task_Group%3A_The_Five_C%27/.

9

Shift in Organizational Practice: Meeting the Needs of an Increasingly Aging Society

PRACTICE

RATIONALE: "Social workers understand that intervention is an ongoing component of the dynamic and interactive process of social work practice with, and on behalf of, diverse individuals, families, groups, organizations, and communities" (CSWE, 2015, p. 9). "Gero social workers address ageism and discrimination at the individual, group, community, and policy levels and aim to reduce inequality based on life-long disparities" (CSWE, 2017, p. 99).

COMPETENCY: "Practitioners in aging with and on behalf of older adults and their constituencies

- provide person-centered and family-directed interventions that take into account life course disparities and are targeted to diverse populations, groups, organizations, and communities.
- assess for quality and access a range of services, supports, and care options, including groups and technology, for older adults and families to assure optimal interdependence." (CSWE, 2017, p. 100)

RESEARCH

RATIONALE: "Social workers are knowledgeable about evidence-informed interventions to achieve the goals of clients and constituencies including individuals, families, groups, organizations, and communities. Social workers recognize the importance of evaluating processes and outcomes to advance practice, policy, and service delivery effectiveness. Social workers understand qualitative and quantitative methods for evaluating outcomes and practice effectiveness." (CSWE, 2015, p. 9)

COMPETENCY: "Practitioners in aging with and on behalf of older adults and their constituencies

- plan and conduct evaluations to continuously improve programs, policies, and practice impacting older adults and their caregivers.
- use and translate evaluation outcomes to enhance the effectiveness and sustainability of programs, policies, and practice for an aging society." (CSWE, 2017, p. 109)

Organizations provide the context and structure in which social workers provide services to individuals, families, groups, and communities. Social workers, whether they are working with individuals or communities, need to understand the interdependency of social welfare organizations and their environment and that "the organization's legitimacy . . . depends on the external environment" (Pillari & Newsome, 1998, p. 133).

The mission, services and services delivery, and funding differ among the three types of human services organizations—public, not-for-profit, and for-profit. Although public and not-for-profit organizations have been the most common sources of services delivery to older adults, for-profit agencies are increasingly assuming an active role in areas such as home health care, assisted living, and geriatric care management.

The aging of U.S. society is challenging many organizations that serve older adults to shift from an inflexible administrative style ("This is the way things always have been done") to a more nurturing role ("How should we do things here to meet our clients' needs?"). Social workers can help an organization respond to this transition by engaging the organization as a client, a target of change, or an ally in the change process. Social workers can also help to challenge the negative and limited public understanding of older adults and the aging process. These attitudes, based on stereotypes and myths about older adults, hamper organizations from developing policies and programs that celebrate older adulthood (Lindland, Fond, Haydon, & Kendall-Taylor, 2015). This chapter addresses the changing role of organizations in serving older clients and the responsibility of organizations to create and expand culturally appropriate age-friendly services to older adults as clients, patients, or customers, staff members, and volunteers and to the larger community.

A CLOSER LOOK AT ORGANIZATIONS

From a theoretical perspective, healthy communities comprise a network of organizations that carry out seven basic functions: (1) production, distribution, and consumption; (2) socialization; (3) social control; (4) social participation; (5) mutual support (Warren, 1978); (6) defense; and (7) sense of community (Pantoja & Perry, 1998). These functions, according to the World Health Organization

(WHO), create healthy organizations, which should provide the "highest attainable standard of health [as] one of the fundamental rights of every human being without distinction of race, religion, political belief, economic or social condition" (WHO, 2006). Healthy systems that promote well-being have been identified as health-responsive organizations and operationalized to include six domains, all of which are reflected in the NASW *Code of Ethics*. These domains are (1) respect for dignity of people, (2) autonomy in health care decision making, (3) ability to select health care team, (4) support services that are accessible and culturally appropriate, (5) respect for privacy, and (6) delivery of usual and acceptable care (Gostin et al., 2003).

CHARACTERISTICS

Organizations, including those serving older adults, share some characteristics. For example, they are made up of people who bring their own values, personalities, experiences, and beliefs into the work environment. Moreover, each organization has its own values, expectations, and beliefs about the people it serves, the people who do the serving, the types of services it offers, and how it provides those services. Is the organization's staff diverse? Do the workers, committee members, clients, and volunteers reflect the population served by the organization?

The organization should have a clearly stated mission and purpose. The organization's mission should include serving older adults and involving older adults in decision making. The structure of organizations should include a division of responsibility and policies that dictate how they will be governed. Social workers, particularly those who serve as staff, board or committee members, or volunteers, can advocate for older adults by helping to increase their visibility within the organizational structure. For example, the organization should periodically assess both written materials and the language used to determine its commitment to challenging negative stereotypes about older adults and to multicultural competence and diversity (NASW, 2015). In meetings and on an individual basis, social workers can promote the image of positive aging and the diversity of the older adult population.

Organizations do not exist in isolation; rather, they are constantly interacting with other organizations, agencies, and individuals in the broader community. An organization may participate in community coalitions to address the fragmented health and social services delivery network for older adults and the lack of coordination of services (Kirst-Ashman, 2000). In general, "a strong organization has a solid mission, a good reputation in the community, family-friendly personnel policies and practices, sound financial management, well-maintained facilities, and receptive administrators" (Miley, O'Melia, & DuBois, 2007, p. 228). The organizational environment is a reflection of the organizational leadership, internal and external resources, the staff, and public policy (Hepworth, Rooney, Rooney, & Strom-Gottfried, 2013). Organizational culture includes policies, programs, procedures, and processes, as well as values, beliefs, and customs of the larger society. An organization that strives to become culturally competent engages people in an organizational change process of realigning the policies, procedures, and programs with the values and goals of the people involved (Joint Commission, 2010; Work Group for Community Health and Development, 2016).

Organizations willing to improve services delivery are called *open systems.* These organizations receive *inputs,* which in social services agencies typically are "critical resources such as funding, staff, and facilities" (Netting, Kettner, & McMurtry, 2011, p. 231). "More subtle but also vital are inputs such as values, expectations, and opinions about the agency that are held by community members, funding agencies, regulatory bodies, and other segments of the environment" (Netting et al., 2011, p. 231). The agency then takes the *throughput* step, in which it processes the inputs and produces *outputs*—its final products or outcomes. Open systems have feedback loops, such as open communication; they are self-correcting or cybernetic systems, meaning each organization is "able to garner information from its surroundings, interpret this information, and adjust its functioning accordingly" (Netting et al., 2011, p. 232). These organizations manage change by balancing risk taking and flexibility, respecting differences, and creating strategies to manage conflict (Hepworth et al., 2013). Consequently, open organizations are in constant contact with their environment. Later, this chapter will describe in more detail open systems such as resilient and elder-friendly organizations.

STRUCTURAL AND CULTURAL LAG

In contrast to open systems, *closed systems* are organizations or agencies that are stuck on how they respond to, or offer limited responses to, shifts in individual or environmental circumstances. *Structural lag,* the "tendency of social structures and norms to lag behind people's rapidly changing lives" (Burkhauser & Quinn, 1994, p. vii), results when social institutions resist transforming social and economic conditions quickly. Consequently, tension or mismatches occur between entrenched existing institutions and desired best practices (Foner, 1994). An example of structural lag, according to Roberts (2003), is the United States' lack of preparation for societal aging and the related fiscal stress in major entitlement programs—Medicaid, Medicare, and Social Security.

When changes in technological or material resources clash with an organization's customs, culture, and symbolic meanings, *cultural lag* has occurred (Bolman & Deal, 1997; Foner, 1994). Until recently, age-differentiated structures had compartmentalized education for young people, work for young and middle-age adults, and retirement for older adults. People received their formal education when they were young, worked during midlife, and were forced to retire between ages 62 and 65 years; retirement symbolized the end of their careers (Reeves, 2005). Thus, ironically, compartmentalization resulted in clear role expectations for people across the life span; however, it may also have limited opportunities for individual or organizational growth (M. W. Riley,

Kahn, & Foner, 1994b; M. W. Riley & Riley, 1994). Another example of cultural lag in organizations is the lack of preparation by some aging and health care providers to serve lesbian, gay, bisexual, and transgender (LGBT) older adults. The demographics about the aging population in general are true for people of color and LGBT older adults. In many areas, neither the traditional organizations serving older adults nor the agencies traditionally serving LGBT clients have developed staff or volunteer training or programs and services to address the unique needs of this population (Hornsby, 2006). Most older adults face institutional and cultural ageism at the same time that they are developing the skills and knowledge necessary to manage the aging process with grace and dignity. However, many LGBT older adults, who may have experienced homophobia, heterosexism, biphobia, transphobia, and other forms of marginalization earlier in their lives, which have exacerbated health issues (IOM, 2011), may now fear aging and go back into the closet for safety because of reports of continued harassment of older LGBT people in long-term care facilities (Fredriksen-Goldsen et al., 2011; National Resource Center on LGBT Aging, 2016; Ranji, Beamesderfer, Kates, & Salganicoff, 2014).

The aging workforce is another issue that has been identified by those who study cultural lag (Taylor, 2014). Many of today's employers and organizations still think in terms of linear, age-stratified approaches to careers, preventing them from preparing creatively for an aging workforce. This translates into limited opportunities for a healthy, active, and diverse workforce that can continue contributing its knowledge and skills beyond retirement age. Such options might include flexible work hours, such as part-time work or time off to care for relatives or friends (Achenbaum, 2005; Haight, 2003; Mosner, Spiezle, & Emerman, 2003; Reeves, 2005; M. W. Riley, Kahn, & Foner, 1994a; Ruiz, 2006).

Age-integrated structures can provide opportunities for education, work, and leisure or retirement to people of all ages across the life span (McCarthy, 2005; M. W. Riley & Riley, 1994). Age integration can alter the person-in-environment fit by tapping into older workers' strengths and assets and by building individual and organizational capacity, reducing the "prolonged 'roleless role' of retirement" (M. W. Riley & Riley, 1994). As system change agents and advocates, social workers can educate organizations and communities about the advantages of age-integrated organizations that build on the strengths of older adults, rather than limit their contributions because of preconceived notions and stereotypes about older adults.

A CHANGING, AGING WORKFORCE

Americans' perception of aging is shifting. In the survey *American Perceptions of Aging in the 21st Century* conducted in 2000, more than 73 percent of the respondents indicated that a decline in physical activity and mental functioning, rather than chronological age, was the most significant indicator of old age (Cutler & Whitelaw, 2002). However, cultural and structural lags still exist in understanding older workers, some of whom are healthy and active and others who will continue working despite various limitations (Merleen, 2006; Ruiz, 2006).

The older workforce today is more heterogeneous. Baby boomers who crossed the age 65 threshold in 2011 have experienced geographic mobility, career opportunities, increased longevity, advances in technology and communication, and sociocultural and historical changes (Mosner et al., 2003; Reeves, 2005). They joined the workforce at the beginning of the technology explosion, which influenced them both positively and negatively. Baby boomer women encountered the women's movement when they were in their twenties or thirties, challenged gender role assignments, and sought to further their education and careers. Political and social movements in the 1960s and again in the 1990s opened doors for people of color and those with disabilities. Today's older workforce reflects older adults' diverse life and work experiences; family responsibilities; and economic, human, and social capital, and "one size does not fit all" for recruiting and retaining older workers (Pitt-Catsouphes & Smyer, 2006b). Also, the current workforce may include multiple generations working together, with different work-related values, communication styles, work habits, and in some cases negative stereotypes about each other (Taylor, 2014).

People still face age discrimination despite the enactment in 1967 of the Age Discrimination in Employment Act, which protects employees and job applicants age 40 years and older from discrimination in hiring, firing, training, compensation, benefits, promotion, and job assignments based on age (Leven, 2004; Pethokoukis, 2006). The legislation applies to organizations, including local, state, and federal governments, with 20 or more employees (Pitt-Catsouphes & Smyer, 2006a, 2006b).

BUILDING BLOCKS OF AN AGE-FRIENDLY, MULTICULTURALLY COMPETENT ORGANIZATION

Multicultural Competence

The significant demographic changes that have occurred during the first part of the 21st century, with projected increases in people of color and older adults during the next four decades, challenge social work practitioners, administrators, researchers, and educators to begin now to prepare for the impact of these changes. Providing culturally competent services to increasingly diverse individuals and communities will require a deeper understanding (beyond demographic information) of the people requesting services, the most effective culturally appropriate strategies in caring for them, and the necessary policy and practice strategies to reduce health and social disparities. This changing cultural landscape and the growing complexity of cultural diversity is reflected in two important social work frameworks: the revised NASW *Code of Ethics* (NASW, 2017) and the *Standards and Indicators for Cultural Competence in Social Work Practice* (NASW, 2016b). The NASW (2017) *Code of Ethics* contains new sections, not contained in the 1999 revisions, that directly address social workers' responsibility (individually and as employees) to understand and practice cultural competence:

1.05 Cultural Awareness and Social Diversity

(c) Social workers should obtain education about and seek to understand the nature of social diversity and oppression with respect to race, ethnicity, national origin, color, sex, sexual orientation, gender identity or expression, age, marital status, political belief, religion, immigration status, and mental or physical [dis]ability.

4.02 Discrimination

Social workers should not practice, condone, facilitate, or collaborate with any form of discrimination on the basis of race, ethnicity, national origin, color, sex, sexual orientation, gender identity or expression, age, marital status, political belief, religion, immigration status, or mental or physical [dis]ability.

6.04 Social and Political Action

(d) Social workers should act to prevent and eliminate domination of, exploitation of, and discrimination against any person, group, or class on the basis of race, ethnicity, national origin, color, sex, sexual orientation, gender identity or expression, age, marital status, political belief, religion, immigration status, or mental or physical [dis]ability.

The revised *Standards and Indicators for Cultural Competence in Social Work Practice* (NASW, 2016b) reflect a stronger emphasis on the importance of culture for all groups. New concepts introduced include cultural humility, intersectionality, linguistic competence, and leadership. Striving to achieve cultural competence is an ongoing, developmental process of learning about others and oneself; it is the journey of lifelong learning, not a single obtainable destination (see chapter 3).

An organization striving to become culturally competent requires thoughtful approaches to address the health and social disparities in its community. Strategies include identifying mechanisms for policy decision making; ensuring appropriate and accessible infrastructure building; and ensuring program administration and evaluation of services delivered in a manner that respects the cultural beliefs, behaviors, and culture of the clients, patients, or consumers and their communities. Other factors that contribute to an organization's cultural competence include respecting and honoring the similarities and differences among people; practicing cultural humility; being self-reflective and understanding dynamics of power and privilege; recognizing that "one size does not fit all" in service delivery; and institutionalizing cultural changes in structures, policies, service delivery, and all forms of communication within the organization (NASW, 2016b; National Center for Cultural Competence, 2016; Tervalon & Murray-Garcia, 1998). Age-friendly organizations are beginning to address the challenges of striving for cultural competence as the aging population increases in numbers, diversity, and complexity.

Characteristics of Age-Friendly Institutions

The organized response to the aging of the population has resulted in greater living options and health care provisions to support older adults aging in place. The CDC defines *aging in place* as "the ability to live in one's own home and community safely, independently, and comfortably, regardless of age, income, or ability level" (CDC, 2013a).

Along with the increased demand for services, the vocabulary used for services to older adults has evolved to reflect changing attitudes and philosophy of service delivery, reinforcing the concepts of freedom of choice and dignity and respect for older adults. For those needing care that cannot be provided in one's own home, options have changed from "nursing home" with the stigma of institutional setting to "assisted living," "independent living," or "senior living" community or home.

This evolution of vocabulary reflects a recognition that older adults can continue to be engaged and contribute to their communities with supportive policies, structures, and programs provided by organizations in their communities. These organizations and communities working together to make the physical, social, and cultural environments welcoming and promoting "aging in place" or "aging in community" have been referred to as "age-friendly communities," "Villages," and "naturally occurring retirement communities" (NORCs) (Greenfield, 2016; Greenfield & Fedor, 2015; Greenfield, Scharlach, & Davitt, 2016; Ivery, 2014).

Organizational characteristics of these initiatives that promote aging in place and engaging older adults as recipients and contributors are those agencies, institutions, and corporations whose policies and practices, external and internal structure, cultural norms, rituals, staff, internal and external lighting, signage, and interior design convey an openness to and affirmation of older adults as customers, consumers, employees, and volunteers. Such organizations acknowledge that people of all ages make contributions to society, and they take responsibility for providing resources to allow older adults to age in place and maintain their quality of life. An aging-in-place philosophy recognizes that people prefer to stay in their community as they age rather than move when their physical, cognitive, or psychological health changes.

Age-responsive organizations are critical to the creation and enhancement of age-friendly cities and communities because they recognize that the aging process is not linear. Some people may experience changes in functioning that may be progressive, such as Alzheimer's disease, whereas others may improve over time through a combination of medications, support, and physical activity. Organizations that promote aging in place communicate to older adults and their families and caregivers that they are concerned with the whole person; they do not have a limited view of the person as an aging body and the organization as a pass-through for people on their way to a nursing home (WHO, 2007). Assessing an organization might begin with a determination of how older adults fit within the organization. It may be that older adults are seen as clients but cannot have any decision-making responsibilities. On the basis of this assessment, a few interventions might be selected, such as involving older adults in the planning, development, and evaluation of services and proposing changes in policies and procedures to reflect the organization's commitment to older adults as resources as well as clients.

RESILIENCY PRINCIPLES

Building organizations that serve older adults effectively and addressing issues related to an aging workforce are critical to a successful response to societal aging. *Organizational resiliency* is the ability of an organization to handle unforeseen or unplanned changes actively, adapt to changing situations, and reinvent strategies and tactics in response to changing circumstances to "bounce back—bounce forward—with speed, grace, determination and precision" as required by changing circumstances or setbacks (M. A. Bell, 2002, p. 2; Center for Organization Effectiveness, 2005a; Curran, 2004; Kline, Schonfeld, & Lichtenstein, 1995). Resilience is "neither ethically good nor bad, it is merely the skill and the capacity to be robust under conditions of enormous stress and change" (Coutu, 2002, p. 52). Resilient organizational culture requires resilient leadership whose influence can be catalytic in creating necessary changes within the organization, using hope, integrity, open communication, and willingness to make decisions (Everly, 2011). Some characteristics of a resilient organization include willingness to invest in clients or customers, to take risks, to develop organizational leaders, and to devote resources to staff and their families (Everly, 2011).

An organization that "hopes to become resilient must address four types of challenges: cognitive, strategic, political, and ideological" (Hamel & Välikangas, 2003, p. 54). The organization must remember that change is constant and dynamic; what worked yesterday may not work tomorrow. An exploration of alternatives rather than the provision of answers will support organizations in their efforts to adapt to changing internal and external pressures. For example, organizations serving older adults who were adults during World War II may need to adjust their services or opportunities to prepare for the contributions of aging baby boomers. An organization that has served mostly white clients may need to train staff and develop culturally appropriate services for older adults of color or LGBT older adults.

An organization has met political challenges when it shows its willingness to move resources from the products of yesterday to the programs and services of tomorrow (Curran, 2004; Hamel & Välikangas, 2003) by investing in human capital and resources. This involves building on the skills and knowledge that older adults bring to the agency, rather than limiting those adults to a role of care recipient or frail elder. As an organization moves from yesterday's best practices to developing "risky" or novel ideas for experimentation, it is addressing ideological challenges—for example, when private geriatric care managers start to charge for their services and organizations serving older adults begin to offer LGBT cultural competency training programs.

The application of the five interdependent principles of organizations—leadership, culture, people, systems, and settings—that build resilient organizations will enable those organizations to transform themselves in an increasingly complex and changing environment (Akabas & Gates, 2006; Azzarto & Smith, 1994; M. A. Bell, 2002; Coutu, 2002; Greene, 2007; Hamel & Välikangas, 2003; Kaplan, 2000; Network, 2004; Pulley, 1997). Although these principles are found in business management literature, they are also social work concepts that provide a framework for assessing and intervening in organizations, particularly organizations that are on the forefront of supporting older adults to age in place (AARP, 2005; Hornsby, 2006).

Leadership

Leaders in organizations "can identify and articulate future directions, persevere in the face of obstacles, treat staff with dignity, communicate well, engender trust, and inspire top level performance" (R. Brody & Nair, 2003, p. 203). Strategic leaders need to know when to collaborate and when to compete (Rothman, Erlich, & Tropman, 2001). Effective leaders must be able to define an organization's key values clearly, set priorities, invest in human capital and allocate resources fairly, balance risk and safety, and cultivate resiliency in themselves and their workforce (Curran, 2004; Kline et al., 1995; Pulley, 1997; Schoenberg, Coward, & Albrecht, 2001; Shirey, 2006; N. Thompson, 2005). In organizational practice with older adults, leadership is about envisioning age-friendly, intergenerational communities, which hear and respect older adults' voices, along with those of all generations, in the planning, implementation, and evaluation of current programs and that build support for current and future programs.

Culture

Organizational culture is the way in which business is conducted and how people and the wider community are treated (Deal & Kennedy, 1982). In resilient organizations, culture represents the core, shared values that guide the organization and the way staff behave and think. Culture encompasses a shared mission, a commitment to learning, and partnerships and strategic alliances with other organizations (Rothman et al., 2001). Organizations may demonstrate those shared values through their mission statements, rituals and ceremonies, traditions, beliefs, metaphors, humor, and stories (Bolman & Deal, 1997; R. Brody & Nair, 2003; Deal & Kennedy, 1982; Taylor, 2014). Although organizational culture may differ between agencies, many health and human services agencies foster a sense of a higher purpose, emotional bonding, trust, stakeholder involvement, and pride in work. Organizations may need to revisit mission, goals, and cultural values to ensure that organizational changes are consistent with their stated purpose and mission (Work Group for Community Health and Development, 2016).

Sometimes internal or external circumstances, such as those related to structural or cultural lag, may challenge the existing organizational culture, but value systems of resilient organizations vary little over time and are used as scaffolding during difficult periods (Coutu, 2002). For example, many nursing homes are now undergoing a cultural change. They are working to improve the quality of life and care for their residents through organizational shifts and environmental modifications (Vourlekis & Simons, 2006). These improvements build on their core value of providing quality care to residents and providing person-centered care. The Green House and Eden Alternative projects, for example, help nursing homes become more resilient rather than extinct. The Green House project involves group homes that use a social and habilitative model of care and maximum staff to serve older adults needing skilled nursing care. The Eden Alternative reconfigures the environment for older adults, emphasizing a more homelike setting with gardens. These projects also aim to give residents and family members increased rights in decision making; develop and nurture intergenerational relationships; and design a comfortable community atmosphere rather than an institutional environment (Kane, 2006; Lustbader & Williams, 2006; Vourlekis & Simons, 2006). The NORCs and Villages supportive services initiatives help to change the organizational culture in the aging service delivery network by providing services and support to help people safely stay in their own homes and, at the same time, engaging older adults as both recipients and volunteers (Greenfield et al., 2016).

People

Resilient organizations need a resilient workforce in which all participants in the organization share decision-making authority rather than having only upper management make the decisions. Organizations must give staff and older adults the skills, support, and services to make decisions and take action to meet the local community's needs (Waite & Richardson, 2004).

Systems

Organizations face challenges as they prepare for an aging workforce and need to plan how to respond with trained staff to the rapid expansion of information and communication technologies. As the baby boomers enter traditional retirement age, organizations must have systems in place to support these older workers. For instance, they will need to make workplace accommodations, devise ways to pass on knowledge and wisdom accumulated over the years, and provide options for continued employment. Resilient organizations must use technology as an asset rather than a barrier to services delivery (M. A. Bell, 2002).

Just as organizations need to improve their planning in the face of an aging workforce, health and social services organizations must plan for a significant increase in volunteers as retired baby boomers seek ways to continue to contribute to society. Health and social work professionals generally recognize that older adults are assets to agencies because of their participation in the planning, development, and evaluation of services. These professionals also realize that organizations must put systems in place to allow older adults to contribute their time, energy, and resources as employees or as volunteers and allow them to move freely between those roles. The NORC supportive services model identifies older adults as social capital, which links the interests of the older adults with the needs of the community (Ivery, 2014). NORCs, as other community organizations, are responsible for developing an infrastructure that permits the organization to match older adults' skills and abilities with the needs of the local community, so older adults will be retiring not from something but to something (Greenfield & Fedor, 2015).

Settings

Older adults are found in multiple settings and environments, and continuous changes in these settings affect both work and retirement. Development of organizational resilience involves confronting and overcoming structural lag within organizations through, for example, cultural changes, much as the Eden Alternative, Green House projects, and the Village and NORC initiatives are proposing, or through collaborative alliances to develop age-friendly communities that provide an environment for older adults to age in place. A social worker concerned with the lack of aging-friendly resources for clients might meet with staffs from other agencies to assess their leadership, culture, people, systems, and settings before referring clients to those agencies (Hornsby, 2006; Moore, Cagle, Croghan, & Smith, 2014).

In sum, age-friendly organizations are resilient, characterized by (a) mutual trust and respect, (b) skilled communication, (c) real collaboration, (d) effective decision making, (e) environments for successful change, and (f) authentic leadership (Center for Organization Effectiveness, 2005b; Pulley, 1997; Shirey, 2006). Such organizations allow older adults to "flourish in ambiguous and uncertain environments" (M. A. Bell, 2002, p. 4) while creating ways to train and retain culturally competent workers to meet the growing demands of the 21st century (Portz et al., 2014).

ACCESSIBLE TECHNOLOGY AND INCREASED WORK FLEXIBILITY

Age-friendly organizations address physiological changes as the body ages, including changes in vision, hearing, mobility, and dexterity; and disabling conditions, such as arthritis or occupational injuries (Haight, 2003). A reduction in the number of physically demanding jobs will allow older workers to remain in the workforce longer. Accessible technology can support employment longevity by, for instance, making working environments more accessible. For example, technology ensures that computer operating systems, software, hardware, and other assistive products are compatible. Technology can also serve "as an equalizer for people with disabilities, removing workplace barriers and increasing employment opportunities while reducing social isolation" (Mosner et al., 2003, p. 12).

Increasing work hour flexibility is another means of addressing structural lag as it relates to older workers. Most employed people, young and old, would like flexible work hours, varying starting and stopping times, the ability to move from full-time to part-time status and back again, time off for education or training, flexibility to exit and reenter the workforce, and extended career breaks to care for family or handle personal responsibilities (Bond, Galinsky, Pitt-Catsouphes, & Smyer, 2005; Kahn, 1994; Mosner et al., 2003; Pitt-Catsouphes & Smyer, 2006b). A balanced relationship between social structures and human lives might produce a future society in which retirement as we know it today will be replaced by periods of leisure interspersed throughout the life course with periods of education and work; a society in which lifelong learning replaces the lockstep of traditional education; a society in which opportunities for paid work are spread more evenly across all ages; a society in which older people, as well as children, will be productive assets, not burdens; a society in which work is valued as much for its intrinsic satisfactions as for it economic returns; a society that can give new meaning not only to leisure but also to all of life—from birth to dying and death (M. W. Riley & Riley, 1994).

ORGANIZATIONAL ANALYSIS

Social work assessment, a skill competent practitioners must possess, is a complex process and product of learning about an individual's or organization's potential and capabilities, the environmental or community resources and characteristics, and changes that will enhance functioning. Just as an individual assessment helps shed light on a person's strengths and resources, an assessment of an organization's external and internal environment will help social workers identify strategies to assist the organization to work in partnership with older adults and other community agencies. An organization may be the client, target of the change, or part of the change agent system. Analysis of an organization is an ongoing and mutual process involving the worker, older adults, community members, and others, depending on the nature of the concern requiring attention (L. C. Johnson & Yanca, 2007). For example, in analyzing the capacity of organizations to provide culturally competent services for LGBT older adults, Portz et al. (2014) recommended that organizations (a) provide LGBT cultural competency training to staff and volunteers, (b) create nondiscriminatory personnel policies, (c) partner with organizations that serve older adults and LGBT older adults to improve service delivery, (d) increase quality and quantity of LGBT older adults specific services, and (e) engage LGBT older adults in roles such as volunteer, employee, and resource developer (Portz et al., 2014).

An examination of an organization's external environment involves gaining an understanding of sources of revenue, regulatory and accrediting agencies, other services providers, and clients and referral sources and discovering what the organization's reputation is in the community. An external analysis might reveal that other agencies are interested in developing a collaborative alliance with the organization to explore how to transform the community into an age-friendly one. Organizations that traditionally serve older adults might join with others that have never before been part of an aging network (Hornsby, 2006; Portz et al., 2014).

An internal environmental analysis should focus on "corporate authority and mission; administrative, management and leadership style; organizational and program structure; planning; delivery and evaluation of programs and services; personnel policies and practices; and adequacy of technology and resources" (Netting et al., 2011, p. 280). For example, if the Alzheimer's Association were considering creating a weekend respite program, a social worker might first conduct an internal assessment, followed by an analysis of the external environment, to determine the level of support in the community for such a service.

STRATEGIES THAT INCREASE ORGANIZATIONAL EFFECTIVENESS

A thorough assessment is needed to plan interventions for organizational change. Such an assessment should determine how ready the organization is for change. Organizational change strategies should include (a) engaging external systems to benefit the clients, workers, or both; (b) removing procedures that inhibit services; (c) developing or modifying programs and projects; and (d) involving clients in setting the direction of the agency (Homan, 2016). The change process may at times require collaborative strategies; at other times, it may call for adversarial strategies or a combination of the two. Both approaches build on an organization's strengths and environmental resources and may be successful in creating change and empowering organizations and older adults.

Collaborative strategies work to establish partnerships. Partner groups contribute resources and move toward common goals while keeping open the possibility of addressing future community problems in new ways. Such strategies include providing information, presenting alternative courses of action, requesting support for experimentation, establishing study committees, creating new opportunities for interaction, making appeals to conscience or professional ethics, using logical arguments and data, and pointing out negative consequences (L. C. Johnson & Yanca, 2007; Resnick & Patti, 1980). For example, community agencies that traditionally serve older adults, such as senior centers, may meet to discuss intergenerational programming that would benefit youths as well as older adults. Agencies that traditionally provide housing for older adults might join with older adults, bankers, and administrators of governmental agencies to discuss intergenerational housing arrangements for grandparents raising grandchildren.

Adversarial or *confrontational strategies* may come into play when decision makers such as agency administrators, legislators, or leaders of social services organizations are unresponsive to older adults, their allies, and their advocates, thus requiring confrontation to initiate change. Adversarial strategists may submit petitions, confront decision makers in open meetings, bring sanctions against an agency, engage in public criticism through the use of the media, encourage noncompliance, go on strike, picket an agency, initiate litigation, or bargain for change (Homan, 2016; L. C. Johnson & Yanca, 2007; Resnick & Patti, 1980). For instance, one might confront absentee landlords about unsatisfactory housing conditions for community-dwelling older adults. Whether collaborative or confrontational strategies are used to achieve change, interventions require careful and thoughtful planning.

USE OF TRADITIONAL AND ALTERNATIVE EVALUATION METHODS

Traditionally, evaluations of organizations serving older adults focus on their ability to provide a "continuum of care" of home- and community-based services to frail and vulnerable older adults, with the goal of preventing premature and inappropriate institutionalization. Program evaluation encourages fiscal responsibility, identifies areas of weakness or concerns that need attention, and provides ethical accountability to boards of directors, funding sources, clients, and the larger community regarding an organization's strengths and resources in meeting its stated goals and objectives (Miley et al., 2007). Common tools for evaluating programs include consumer satisfaction questionnaires, review of client files, and peer reviews, often using outside experts (Miley et al., 2007). In addition to applying traditional program evaluation approaches, it is critical that evaluators ask about how an agency is planning for and responding to older clients, aging staff, and policies affecting older adults, as well as about the organization's participation in the provision of services to help older adults age in place.

An alternative to traditional program evaluation methods is the *empowering evaluation* approach, which is designed to assist people in helping themselves and improving programs by using a form of self-evaluation and reflection (Fetterman, 2007). This form of evaluation encourages self-determination and supports successful aging, vital involvement, and age-friendly paradigms by fostering the involvement of clients (that is, consumers or customers) as partners in all aspects of the evaluation process and by building organizational capacity (Miley et al., 2007).

The initial step in conducting an empowerment evaluation is to establish a mission or vision that focuses on the results clients or consumers would like and specifying the tasks and processes to accomplish these results. In the second step, staff and program participants work together to identify the most critical program activities and then meet to discuss the activities' strengths and weaknesses. During the third step, staff and participants address program improvement by identifying future directions for the program and strategies to help them achieve their goals and discuss how they will evaluate their progress (Fetterman, 2007). Empowerment evaluation not only involves assessment of the external but also includes an internal component, with input from the program participants themselves (J. W. Brown, 1997). Agencies that serve older adults and use empowerment evaluation affirm, empower, and demonstrate "respect for people's capacity to create knowledge about, and solutions to, their own experiences" (Fetterman, 2007, p. 147) and strengthen the organization's capacity for services delivery in the community. In addition to the three steps of the empowerment evaluation, Chinman, Imm, and Wandersman (2004) identified 10 questions that help to establish accountability in organizations. Older volunteers, board members, and community members can participate in this empowerment evaluation by answering these questions and providing feedback in program planning, implementation, evaluation, and sustainability, making the organization more age friendly:

1. What are the needs and resources for older adults (clients/patients/ consumers, volunteers, and staff) in my organization/school/community/ state? (NEEDS AND RESOURCES)

2. What are the goals, target population, and desired outcomes for older adults (OBJECTIVES) for my school/community/state? Who defined the goals? Were members of the target population (older adults, people of color, LGBT older adults, and so on) actively involved in defining objectives and goals? (GOALS)

3. How does this program incorporate knowledge of science and best practice in serving older adults in this area? Were ethnically, culturally, and LGBT older adults engaged in the planning, implementation, and evaluation? (BEST PRACTICE)

4. How does this program fit with other programs already being offered to and for older adults? (FIT)

5. What capacities do I need to put this program for older adults into place with quality? (CAPACITIES)

6. How will this program be carried out in a culturally competent manner? Are there organizational changes needed? (PLAN)

7. How will the quality of program implementation be assessed, including cultural and linguistic culturally competent assessment, intervention, and evaluation? (IMPLEMENTATION)

8. How well did the program work based on stated objectives and goals? (OUTCOMES)

9. How will continuous quality improvement strategies be incorporated? (CQI)

10. If the program (or components of the program) is successful, how will the program be sustained? If it wasn't successful, how will the program or service be changed? (SUSTAINING)

Finally, integral to the empowerment evaluation technique are the following five dimensions identified by Fetterman (2007): training, facilitation, advocacy, illumination, and liberation. *Training* involves teaching participants how to conduct their own evaluations and increasing their skills, knowledge, and confidence as evaluators. *Facilitation* is the process of empowering program participants by offering suggestions and assisting them to create the evaluation design. *Advocacy* involves helping marginalized people to advocate for themselves and for disenfranchised people regarding policies, economic development, and services. *Illumination* means that program participants have gained insight and understanding in their ability to assess problems and develop intervention strategies. *Liberation* "enables participants to find new opportunities, see existing resources in a new light, and redefine their identities and future roles" (Fetterman, 2007, p. 16), thereby taking charge of their own lives (Miley et al., 2007).

CONCLUSION

This chapter presented information on organizations and their type, purpose, structure, and function. Of paramount importance is the ability of organizations to respond to and provide services for older adults. Models, tools, and techniques that can be used to address cultural competence and age friendliness were discussed and applied to organizational practice. Responding to an increasing aging population is necessary for organizations to remain relevant. It is social work's professional responsibility to do so. In the words of Putnam (2000),

> In the end, however, institutional reform will not work—indeed, it will not happen—unless you and I, along with our fellow citizens, resolve to become reconnected with our friends and neighbors. Henry Ward Beecher's advice a century ago to "multiply picnics" is not entirely ridiculous today. We should do this, ironically, not because it will be good for America—though it will be—but because it will be good for us. (p. 414)

Case Study: Organizations That Support Grandparent-Headed Families

The increase in the number of grandparents who are raising their children creates a need for organizations to provide more intergenerational support. In this way, the community where the Stanley family lives has addressed this need by providing services across age categories, as typically offered. In addition, networks across different services have been formed to broaden communication and interaction to more comprehensively meet the needs of intergenerational families.

For example, the Area Agency on Aging (AAA) organized services to increase support of custodial grandparents. Although supports for caregivers of older adults are typical services in the AAA network, this organization has established supports for aging adults who remain in caregiving roles for younger generations. In addition to custodial grandparents, the AAA program also provides support to parents who are in care provision roles for sons and daughters with intellectual disabilities, psychiatric diagnoses, and traumatic physical disabilities. Because family constellations have more diversity, this is a way for families like the Stanleys to receive support.

In addition, child-based organizations need to respond to changes in caregiving. At the school that Jasmine and Terrell attend, for example, the AAA has provided training to teachers about working with grandparents. These sessions include an overview of aging-related issues, understanding the grandparent–grandchild relationship, and helping grandparents understand the changing complexities of the contemporary educational system. In this way, the schools are working to promote an environment where teachers and grandparents can work together to help students who are being raised in intergenerational families to be successful in education.

As these two examples highlight, part of organizational change is creating a network where programs and services are not delivered in isolation. For example, the school system and AAA jointly plan and sponsor a "Grandparent/Grandkid Day" once a year where there is a full day of activities for grandparents and grandchildren. There are opportunities for the adults and children to do things together, such as make tie-dye shirts commemorating the day. There are other activities where the children and adults can have fellowship with their peers. Children participate in activities such as games or field trips while the grandparents participate in their own activities such as a musical program. In this way, the educational and aging networks take responsibility to provide support for custodial grandparents.

WHAT WE LEARNED IN THIS CHAPTER

- The functions and characteristics of organizations
- How structural and cultural lag affect organizations
- How changing aging demographics will affect organizations
- Techniques to assess organizational cultural competence
- Techniques to assess age friendliness in organizations

SUGGESTED EXERCISE TO EVALUATE STUDENT COMPETENCY

Select an organization, and using Chinman et al.'s (2004) 10 questions, assess the aging friendliness of the organization. Or select an organization and assess the cultural competence of the organization by using the Promoting Cultural and Linguistic Competency Self-Assessment Checklist for Personnel Providing Primary Health Care Services (http://nccc.georgetown.edu/documents/Checklist%20PHC.pdf).

ADDITIONAL RESOURCES

The Association for Community Organization and Social Administration is a membership organization for professional organizers, advocates, and administrators. Resources and information can be accessed at http://www.acosa.org/joomla/.

The Eden Alternative is an international nonprofit organization whose mission is to create quality of life for older adults and their significant others. For more information, see http://www.edenalt.org.

The National Association of Social Workers offers tools and standards for professional practice in 14 topic areas including aging, health, and hospice and palliative care: https://www.socialworkers.org/practice/practice_tools/index.asp

The National Center for Cultural Competence is committed to increasing the capacity of health and mental health programs to design, implement, and evaluate culturally competent services and systems. For resources and educational materials, visit https://nccc.georgetown.edu/.

The National Network for Social Work Managers is a free membership organization for human services professionals in management positions within human services organizations. For tools and resources, visit https://social-workmanager.org/.

The Society for Social Work Leadership in Healthcare is a member organization that supports leaders in health care through networking, resource development, advocacy, and education. Visit http://sswlhc.org/.

The goal of the World Health Organization is to build a healthier future for people across the globe. Health data, tools and resources, and information on political initiatives can be found at http://www.who.int.

Village to Village Network helps communities establish and manage aging-in-place initiatives. For more information, visit http://www.vtvnetwork.org.

10

Building Community Capacity

RATIONALE: "Social workers value principles of relationship building and inter-professional collaboration to facilitate engagement with clients, constituencies, and other professionals as appropriate" (CSWE, 2015, p. 9). "Gero social workers address ageism and discrimination at the individual, group, community, and policy levels and aim to reduce inequality based on life-long disparities" (CSWE, 2017, p. 99).

COMPETENCY: "Practitioners in aging with, and on behalf of, older adults and their constituencies

- promote older adult's support systems and engagement in families, groups, and communities.

- provide person-centered and family-directed interventions that take into account life course disparities and are targeted to diverse populations, groups, organizations, and communities.

- assess for quality and access a range of services, supports, and care options, including groups and technology, for older adults and families to assure optimal interdependence.

- monitor and modify interventions as needed to respond to individuals, family, and environmental challenges." (CSWE, 2017, pp. 99–100)

Much has been written about the development of the older adult and the effects of psychological, biological, and social systems on later adulthood. In the past, scholars occasionally made reference to the effect of older adults' living environments, but research failed to examine how communities and neighborhoods influenced physical, social, and psychological adjustment in older adulthood (Berk, 2014; Glicken, 2004; Hutchison, 2015). Until recently, gerontological social work used a social planning model that relied on "experts" and "professionals" in the planning, development, or implementation of home- and community-based services, without recognizing the assets and contributions that older adults bring to the community (Atchley & Barusch, 2004; Kochera, Straight, & Guterbock, 2005; Netting et al., 2011; Richardson & Barusch, 2006).

Older adults were viewed as recipients of services and not as contributing members of society. The social work profession's efforts to plan proactively for ways to engage older adults as active community members were limited. The response of older adults and others to adverse conditions created by individual and societal ageism has played a significant role in hindering the development of individual and community resiliency. The one-size-fits-all model for community planning has become increasingly ineffective and presents new challenges and opportunities to the social work profession.

During the first two decades of the 21st century, demographic changes have caused a paradigm shift in understanding the interaction between community members and their environment and in challenging myths and stereotypes about aging and older adults. The following three factors reflect this paradigm shift, which are very positive changes for older adults and challenging ageism. First, there is a national and international movement to promote the health and well-being of all Americans through community initiatives such as Healthy People 2020 (U.S. Department of Health and Human Services, Office of Disease Prevention and Health Promotion, 2010) and Partnership to Improve Community Health (CDC, 2016b). These and other initiatives encourage local communities to develop strategies for reducing chronic diseases, such as cardiovascular disease, hypertension, cancer, and Type 2 diabetes, which affect the quality of life of all community residents. Some of the strategies include implementation of smoking cessation programs, increased physical activity, enhanced interdisciplinary teams to help patients and clients manage chronic illnesses, and private–public partnerships to support older adults aging in place. Second, advances in medical and health care, behavioral changes that support healthy lifestyles, enhanced environmental conditions, and increased longevity of older ethnic minorities have resulted in an older adult population that chooses to age in place in their homes and communities, living more active, productive, or successful lives. The projection that the world's population over age 60 will double to nearly 2 billion people has created an urgency for cities and communities to begin creating age-friendly environments to support, contribute, and enable older adults in maintaining their independence and health (Officer et al., 2016).

The third factor is a response to this dramatic population shift. In 2006, the World Health Organization (WHO) launched its Aging Friendly Cities and Communities initiative "to help cities prepare for rapid population aging and the parallel trend of urbanization . . . in more than 20 nations as well as 10 affiliates representing more than 1,000 communities" (AARP, 2015). The age-friendly community initiative is designed to promote and maintain a healthy lifestyle for all of a community's residents and to address the diverse needs and wants of older adults wishing to age in place. By providing community support and health services, age-friendly communities can prevent or delay age-related illnesses and prevent premature or inappropriate institutionalization, while continuing to benefit from the contributions of older adults who have learned how to adapt and change as they have overcome adversity in the past (Greene & Cohen, 2005). WHO, the Centers for Disease Control and Prevention (CDC), AARP, and private foundations are involved in identifying those community factors that promote healthy lifestyles and positive aging (AARP, 2014; CDC, 2013a; Cusato, 2015; Harrell, Lynott, & Guzman, 2014; WHO, 2013).

Because the aging process knows no race, ethnicity, gender, class, sexual orientation, or geographic boundaries, social workers now have the opportunity to support older adults and community members to determine a vision and plan that builds on assets and resources unique to their community. As the population ages, new definitions are needed to challenge the negative narrative about older adults and the aging process in this country (Lindland et al., 2015). The new paradigm of successful community aging (Greene & Cohen, 2005) shifts the social work lens from a limited view of older adults as vulnerable, burdensome, and a drain on community resources to a wider, more positive perspective that recognizes older adults as community assets that have the capacity and desire to make communities better places in which to live, work, and play (Achenbaum, 2005; Austin, Camp, Flux, McClelland, & Sieppert, 2005; Billig, 2004). This new perspective recognizes vital communities that support older adults aging in place and includes a vision of resilient, intergenerational communities that support all members. Social work, with its focus on the person in environment (Kirst-Ashman, 2000), is in the best position to work collaboratively with others in rebuilding and revitalizing communities by drawing on community members' skills and talents (Saleebey, 2002). By recognizing and using older adults' resources and assets, social workers can foster individual and community resiliency (Greene, 2007) and build age-friendly communities that serve the needs of community members. They can also help to build community capacity, when necessary.

This chapter explores new approaches to social work practice with older adults and communities, based on two critical factors: (1) an understanding that communities are changing, aging, and engaged in a transformative process that recognizes the contributions of older adults as valuable community resources, and (2) a response to the research documenting that older adults want to age in place. Although certain roles and tasks have been associated with past community practice, the knowledge, skills, and values—that is, the competencies—presented in this chapter will provide social workers with the knowledge and skills to assist communities in preparing to become age-friendly environments, supporting all of a community's residents, based on a person-in-environment perspective.

Social work students will investigate how intergenerational livable communities can contribute to active aging and improve the quality of life for all their residents, developing strategies to help older adults become community resources, not just services recipients. The chapter also highlights the domains of living for livable communities; the evidence-based tools, resources, and information for helping professionals to make communities livable and age friendly; and two evidence-based models of age-friendly community initiatives, Naturally Occurring Retirement Community (NORC) supportive services programs (Greenfield & Fedor, 2015) and the Village (AARP, 2015).

WHAT IS AN AGE-FRIENDLY COMMUNITY?

Definitions

There are numerous definitions of community. One definition is a group of people who are bound by geography or by communication network, share mutual connections, and relate to each other (Homan, 2016). The oldest definitions of community come from Ferdinand Tonnies, who described the move from *gemeinschaft* (rural) communities, in which identification with the community is strong and informal, relationships are personal, and authority is based on tradition, to *gesellschaft* (structured) communities, in which people have limited identification with community, authority is rational, and relationships are impersonal (Hutchison, 2015; L. C. Johnson & Yanca, 2007). After years of discussion about the breakdown of communities (Putnam, 2000; van Wormer, Besthorn, & Keefe, 2007), the development of age-friendly communities is a return to the sense of belonging that is a signature feature of *gemeinschaft* communities.

Communities are often multifaceted and complex and act and are acted on by their residents (Hardcastle, Wenocur, & Powers, 2011). People may belong to several different communities; membership in some may overlap, whereas others may have select distinct memberships. Physical boundaries define the geographic community or community of place. Identification or interest defines some "nonplace" communities, such as sororities or fraternities and certain ethnic or cultural groups, such as the African American community or the Jewish community. Communities of personal networks may include professional associations, such as the National Association of Social Workers (Homan, 2016; L. C. Johnson & Yanca, 2007; Netting et al., 2011). This chapter defines *community* as a social system with shared values and beliefs, a defined population, and significant relationships between members of the community and between community members and community institutions (L. C. Johnson & Yanca, 2007).

Age-friendly communities are those communities that are developing policies, structures, and services that will create or adapt the social and physical environment in ways that assist older community members to remain active, healthy, and safe, and to contribute to the well-being of the community as they age (Public Health Agency of Canada, 2015). This chapter uses "age-friendly communities" as an umbrella term for communities that share an underlying philosophy centered on positive beliefs about, and images of, older adults as valuable members of society. These communities strive to create a place in which community residents of all ages can live comfortably; enjoy meaningful work and volunteer experiences; and have access to health, educational, and supportive services.

Social Work's Role in Community Practice

Since the late 19th century, community organization, the foundation of social work practice, has struggled to define and redefine itself in relation to the larger society. Currently, community practice involves changing policy, practice, or legislation by working directly with clients to identify and address community projects and by advocating for community change. The focus of community practice may address strategies to improve the community's social, economic, and physical health or to enhance the well-being of individuals and families living in the community.

Although community practice is articulated in social work's code of ethics and has continued to evolve, disagreements about the social work role in community work continue to exist (Homan, 2016; Hutchison, 2015). In particular, the following four areas of tension affect community practice with older adults.

Community as Context for Practice versus Target of Practice

In practice, social workers may view community as both the target of and the vehicle for change (Long & Holle, 1997; Lyons & Zarit, 1999). The position that the community is the context in which work with families and individuals occurs emphasizes the need to create healthy individuals, recognizing that communities and organizations can create both challenges and assets for clients. Practitioners demonstrate the importance of the community as context by enhancing the assets of older adults, reducing their liabilities, and allowing them to age in place (Kivnick & Murray, 1997).

In contrast, the view that the community is the client or target of practice highlights the importance of developing healthy communities. Similar to individuals, communities have resources, limitations, coping skills, a culture, and problem-solving skills. To engage in the change process, communities must be motivated to change and be able to demonstrate responsibility and accountability (Homan, 2016). For example, neighborhood watch programs, a community coping mechanism, increases the safety and reduces victimization of older adults and other community members.

Hardcastle and colleagues (2011) have suggested that social workers view community as both the context and target of practice. The age-friendly community initiative (discussed later in this chapter), which supports the empowerment of older adults and enables the community to begin recognizing its older members' contributions, incorporates this integrated approach.

AGENCY-BASED MODEL VERSUS SOCIAL ACTION MODEL

The tension between the agency-based and social action models results from a controversy between two beliefs: the view, which evolved from Jane Adams's settlement house movement, that social reform efforts and change are necessary to improve community functioning, and the belief that community services are best delivered through a coordinated network of social and human services. Although this conflict is sometimes framed as an either–or dilemma, social workers can more effectively address community problems and draw on community resources by using an integrated strategy to community social work practice that builds on traditional community-based services, enhances sense of community, and advocates for social change (Hutchison, 2013).

Older adults, for instance, have benefited from a network of home- and community-based services provided through Area Agencies on Aging. Moreover, grassroots organizations have supported the older adult population. For example, the Older Women's League, founded in 1980 after a White House miniconference on aging, creates social change by raising awareness about older women. The Gray Panthers, started by Maggie Kuhn in 1970, advocates for older adults and educates others about both intergenerational issues and the marginalization and oppression of older women.

CONFLICT MODEL VERSUS COLLABORATIVE MODEL

The conflict model emphasizes the need to challenge social and economic injustice and to fight for and at the side of marginalized and oppressed populations. An illustration of this model in action is the Gray Panthers' work with the U.S. Food and Drug Administration to help reform the pharmaceutical market so that less costly generic drugs are more readily available.

The development of nontraditional, collaborative partnerships that cross economic, religious, age, and cultural lines may lead to the identification of creative new problem-solving approaches (Hutchison, 2015). The Gray Panthers, for example, built a coalition of more than 125 local, state, and national organizations to address a number of issues and to build community capacity. The age-friendly community movement also illustrates the effective use of the collaborative model by bringing community members together with formal and informal organizations to create and implement a common vision of the community.

SOCIAL WORKER AS EXPERT VERSUS PARTNER IN THE CHANGE PROCESS

Social workers may be viewed as either experts or partners, depending on their approach to a community—its resources, strengths, and assets. Although social workers may have expertise in areas such as public and private funding and work within formal systems, community members also are the experts on their own community's resources and solutions. Community work involves recognizing and affirming the strengths that each partner—community and social worker—brings to the relationship (Hutchison, 2015). In the new paradigm of successful aging and livable communities, practitioners view older adults as partners and contributors to the development and implementation of a community vision that supports and nurtures all members (McNulty, 2005). Social workers can help reduce or remove the psychological, social, and physical obstacles restricting older adults from contributing to the community.

NEW APPROACHES

How can social work community practitioners work with older adults who want to remain active members of their communities but will need a more supportive environment that provides resources, safety, and security for them to age in place (Austin et al., 2005; E. O. Cox, 2001; J. L. Johnson & Grant, 2005; Zastrow & Kirst-Ashman, 2016)? In social work practice, often the individual and family are the starting place for assessment, surrounded by the community or communities, larger society, and global concerns. A. K. Johnson (1999) has identified a different perspective through the Community Practice Pilot Project (CPPP). Students who participated in the CPPP reported that by first assessing the "environment-surrounding-the-person"—that is, the multiple communities to which the individual or family belonged—they could better understand the individual and the family.

Traditionally, gerontological social work and community practice have overlooked older adults as partners in building community capacity and social capital (Austin et al., 2005). The basis of that traditional approach is the medical model, a problem-oriented framework whose users mediate psychosocial concerns and view older adults as generally in need of care and as an economic drain on community resources.

The traditional medical model does not give sufficient attention to the development of community capacity, even when practitioners consider older adults to be key informants. Instead, in that model, social workers conduct a community needs assessment by identifying unmet needs and community problems (L. C. Johnson & Yanca, 2007). The model acknowledges social workers as "experts" who should plan for older adults; professionals conduct the assessment and frequently gather the data.

In contrast, contemporary approaches to community practice give more attention to building community capacity, social justice, and empowerment. Social workers who have successfully implemented new community practice models with minority and disenfranchised populations can also use these models as effective strategies to engage and empower older adults. Community workers can learn to become effective change agents with older adults by focusing on "the capacities and strengths within a community, for doing so empowers people in the community" (G. Corey, Corey, & Callanan, 2007, p. 446).

More than simple semantics, shifting from a community needs assessment to community assessment, which is the foundation for developing age-friendly communities, reflects a philosophical and practical transformation in the role of social workers who are involved in community development. The move to an increasingly participatory, person-centered, strengths-based resilience approach to gathering information about the community begins with an identification of community assets and resources, not community problems or needs. Rather than comprising discrete phases, the community engagement, assessment, intervention, and evaluation processes are interactive, dynamic, and overlapping. They involve older adults and other community members in defining the community, designing and implementing the assessment, and making decisions about community interventions (CSWE, 2015; Gutierrez & Lewis, 1998; Homan, 2016; Rivera & Erlich, 1998). The questions that social workers may ask in a community engagement assessment include the following:

- What has been the community's past experience with social workers?
- Have I been brought into the community to solve a community problem or to help build community capacity? What information do I have available to answer this question?
- How will I develop a relationship with the community? How will I build a trusting relationship with older community members? Where and how will I learn about the community's cultural, social, economic, and historical trends?
- How can I support older adults and other community members as they make the transition from service recipients or service provider to participants in planning and implementing an elder-friendly community?
- Using the strengths perspective and resiliency approach, how will I engage older adults and their families and community partners?
- What can I say or do as a culturally competent practitioner to convey my belief that each community, each older person, and each local provider is unique and needs time to share his or her own story and to be affirmed?
- As I engage and begin working with communities, how can I recognize barriers and resistance to the change process? When I get excited about the possibilities for an intergenerational community that welcomes and respects all members, how can I remember that I am not the expert in this community and, regardless of how frustrated and impatient I may feel, remember that the community-change process involves building collaborative relationships and meeting any outcome goals? Older adults and community members need time to connect and may need time to heal from negative relationships of the past.
- How can I communicate in oral and written form in a language that community members and older adults can understand without a lot of social work jargon? Information is a powerful tool. Empowered people and communities have the information they need to make informed decisions.

ENGAGEMENT AS RELATIONSHIP BUILDING

Social work practice with older adults in communities involves developing professional relationships with community members and understanding what role the practitioner is expected to perform and what goals he or she is trying to achieve. Social workers need to engage and access older adults where they live and engage informal and formal public and private organizations where they conduct business. Doing so will enable social workers to understand how older community members perceive and give meaning to their communities and allow practitioners to appreciate the benefits and challenges of community in the lives of older adults and their families (Shulman, 2016). According to Rose (2000), in working with any community population,

> The challenge [is] to create relationships in which meaning [is] being produced, not received, where the participants [are] equally valid contributors to defining and shaping the process, product, and purpose of their interaction, not simply functional consumers of concealed, still dominated relationships, and where action [is] derived from the entire dynamic and [is] reflected [in] its values. (p. 411)

The engagement process supports the beginning of collaboration building among potential community partners. The creation of collaborative partnerships may involve assessment, intervention, and evaluation skills and knowledge. The engagement of older adults, their families, and other community members empowers all of them and increases older adults' capacity to participate in the change process, thereby enhancing community capacity.

ASSESSMENT AS RECOGNITION OF A COMMUNITY'S STRENGTHS AND ASSETS

Assessment, a critical component of the social work process with individuals, families, and groups, is equally fundamental in working with communities. It is just as essential to involve community members and the community as an entity in decision making as it is to include individuals. Assessment allows community members to tell their stories; that storytelling may lead to the emergence of community resiliency (Greene & Cohen, 2005). Frequently, individual, family, and community resilience are interconnected (Saleebey, 2012).

Resiliency is "the potential that comes for the energy and skill required by ongoing problem solving" (Netting et al., 2011, p. 149). Community resiliency is "a measure of the sustained ability of a community to utilize available resources to respond to, withstand, and recover from adverse situations" (Rand Corporation, 2017). The Community & Regional Resilience Institute (CARRI) (2017) defines *community resilience* as "the ability to anticipate risk, limit impact, and bounce back rapidly through survival, adaptability, evolution, and growth in the face of turbulent change." Regular news programs report a variety of threats to American communities, from acts of terrorism; to tornadoes, flooding, and other natural disasters; to oil spills and slow economic growth in certain parts of the country. In addition, other threats to communities have been identified, including the demographic shifts as baby boomers retire, the need to transform traditional communities into age-friendly communities, and the need to anticipate what services might be disrupted and what new modules of service delivery need to be created. The Community Resilience System Initiative (CRSI), working with the U.S. Department of Homeland Security, Oak Ridge National

Laboratory, and the Meridian Institute, examined how to support communities to develop and strengthen their community resiliency–building responses to these disruptions and threats. Although the CRSI report did not specifically mention age-friendly communities, the way to build community resilience and prevent the "silver tsunami" is to help communities assess their strengths and build resiliency; determine how to measure their progress; adapt evidence-based tools, strategies, and processes to move the community forward; and identify the outcomes and benefits from building age-friendly resilient communities now (CARRI, 2011; Public Health Agency of Canada, 2015). Planners project a "silver tsunami" when the baby boomers (born 1946–1964) join the World War II generation in retirement. It is important, therefore, that social workers work toward the achievement of community resiliency.

The strengths perspective in community practice has shifted the focus from identifying unmet needs to recognizing community assets and strengths (Glicken, 2004; Greene, 2007; Gutheil & Congress, 2000; Norman, 2000), a process that Beaulieu (2012) called the "development of the community"—that is, the transformation of the community. Examples of strengths-based questions to use to determine community resources include the following: (a) What does an age-friendly community look like to its community residents? (b) What are the assets and resources that older adults can provide their community? (c) What do older adults need to continue to contribute to the community? (d) How can older adults participate in the design and implementation of research to learn about community capacity? (e) How can the community build a social infrastructure that supports successful aging and that facilitates aging well throughout the life course? (f) What are attitudes toward older adults in your community? (g) What knowledge, skills, and values do social workers bring to the community setting in work with older adults and other community members that can bring about social justice and community change?

Community assets are the individuals, formal and informal organizations, physical environment, and other resources that can improve a community's quality of life (Saleebey, 2012). They may also include capacities of individuals; gifts of "strangers" that recognize the contribution of both young and old; associations of community members; local, public, private, and not-for-profit institutions; physical assets; and community resource developers (Kretzmann & McKnight, 1993). Older adults bring a wealth of resources to the community setting. According to Kretzmann and McKnight (1993), these include economic potential; culture, history, and tradition; knowledge gained from a variety of personal and professional life experiences; time; and a connection with other older adults through senior centers, living arrangements, or social ties. Identifying community assets means looking at not only what older adults can provide the community, but also what the community can offer older adults. For example, the community may assist older adults to develop skills and learn new ways of contributing to the community, whether through their income, education, or social or professional stature.

Social work community practice with older adults involves helping older adults actively engage in problem solving to improve quality of life for themselves and others in communities and by educating, mobilizing, and organizing older adults and their allies to address shared community concerns. When older adults realize that others share some of their individual issues, it can reduce the isolation and stigma associated with advancing age; it can also empower older adults to recognize their continuing contribution to the well-being of others (McInnis-Dittrich, 2014). Community members and vital older adults might advocate for improved public transportation, better access to health care and health prevention programs, or building sidewalks with benches along them for older adults to use when they are exercising.

The baby boomer generation, who turn 65 between 2011 and 2029, will be better educated and more diverse than previous older adult cohorts. This cohort has challenged society institutions such as education, marriage, and the workplace. There is little doubt that they will also challenge the traditional notions of aging and older adults, including the workforce, the delivery of housing, transportation, social services, nutrition to older adults, and health care. In fact, "tsunami" may not be such an appropriate term for this demographic shift because "a tsunami is something that strikes without warning and sucks everything out to sea. . . . In fact, the demographic wave that we're looking at is an extremely well-documented phenomenon that is washing gently across a flood plain" (NPR Staff, 2014). Social work is well positioned to prevent a tsunami by assisting communities to transition into age-friendly communities that recognize the contributions of all community members. Social workers have a significant and important set of skills and knowledge to facilitate a vital aging perspective, in which older adults engage in activities that benefit themselves and society, and the physical and philosophical transformation of communities to become age-friendly places to live. According to R. N. Butler, "Social work's role will be to help older individuals and society prepare for the growing numbers of older people as the 21st century becomes the century of productive old age" (2005, p. x). Social workers bring skills and knowledge to working with older adults, including a strengths-based approach and client empowerment strategies; knowledge of traditional and nontraditional home- and community-based services; innovative approaches to problem solving; assessment and interventions skills and knowledge based on evidence-based practice; knowledge of human and organizational behavior; ability to intervene across multiple systems; the ability to work on interdisciplinary teams and to develop partnerships (Kaye, 2005); respect for diversity; and commitment to engage in practice that promotes human rights and social justice for older adults (see chapter 4).

AGING IN PLACE AND AGE-FRIENDLY COMMUNITIES

Aging in Place

The national movement to promote aging in place began in the United States during the early years of the 21st century. Founders of the movement saw that community-based long-term care networks were often fragmented. Consequently, they recognized that communities were ill prepared to meet long-term care demands of an aging society (Bolda, Lowe, Maddox, & Patnaik, 2005).

Research has indicated that aging in place has a number of advantages over moving older adults into long-term care facilities (McNulty, 2005). For one, many older adults want to stay in their own homes and communities, in which the environment and relationships are familiar and predictable. In addition, home- and community-based services are more cost-effective than residential and institutional ones, and because these services support older adults aging in place, they frequently prevent premature or inappropriate institutionalization. Furthermore, older adults who stay in their homes and communities may have increased opportunities to remain socially and civically engaged as contributing members of the community. The development of aging-in-place communities is consistent with the social work value of the right of self-determination (NASW, 2017), as long as older adults have access to needed resources and services.

Aging in place recognizes older adults' desire to remain in their home or neighborhood as long as possible, to continue to contribute to their communities, and to live independently, safely, and comfortably, regardless of age, income, or ability level (CDC, 2017; Rantz et al., 2013). The concept has gained momentum because it provides an alternative to costly and sometimes premature or inappropriate institutionalization and allows people to remain independent, self-sufficient, and close to natural support systems, such as friends and neighbors (WHO, 2007). From a social work perspective, aging in place recognizes the person in environment. For older adults, "home" represents more than just the physical dwelling place; it involves the symbolic and emotional renegotiation of the meaning of one's identity. The attachment to one's home provides a sense of connection to the past, present, and future; autonomy to make one's own decisions; and familiarity with one's neighborhood and larger environment (Wiles, Leibing, Guberman, Reeve, & Allen, 2012).

AARP and the National Council for State Legislatures found that almost 90 percent of older adults over the age of 65 expressed a desire to remain in their own homes as they continue to age, and 80 percent believe their current residence is where they will always live (AARP, 2017). For those in midlife (ages 50–65) who were still working, 91 percent reported a wish to live in their own homes during their postretirement years (MetLife Mature Market Institute, 2010). Older adults have made important decisions all their lives about where and how they want to live. Now as older adults, they want to continue to make their own decisions (Wiles et al., 2012). One of the top three reasons that older adults want to stay in their own homes is to be able to set and maintain their own rules, rather than giving up control of decisions about their daily schedule (MetLife Mature Market Institute, 2010).

Home- and Community-Based Services

For older adults to age in place in the home of their choosing, they must understand the importance and function of home- and community-based services, including health services, care support services, and home maintenance services. Assessment and interventions at multiple levels are needed. First, many older adults and their families lack awareness of the availability of home- and community-based services, which provide the support and assistance needed for these older adults to remain at home. In addition to accessibility of these services, older adults may require home modifications to compensate for reduced vision, hearing, mobility, or balance as they age. Social workers can serve to educate older adults and their families about the availability and accessibility of these services and about the importance of home improvements, such as adding grab bars, a ramped entrance, non-slip floors, level-handed doorknobs, lower electrical plugs, and an emergency alert system (Cusato, 2015).

HomeAdvisor's Aging in Place Survey (Cusato, 2015) found that although 74 percent of home service professionals who specialize in home modifications, disability projects, and redesign of homes reported that they could explain the benefits of home modifications to allow people to stay in their homes, only 17 percent knew about Medicare and Medicaid benefits for in-home services. The National Association of Home Builders forecasts that about 70 percent of home modifying projects are related to aging-related changes (National Aging in Place Council, 2015), and the home improvement business could become a $20 to $25 billion market (Cusato, 2015). Creating home environments that are conducive to the social, emotional, and physical changes that older adults may experience in their later ages allows them to remain safe and secure in the home of their choice, as long as possible.

With the increasing diversity of the older adult population, a second factor that must be considered in the delivery of home- and community-based services is whether services are delivered in ways that are culturally responsive to the target populations. The Administration on Aging (AoA) has historically targeted groups with the greatest social and economic need to ensure that organizations receiving federal funding direct programs and resources to serve these populations. In addition to racial and ethnic people of color, the AoA has included LGBT older adults in the historically disadvantaged group because of higher levels of disability, illness, and premature death (Fredriksen-Goldsen et al., 2011; IOM, 2011). Like all older Americans, older lesbian, gay men, and bisexual and transgender older adults face challenges because of negative stereotypes and misinformation about aging and older adults in society; however, LGBT older adults also have faced a lifetime of heterosexist and homophobic attitudes and threats of violence, harassment, and abuse. They are more likely than their aging cohort to have experienced workplace discrimination and economic insecurity, been refused medical care, and postponed needed medical care because of real or perceived discrimination. For older LGBT adults of color, the discrimination is even more disturbing. Developing LGBT culturally competent training is critically needed to overcome their negative earlier experiences and to prevent LGBT older adults from retreating to the closet to receive the services they need to remain in their homes and communities, where they feel safe (Fredriksen-Goldsen et al., 2011).

Older adults may have moved into a neighborhood many years earlier because they shared values or beliefs similar to those of others living in that neighborhood. Cultural values might determine whether an older Korean woman is willing to accept Meals on Wheels when the food is cooked very differently than the food she has eaten all of her life, whether an older Jewish woman will accept help from a volunteer of German descent, or whether an older gay couple welcomes a geriatric care manager into their home when they have previously experienced discrimination by health care providers. Harrell et al. (2014) conducted research with 4,500 older adults and found that "preferences of older adults are complex, intertwined, and sometimes conflicting" (p. 2).

The third factor that must be considered is that at a national and international level, the terms "a livable community for all ages," "age-friendly communities," and "aging in place" or "aging in community" refer to the attempt by communities to meet the diverse needs and wants of its members, regardless of the community members' age, income, ethnicity, physical ability, or other factors, so that they can continue living productive lives. For example, one community might decide it needs better sidewalks with lighting and seating so that its members can walk safely and stop to rest when needed, whereas another community might need transportation services for community members who no longer drive or who have disabilities (Harrell et al., 2014).

Age-Friendly Communities

The age-friendly community initiative represents a paradigm shift from the delivery of services and programs targeted specifically to the needs of older individuals usually defined by an agency or funding body. The new paradigm asks communities and the residents living in those communities what they need and want, and then resources and programs are developed based on community-identified need (Greenfield, 2015a). This approach changes the perception of the aging process from a belief that older adults are sick, frail, and no longer able to contribute to a more positive one in which older adults can continue to contribute to their community and participate in decisions affecting their lives when their physical and social environments better support their changing needs (Greenfield, Oberlink, Scharlach, Neal, & Stafford, 2015). The "broader social fabric is aging," says Achenbaum (2005, p. xi), and will consequently influence communities and result in their transformation. The majority of older adults live in households. However, the probability of living in a nursing home increases with age—less than 1.1 percent for 65- to 74-year-olds, 3.5 percent for 75- to 84-year-olds, and 13.2 percent for those 85 and older (AoA, 2011). The nature of the community, whether robust or weak, can dramatically affect older adults' quality of life. This idea is grounded in the person-in-environment lens that emerged from the ecological perspective and systems theory (A. K. Johnson, 1998) and "enables social workers to understand the complexities of clients' lives by emphasizing the impact of the physical and social environment on the person" (Berg-Weger 2005, p. 152). For older adults, it can determine whether an older adult can age in place or will be forced to leave the community because of lack of support. Communities have since started to transform themselves, planning the services and programs they must develop, modify, or expand to create age-friendly communities that can respond to the dramatic increase in the older population. AARP has identified eight domains of living critical to every age-friendly community: (1) outside space and buildings for people to gather; (2) transportation options that move beyond driving and owning a car; (3) housing options that are affordable, accessible, and allow people to age in place safely; (4) opportunities for social participation to maintain or enhance one's sense of well-being and prevent loneliness; (5) respect for older adults and provision of opportunities for social inclusion, such as intergenerational activities; (6) paid or volunteer civic participation and employment; (7) communication and information provided in an age-friendly manner, that is educationally and culturally appropriate; and (8) community and health services that are available, affordable, and accessible. AARP recommends that cities and communities consider these eight domains to create an age-friendly community that improves well-being for older adults and the community itself (AARP, 2015; WHO, 2007).

Building community capacity involves changing the paradigm about community change (see Kretzmann & McKnight, 1997, for capacity inventories). Rather than engaging experts to solve community problems, local community members can develop community partnerships in which people can work together to solve problems that affect their daily lives. Community changes should focus on programs and policies that build healthier communities and transform health behaviors for all community residents.

AARP has identified 10 principles for creating age-friendly communities, in which all members have opportunities for engagement in the life of the community, social connectedness, and opportunities for health care prevention and maintenance. The 10 principles include the following:

- Leverage the current and potential contributions of older adults in the community as entrepreneurs, volunteers, or other talents or interests.
- Acknowledge the significance of maintaining older adults' connection to both people and community, as a context for their past and present.
- Provide safe and affordable housing and surrounding environment, including streets, sidewalks, and access to transportation.
- Improve health through access to healthy food options, exercise and recreation options, and health facilities.
- Provide transportation alternatives, recognizing that one in five people over age 65 does not drive and may need dependable paratransit services, reduced taxi fares, or volunteers to accompany them to doctors' appointments or shopping.
- Promote community and personal safety to prevent injuries and ensure the security for all community members.
- Support older adults and their family caregivers through access to long-term care resources, programs, and services.
- Partner with other community groups in the planning process for transportation, supportive services, land use, housing, health planning services, and safety.

- Community land use should be interconnected with housing, transportation, social services, and health. (Adapted from Harrell et al., 2014)

Age-Friendly Communities and Social Work

Social workers have the professional skills and knowledge to support communities as they transform into aging-friendly ones. National aging organizations and city and county government agencies have joined with formal and informal organizations, local government, private foundations, and the federal government to fund demonstration projects to assist communities in initiating dialogues with older adults. The goals of these partnerships are to create a mutually agreed-on vision for aging in place and to develop a plan of action. These innovative community demonstration projects, based on the strengths perspective or resiliency approach, are called Community Partnerships for Older Adults, Livable Communities for All Ages, and the Aging in Place Initiative. According to L. C. Johnson and Yanca (2007), for age-friendly communities to develop successfully and sustain themselves, they must have the following nine characteristics:

1. At least some primary relationships must exist.
2. The community must be comparatively autonomous.
3. The community must have the capacity to face problems and engage in problem solving.
4. A broad distribution of power must be apparent.
5. Citizens must be committed to the community.
6. Citizen participation is possible and the community encourages it.
7. More homogenous than heterogeneous relationships exist.
8. Community members have developed ways of dealing with conflict.
9. The community tolerates and values diversity.

Two major age-friendly community initiatives have evolved to promote aging in place and to engage older adults as contributors, as well as recipients, of these initiatives (Greenfield, 2015; Greenfield et al., 2016; Ivery, 2014; Thomas, 2011; Village to Village Network, n.d.). Social workers can play a central role in helping older adults achieve their goal of aging in place.

Two integrated models of age-friendly community initiatives that help older adults age in their own homes safely are the NORC supportive services programs and the Villages. Both require social work community practice skills and knowledge to transform traditional communities into innovative strategies to increase community capacity, services, and resources that are accessible, affordable, appropriate, responsive, and consumer driven (Greenfield et al., 2016). Villages and NORCs share common characteristics of engaging community members as informal supports, serving both as contributors and recipients of support, and developing social capital for older adults and other community members (Greenfield et al., 2016; Ivery, 2014), an approach consistent with the healthy aging paradigm. Informal supports are those resources that function outside the formal social services delivery system or family caregivers and are often neighbors helping neighbors. Recent studies have identified the importance of support from neighbors, particularly when one neighbor experiences an emergency; however, the research on the meaning of neighbor relationships to promote aging in place is fairly recent (Greenfield & Fedor, 2015).

The first NORC began in New York City in 1986 in a low-income cooperative housing complex. Like most NORCs today, the housing complex was not designated as senior housing originally. Many of its residents moved into the complex when they were younger but stayed because of the relationships they had developed over the years. Private, nonprofit organizations and their professional staff members who help to develop important partnerships with stakeholders—older adults, building managers, aging and health care service providers, and local government—provide funding for NORC programs. Staff may provide direct and indirect services to ensure that neighbors are receiving the support they need to age in place safely (Greenfield, 2016).

There are two main types of NORCs in large cities, small towns, suburbs, and rural areas. The housing base, also called the vertical or classic NORC, refers to communities in which residents live in the same building or a housing complex with multiple buildings under one management. The neighborhood, horizontal or open NORC, typically consists of one- and two-family homes in age-integrated neighborhoods. A designated NORC will have at least half of its residents at least 60 years old. Older adults, whether as volunteers or recipients of support, contribute their ideas and suggestions to ways the community can promote healthy behaviors, reduce isolation, and create an age-friendly environment that is sustainable (Ivery, 2014). NORC programs offer a variety of benefits to older community members, including direct and indirect services, group activities, and larger community activities, to create person-centered, consumer-driven options that respond to the residents' needs, interests, and preferences. NORC programs provide social and health care services to the older community residents on-site at no charge. This allows the programs to respond to the changing needs of the resident and to encourage community changes needed for healthy aging by the residents. Older community members actively participate in decision making regarding services and activities offered by the NORCs. There is no central database of NORC programs.

Villages began in 2001 in Boston's Beacon Hill to help older adults access services that allow them to age in their own homes safely. In 2011, there were 56 community villages in the United States and another 120 in development (Thomas, 2011). As with the NORCs, members of the Village pay an annual fee (roughly $600–$1,000) for services such as yard work, transportation, and bookkeeping. Each Village may have one to two paid staff, but they do not provide direct services. Other able-bodied community residents, younger neighbors, or youth groups doing community service often provide the services. In addition, the Village often recommends contractors who give discounts to Village members.

Both the Village and the NORC programs respect the contributions of older adults and offer intergenerational relationships, unlike most retirement housing options, which are age segregated. These age-friendly community models are inclusive and culturally responsive to the needs of its diverse members, an important theme articulated by participants in the 2015 White House Conference on Aging. NORCs and Villages promote independence, interdependence, and reciprocity, which give older adults agency and control over their lives. Independence also includes the values of choice, dignity, respect, control, and self-empowerment. Those values are at the base of the successful Village concept and are often missing from the lives of older adults. Studies have found that aging in place improves older people's physical health, self-esteem, and quality of life, reduces isolation, and is cost-effective.

These community initiatives create a culture change that challenges the negative stereotypes of older adults as frail and a drain on society and serves to empower them by restoring meaning and purpose to the lives of both older community members and volunteers and by finding ways for them to contribute to the well-being of one another and their community (Village to Village Network, n.d.; White House Conference on Aging, 2015). The biggest difference between NORCs and Villages is the intentionality with which they are started. Residents generally start Villages, while the NORCs occur by default.

Community-Based Research

Community-based participatory research views community members, whether formal organizations or informal groups of community residents, as research partners—not research subjects. Community members bring their perspective of and hope for their community to the table as full participants in the planning, design, and implementation of research and distribution of the final report. The community-based participatory research model recognizes a community's resources and assets by acknowledging community members as experts and consultants and by building community capacity (U.S. Department of Health and Human Services, Agency for Healthcare Research and Quality, 2003).

Community practice with older adults is a process of building trusting relationships and community capacity as members learn how to relate to each other and the social worker learns how best to work with the community. Through asset mapping, practitioners identify the capacity of individuals and formal and informal groups and use that information during the community assessment and intervention process, which in turn builds capacity for later interventions. The strengths-based perspective and resiliency approach provides social workers with tools to help communities define and implement a vision that builds on the strengths of all community members and supports older adults and their families to age in place.

CONCLUSION

Community practice with older adults builds on the new gerontology paradigm, which begins by identifying community assets or resources, rather than unmet problems, needs, and deficits, through a community assessment (Greene & Cohen, 2005). An assessment of community capacity embraces older adults as members of society who have the ability to make communities better places to live and work and in which they can connect with others. This empowerment approach provides an environment for older adults to remain engaged in their community and age in place, recognizing how environmental factors can affect the mental and physical health and well-being of older adults. Social workers bring to this new paradigm their knowledge and experience with assessment and intervention; a strengths approach and resiliency perspective; an understanding of the person in environment; values of self-determination and cultural competence; and skills in communication, problem solving, negotiation, and advocacy—all of which are critical to the successful development of age-friendly communities.

Changes in the community will occur only if social workers join as partners with community members of all ages and with public and private community organizations to make significant structural and attitudinal changes with the goal of developing age-friendly and livable communities. "The vision of a livable community is more than a goal; it is a call to boomers and their parents to become involved in their community as well as to public officials to seek out residents when planning and making change" (Kochera et al., 2005, p. 90).

Social work practice has its roots in the settlement house movement (Berg-Weger, 2005), and it is time to return to those roots as the 21st-century vision of settlement houses evolves—now as livable or age-friendly communities. Older adults have expressed their strong desire to age in place. Social workers are well equipped as leaders and advocates to intervene in communities and assist older adults to remain in their own homes as they continue to contribute to their communities and maintain their independence, while they assist community members to create livable communities that will improve the quality of life for older adults and people of all ages.

Case Study: Geographic and Nonplace Communities in the Stanley Family

In the case of the Stanley family, there are multiple communities involved. One is the nonplace community of intergenerational families where children are in the primary care of their grandparents. The members in this community share similar characteristics of being in an off-time caregiving role, dealing with the complex issues of missing parents, and often coping with the interaction of aging and caregiving responsibilities. Although significant diversity exists within the community—based on ages and functional status of the grandparents and grandchildren; race, ethnicity, and gender characteristics; and pathways into care—the commonalities shared by these families gives them membership in the community of caregivers.

Likewise, the Stanley situation also involves geographic communities. To live with their grandmother, Jasmine and Terrell had to leave one community and relocate to another. Although this move was not a long distance, it involved going to a new school and making new friends. For children of their age, this experience was disrupting as it took place in the middle of a school year when routines and relationships were already established.

Mrs. Stanley's community is important to her. Although the neighborhood has changed over time, the location holds many memories of raising her children with her husband. In addition, her church is in her community and is a source of support and spiritual fellowship for her. For those families that have lived in this community for numerous years and are aging in place, there is a system of mutual aid and watching out for each other. When her grandchildren first moved in with her, for example, two men in the neighborhood found two beds and dressers at a flea market. They moved, assembled, and repaired the furniture so the children would have a place to sleep and store clothing.

In some cities, a geographic community for custodial grandparents has been developed. An example is Grandfamily Housing (A. S. Gottlieb, Silverstein, Bruner-Canhoto, & Montgomery, 2000) in Boston, where a housing complex specifically for these families has been developed. This type of "elder-friendly community" provides mutual aid between grandfamilies and normalizes the experience of raising grandchildren. In this way, the purposeful creation of a place for custodial grandparents to live in close proximity fosters a sense of community.

WHAT WE LEARNED IN THIS CHAPTER

- The definition, description, functions, and types of age-friendly communities
- The social work role in developing responsive aging-friendly communities
- Models, tactics, and techniques to use when promoting age-friendly community change
- Assessment techniques to use to evaluate communities for age friendliness
- The use of community-based participation research to study community issues

SUGGESTED EXERCISE TO EVALUATE STUDENT COMPETENCY

Students will use L. C. Johnson and Yanca's (2007) nine characteristics of successful age-friendly communities to explore how many of these characteristics exist in their community. Based on this assessment, what are some suggestions for how to make the community more responsive to older adults?

ADDITIONAL RESOURCES

The Association for Community Organization and Social Administration is a membership organization for professional organizers, advocates, and administrators. Resources and information can be accessed at http://www.acosa.org/joomla/.

An example of how community-based participatory research is utilized can be found in the article by Minkler, Blackwell, Thompson, and Tamir (2003), accessed here: https://www.ncbi.nlm.nih.gov/pmc/articles/PMC1447939/.

The Community-Campus Partnerships for Health is a nonprofit organization that promotes health equity and social justice through community and academic institution partnerships. Visit https://ccph.memberclicks.net/.

The National Aging in Place Council's Web site provides information and resources to assist persons to age in place. Visit http://www.ageinplace.org.

The NORC Blueprint: A Guide to Community Action outlines steps to developing a naturally occurring retirement community and other tools and resources. Visit http://www.norcblueprint.org/.

The Partnership to Improve Community Health supports the implementation of evidence-based strategies to improve the health of communities. For additional information, visit https://www.cdc.gov/nccdphp/dch/programs/partnershipstoimprovecommunityhealth/index.html

The Social Welfare Action Alliance, formerly the Bertha Capen Reynolds Society, is a national organization of progressive workers in human services who promote social justice, peace, and coalition building. Information on educational and publishing opportunities can be found at http://www.socialwelfareactionalliance.org/.

Successful Models of Community-Based Participatory Research (O'Fallon, Tyson, & Dearry, 2000), published by the National Institutes of Health, provides information on the value of community-based participatory research and recommendations for best practices and can be accessed at https://www.hud.gov/offices/lead/library/hhts/NIEHS_Successful_Models.pdf.

11

Policy Practice: Advocating for Older Adults

RATIONALE: Social workers "understand the history and current structures of social policies and services, the role of policy in service delivery, and the role of practice in policy development" (CSWE, 2015, p. 8). "Practitioners in aging understand how a vast array of policies at the local, state, national, and global levels influence the design and delivery of services for older adults and caregivers, as well as how policy shapes the extent to which environments are supportive and inclusive of diverse subgroups of older adults and caregivers. They apply critical thinking to analyze the effects of social policy on interconnected domains of well-being in later life, with special attention to older adults from marginalized groups and facing cumulative disadvantages." (CSWE, 2017, p. 57)

COMPETENCY: "Practitioners in aging with, and on behalf of, older adults and their constituencies

- educate key stakeholders on how policy for an aging society relates to human rights and social, economic, and environmental justice from the local to the international level.
- advocate for policies across all levels to enhance service delivery to promote well-being among all older adults and constituencies." (CSWE, 2017, p. 57)

A POLICY PRACTICE FRAMEWORK

Social workers practice within a larger environment—regarded as a set of systems—that encompasses organizations, communities, and the general society. A *system* comprises objects that are ordered and bound together by a form of regular interaction or interdependence (Bardill & Ryan, 1973). A *social system*, according to Greene (1999a), is a defined structure of interacting and interdependent parts that has the capacity for organized activities. Each system possesses unique characteristics, and each member of a system carries out specific but different roles. Systems theory informs social workers that a social system is more than the sum of its parts and the activities of any one member. Rather, it is a network of differing interlocking relationships with discernible structural and communication patterns.

Services delivery systems for older adults are entities within the community that provide structured programs and resources based on that population's needs. Each organization delivers services that are influenced by a particular entity and its rules or guidelines. Further affecting the services delivery systems are organizational and public policy, which bring order and provide direction to those entities. In a systems model of policy development, the policy process is a total system—the various parts, including governmental representatives, legislatures, organizations, interest groups, and political parties, operate together to determine policy (Brueggemann, 2014).

Because policy organizes and affects systems, a practitioner's competency in influencing, revising, and developing policy is important to the well-being of older adults within the larger context of society. The profession calls this *policy practice.* What policy practice functions do social workers perform, and how do they work within a larger context? The following framework, provided by Jansson (2014), offers an organized approach to engaging in policy practice:

- Know the contextual setting of the environment to identify factors that affect policy.
- Be prepared to analyze and use multiple participants in the process who will shape choices and outcomes—allow policy deliberations to occur.
- Become familiar with and undertake these tasks of policy practice: agenda setting, problem analysis, proposal writing, policy enactment, policy implementation, and policy assessment
- Become familiar with and use analytical, political, interactional, and value-clarifying policy practice skills.
- Become familiar with and develop policy competency skills. (p. 455)

Social workers must not only become acquainted with this framework, but also learn about services providers within a community. To practice effectively, it is critical that practitioners have working knowledge of community agencies and their policies. They need to seek information such as the type of services an agency offers, an agency's eligibility criteria, its service delivery restrictions, whether a waiting list exists, and the length and duration of services. Practitioners also must educate themselves about local, state, and federal policies. Primary policies, such as the Older Americans Act of 1965 (P.L. 89-73), protect older adults' interests and well-being, whereas secondary policies, such as kinship care bills, indirectly affect those elders. Practitioners need to be aware of the consequences policies may have for the older adult population in terms of creating opportunities and constraints.

Furthermore, as the aging population increases, older adults will need new policies and programs created or modified to meet their needs. Therefore, social workers will find they must keep abreast of these new or revised policies and programs so they may evaluate whether they assist or hinder the helping process. To assess policies and services effectively, practitioners will need to develop skills in policy identification, analysis, development, and advocacy.

The practice competencies described in this chapter will help social workers learn how to identify the following: advantages and disadvantages of a policy, the target populations affected by a policy, the gaps in services created by a policy, how a policy addresses community and individual well-being, and the skills needed to effect policy change at both the organizational and societal levels. Practitioners may use Jansson's (2014) policy practice framework in conjunction with these competencies.

INFORMATION GATHERING

An important role for any social worker is to identify and tap into resources that will enable clients to function optimally. To connect a client to needed resources, the practitioner must first assess the client's needs. The next task is to familiarize oneself with the specific policies and programs in the community where the client resides and determine what resources are available to meet those needs.

Community Resources and Programs

Practitioners have a number of tools at their disposal to assist them in information gathering. Community-developed resource booklets provide basic information about available services. These resources often include contact information that allows social workers to seek more detailed data from a service provider.

Another resource is the professional network of social workers and other human services providers that exists within the practice community. This network might include members of the local chapter of the NASW, members of community welfare organizations or other professional organizations, hospice and palliative care organizations, gerontology and long-term care organizations, networks of organizations that provide services to older adults, or special-interest groups. Participation in this network will ensure connection with experts who have invaluable knowledge about community resources and who work in the very agencies that provide services to older adults. To locate professional, organizational, and advocacy resources, social workers may wish to consult directories such as those provided in the Additional Resources section at the end of this chapter.

In addition, the practitioner's employer and network of fellow employees are other resources available to the social worker. Networking with colleagues provides opportunities to learn about resources that are used by fellow professionals in providing services to older adults. Some questions to ask when inquiring about existing resources include the following: What are the difficulties and successes you have encountered with other agencies? What are the admissions criteria, and do these criteria fit the client's needs?

Other information about services and programs is available on the Internet, Facebook pages, and other social media venues. Social workers can search for admissions criteria, agency location, hours of operation, and so forth. Using this medium, practitioners may locate services for older adults more expeditiously by entering key words or phrases, such as the name of the community or "services for older adults."

After gathering information about available community resources for their older adult clients, social workers then assess whether any gaps exist in those services and if the services apply to all older adults. If needs are identified through this process, all entities may collaborate and advocate to develop additional services, reduce resource gaps, change eligibility criteria, or develop needed services.

Federal, State, and Local Policies

As part of their knowledge base, social workers require an operating knowledge of federal, state, and local policies affecting older adults. Information on regulations, policies, laws, and codes is generally available in public and law libraries, which typically have copies of federal and state codes, and through the Internet. The Additional Resources section at the end of this chapter contains a list of informative Web sites for policy practitioners. Several sites enable users to search for specific federal regulations and bills that have been introduced to the U.S. Congress. The home pages of state governments customarily provide information on regulations and pending legislation. Similarly, county regulations appear on the home pages of county governments.

The following federal laws mandate the provision of services and resources for older adults. It is essential that gerontological social workers gain familiarity with these key policies. Obtaining knowledge about how they translate into services for older clients will help social workers to become more responsive to meeting the needs of individuals and the community.

Social Security Act (enacted 1935)

- a sweeping federal policy passed to help ensure economic security for the aged and, later, indigent populations; for surviving spouses and children; and for individuals with disabilities
- originally included social insurance, unemployment insurance, old age assistance, and aid to dependent children; later additions included Medicare, Medicaid, Supplemental Security Income (SSI), and Supplemental Security Disability Income
- For 2016 financial status of social security, see http://www.ssa.gov/OACT/TRSUMl

Food Stamp Program (Supplemental Nutrition Assistance Program, or SNAP) (enacted 1961 by executive order)

- relief program, administered by the U.S. Department of Agriculture, to help people buy food
- eligibility rules less stringent for older people because of their generally high medical costs and fixed-income status
- older adults who meet the eligibility requirements for the SSI program automatically meet the eligibility requirements for SNAP

Older Americans Act (enacted 1965)

- for individuals age 60 years and older, an entitlement based on age regardless of health or other personal characteristics
- provides access, in-home, senior center, nutrition, employment, family caregiver support, transportation and legal assistance, and additional services based on local needs and resources
- established the federal Administration on Aging and the aging network comprising federal, state, and Area Agencies on Aging network
- 2015 appropriations: $1.9 billion

See Congressional Budget Office Cost Estimate (2015).

Medicare (established in 1965 under Social Security Act—Title XVIII)

- makes those eligible for old age insurance (commonly called Social Security) also eligible for the following health benefits:

  - Part A: coverage for hospital care

  - Part B: voluntary supplemental health insurance

  - Part C: Medicare + Choice: private insurance companies offering alternatives to the original Medicare plan

  - Part D: subsidization of prescription medication purchases for seniors

Medicaid (established in 1965 under Social Security Act—Title XIX)

- is a means-tested medical assistance program for categorically needy populations
- pays a significant amount of long-term care expenses and other health-related expenses for the older population

- allows waiver programs approved by the federal government to be used to support community-based programs for older adults

Patient Protection and Affordable Care Act (enacted 2010)

- mandated comprehensive health insurance reforms
- emphasized improved access, affordability, and quality in health care for Americans.
- included major initiatives to reduce health care spending
- added improvements to prescription drug coverage for seniors

SSI (established in 1972, began operations in 1974)

- means-tested program for low-income individuals
- a monthly amount is provided to people with limited income who are disabled, blind, or age 65 or older
- cash benefits are provided to assist with basic needs of food, clothing, and shelter
- persons who receive SSI benefits are eligible for Medicaid

Tax Code Provisions Related to Older Americans

- Social Security benefit payments taxed if individual's income is above a certain threshold
- credit given for elderly or disabled individual if person is age 65 years or older and if individual's income is below a certain threshold

Age Discrimination in Employment Act (enacted 1967)

- promotes the hiring of workers based on ability, not age, and prohibits age discrimination in employment
- later includes government employers under these requirements

Housing and Community Development Act (enacted 1974)

- introduced Section 8 subsidy program
- eligible individuals pay 30 percent of their adjusted monthly income for rent, and government subsidy pays the rest
- reinstated Section 202, which offers low-interest loans for construction of residential projects, resulting in reduced rental costs

Employee Retirement Income Security Act (enacted 1974)

- strengthens workers' rights regarding private pension plans
- requires employers to inform participants of their pension plan status, outlaws discrimination regarding who may participate, sets minimum standards for vesting, requires accountability in management of pension plans, and guarantees payment of certain benefits on termination of a plan

Consolidated Omnibus Budget Reconciliation Act (1986 and 1987)

- 1986: requires employers to continue accruing benefits for workers who continue past the normal retirement age
- 1987: lays out requirements for nursing homes, including minimum standards of care, staffing, and training; protects residents' rights and imposes a survey and certification process

Americans with Disabilities Act (enacted 1990)

- intends to end discrimination for individuals with disabilities
- prohibits discrimination in employment and in services, such as transportation, provided by public entities
- requires private businesses to be accessible for individuals with disabilities when it is "readily achievable"
- mandates access to telecommunications for those with hearing- or speech-related disabilities

National Affordable Housing Act (enacted 1990)

- separates housing development programs for older people from those of people with disabilities
- provides block grants for housing project improvements and rehabilitation

Family and Medical Leave Act (enacted 1993)

- requires employers with 50 or more employees to offer eligible workers up to 12 weeks of unpaid leave for various emergencies, including the care of an ill parent

Health Insurance Portability and Accountability Act (enacted 1996)

- includes protections for individuals who may have difficulty obtaining insurance because of health conditions

OBJECTIVE APPROACH TO POLICY ANALYSIS

To mitigate political reactions or emotional responses biasing policy-making decisions, practitioners can ensure a more objective process using a framework that systematically analyzes existing or proposed policies. A *policy analysis framework* is a model that proffers a set of questions whose answers will help practitioners determine whether the policy addresses the problem. An analysis of policy affecting older adults should focus on ascertaining whether a policy adequately attends to the needs of that population or target group. As advocates for older adults, social workers must ask how the policy will affect older Americans.

Policy Analysis Models

Karger and Stoesz Model. A number of policy analysis models exist. The Karger and Stoesz (2014) model contains a four-section framework:

1. Historical background of the policy, focusing on identifying the historical events that led up to the policy's development.
2. Description of the problem that necessitated the policy, identifying the problem's parameters: What is the nature, scope, and magnitude of the problem? How is the aging population affected by the problem?
3. Description of the policy, providing critical information such as how the policy works, the resources or opportunities it provides, who is covered by the policy, how it is to be implemented, expected goals and outcomes, funding issues, organizational auspices, and policy time frames.
4. Policy analysis, involving an in-depth and systematic examination of the policy goals and their political, economic, and administrative feasibility.

After examining these four areas, social workers then identify alternative policy options. It is recommended that social workers move forward with the policy alternative that is the most feasible from a political, economic, and administrative standpoint (Karger & Stoesz, 2014).

Kraft and Furlong Model. The straightforward model of Kraft and Furlong (2015) follows these five steps:

1. Define and analyze the problem.
2. Identify policy alternatives.
3. Develop criteria to evaluate the policy alternatives.
4. Use established evaluative criteria to assess the policy alternatives.
5. Make recommendations based on the assessment results.

Table 11.1 illustrates how practitioners may use Kraft and Furlong's (2015) model to analyze independent living options for older adults, including what type of information to obtain in conducting such an analysis.

Table 11.1: Analysis of Older Adults' Independent Living Options Using Policy Analysis Model

Step	Analysis of Specific Issues	Applications to Living Options
Define and analyze the problem	• What is the problem? • How did it develop? • Who is affected by it? • What are the major causes? • How might policy options affect the problem?	• How can older adults remain independent in the community after experiencing functional impairments? • How can older adults remain in the community safely? • Are family and friends affected by increased dependency?
Construct policy alternatives	• What are the policy options to consider?	• Does Medicare reimburse for assisted living to avoid nursing home placement? • Does Medicare pay for extended home care services to avoid nursing home placement? • Will the Senior Independence Act of 2006 (H.R. 5293) provide enough resources to support older adults in the community?
Develop evaluative criteria	• What are the costs? • How are societal values affected? Effectiveness? Efficiency? Equity? Social and political feasibility?	• What is the expense to society to preserve an older adult's independence? • Is it feasible for older adults to remain in the community with services? From a social perspective? From a political perspective? • What are the resources needed to keep older adults in the community?
Assess alternatives	• How does one distinguish between better and worse alternatives? • Does enough evidence exist to assess the alternatives? • Which are the better alternatives?	• Is it less expensive to provide community services over nursing home placement? • Are there enough community resources to enable elders to remain in the community? • Will the creation of aging and disability resource centers provide the support needed by older adults in the community?
Draw conclusions	• Which is the best or most desirable option given the political circumstances? • Which option performs the best in the evaluative criteria established?	• Could Medicare charge additional fees to support an increase in community services? • Are the services included under the Senior Independence Act comprehensive enough to enable older adults to remain at home?

DiNitto and Johnson Rational Model. DiNitto and Johnson (2016) offer a rational model of policy analysis, which emphasizes a cost–benefit approach to evaluation. The policy alternative that presents the most benefit for the least cost is the one recommended for adoption. Users of this model typically measure benefits and costs in economic terms; however, they may also apply this model to an evaluation of the social values of an approach. The rational model follows six steps:

1. Identify and define the social problem.
2. Identify and weigh all the values of society.
3. Identify and consider all alternative policies.
4. Weigh the consequences of each alternative as it relates to the target group affected and to society, and consider the effects each alternative will have on the present and future.
5. Conduct a cost–benefit analysis for each alternative.
6. Choose the policy alternative that yields the greatest benefit for the lowest cost. (DiNitto & Johnson, 2016, p. 5)

Bounded Rationality. The rational model requires the policy analyst to identify all values of the society and all possible alternative policies. Such an effort, including weighing the consequences of each alternative, is frequently more time-consuming than is feasible for the average practitioner. Consequently, policy analysts often use the more practical bounded rationality approach. This model, developed by Herbert A. Simon (1945), uses the principles of the rational model to analyze only a select number of alternatives. The practitioner evaluates a reasonable number of consequences and values and subsequently chooses the alternative that offers a desired benefit at the most reasonable cost (Simon, 1945).

Evaluation Frameworks

Social workers should systematically evaluate programs that provide services to older adults to determine whether these programs are meeting their goals and objectives and whether they are indeed providing services as intended. This process, called *program evaluation,* focuses on policy results or outcomes. One model, created by Rossi, Lipsey, and Freeman (2004), follows seven steps:

1. Identify program goals.
2. Identify the means by which the practitioner can measure the goals.
3. Identify the target group for which the program was designed—older adults in general or older adults who meet some predetermined criteria, such as income level or disability.
4. Identify the nontarget groups that might be affected by the program, such as family members or neighbors.

5. Using the measures developed in step 2, evaluate the program's effects on both the target and nontarget groups.
6. Evaluate the costs of the program compared with the allocated resources.
7. Identify indirect costs.

The following list provides a summary of the questions to ask in the program evaluation process (Rossi et al., 2004):

Program Conceptualization and Design Questions

- Is a social problem appropriately conceptualized?
- What is the extent of the problem and the distribution of the target population?
- Is the program designed to meet its intended objectives?
- Is there a coherent rationale underlying it?
- Have chances of successful delivery been maximized?
- What are the projected or existing costs?
- What is the relationship between costs and benefits?

Program Monitoring Questions

- Is the program reaching the specified target population?
- Are the intervention efforts being conducted as specified in the program design?

Program Utility Questions

- Is the program effective in achieving its intended goals?
- Can the results of the program be explained by some alternative process that does not include the program?
- What are the costs of delivery of services and benefits to program participants?
- Is the program an efficient use of resources compared with alternative uses of resources?

Using evaluation frameworks, social work practitioners can make informed decisions about which policies and programs are most effective and responsive to older adults. They can determine whether the available resources within a community are indeed meeting the needs of older adults and family members. Furthermore, evaluation frameworks allow social workers to analyze proposed revisions to existing policies to ascertain the benefits those revisions may have for older citizens.

Fairness in Practice

An evaluation may reveal inequities in the provision of resources and services to older adults. According to McNutt and Hoefer (2016), inequities related to gender and class still exist. For instance, the American retirement system currently disregards the contributions of both retired female caregivers and women who were career homemakers but were not compensated monetarily for their accomplishments. Similarly, the labor market devalues working-class elders as they age (Estes, 2001; McNutt & Hoefer, 2016).

Social workers can infuse equity into policy practice in a number of ways. One way is through the decision-making process involved in policy development (Kraft & Furlong, 2015). Practitioners may consider whether that process was fair and open. Did the decision makers come to their decision voluntarily, or were they coerced into making the decision? If practitioners find that the decision-making process did indeed meet the criteria of being fair, open, and voluntary, they may conclude that the process was equitable. This means of applying equity to policy practice concerns the policy-making process only; practitioners may judge the process as equitable, even though some individuals may fare better or worse as a result of the process (Noziak, 1974).

Social workers may also measure equity in terms of outcomes: Were the outcomes just, or was there a fair distribution of goods and services (Rawls, 1971)? Practitioners focus on programmatic equity—that is, from a service perspective how individuals are treated and how goods are distributed—and whether one group of individuals fares better or worse than another. Key to this focus is fair treatment, which J. P. Flynn (1985) defined as "the extent to which situations in similar circumstances are dealt with similarly" (p. 54). Chipungu (1991) pointed out that a program is inequitable if two people receive different services even though all other factors are the same.

Policy analysis frameworks may include equity as a process or outcome criterion. When analyzing a policy, practitioners may systematically review equity and its relationship to proposed policies and policy revisions. Equity is an important criterion for the evaluation of redistribution policies, such as tax reforms, enhancement of health services, or assistance to people with low income, and in debates in which one population clearly gains while another loses, such as the intergenerational equity conflict, which emphasizes what is fair for future generations (Kraft & Furlong, 2015). The intergenerational equity issue has created conflict between younger and older generations. The real issue is that all generations have needs that future policy development must address. An examination of equity in a particular policy might involve determining which group or category of people gains or loses as a result of the policy and which pays for the cost of the program.

Equity issues are dominant in the intergenerational equity debate (Kraft & Furlong, 2015), which, for example, is central in the dialogue over whether to preserve Social Security and Medicare. One side views these programs as a contract between the U.S. government and workers—a promise made to the older generation. The other side views the programs as an unfair burden to future generations, who will need to manage debt they had no role in creating (Kraft & Furlong, 2015).

Clearly, intergenerational equity issues are present in many national debates, including those on environmental and conservation issues. As the country continues to contend with the distribution of scarcer social and natural resources to accommodate a growing aging population, the intergeneration equity debate will continue to gain importance in policy practice.

Attention to Well-Being

Like equity in practice, another factor in the policy analysis process deserves social workers' attention—whether a policy benefits individual and societal well-being. How one defines well-being varies, making it difficult to ensure the well-being of all because policies affect people differently. Therefore, applying the teleological theory of utilitarianism to policy analysis may be the most effective way to protect the well-being of most older adults.

Users of a utilitarian approach decide what action to take and what rule to create by determining which one they expect will promote the greatest good (Frankena, 1973). The principle of utility directs that the result achieved be the greatest balance of good over evil (Frankena, 1973). Whatever satisfies that principle, Mill (1863/1957) has argued, also satisfies the principle of justice, which, according to Frankena (1973), is built into the principle of utility. Rule utilitarianism directs geriatric social workers to consider which rule, or in this case policy or policy alternative, will advance the general good for older adults. A critical question to ask is how do we achieve the greatest good for the greatest number of individuals? Consider the concept of aging in place. If policies and programs were reorganized around aging-in-place models, older adults would be able to remain independent longer, ensuring their good health while at the same time lowering health care costs (Rantz, 2016). More resources would then be available to assist a larger portion of older adults.

SHAPING POLICY THROUGH MACRO-PRACTICE

Social problems such as racism, sexism, classism, and ageism affect individuals and groups and may be embedded in institutions, policies, regulations, and communities. Therefore, they require broad interventions. Of all these problems, ageism has the widest effect on older adults, especially among minority elders. Ageism, or age prejudice, is a negative attitude toward or disposition about aging and older people based on the belief that aging makes people unattractive, unintelligent, asexual, unemployable, and mentally incompetent (Atchley & Barusch, 2004). Ageism may lead to age discrimination, the act of treating people unjustly based on their chronological age or older appearance (Atchley & Barusch, 2004), which promotes the exclusion of older adults from society.

To meet the needs of the older adult population effectively, practitioners may address ageism and age discrimination in practice by using political advocacy and community organization skills. These skills form what is called *macro–social work practice,* defined by Brueggemann (2014) as helping people resolve issues and problems through community, organizational, societal, and global interventions.

POLITICAL ADVOCACY

The intent of political advocacy is to eliminate or lessen the inequalities that exist in society for older adults. Inequalities, according to Jansson (2014), result from a deprivation of material resources; mental, emotional, or cognitive abilities; opportunities; interpersonal connections; personal rights; and physical abilities. Political advocacy focuses on efforts to help powerless individuals and groups improve their situation (Jansson, 2014).

Social workers as political advocates must start with this question: What are the structural or environmental factors that create or intensify the problems of older adults? Once they have identified the problem, practitioners must establish what policies or regulations require change. Does policy change need to occur at the federal, state, local, or organizational level? To be effective in changing policy, advocates must be skilled at

- Developing a vision: They must ask, what is the ideal state for which they strive? The ideal state is shaped by values, beliefs, and ideology.

- Seeking opportunities for policy advocacy: Practitioners must identify where change needs to occur. They might join interest groups or other organizations to effect policy change. They might help mobilize change by participating in community forums, writing letters, working with the media, or using other resources.

- Taking sensible risks: They ought to assess what is a doable and reasonable change and move toward effecting that change.

- Balancing flexibility with planning: Political advocates need to develop a plan of action that includes tasks to be accomplished but must be prepared to change the plan based on the situational realities they encounter.

- Developing multiple skills: Social workers must possess analytic, political, interactional, and value-clarification skills to affect the policy process.

- Being persistent: Perseverance is required even when facing defeats and obstacles. Practitioners must be mindful of their original vision.

- Tolerating uncertainty: The political process is unpredictable. Advocates must learn to deal with changes in the process.

- Combining pragmatism with principles: Frequently, people must make mutual concessions during the political process. Political advocates must be able to consider alternative options and choose the solution that does not substantially compromise their vision. (Jansson, 2014)

Political advocacy requires skills and competencies different from social work practice skills used with individuals. Political advocacy is a much needed intervention that, when used appropriately, can protect the rights of older adults and move society toward equality of treatment of older adults.

COMMUNITY ORGANIZATION

Community organization is another practice method that allows social workers to lessen the effects of ageism. It is a process by which people in neighborhood organizations, associations, and places of worship join forces to combat community social problems and, with the help of government and corporations, implement solutions to those problems.

The following five-step model, proposed by Brueggemann (2014), enables social workers to help resolve community issues affecting older adults:

1. Define the problem: Assist the community in identifying areas of oppression on which they wish to work. Keep in mind that it is important that members of the community themselves define the problem. For example, they might choose a senior housing project in need of repair, recommend that the community's senior center increase services, or suggest that the community develop an intergenerational day care program.

2. Engage the community: Gain an understanding of the community and its people. How do people really feel about an issue? How can the practitioner or organizer join with the community so that he or she is perceived as a helping agent rather than an intruder?

3. Empower forces of change: Enable people to mobilize so that they may move their community into a position of change. The organizer needs to think of ways to entice people to be a part of the solution. Perhaps he or she may point out the injustices that older adults experience or emphasize how important community members' involvement is in effecting change.

4. Build an organization: As people become interested in being part of the change process, schedule a series of meetings to build a structure, such as a task force or coalition, to guide the operation, assignments, strategies, and time lines. The focus of the meetings should be on moving people toward decision making and action. Help participants to identify leaders and then train those leaders. Review and evaluate strategies, celebrate victories, regroup, and move on to other issues.

5. Evaluate and terminate: Evaluate progress toward resolving the problem and facilitate an organizational assessment. It is important that the organizer spend considerable time disengaging from the process.

CONCLUSION

Finally, practitioners may involve a number of community organizations in efforts to evoke positive change. Those organizations known for their advocacy work on behalf of older adults include AARP, Gray Panthers, and the Older

Women's League. Among the professional organizations that advance the aging agenda are the American Society on Aging, National Council on Aging, Gerontological Society of America, and Association for Gerontology in Higher Education (see list in Additional Resources for a brief description of the aforementioned organizations' Web sites). Many of the professional and advocacy organizations listed at the end of this chapter have been and continue to be instrumental in moving the aging agenda forward and in the promotion of political activism. Connecting with these groups is a good starting point for gerontological social workers to become politically active so that they may begin to define the problems and issues requiring change.

As the United States grapples with an increasing older adult population, society will be in a quandary about how it can continue to provide needed services at an affordable level. Public retirement income, private pensions, the financing of health care, and how to encourage older people to remain in the workforce are but a few of the policy issues society will face (Atchley & Barusch, 2004). Social workers have much to contribute to the debates on these issues and are in an important position to influence and shape policy affecting older adults.

Case Study: Macro Issues That Affect the Stanley Family

There are several policy issues that are related to grandparents who are raising their grandchildren (cf. C. B. Cox, 2010). One is the lack of financial resources that are available to custodial grandparents if they are raising their grandchildren outside of formal systems (for example, adoption, legal guardianship). Individuals like Mrs. Stanley are making an extremely large contribution to the child welfare system. One estimate is that grandparents and other caregivers save the United States $6.5 billion per year by keeping children out of the foster care system (Generations United, 2016). Mrs. Stanley assumed care when her grandchildren were about to enter the foster care system because of severe neglect from their mother. With this type of crisis, there is limited time to prepare or even consider various options. As with Mrs. Stanley, the goal was to get Jasmine and Terrell into a safe environment.

Housing is a huge policy issue for many custodial grandparents, especially for those who rent their home. Social workers in this area of practice often face situations where grandparents may not be able to stay in public housing when multiple grandchildren come into their care. Two policy initiatives are available to help families be able to stay in their home. The U.S. Department of Housing and Urban Development administers a Family Unification Program that prioritizes providing housing to families who are at risk of losing custody of their children because of inadequate housing arrangements. In addition, Section 202 Supportive Housing for the Elderly Program funds nonprofit developers to build subsidized rental housing for older people. Children are allowed to live with family members; however, there are long waiting lists for this type of housing. For example, C. B. Cox (2010) cited data from New York City showing that the average wait for Section 202 housing is between eight and 10 years.

Part of policy practice is helping custodial grandparents themselves share their experience and advocate for more supportive policy. One way is to bring these grandparents together to "speak in a united voice" about their experiences. An example of political action for grandparent-headed families were the GrandRallys, held in Washington, DC (http://cdf.childrensdefense.org/site/PageServer?pagename=grandrally_action). Cosponsored by a number of organizations in aging, child welfare, and family services, the rallies brought over 1,000 grandparents together to share their stories and meet elected officials. Although Mrs. Stanley did not attend one of the national rallies, smaller local initiatives were developed and Mrs. Stanley was able to attend one of these events and meet with her national officials in her own state.

WHAT WE LEARNED IN THIS CHAPTER

- The elements of a policy practice framework
- How to gather information about community policies and programs to identify gaps in services and resources for older adults
- How to conduct a policy analysis on policies relevant to older adults, using several policy analysis models
- How to apply program evaluation models to determine program effectiveness
- Fairness-in-practice concepts as they relate to older adults
- How to address ageism through macro-practice, including policy advocacy and community organization

SUGGESTED EXERCISE TO EVALUATE STUDENT COMPETENCE

Using Jansson's (2014) policy analysis framework discussed in this chapter, students will select and analyze a policy under consideration nationally or in their state. The following framework offers an organized approach to engaging in policy practice:

- Learn the contextual setting of the environment, and identify factors that affect policy.
- Obtain, analyze, and use the opinions of multiple participants engaged in policy formation.

- Perform at least one policy practice task: agenda setting, problem analysis, proposal writing, or policy assessment.

ADDITIONAL RESOURCES

The Centers for Medicare and Medicaid Services administers such health programs as Medicare, Medicaid, and the health insurance marketplace. For policy information, regulations, research, reports, and educational opportunities, go to https://www.cms.gov.

The Henry J. Kaiser Family Foundation Health Reform Section provides current information on research and analyses on health reform initiatives, including policy analysis reports, public polls, and position papers. Visit http://healthreform.kff.org.

The Henry J. Kaiser Family Foundation's Web page on Medicare provides current information on Medicare, including policy analysis reports, public polls, and position papers. Go to http://www.kff.org/medicare/.

A document that explains the Housing for Older Persons Act may be located at www.hud.gov/offices/fheo/library/hopa95.pdf.

Influencing State Policy is a nonprofit organization whose mission is to prepare social workers for active roles in shaping social policies. For more information, go to http://www.statepolicy.org/.

Justice in Aging works to reduce senior poverty and health and wealth disparities through legal means. For training and resource information, go to http://www.nsclc.org.

The National Aging and Disability Transportation Center promotes availability and accessibility of transportation options for older adults, people with disabilities, caregivers, and communities. For training, resources, and grant information, visit http://www.nadtc.org/.

The National Caucus and Center on Black Aging is an advocacy organization dedicated to aging issues, with a special focus on minority and low-income aging. For resources and other information, visit http://www.ncba-aged.org/.

The National Resource Center on Nutrition and Aging's purpose is to build capacity of the aging services network to provide nutritional services to older adults and to provide training and technical assistance on nutritional services to the aging network. Visit http://nutritionandaging.org.

National trade and professional associations of the United States. (2016). Bethesda, MD: Association Executives.

Notten, L. (Ed.). (2014–2015). *Washington information directory.* Thousand Oaks, CA: CQ Press.

The RAND Corporation is a research organization that focuses on public policy challenges. One policy focus area is population and aging. For resources, educational opportunities, articles, and reports, go to https://www.rand.org/.

Swartout, K. (Ed.). (2015). *Encyclopedia of associations: National organizations of the U.S.* (54th ed., Vols. 1–3). Farmington Hills, MI: Thompson Gale.

The Urban Institute provides resources in the form of policy briefs, policy analyses, research, training, and education on social and economic policy, including retirement, health care, aging, and poverty. Visit www.urban.org.

The U.S. Department of Housing and Urban Development provides information and resources for senior citizens, including federal housing programs for seniors, reverse mortgages, affordable housing, and housing discrimination. Visit https://portal.hud.gov/hudportal/HUD?src=/topics/information_for_senior_citizens.

WEB SITES OF PROFESSIONAL, GOVERNMENT, AND ADVOCACY ORGANIZATIONS (ALPHABETICAL BY URL):

http://www.aagponline.org/   The American Association for Geriatric Psychiatry is an organization composed of practitioners, researchers, educators, students, and anyone who is interested in improving the mental health of older people.

https://www.aarp.org   AARP, formerly known as the American Association of Retired Persons, is an advocacy organization for older Americans. This Web site contains data and research on a variety of issues.

https://www.access.gpo.gov   This site provides access to the federal Government Printing Office and is a source for locating government documents.

https://www.acl.gov   The Administration for Community Living's government Web site features resources and information on programs and services related to the Older Americans Act.

https://www.aghe.org   The Association for Gerontology in Higher Education features programs and resources to advance aging content in higher education curricula.

http://agingsociety.org   The National Academy on an Aging Society, a nonpartisan public policy institute, contains information on issues related to population aging.

http://www.alz.org/index.asp   The Alzheimer's Association is the leading voluntary health organization in Alzheimer's care, support, and research.

https://www.americangeriatrics.org   The American Geriatrics Society is a not-for-profit organization of health professionals dedicated to improving the health, independence, and quality of life of older adults.

http://asaging.org   The American Society on Aging offers educational resources for professionals working in gerontology.

http://cbo.gov   The Congressional Budget Office provides analyses of economic and budget issues.

http://cms.hhs.gov   The U.S. Department of Health and Human Services Web site features access to the Centers for Medicare and Medicaid Services. It includes links to federal and state health care programs.

http://csg.org   The Council of State Governments features links to the government home pages for all 50 states and to public policy think tanks.

https://www.fedstats.sites.usa.gov   This site contains federal data on policy problems.

http://www.gao.gov   The Government Accountability Office, formerly called the General Accounting Office, provides access to government agency and program reports, including evaluation studies.

http://geron.org   The Gerontological Society of America provides information on research and educational resources that focus on older adults.

http://graypanthers.org   The Gray Panthers, an advocacy group that works on a variety of issues affecting older adults, offers information and resources on advocacy and includes a guide to local networks.

http://ncoa.org   The National Council on Aging, which is dedicated to improving the health and independence of older persons, provides information on programs, action alerts, and policies affecting older adults.

http://www.ncpssm.org/   The National Committee to Preserve Social Security and Medicare is an advocacy organization dedicated to preserving Social Security, Medicare, and Medicaid.

http://owl-national.org   The Older Women's League, the only organization that currently focuses on issues unique to women as they age, features advocacy and policy information and contains a directory of local chapters.

http://publicagenda.org   This Web site features nonpartisan briefings on policy, polls, news, legislation, studies, and research.

https://www.sageusa.org   SAGE is an advocacy organization for lesbian, gay, bisexual, and transgender senior citizens.

http://socsec.org   The Social Security Network features reports and analyses on social security and offers links to other Web sites containing information on social security.

https://www.ssa.gov   The Social Security Administration offers comprehensive information on the Social Security program.

http://www.congress.gov   This site features a comprehensive search engine for locating congressional documents in the Library of Congress collection.

https://www.usa.gov   This Web site is the online guide to government information and services.

http://www.uscourts.gov   This is the Web site for the U.S. judiciary system.

https://www.whitehouse.gov   This is the site for the White House.

12

Geriatric Case Management: Assembling a Broad Repertoire of Practice Skills

CASE MANAGEMENT

RATIONALE: "Social workers value the importance of interprofessional team-work and communication in interventions, recognizing that beneficial outcomes may require interdisciplinary, interprofessional, and interorganizational collaboration" (CSWE, 2015, p. 9). "Gerosocial workers value and draw on strengths-based and person/family-centered approaches to ensure that interventions are consistent with mutually agreed on goals at the individual, family, group, organization, and community level. They use technological resources, when appropriate, to improve quality of care. Practitioners in aging advocate to improve access, coordination, and quality across a continuum of medical, community, and social services" (CSWE, 2017, p. 99).

COMPETENCY: "Practitioners in aging with, and on behalf of, older adults and their constituencies

- promote older adults' social support systems and engagement in families, groups, and communities.

- provide person-centered and family-directed interventions that take into account life course disparities and are targeted to diverse populations, groups, organizations, and communities.

- assess for quality and access a range of services, supports, and care options including groups and technology, for older adults and their families to assure optimal interdependence.

- monitor and modify interventions as needed to respond to individual, family, and environmental challenges." (CSWE, 2017, pp. 99–100)

RESEARCH

RATIONALE: "Social workers understand that evidence that informs practice derives from multi-disciplinary sources and multiple ways of knowing. They also understand the processes for translating research findings into effective practice" (CSWE, 2015, p. 8).

COMPETENCY: "Practitioners in aging with, and on behalf of, older adults and their constituencies

- understand and build knowledge central to maximizing the well-being of older adults and their caregivers.
- adopt, modify, and translate evidence informed practices that are most appropriate to particular aging focused practice settings" (CSWE, 2017, p. 49).

EVALUATION

RATIONALE: "Social workers recognize the importance of evaluating processes and outcomes to advance practice, policy, and service delivery effectiveness. Social workers understand qualitative and quantitative methods for evaluating outcomes and practice effectiveness" (CSWE, 2015, p. 9).

COMPETENCY: "Practitioners in aging with, and on behalf of, older adults and their constituencies

- plan and conduct evaluations to continuously improve programs, policies, and practice impacting older adults and their caregivers.
- use and translate evaluation outcomes to enhance the effectiveness and sustainability of programs, policies, and practice for an aging society." (CSWE, 2017, p. 109)

Case managers may come from various disciplines and backgrounds; however, they are typically either graduate-level nurses or social workers with professional designations or certifications. Several job titles may be used to classify positions that are similar to case management, such as care manager, care coordinator, or patient navigator (NASW, 2013). The basis for these roles is historically rooted in the social work profession. Case coordination—the precursor to the current practice method—is one of the earliest forms of professional social work practice. A part of the first Board of Charities, case coordination involved organizing services and conserving funds to provide care for sick and impoverished people. During the late 1800s and early 1900s, *charity organization societies* sprang up in the United States, largely as a response to the social conditions that were occurring as a result of increased industrialization (Popple, 2013). These included poverty, urbanization, immigration, and population growth. Case management was a practice role that was prominent in the settlement house movement, which also occurred during this period (Frankel & Gelman, 1998; Naleppa & Reid, 2003). Case managers have historically been part of social work practice with clients who have multiple and complex service needs that span various service delivery sectors.

As a result of demographic trends, an increasingly aging population calls for even greater numbers of case managers (Greene & Kropf, 2017). Social workers, with their dual focus on the person-in-environment configuration, have the requisite knowledge and skill set to function as geriatric case managers or to serve other populations that may be considered vulnerable because of limited cognitive or physical ability (Rothman, 1994). Geriatric case managers play an important role in promoting and preserving older adults' functioning, helping older clients and families in complex decision making, and securing resources to promote safety and security for individuals and their caregivers.

The competencies defined in this chapter address the social work roles and skills necessary for effective case management practice. As case manager, the social worker must be able to complete a comprehensive biopsychosocial assessment of the older client to determine that person's needs or challenges and strengths or assets. Too often, case management services focus primarily on an older client's limitations or problem situations. Older adults, however, are resilient; therefore, case managers must include clients' survivorship within their understanding of each older adult's history and current life situation. Lewis and Harrell (2002) offered a model to foster resilience in practice with older adults. The model, which provides a framework for case management with that particular population, has three components:

1. promoting affiliations, which involves expanding the meaning of social relationships; being sensitive to issues related to one's culture, ethnicity, and sexual orientation; and creating culturally responsive services for the older population within services systems;

2. enhancing safety and support, such as including the client's perception of his or her interpersonal functioning; promoting trust within the worker–client relationship; exploring environmental and cultural dynamics; and being sensitive to the client's expression of self-determination; and

3. fostering altruism, that is, focusing on reciprocity within the client's social relationships; exploring the client's need for social connectedness and related values; and identifying the client's linkages with extended family and indigenous groups, including clubs, self-help groups, churches, synagogues, and mosques.

These three principles assist the case manager in understanding the older client's social and emotional values and history as they relate to that person's physical and environmental resource needs.

Effective case managers must have a thorough knowledge of resources within the environment that may benefit the client and family. To enhance client functioning, managers may use formal sources of support (for example, respite care, volunteer opportunities, or health care options) and informal sources (such as social support systems or personal assets). They can then construct the information they have acquired from those resources into a services plan with measurable goals and objectives to be evaluated later. Furthermore, they can be change agents, helping to transform fragmented services delivery practices into comprehensive services systems.

WHAT IS GERIATRIC CASE MANAGEMENT?

Case Management Defined

Because social work is one of the primary disciplines to serve in case management roles, the National Association of Social Workers (NASW) has promulgated standards for social work case management (NASW, 2013). Within these standards, *case management* is defined as

> a process to plan, seek, advocate for, and monitor services from different social services or health care organizations and staff on behalf of a client. The process enables social workers in an organization, or in different organizations, to coordinate their efforts to serve a given client through professional teamwork, thus expanding the range of needed services offered. Case management limits problems arising from fragmentation of services, staff turnover, and inadequate coordination among providers. (NASW, 2013, p. 13)

As this definition suggestions, case management includes broad and diverse activities and outcomes (Sullivan & Fisher, 1994).

In an attempt to determine the core content of case management, Genrich and Neatherlin (2001) performed a content analysis of published literature on that practice method. After reviewing a total of 228 published articles, they determined that the common role components were

- being able to establish strong interpersonal relationships
- developing plans that foster appropriate use of resources
- engaging in the study of populations for problem identification and plans of action
- pursuing activities directed at monitoring and tracking institutional and community efforts
- implementing research to measure outcomes
- developing and implementing plans that reflect awareness of fiscal issues and trends
- conducting cost-effectiveness analysis.

In a similar study, Bowers and Jacobson (2002) interviewed long-term care case managers who were identified as "excellent" or "very good" by professional supervisors, colleagues, and consumers of their services. The goal of the interviews was to determine how this small group of case managers (N = 16) viewed their positions. An analysis of the transcripts revealed a number of common principles identified by the highly rated case managers and included (a) honoring rules and regulations, allowing for some flexibility when possible; (b) supporting their clients who were taking risks; (c) cultivating and maintaining good, positive relationships; (d) managing with flexibility; (e) listening to and engaging with their clients, basing their approach on the knowledge of who their clients are; and (f) relating to and relying on their supervisors (Bowers & Jacobson, 2002).

Geriatric Case Management

Although geriatric case management is certainly a form of case management, some of its practice aspects are unique. An important focus of case management with the older population is the preservation of functioning and emphasis on quality of life issues for both the older adult and family members. Cress (2015) defined a *geriatric case manager* as a professional who typically intervenes with the older individual or family to remediate a crisis, prevent challenges from occurring, or enhance peace of mind and quality of life. Aspects of geriatric case management include smaller caseloads than those of case managers working in other settings and personalized service plans to promote and preserve functioning for older clients. In addition, geriatric case managers may work with families who are geographically distant from their older family member, helping them connect to services and address complicated decisions about care. As Cress stressed, "The [geriatric case manager's] product is service, and that product must be available at all times to be useful to older people [and], their families" (2015, p. 3).

Other authors have promoted strengths-based case management models for older adults. Fast and Chapin (2000) stressed that illness, disease, or other challenges in functioning are only one part of the picture—and not the most important part. In their conceptualization,

> problems become a backdrop rather than the foreground of the client–care manager relationship. The client is perceived as having a range of experiences, characteristics, and roles that determine who he or she is, rather than as someone who is old, disabled, or chronically ill. (pp. 1–2)

Optimal outcomes achieved through strengths-based case management include optimizing client living arrangements, vocational activities, and use of leisure time (Sullivan & Fisher, 1994). Fast and Chapin (2000) presented those principles forming the foundation of strengths-based case management practice as

- discovering and building on strengths rather than problems, which facilitates hope and self-reliance
- recognizing that older adults have the power to learn, grow, and change

- realizing that relationship building is essential to effective efforts to help clients
- encouraging older people to participate in decisions, make choices, and determine the direction of the helping process
- reaching out assertively to all community agencies for resources. (pp. 7–9)

CONTEXTS

As people age, physical, emotional, and social issues may present challenges requiring resources beyond those currently available to them. Geriatric case managers can assist older adults during transitions—such as retirement or widowhood—by connecting them to additional sources of support, providing continuous monitoring to determine whether current levels of support and functioning are adequate, and offering assistance to care providers. Case managers may also support families in their decision making about issues involving possible transitions; for instance, they may help older parents of adult sons or daughters with disabilities by addressing the need for permanency planning.

Crises and transitions are frequently a gateway for case managers to intervene and assist older clients to deal with complex care plans or comorbidity issues. A recent health diagnosis, for example, may necessitate that an older adult restructure lifestyle patterns by increasing exercise or using supportive or adaptive equipment, or the diagnosis may lead to a struggle with other challenges, such as the onset of depression or fatigue. After summarizing several case management models for older diabetics, DeCoster (2008) reported that case management is effective in reducing depression, enhancing functional abilities, and increasing knowledge about the disease. Another area where there is a need for coordinated care services is the transition from an acute setting, such as after discharge from a hospitalization. During this critical period, care plans need to be carefully established and monitored to avoid additional health risks and readmissions (Engel, Spencer, Paul, & Boardman, 2016; Volland & Blockberger-Miller, 2015).

Other case management programs focus on care provision. Project Healthy Grandparents is one such program that has received international attention (Whitley, Kelley, & Campos, 2013). Using a strengths-based model, practitioners partner with medical and legal professionals to provide health, social, and legal services to grandparents who are raising their grandchildren. Program results have suggested that the model fosters a sense of independence and self-assurance among grandparents, thus enhancing their level of confidence to nurture and support their grandchildren, and enables social workers and grandparents to establish linkages and supports with other families and resources within the community (Campbell, Carthron, Miles, & Brown, 2012; Kelley & Whitley, 2003; Robinson, Kropf, & Myers, 2000).

CASE MANAGERS' REPERTOIRE OF SKILLS

To serve older adults who are fast becoming part of a number of service delivery sectors effectively, the case manager will need to assemble a broad repertoire of practice skills. Because the focus of case management is on both the individual and the larger environment, social workers striving to become effective, competent geriatric case managers must draw skills from their work with individuals, families, and the community and from their roles as advocates and change agents.

Sensitive Relationship Building

The skill of engagement is critical to social work practice; therefore, it is not surprising that case managers must be especially sensitive in initial interactions with their clients. The complexity of service needs in many situations involving older clients with multiple needs requires practitioners to have a solid understanding of functioning and abilities. This comprehensive knowledge is based on a relationship that is established between the case manager and client and includes an assessment of assets and functional abilities, as well as needs and challenges (Cristofalo et al., 2016).

A frequent point of intervention by case managers is during major transitions or crises, when an older adult is dealing with change on many levels. As the strengths-based approach indicates, the client is an individual with a unique life history, current set of strengths and resources, and particular needs and challenges. These client dimensions are an essential part in structuring the initial engagement and relationship development phases.

It is not unusual for a case manager to initially engage with an older adult in the client's home. Households may be dangerous environments for older adults because the older body may be less able to manage some of the more difficult household tasks—for example, carrying laundry into the basement, reaching top shelves, or navigating dark hallways—as efficiently as during younger years. The CDC's (2005) "Check for Safety: A Home Fall Prevention Checklist for Older Adults" demonstrate how critical this issue is for older adults, their families, and health care costs:

- Every year more than 2.5 million older adults are treated in emergency departments for falls.
- Twenty percent of these falls result in a serious injury such as a traumatic brain injury or hip fracture.
- Direct costs for fall injuries is $31 billion annually, with two-thirds of this amount for hospitalizations.
- Even if a person is not seriously injured, the increased fear of falling raises the probability of future falls.

With a comprehensive assessment, many falls are preventable with modifications in behavior and the environment (Ambrose, Paul, & Hausdorff, 2013). For example, a retrospective study of emergency department records over a seven-year period reported that 72.8 percent of those recorded fell within the home. The majority of those treated were associated with worn or unsecured carpeting, and a frequent problem was the transition between two surfaces, such as carpeted to noncarpeted areas (Rosen, Macka, & Noonan, 2013). Case managers work within an older adult's home environment to keep the client safe and reduce the risk of accidents. As people face increasingly difficult living conditions, managers can assess what environmental modifications or required home maintenance is necessary to help older adults remain in their homes and communities. In addition, case managers can help older clients modify behaviors, such as wearing sturdy shoes instead of bedroom slippers (which are less substantial) while walking down stairs.

Older homeowners often live in older structures of a size more suitable to when their children lived with them. Now those homeowners may no longer be able to carry out regular maintenance or required repairs, thus leading to safety problems. If the situation is left unchanged, deteriorating conditions may lead to the condemnation of the houses.

Reasons for not undertaking needed maintenance and repairs include high cost, inability to make repairs because of poor health, and not knowing how to make repairs. Types of formal assistance include the following programs: neighborhood conservation, emergency repair, repair and maintenance, and weatherization. Local private businesses may undertake smaller repair and maintenance jobs. The following list provides a task-centered case management example from Naleppa and Reid (2000) for working with older clients living in households with deteriorating conditions.

- Assess the home for safety and need for repairs. As necessary, refer to a resource index on home safety issues, such as the Safety for Older Consumers: Home Safety Checklist (document no. 701), available online from the U.S. Consumer Product Safety Commission at https://www.cpsc.gov/home/safety-older-consumers-home-checklist.

- Discuss potentially required repairs with the client and indicate which repairs are health and safety priorities.

- Assist the client in selecting the repairs that should be undertaken.

- Identify whether informal support systems can help with the repairs.

- If the home requires professional repair or maintenance help is needed, assist with the contact as needed and help the client research prices. (Note that AARP or Area Agencies on Aging, among other organizations, may provide information on discount plans.)

- Establish whether maintenance or repair programs are available and establish eligibility.

- Assist the client with arranging for repairs to be completed.

Case managers not only work with community-based clients but also serve older adults in long-term care facilities. In this practice context, they may be responsible for coordinating services, for example, acute care and long-term care resources. In an evaluation of case manager services in rural long-term care models, Schrader and Britt (2001) found that working in long-term care, especially in areas with limited resources, requires an integrated model of care. Case managers play a vital role: They may provide information across multiple and geographically disparate health care providers.

Furthermore, they may help clients and older adults in complex decision making, such as when a person with dementia needs to move into a more safe and secure residential situation. Relocations can be difficult and traumatic for older adults, especially if there is cognitive decline. Case managers can introduce strategies to decrease negative outcomes and facilitate adjustment into long-term care settings, to help clients transition into their new environment (Aminzadeh, Molnar, Dalziel, & Garcia, 2013; Löfqvist et al., 2013).

Regardless of the context, a challenge for a case manager is to engage with clients who may be challenging or resistant to intervention. As part of the assessment process, the practitioner should consider these dynamics within the relationship—that is, what might be happening with the older client that could create a sense of mistrust or reluctance to receive assistance or aid?

There are many possible reasons that should be considered within the assessment process. One possibility is that older clients fear that their independence might be curtailed. If the reason is to provide additional support, such as contracting with home care providers, the older adult might be hesitant to engage with the practitioner. Another reason might be transference or countertransference issues between the older client and the case manager. In these situations, an older client might believe that the case manager cannot possibly be helpful—for example, she or he is too young to understand or is of a different race, ethnicity, or gender. Likewise, the case manager might display countertransference that also hinders relationship development. If the case manager is experiencing challenges in developing a relationship, it is a good practice for him or her to seek supervision about the situation. The perspective of a supervisor can be helpful in understanding the dynamics and providing useful assistance in this phase of building a relationship with the client.

Appropriate Resources and Services

The most important service that social workers provide to older adults and their caregivers is assisting clients to locate needed resources (Naito-Chan, Damron-Rodriguez, & Simmons, 2004). On face value, linking clients and their families with resources within their environment may sound like a relatively simple task: The client presents with a particular need, the social worker finds a resource in the community that delivers services in that area, and the two are connected. That process, though, is frequently much more involved and complicated than it might appear at first. Case managers must possess a multitude of skills to successfully link clients with resources, including the ability to motivate clients to access resources, convince clients to accept help, and advocate on behalf of clients to ensure that their needs are adequately served.

Consider the older adult who requires support from in-home services, such as a homemaker or a home health care worker. Although such services may be necessary to ensure the client's safety and well-being, the older adult may find it difficult to accept such a level of "intrusion." In this case, the compassionate case manager can assist with the client's perceptions of his or her own declining health or functional status—termed "brokenness" by Nowitz (2005). It is apparent that case managers must intervene in the psychosocial issues that clients face in receiving services. Instead of viewing clients as "resistive" or "uncooperative," managers must listen for ways in which clients are asking for help in relinquishing aspects of their independence.

Case managers also need to intervene to ensure that older clients do indeed receive services. Ageism, oppression and discrimination based on chronological age, can compromise older adults' ability to receive adequate services, particularly in health care. When health care providers use age to explain the cause of an older adult's health condition, that health issue and perhaps other conditions that might be amenable to treatment or cure might go undiagnosed.

Sadly, inattention or neglect is not limited to an older client's physical health. Significant numbers of older adults have mental health needs, with geriatric depression and anxiety being the two most prevalent conditions (Adamek & Slater, 2009). Unfortunately, older adults are less likely than younger cohorts to receive professional treatment for a mental health diagnosis. Estimates suggest that less than 30 percent of older adults who experience a mental health disorder receive treatment for their condition (Akincigil et al., 2011; Byers, Arean, & Yaffe, 2012). Clearly, many older adults would benefit from connection to mental health services and coordination with other services that they are receiving (for example, health care, insurance) (Choi, Kunik, & Wilson, 2013).

Case managers play an essential role in coordinating health and mental health providers to ensure comprehensive care of older clients. An example of a geriatric case management system for adults who are depressed was described by Enguidanos, Davis, and Katz (2005). In their model, the case manager performed a number of tasks, including communicating with the primary care physician about the client's mental health issues, obtaining a referral to a geriatrician for psychiatric evaluation of the client, holding a family conference to discuss treatment issues, and identifying safety issues for remaining in the home. Clearly, the case manager plays an important role in ensuring that older clients receive comprehensive and appropriate support in dealing with depression.

A Network of Alliances

Knowledge about resources within the community is a vital case management tool. Case managers must develop positive relationships with other services providers to create a robust network of alliances within the community. Such relationships are invaluable when working to connect clients with existing resources.

Ample opportunities exist to be creative in securing resources. Case managers, however, need to look beyond the "usual suspects" of available services to other sources of support for families. For example, consider the situation of an older couple who was raising their grandson (Myers, Kropf, & Robinson, 2002). The family lived in a rural county and was very isolated. As part of the services plan, the case manager identified recreational and leisure opportunities for the grandson. The grandson decided that he wanted to join a Little League baseball team, so the case manager assisted the grandparents with getting him signed up, secured a donation of a uniform (which the family could not afford), and even attended a few games with the family. That recreational outlet provided the grandparents with a respite from the caregiving role, a social outlet to meet other families with similarly aged children, and integration into their community. The most poignant moment came when their grandson hit a home run and got to be the team hero. The sense of pride shared by the whole family was immeasurable.

Clients themselves may have resources to contribute to a care management plan, and case managers can assist them in identifying those potential resources, which may include friends and neighbors. Moreover, managers can help older clients and their families handle the coordination of informal support systems. For example, the manager may work with "distant caregivers" who live away from their older family member (Cress, 2015). In such a situation, the social worker might ask the older adult to identify neighbors who could keep an eye on the older adult and contact the family if something seems amiss (for example, if newspapers and mail pile up or no lights are on in the home). If a risky situation should arise, the case manager could mobilize the client's informal network to articulate an action plan.

Services Plan

An important case management role is assessing clients' level of functioning and presenting need and investigating available resources and supports. The case manager and the client, with the family, if appropriate, should establish the services plan together. According to systems theory, one can achieve an outcome in a number of ways—a concept known as *equifinality* (Anderson & Carter, 1990). Therefore, in choosing a particular course of action, the case manager should encourage the older client's input as much as possible and allow the client to state his or her preferences. For example, some older adults may find that support groups are extremely helpful in enabling them to cope after a significant loss, such as the death of a spouse or partner. Other older individuals, though, may not be "joiners" and thus may perceive group interactions as stressful or intrusive. If a goal is to enhance the older adult's coping skills, strategies might include suggesting that the client participate in an online discussion board or group; read helpful works on grief, loss, and recovery; or engage in journaling.

Even the most comprehensive services plans need periodic review and reevaluation. For some clients, the services plan may provide relief or have a restorative function, or a review of the plan might indicate it is no longer needed.

For example, a widowed client may reach a point at which he or she is incorporating the loss and is ready to resume relationships and roles. After attending a grief and loss support group, the client might decide he or she is ready to leave the group and assume a volunteer position within the community. Such an outcome is a good indicator that the intervention successfully provided support to the client when needed during the grief process.

The case manager, though, must continually reevaluate services plans addressing physical or cognitive changes that are part of a disease process—especially for clients with dementia, a progressive and incurable condition. Services plans must take into account multiple factors, including clients' level of safety in the current environment, other existing health issues, and care providers' quality of life (Reilly et al., 2015). As a client's condition changes, the case manager will need to review and revise the services plan to ensure that it is relevant and continues to meet the client's and family's level of need.

Cost-Effectiveness of Services Delivery

The competencies discussed thus far have described practice-related knowledge and skills. Another major case management responsibility, involves work from a more fiscal or budgetary point of view: determining cost-effective methods of delivering services to clients. As health care services continue to shrink, services are being organized around acute care versus chronic care needs. However, many older adults require case management for long-term and progressive conditions, such as dementia.

A variety of sources may pay for case management services (Cress, 2015). Some services are funded by federal dollars from agencies such as the U.S. Department of Veteran Affairs, others are funded through various community-based aging agencies, and clients themselves may be private-pay recipients. In dealing with cost issues, case managers can be creative in leveraging current resources to garner additional sources of support.

As a method of intervention, cost effectiveness of case management has also been evaluated and seems to vary across different client populations and problem situations. Case management appears to be less effective in reducing the risk of unplanned hospitalizations in older adults (Huntley, Mann, Huws, Paranjothy, & Purdy, 2013). However, there is significant evidence that case management improves the quality of life for frail, community-dwelling older adults without substantially increasing service costs (You, Dunt, & Doyle, 2013). Therefore, policy makers should consider ways to target resources to programs that focus on community-dwelling older adults, as case management has an important role to play in keeping this group functioning as well as possible.

Changes in Services Delivery

Quality services delivery systems are essential for older adults. To ensure that the delivery of services is responsive to this population, case managers must actively promote changes that support the client, such as modifying programs to be more accessible to or appropriate for older clients. Because many older adults cannot access programs, or programs are unavailable in their communities, these adults are faced with particular challenges. Consider the basic issue of transportation, for example, which is a major barrier to services provision for a number of older adults residing in communities with limited resources. If a client cannot physically get to a senior center, for example, there is no probability that he or she can benefit from the services provided at the site.

Geriatric case managers are in a good position to determine ways to eradicate gaps such as this one in neighborhoods and communities. By having a good knowledge of resources, they could locate untapped resources: for instance, having a local church assist with transporting older adults to a senior center in their church bus. In addition, case managers might also be able to coordinate individual clients' resources into a plan—such as forming a cooperative in which families share responsibilities for transportation of older adults. Although it might not be possible to institute a comprehensive system of public transportation within the community, case managers can creatively construct other methods of providing service.

A fairly recent policy change has broad implications for case management with older populations. In March 2010, President Barack Obama signed the Patient Protection and Affordable Care Act (ACA) (P.L. 111-148) into law. Long before the ACA became law, geriatric case managers were working to improve service coordination across disparate service networks. However, the ACA initiated a "seismic shift in the way that health care is delivered" (Greene & Kropf, 2014, p. 218), in part by increasing the importance of comprehensive and coordinated services in health care delivery. The ACA stresses the interface and congruence between health care patients and their social environment. For older adults, this shift has prompted various new initiatives, including Medicare community-based transitions programs, accountable care organizations that stress continuity of care, and reduction of avoidable hospitalizations among nursing home patients, among other innovative programs (Emmer, 2013). In these examples, a prominent role is played by the geriatric case manager, who is involved with a health care team to provide services that will keep older adults well and functional, coordinate care across different service systems, and work to reduce unnecessary and duplicative costs.

Case managers can be change agents within their own programs and agencies. Kropf (2006) described how case managers can forge relationships to enhance service delivery by creating coalitions, bringing together nontraditional partners, and working across service sectors. For example, older adults with lifelong psychiatric conditions often fall through the cracks of both aging and mental health services. Efforts to identify resources that specifically meet the complex needs of this population and their families are needed (Crowe & Lyness, 2014; Cummings & Kropf, 2011).

Advocacy Role

Advocacy, according to Frankel and Gelman (1998), is when "a case manager acts on behalf of clients who are unable or unwilling to act on their own behalf

. . . or when clients are able to act on their own, but when it is judged that a case manager could intervene more effectively" (p. 38). The advocacy role is a vitally important part of case management; Frankel and Gelman have argued that, compared with the role of advocate, other case management roles are subsidiary. Unfortunately, ageism is a part of the culture, and other professionals are not immune to engaging in oppressive behaviors. Therefore, in addition to helping connect clients with various resources, case managers may need to advocate for improved responsiveness of those resources to their clients.

Acting as an advocate requires numerous social work skills. Fast and Chapin (2000) have suggested that a case manager first needs to acquire thorough knowledge about available resources in the client's environment, the client's preferences for using services, and any barriers or obstacles to using or accessing these services. The manager then must use his or her influence to assist the client in connecting with these resources. Consider the example of older adults with developmental disabilities—these clients receive services through aging initiatives, such as leisure-based options or meal programs. As adults with lifelong disabilities age, it makes little sense for them to continue with vocational or habilitation services, such as supported employment or workshops. Yet few agencies offer later life leisure-based options, thus leaving many older adults with nothing to do.

Clearly, geriatric case managers must have a set of competencies to practice with older adults successfully and effectively. As the older population grows in both size and diversity, case managers will continue to play increasingly important roles in services delivery. They must have the skills to intervene effectively with older clients and their families, provide needed linkages to traditional and innovative resources, and serve as change agents to promote a comprehensive system of programs and services. Although case coordination was one of the earliest functions within the social work profession, this role continues to hold an important place in today's services delivery systems.

CONCLUSION

Case management has been a part of social work practice since the earliest days of the profession. Beginning with charity organization societies and the settlement house movement, this type of intervention approach continues to be an important part of social workers' professional role. Geriatric case managers tend to focus on promoting functioning with older adults and providing linkages to needed resources within the environment.

Because the issues faced by older adults often straddle multiple services sectors (for example, health, mental health, and aging services), case managers need to have an extensive network of other providers. A person who has dementia, for example, may require a safe residence, support for care providers, and linkage to health care providers who understand this disease. An effective case manager will have skills to assess and intervene effectively with the older client and family, as well as be able to attend to issues in services delivery. The competencies that are part of this chapter highlight the breadth of skills that the geriatric case manager must possess.

Case Study: Resources and Advocacy for the Stanley Family

Examples of ways that geriatric case managers provide service to custodial grandparents were presented within this chapter. Because of the multiple issues that grandparent-headed families face, case managers fill a vital role in working across service delivery sectors to ensure that these families are linked to needed resources. Often, these practitioners need to create service plans for families that include educational, aging, health care, and mental health services. Without the support and involvement of case managers, the complexity of these services can overwhelm caregivers who often have limited time and energy.

   With the Stanley family, a case manager helped the family with some of its health and mental health needs. As discussed in an earlier chapter, Mrs. Stanley had unregulated hypertension. The case manager was able to locate a physician who accepted Medicare, and Mrs. Stanley was able to get assistance to afford her medication. The case manager also located a clinical social worker who was able to see Jasmine about some of her early life trauma experiences. In addition to locating a therapist who had expertise in this area, the case manager also worked with Mrs. Stanley, who was initially reluctant to have her granddaughter involved in therapy as she was afraid that this might overwhelm Jasmine. The case manager prepared both the grandmother and granddaughter for the process of therapy.

   The case manager also became involved in advocating for additional resources for grandparents. Working with the local Area Agency on Aging, she was able to secure the use of its van to take the grandparents to a thrift store once a month, where the families could shop for low-cost clothes and household needs. This nontraditional resource became a form of assistance for the grandparents but also increased the commitment of the AAA to this group of care providers.

WHAT WE LEARNED IN THIS CHAPTER

- What case management is and how it applies to an older adult population
- The emphasis on person in environment and the ecological perspective within the case management practice model
- Skills necessary to conduct case management services

- Services provided by geriatric case managers
- Case management's effectiveness both in service delivery and in containing costs.

SUGGESTED EXERCISE TO EVALUATE STUDENT COMPETENCY

Students will write a care plan to meet the needs of Mrs. Vishnick and her daughter Meta.

Case Study: Mrs. Vishnick

Mrs. Vishnick is an 87-year-old widow who is the primary caregiver for her 64-year-old daughter, Meta, who has intellectual disability. Meta has very limited functional ability, as she requires total support in all activities of daily living, including dressing, feeding, toileting, and bathing. Meta does not participate in any services for people with developmental disabilities and has never been involved in any community programs.

This family approached the county developmental disability service when Mrs. Vishnick became ill and required hospitalization. The only other family member is Mrs. Vishnick's younger daughter, Teresa, who is married and lives in the same neighborhood. Although Teresa spends time with Meta, she has been adamant that she and her husband will not become the primary care providers for Meta when their mother can no longer function in this role. Teresa was the person who contacted the disability services agency in the present situation.

In understanding the family history, several events and situations have important meaning for the family's current situation. First of all, Mrs. Vishnick and her husband immigrated to the United States from Eastern Europe when they were first married. When the couple arrived in this country, Mr. Vishnick secured a job at an automotive manufacturing plant, and the couple had Meta. When Meta did not seem to be making developmental progress, the Vishnicks' physician encouraged them to place her in an institution, which they did not do. After the birth of Teresa, the demands of raising two children became overwhelming for Mrs. Vishnick, and Meta was moved to the state institution, about 75 miles from the family home. One year after this move, a fire destroyed much of the institution. Although Meta was uninjured, Mrs. Vishnick was so consumed with anxiety about her daughter's safety that Meta returned to the family home. Since this time, Meta and Mrs. Vishnick have not spent a single night apart until the recent hospitalization.

If you were the case manager in the agency, how would you proceed in working with this family? Consider the following questions:

- How would you develop a relationship with the family? What might be some issues or challenges in developing a trusting relationship?

- What resources would be appropriate for this family? How would you link to services in different networks (for example, aging services and health resources)?

- From a macro-practice perspective, what are some ways that case managers from different services delivery networks could work more effectively to assist families like the Vishnicks?

- How would you evaluate your practice as a case manager with this family? What would be some measurable outcomes that you could establish?

ADDITIONAL RESOURCES

The Aging Life Care Association Web site features standards of practice and a code of ethics at http://www.aginglifecare.org/ALCA/About_ALCA/ Code_of_Ethics_and_Standards_of_Practice/ALCA/About_Us/Code_of_ Ethics_and_Standards_of_Practice.aspx.

The American Case Management Association is a membership organization that strives to provide practitioners with professional development services, including mentoring, education, and resource information. Visit http:// www.acmaweb.org/.

The American Society on Aging: Healthcare and Aging Network facilitates information exchange and collaboration among policy makers, researchers, and service providers on the needs of older adults and best practices. Visit http://www.asaging.org/han.

The Case Management Society of America is a membership association dedicated to fostering case management growth and development by affecting policy and providing evidence-based tools and resources. Go to http:// www.cmsa.org/.

The Case Management Society of America Standards of Practice for Case Management can be found at http://www.cmsa.org/portals/0/pdf/member-only/standardsofpractice.pdf.

The Eldercare Locator connects users with services for older adults and their families and is sponsored by the U.S. Administration on Aging. Visit http:// www.eldercare.gov/Eldercare.NET/Public/Index.aspx.

The NASW Standards for Social Work Case Management can be found at http:// www.socialworkers.org/practice/practice_tools/case-management-stand-ards.asp.

The U.S. Department of Veterans Affairs offers a variety of resources to older adult veterans, including health and mental health care, survivors' benefits, and burial and memorial benefits. For more details, see https://www .va.gov.

References

AARP. (2005). *Reimagining America: How America can grow older and prosper.* Retrieved from http://assets.aarp.org/www.aarp.org_/articles/legpolicy/blueprint200508.pdf

AARP. (2014, April). *Age discrimination fact sheet.* Retrieved from http://www.aarp.org/work/employee-rights/info-02-2009/age_discrimination_fact_sheet.html

AARP. (2015, August). *The AARP network of age friendly communities: An introduction.* Retrieved from http://www.aarp.org/livable-communities/network-age-friendly-communities/info-2015/8-domains-of-livability-case-studies.html

AARP. (2017). *Aging in place: A state survey of livability policies and practices.* Retrieved from https://assets.aarp.org/rgcenter/ppi/liv-com/aging-in-place-2011-full.pdf

Achenbaum, W. A. (2005). *Older Americans, vital communities: A bold vision for societal aging.* Baltimore: Johns Hopkins University Press.

Adamek, M. E., & Slater, G. Y. (2009). Depression and anxiety. In S. M. Cummings & N. P. Kropf (Eds.), *Handbook of psychosocial interentions with older adults: Evidence-based approaches* (pp. 146–180). New York: Haworth Press.

Administration on Aging. (2011). *A profile of older Americans: 2011.* Retrieved from https://aging.ca.gov/docs/DataAndStatistics/Statistics/OtherStatistics/Profile_of_Older_Americans_2011.pdf

Administration on Aging, Administration for Community Living (2016). *A profile of older Americans: 2015.* Retrieved from https://www.acl.gov/sites/default/files/Aging%20and%20Disability%20in%20America/2015-Profile.pdf

Advocates for Human Rights. (2013). *Discover human rights: A human rights approach to social justice training manual.* Retrieved from http://discover humanrights.org/uploads/dhr_training_manual_2011.pdf

Advocates for Human Rights. (n.d.). *Human rights and the United States law.* Retrieved from www.theadvocatesforhumanrights.org/ human_rights_and_the_united_states

AgeUK. (2011). *Older people and human rights: A reference guide for professionals working with older people.* Retrieved from http://www.ageuk.org.uk/ documents/en-gb/for-professionals/equality-and-human-rights/older_ people_human_rights__expert_series_pro.pdf?dtrk=true

Agich, G. J. (1993). *Autonomy and long-term care.* New York: Oxford University Press.

Akabas, S. H., & Gates, L. B. (2006). The workplace. In B. Berkman & S. D'Ambruoso (Eds.), *Handbook of social work in health and aging* (pp. 499–508). New York: Oxford University Press.

Akincigil, A., Olfson, M., Walkup, J. T., Siegel, M. J., Kalay, E., Amin, S., & Crystal, S. (2011). Diagnosis and treatment of depression in older community-dwelling adults: 1992–2005. *Journal of the American Geriatrics Society, 59,* 1042–1051.

Ambrose, A. F., Paul, G., & Hausdorff, J. M. (2013). Risk factors for falls among older adults: A review of the literature. *Maturitas, 75*(1), 51–61.

American Academy of Social Work and Social Welfare. (2016). *Grand challenges for social work.* Retrieved from http://aaswsw.org/grand-challenges-initiative/

Aminzadeh, F., Molnar, F. J., Dalziel, W. B., & Garcia, L. J. (2013). An exploration of adjustment needs and efforts of persons with dementia after relocation to a residential care facility. *Journal of Housing for the Elderly, 27,* 221–240.

Andersen, S. M., Reznik, I., & Chen, S. (1997). The self in relation to others: Cognitive and motivational underpinnings. In J. G. Snodgrass & R. L. Thompson (Eds.), *The self across psychology: Self-recognition, self-awareness, and the self-concept* (pp. 233–275). New York: New York Academy of Sciences.

Anderson, R. E., & Carter, I. E. (1990). *Human behavior in the social environment: A social systems approach* (4th ed.). Hawthorne, NY: Aldine de Gruyter.

Andrada, P. A., & Korte, A. O. (1993). En aquellos tiempos (In those times): A reminiscing group with Hispanic elderly. *Journal of Gerontological Social Work, 20*(3–4), 25–42.

Angell, G. B., Dennis, B. G., & Dumain, L. E. (1998). Spirituality, resilience, and narrative: Coping with parental death. *Families in Society, 79,* 615–630.

Antonovsky, A., & Sourani, T. (1988). Family sense of coherence and family adaptation. *Journal of Marriage and Family, 50,* 79–92.

Applewhite, S. L. (1998). Culturally competent practice with elderly Latinos. *Journal of Gerontological Social Work, 30*(1–2), 1–15.

Asay, T. P., & Lambert, M. J. (1999). The empirical case for the common factors in therapy: Quantitative findings. In M. A. Hubble, B. L. Duncan, & D. Miller (Eds.), *The heart & soul of change: What works in therapy* (pp. 23–55). Washington, DC: American Psychological Association.

Atchley, R. C., & Barusch, A. S. (2004). *Social forces and aging: An introduction to social gerontology* (10th ed.). Belmont, CA: Wadsworth.

Austin, C. D., Camp, E. D., Flux, D., McClelland, R. W., & Sieppert, J. (2005). Community development with older adults in their neighborhoods: The Elder Friendly Communities Program. *Families in Society, 86,* 401–409.

Australian Human Rights Commission. (2012). *Respect and choice: A human rights approach for ageing and health.* Retrieved from https://www.humanrights.gov.au/sites/default/files/document/publication/human_rights_framework_for_ageing_and_health.pdf

Australian Human Rights Commission. (2016). *Human rights and older people.* Retrieved from https://www.humanrights.gov.au

Azzarto, J., & Smith, M. F. (1994). Should health and human services be decentralized into neighborhood social health centers managed by the community? In M. J. Austin & J. I. Lowe (Eds.), *Controversial issues in communities and organizations* (pp. 73–85). Boston: Allyn & Bacon.

Baer, B., Bhushan, A., Taleb, H. A., Vasquez, J., & Thomas, R. (2016). The right to health of older people. *Gerontologist, 56*(2), S206–S217.

Bailey, D. J., & DePoy, E. (1995). Older people's responses to education about advance directives. *Health & Social Work, 20,* 223–228.

Bardill, D. R., & Ryan, F. J. (1973). *Family group casework.* Washington, DC: National Association of Social Workers.

Barnett, A., Smith, B., Lord, S. R., Williams, M., & Baumand, A. (2003). Community-based group exercise improves balance and reduces falls in at-risk older people: A randomized controlled trial. *Age and Aging, 32,* 407–414.

Barranti, C., & Cohen, H. (2000). Lesbian and gay elders: An invisible minority. In R. Schneider, N. Kropf, & A. Kisor (Eds.), *Gerontological social work* (pp. 343–368). Belmont, CA: Wadsworth.

Beauchamp, T. L., Walters, L., Kahn, J., & Mastroianni, A. (2014). *Contemporary issues in bioethics.* Boston: Wadsworth.

Beaulieu, E. M. (2012). *A guide for nursing home social workers* (2nd ed.). New York: Springer.

Begun, A. (1993). Human behavior and the social environment: The vulnerability, risk, and resilience model. *Journal of Social Work Education, 29,* 26–35.

Bell, M. A. (2002, January 7). *The five principles of organizational resilience.* Retrieved from https://www.gartner.com/doc/351410/principles-organizational-resilience

Bell, W. G., Schmidt, W., & Miller, K. (1981). Public guardianship and the elderly: Findings from a national study. *Gerontologist, 2,* 194–202.

Berg-Weger, M. (2005). *Social work and social welfare: An invitation.* Boston: McGraw-Hill.

Berk, L. E. (2014). *Development through the lifespan* (6th ed.). Boston: Pearson.

Berman, J., & Furst, L. M. (2011). *Depressed older adults: Education and screening.* New York: Springer.

Berry, J. (1997). Immigration, acculturation, and adaptation. *Applied Psychology: An International Review, 46,* 5–33.

Billig, M. (2004). Supportive communities, an optimum arrangement for the older population? *Journal of Sociology and Social Welfare, 31*, 131–151.

Blieszner, R., & Bedford, V. H. (Eds.). (2012). *Handbook of families and aging* (2nd ed.). Santa Barbara, CA: Praeger.

Blow, F. C., Walton, M. A., Chermack, S. T., Mudd, S. A., & Brower, K. J. (2000). Older adult treatment outcome following elder-specific inpatient alcoholism treatment. *Journal of Substance Abuse Treatment, 19*, 67–75.

Bohlmeijer, E., Roemer, M., Cuijpers, P., & Smit, F. (2007). The effects of reminiscence on psychological well-being in older adults: A meta-analysis. *Aging & Mental Health, 11*, 291–300.

Bolda, E. J., Lowe, J. I., Maddox, G. L., & Patnaik, B. S. (2005). Community partnerships for older adults: A case study. *Families in Society, 86*, 411–418.

Bolman, L. G., & Deal, T. E. (1997). *Reframing organizations: Artistry, choice, and leadership* (2nd ed.). San Francisco: Jossey-Bass.

Bond, J. T., Galinsky, E. M., Pitt-Catsouphes, M., & Smyer, M. A. (2005, November). The diverse employment experiences of older men and women in the workforce. *Research Highlights, 2005*(02). Retrieved from https://www.bc.edu/content/dam/files/research_sites/agingandwork/pdf/publications/RH02_DiverseEmployExper.pdf

Borden, W. (1992). Narrative perspectives in psychosocial intervention following adverse life events. *Social Work, 37*, 135–141.

Boszormenyi-Nagy, I., & Spark, G. (1973). *Invisible loyalties.* New York: Harper & Row.

Bourgeois, M., Schulz, R., & Burgio, L. (1996). Interventions for caregivers of patients with Alzheimer' disease: A review and analysis of content, process, and outcomes. *International Journal of Aging: Human Behavior, 43*, 35–92.

Bowers, B. J., & Jacobson, N. (2002). Best practice in long-term care case management: How excellent case managers do their jobs. *Journal of Social Work in Long-Term Care, 1*, 55–72.

Brandl, B., Hebert, M., Rozwadowski, J., & Spangler, D. (2003). Feeling safe, feeling strong: Support groups for older abused women. *Violence against Women, 9*, 1490–1503.

Brodie, K., & Gadling-Cole, C. (2003). The use of family decision meetings when addressing caregiver stress. *Journal of Gerontological Social Work, 42*(1), 89–99.

Brody, E. (1985). Parent care as normative family stress. *Gerontologist, 25*, 19–29.

Brody, R., & Nair, M. D. (2003). *Macro practice: A generalist approach* (6th ed.). Wheaton, IL: Gregory.

Bronfenbrenner, U. (1979). *The ecology of human development.* Cambridge, MA: Harvard University Press.

Bronfenbrenner, U. (1989). Ecological systems theory. *Annals of Child Development, 6*, 187–249.

Brooks, J. S., Nomura, C., & Cohen, P. (1989). A network of influences on adolescent drug involvement: Neighborhood, school, peer, and family. *Genetic, Social, and General Psychology Monographs, 115*, 125–145.

Brown, J. W. (1997). Empowerment evaluation: Knowledge and tools for self-assessment and accountability [Book review]. *Health Education & Behavior, 24*, 388–391.

Brown, K. L, & Browne, C. V. (1998). Perceptions of dementia, caregiving, and help seeking among Asian and Pacific Islander Americans. *Health & Social Work, 23*, 262–274.

Brownell, P., & Heiser, D. (2006). Psycho-educational support groups for older women victims of family mistreatment: A pilot study. *Journal of Gerontological Social Work, 46*(3–4), 145–160.

Brueggemann, W. G. (2014). *The practice of macro social work* (4th ed.). Belmont, CA: Brooks/Cole.

Buckley, W. (1967). Systems and entities. In W. Buckley (Ed.), *Sociology and modern systems theory* (pp. 42–66). Englewood Cliffs, NJ: Prentice Hall.

Bullock, K., Crawford, S. L., & Tennstedt, S. L. (2003). Employment and caregiving: Exploration of African American caregivers. *Social Work, 48*, 150–162.

Burkhauser, R. V., & Quinn, J. F. (1994). Changing policy signals. In M. W. Riley, R. L. Kahn, & A. Foner (Eds.), *Age and structural lag: Society's failure to provide meaningful opportunities in work, family, and leisure* (pp. 237–263). New York: Wiley.

Butler, K. (1997). The anatomy of resilience. *Family Therapy Networker, 21*, 22–31.

Butler, R. N. (1963). The life review: An interpretation of reminiscence in the aged. *Psychiatry, 26*, 65–76.

Butler, R. N. (1968). Toward a psychiatry of the life-cycle: Implications of socio-psychologic studies of the aging process for the psychotherapeutic situation. In A. Simon & L. Epstein (Eds.), *Aging in modern society* (pp. 233–248). Washington, DC: American Psychiatric Association.

Butler, R. N. (1975). *Why survive? Being old in America.* New York: Harper & Row.

Butler, R. N. (2005). Foreword. In L. W. Kaye (Ed.). *Perspectives on productive aging: Social work with the new aged* (pp. xi–xiii). Washington, DC: NASW Press.

Byers, A. L., Arean, P. A., & Yaffe, K. (2012). Low use of mental health services among older Americans with mood and anxiety disorders. *Psychiatric Services, 63*(1), 66–72.

Caldwell, R. L. (2005). At the confluence of memory and meaning—Life review with older adults and families: Using narrative therapy and the expressive arts to remember and re-author stories of resilience. *Family Journal: Counseling and Therapy for Couples and Families, 13*, 172–175.

Campbell, L., Carthron, D. L., Miles, M. S., & Brown, L. (2012). Examining the effectiveness of a case management program for custodial grandparent families. *Nursing Research and Practice.* doi:10.1155/2012/124230

Canda, E. R., & Furman, L. D. (1999). *Spiritual diversity in social work practice.* New York: Free Press.

Carter, E. A., & McGoldrick, M. (1999). *The expanded family life cycle: Individual, family, and social perspectives* (3rd ed.). Boston: Allyn & Bacon.

Center for Organization Effectiveness. (2005a). *Guidelines for assessing organizational culture.* Retrieved from http://www.greatorganizations.com/pdf/spGuidelinesCulture.pdf

Center for Organization Effectiveness. (2005b). *Leading change.* Retrieved from http://www.greatorganizations.com/leadingchange.htm

Centers for Disease Control and Prevention. (2005). *Check for safety: A home fall prevention checklist for older adults.* Retrieved from https://www.cdc.gov/HomeandRecreationalSafety/pubs/English/booklet_Eng_desktop-a.pdf

Centers for Disease Control and Prevention. (2013a). *Healthy places terminology.* Retrieved from http://www.cdc.gov/healthyplaces/terminology.htm

Centers for Disease Control and Prevention. (2013b). *The state of aging and health in America 2013.* Atlanta: Author.

Centers for Disease Control and Prevention. (2016a). *The community guide—Mental health.* Retrieved from https://www.thecommunityguide.org/topic/mental-health

Centers for Disease Control and Prevention. (2016b). *Partnerships to improve community health.* Retrieved from https://www.cdc.gov/needphp/dch/programs/

Centers for Disease Control and Prevention. (2016c). *The state of mental health and aging.* Retrieved from https://www.cdc.gov/aging/pdf/mental_health.pdf

Centers for Disease Control and Prevention. (2017). *Healthy places terminology.* Retrieved from https://www.cdc.gov/healthyplaces/terminology.htm

Chadiha, L. A., & Fisher, R. H. (2002). Contributing factors to African American women caregivers' mental well-being. *African American Research Perspectives, 8*(1), 72–84.

Chestang, L. W. (1972). *Character development in a hostile society* (Occasional Paper No. 3). Chicago: School of Social Services Administration, University of Chicago.

Chinman, M., Imm, P., & Wandersman, A. (2004). *Getting to outcomes 2004: Promoting accountability through methods and tools for planning, implementation, and evaluation.* Retrieved from http://www.rand.org/pubs/technical_reports/TR101.html

Chipungu, S. (1991). A value-based policy framework. In J. E. Everett, S. S. Chipungu, & B. R. Leashore (Eds.), *Child welfare: An Africentric perspective* (pp. 290–305). New Brunswick, NJ: Rutgers University Press.

Choi, N. G., Kunik, M. E., & Wilson, N. (2013). Mental health service use among depressed, low-income homebound middle-aged and older adults. *Journal of Aging and Health, 24*, 638–655.

Cohen, H. L., & Greene, R. R. (2006). Older adults who overcame oppression. *Families in Society, 87*, 1–8.

Cohen, J. F., Parpura, G. A., Campbell, K. M., Vass, J., & Rosenberg, F. R. (2005). Elderly persons' preferences for topics of discussion and shared interest groups. *Journal of Gerontological Social Work, 44*(3–4), 39–57.

Community & Regional Resilience Institute. (2011). *Community Resilience System Initiative (CRSI) Steering Committee final report—A roadmap to increased community resilience.* Retrieved from http://www.resilientus.org/wp-content/uploads/2015/04/CRSI-Final-Report-1.pdf

Community & Regional Resilience Institute. (2017). *What is community resilience?* Retrieved from http://www.resilientus.org/about-us/what-is-community-resilience

Congress, E. P. (1994). The use of culturagrams to assess and empower culturally diverse families. *Families in Society, 75*, 531–540.

Congress, E. P. (1999). *Social work values and ethics.* Belmont, CA: Wadsworth.

Congressional Budget Office Cost Estimate. (2015, February 10). S. 192 Older Americans Act Reauthorization Act of 2015 (p. 2). Retrieved from https://www.cbo.gov/sites/default/files/114th-congress-2015-2016/costestimate/s192.pdf

Conrad, A. P. (1999). Professional tools for religiously and spiritually sensitive social work practice. In R. R. Greene (Ed.), *Human behavior theory and social work practice* (2nd ed., pp. 63–72). Hawthorne, NY: Aldine de Gruyter.

Corey, G., Corey, M. S., & Callanan, P. (2007). *Issues and ethics in the helping professions* (7th ed.). Belmont, CA: Thomson Brooks/Cole.

Corey, G., Corey, M. S., & Callanan, P. (2011). *Issues and ethics in the helping professions* (9th ed.). Belmont, CA: Brooks/Cole.

Corey, M. S., & Corey, G. (1997). *Groups: Process and practice* (5th ed.). Pacific Grove, CA: Brooks/Cole.

Council on Social Work Education. (2015). *2015 educational policy and accreditation standards for baccalaureate and master's social work programs.* Alexandria, VA: Author.

Council on Social Work Education. (2017). *Specialized practice curricular guide for gero social work practice.* Retrieved from http://cswe.org/CSWE/media/GeroEdResources/Gero_Guide_WEB_final_NewSite.pdf

Cournoyer, B. (2000). *The social work skills workbook.* Belmont, CA: Wadsworth.

Coutu, D. L. (2002, May). How resilience works. *Harvard Business Review, 80*, 46.

Cox, C. B. (2010). Policy and custodial grandparents. *Marquette Elder's Advisor, 11*, 281–305.

Cox, E. O. (2001). Community practice issues in the 21st century: Questions and challenges for empowerment-oriented practitioners. *Journal of Community Practice, 9*, 37–55.

Cox, E. O., & Parsons, R. R. (1996). Empowerment-oriented social work practice: Impact on late life relationships of women. *Journal of Women and Aging, 8*(3–4), 129–143.

Cress, C. (2015). *Handbook of geriatric care management.* Gaithersburg, MD: Aspen.

Creswell, J. W. (1998). *Qualitative inquiry and research design: Choosing among five traditions.* Thousand Oaks, CA: Sage Publications.

Cristofalo, M., Krupski, A., West, I. I., Atkins, D. C., Joesch, J. M., Jenkins, L., & Roy-Byrne, P. (2016). Barriers and facilitators to coordinating care with high-risk, high-cost disabled Medicaid beneficiaries: Perspectives of front-line staff and participating clients. *Care Management Journals, 17*(1), 24–36.

Cross, T. (1998). Understanding family resiliency from a relational world view. In H. I. McCubbin, E. A. Thompson, A. I. Thompson, & J. E. Fromer (Eds.), *Resiliency in Native American and immigrant families* (pp. 143–158). Thousand Oaks, CA: Sage Publications.

Crowe, A., & Lyness, K. P. (2014). Family functioning, coping, and distress in families with serious mental illness. *Family Journal, 22*, 186–197.

Cummings, S. M., & Kropf, N. P. (Eds.). (2008). *Evidence-based psychosocial treatments for older adults.* New York: Haworth Press.

Cummings, S. M., & Kropf, N. P. (2011). Aging with a severe mental illness: Challenges and treatments. *Journal of Gerontological Social Work, 54,* 175–188.

Curran, C. R. (2004). Bad news for the custodians of convention. *Nursing Economics, 22,* 109–110.

Cusato, M. (2015). *Aging in place survey report October 2015.* Retrieved from http://www.homeadvisor.com/r/wp-content/uploads/2015/10/HomeAdvisor-Aging-in-Place.pdf

Cusicanqui, M., & Salmon, R. (2004). Seniors, small fry, and song: A group work libretto of an intergenerational singing group. *Journal of Gerontological Social Work, 44*(1–2), 189–210.

Cutler, N. E., & Whitelaw, N. A. (2002). American perceptions of aging in the 21st century [APA21], 2000. ICPSR03326-v1. Ann Arbor, MI: Inter-university Consortium for Political and Social Research [distributor]. http://doi.org/10.3886/ICPSR03326.v1

Daly, A., Jennings, J., Beckett, J. O., & Leashore, B. R. (1995). Effective coping strategies of African Americans. *Social Work, 40,* 240–248.

Davis, K., Leijenaar, M., & Oldersma, J. (Eds.). (1991). *The gender of power.* Newbury Park, CA: Sage Publications.

Deal, T. E., & Kennedy, A. A. (1982). *Corporate cultures.* Reading, MA: Addison-Wesley.

DeCoster, V. (2008). Diabetes treatments. In S. M. Cummings & N. P. Kropf (Eds.), *Handbook of psychosocial interventions with older adults: Evidence-based approaches* (pp. 105–129). New York: Haworth Press.

Devore, W., & Schlesinger, E. G. (1996). *Ethnic-sensitive social work practice.* Boston: Allyn & Bacon.

Diehl, M. (1998). Everyday competence in later life: Current status and future directions. *Gerontologist, 38,* 422–433.

Diehl, M. (1999). Self-development in adulthood and aging: The role of critical life events. In C. D. Ryff & V. W. Marshall (Eds.), *The self and society in aging processes* (pp. 150–183). New York: Springer.

Dilworth-Anderson, P., Williams, I., & Gibson, B. (2002). Issues of race, ethnicity, and culture in caregiving research: A 20-year review (1980–2000). *Gerontologist, 42,* 237–272.

DiNitto, D. M., & Johnson, D. H. (2016). *Social welfare: Politics and public policy* (8th ed.). New York: Pearson.

Dolgoff, R., Harrington, D., & Loewenberg, F. M. (2012). *Ethical decisions for social work practice* (9th ed.). Belmont, CA: Brooks/Cole.

Duncan, B. L., & Miller, S. D. (2000). *The heroic client.* San Francisco: Jossey-Bass.

Dupree, L. W., & Schonfeld, L. (1998). The value of behavioral perspectives in treating older adults. In M. Hersen & V. B. Van Hasselt (Eds.), *Handbook of clinical geropsychology* (pp. 51–70). New York: Plenum Press.

Ellis, R. R., & Simmons, T. (2014). *Coresident grandparents and their grandchildren 2012: Population characteristics.* Retrieved from http://www.census.gov/content/dam/Census/library/publications/2014/demo/p20-576.pdf

Emmer, S. (2013, Fall). Care coordination under the Affordable Care Act: Opportunities and challenges for geriatric care managers. *Journal of Aging Life Care*. Retrieved from http://www.aginglifecarejournal.org/fall-issue-article-title-goes-here-and-is-pretty-long-so-thats-that/

Engel, P. A., Spencer, J., Paul, T., & Boardman, J. B. (2016). The geriatrics in primary care demonstration: Integrating comprehensive geriatric care into the medical home: Preliminary data. *Journal of the American Geriatrics Society, 64*, 875–879.

Enguidanos, S. M., Davis, C., & Katz, L. (2005). Shifting the paradigm in geriatric care management: Moving from the medical model to patient-centered care. *Social Work in Health Care, 41*(1), 1–16.

Erikson, E. H. (1980). *Identity and the life cycle.* New York: W. W. Norton. (Original work published 1959)

Estes, C. L. (2001). *Social policy and aging: A critical perspective.* Thousand Oaks, CA: Sage Publications.

Everly, G. S. (2011), June 24. Building a resilient organizational culture. *Harvard Business Review*. Retrieved from https://hbr.org/2011/06/building-a-resilient-organizat

Falk, E., & Hoffman, N. (2014). The role of capacity assessments in elder abuse investigations and guardianships. *Clinics in Geriatric Medicine, 30*, 851–868. doi: 10.1016/j.cger.2014.08.009

Farris, K. (2006). The role of African-American pastors in mental health care. *Journal of Human Behavior in the Social Environment, 14*(1–2), 159–182.

Fast, B., & Chapin, R. (2000). *Strengths-based care management for older adults.* Baltimore: Health Professions.

Federal Interagency Forum on Aging Related Statistics. (2016). *Older Americans 2016: Key indicators of well-being*. Washington, DC: U.S. Government Printing Office.

Fetterman, D. M. (2007). *Collaborative, participatory, & empowerment evaluation* [Empowerment Evaluation Blog]. Retrieved from http://eevaluation.blogspot.com/

Flynn, D. (2005). What's wrong with rights? Rethinking human rights and responsibilities. *Australian Social Work, 58*, 244–255.

Flynn, J. P. (1985). *Social agency policy: Analysis and presentation for community practice.* Chicago: Nelson-Hall.

Folkman, S., Cheney, M., McKusick, L., Ironson, G., Johnson, D. S., & Coates, T. J. (1991). Translating coping theory into an intervention. In J. Eckenrode (Ed.), *The social context of coping* (pp. 239–260). New York: Plenum Press.

Fonagy, P., Steele, M., Steele, H., Higgitt, A., & Target, M. (1994). The Emanuel Miller memorial lecture 1992: The theory and practice of resilience. *Journal of Child Psychology and Psychiatry and Allied Disciplines, 35*, 231–257.

Foner, A. (1994). Endnote: The reach of an idea. In M. W. Riley, R. L. Kahn, & A. Foner (Eds.), *Age and structural lag: Society's failure to provide meaningful opportunities in work, family, and leisure* (pp. 263–280). New York: Wiley.

Fong, R. (2001). Culturally competent social work practice: Past and present. In R. F. Fong & S. Furuto (Eds.), *Culturally competent practice: Skills, interventions, and evaluations* (pp. 1–9). Needham Heights, MA: Allyn & Bacon.

Frank, C., Kurland, J., & Goldman, B. (1978). Tips for getting the best from the rest. Baltimore: Jewish Community Services.

Frankel, A. J., & Gelman, S. R. (1998). *Case management: An introduction to concepts and skills.* Chicago: Lyceum Books.

Frankena, W. (1973). *Ethics* (2nd ed.). Englewood Cliffs, NJ: Prentice Hall.

Fraser, M. W., Richman, J. M., & Galinsky, M. J. (1999). Risk, protection, and resilience: Toward a conceptual framework for social work practice. *Social Work Research, 23,* 131–143.

Fredriksen-Goldsen, K. I., Kim, H.-J., Emlet, C. A., Muraco, A., Erosheva, E. A., Hoy-Ellis, C. P., et al. (2011). *The aging and health report: Disparities and resilience among lesbian, gay, bisexual, and transgender older adults.* Seattle: Institute for Multigenerational Health.

Galambos, C. (1997). Resolving ethical conflicts in providing case management services to the elderly. *Journal of Gerontological Social Work, 27*(4), 57–67.

Galambos, C. M. (1998). Preserving end-of-life autonomy: The Patient Self-Determination Act and the Uniform Health Care Decisions Act. *Health & Social Work, 23,* 275–281.

Galambos, C. (1999). Resolving ethical conflicts in a managed health care environment. *Health & Social Work, 24,* 191–197.

Galambos, C., Starr, J., Rantz, M. J., & Petroski, G. F. (2016). Analysis of advance directive documentation to support palliative care activity in nursing homes. *Health & Social Work, 41,* 228–234. doi:10.1093/hsw/hlw042

Galambos, C., Watt, J. W., Anderson, K., & Danis, F. (2005). Rural social work practice: Maintaining confidentiality in the face of dual relationships. *Journal of Social Work Values and Ethics, 2*(2), 1–5.

Gallagher-Thompson, D., Coon, D. W., Rivera, P., Powers, D., & Zeiss, A. M. (1998). Family caregiving: Stress, coping, and intervention. In M. Hersen & V. B. Van Hasselt (Eds.), *Handbook of clinical geropsychology* (pp. 469–493). New York: Plenum Press.

Garbarino, J. (1982). Children and families in the social environment. New York: Aldine.

Garmezy, N. (1991). Resiliency and vulnerability to adverse developmental outcomes associated with poverty. *American Behavioral Scientist, 34,* 416–430.

Gaugler, J. E., Kane, R. J., & Newcomer, R. (2007). Resilience and transitions from dementia caregiving. *Journals of Gerontology, Series B: Psychological Sciences and Social Sciences, 62*(1), 38–44.

Generations United. (2016). *Grandfamilies.* Retrieved from http://www.gu.org/OURWORK/Grandfamilies.aspx

Genrich, S. J., & Neatherlin, J. S. (2001). Case manager role: A content analysis of published literature. *Care Management Journals, 3,* 14–19.

George, L. K., & Gwyther, L. P. (1986). Caregiver well-being: A multidimensional examination of family caregivers of demented adults. *Gerontologist, 26,* 253–259.

Gergen, K. J. (1985). The social construction movement in modern psychology. *American Psychologist, 40*, 266–275.

Geriatric Mental Health Foundation. (2016). *Caring for the Alzheimer's disease patient.* Retrieved from http://www.gmhfonline.org/

Germain, C. B. (1991). *Human behavior in the social environment.* New York: Columbia University Press.

Germain, C. B., & Gitterman, A. (1995). *The life model of social work practice* (2nd ed.). New York: Columbia University Press.

Gibbs, L., & Gambrill, E. (1996). *Critical thinking for social workers: A workbook.* Thousand Oaks, CA: Pine Forge.

Gibson, L. (2011). Giving courts the information necessary to implement limited guardianships: Are we there yet? *Journal of Gerontological Social Work, 54*, 803–818. doi:10.1080/01634372.2011.604668

Gironda, M., Lubben, J., & Atchison, K. (1999). Social networks of elders without children. *Journal of Gerontological Social Work, 31*(1/2), 63–83.

Gitlin, L. N., & Rose, K. (2014). Factors associated with caregiver readiness to use nonpharmacologic strategies to manage dementia-related behavioral symptoms. *International Journal of Geriatric Psychiatry, 29*, 93–102. doi:10.1002/gps.3979

Glicken, M. D. (2004). *Using the strengths perspective in social work practice: A positive approach for helping professions.* Boston: Pearson Education.

Goelitz, A. (2004). Using the end of groups as an intervention at end-of-life. *Journal of Gerontological Social Work, 44*(1–2), 211–221.

Gonyea, J. G., Hudson, R. B., & Curley, A. (2004, Spring). The geriatric social work labor force: Challenges and opportunities in responding to an aging society. In *Institute for Geriatric Social Work issue brief* (pp. 1–7). Boston: Boston University School of Social Work.

Goodman, C. C. (2007). Intergenerational triads in skipped-generation grandfamilies. *International Journal of Aging and Human Development, 65*, 231–258.

Gostin, L., Hodge, J. G., Valentine, N. B., & Nygren-Krug, H. (2003). *The domains of health responsiveness: A human rights analysis* (EIP Discussion Paper No. 53). Geneva: World Health Organization.

Gottlieb, A. S., Silverstein, N. M., Bruner-Canhoto, L., & Montgomery, S. (2000). *Life at GrandFamilies House: The first six months.* Retrieved from http://www.umb.edu/editor_uploads/images/centers_institutes/institute_gerontology/Gfreport.pdf

Gottlieb, B. H. (2000). Self-help, mutual aid, and support groups among older adults. *Canadian Journal on Aging, 19*, 58–74.

Goyer, A. (2010, December 20). *More grandparents raising grandkids: New census data shows an increase in children being raised by extended family.* Retrieved from http://www.aarp.org/relationships/grandparenting/info-12-2010/more_grandparents_raising_grandchildren.html

Graybeal, C. (2001). Strengths-based social work assessment: Transforming the dominant paradigm. *Families in Society, 82*, 233–241.

Green, J. (1999). *Cultural awareness in the human services: A multi-ethnic approach* (3rd ed.). Needham Heights, MA: Allyn & Bacon.

Greene, R. R. (1999a). General systems theory. In R. R. Greene (Ed.), *Human behavior and social work practice* (pp. 215–249). Hawthorne, NY: Aldine de Gruyter.

Greene, R. R. (1999b). *Human behavior theory and social work practice.* New Brunswick, NJ: Aldine Transaction Press.

Greene, R. R. (2000). *Social work with the aged and their families* (2nd ed.). Hawthorne, NY: Aldine de Gruyter. (Original work published 1986)

Greene, R. R. (Ed.). (2002). *Resiliency: An integrated approach to practice, policy, and research.* Washington, DC: NASW Press.

Greene, R. R. (2005a). Family life. In L. W. Kaye (Ed.), *Perspectives on productive aging: Social work with the new aged* (pp. 107–122). Washington, DC: NASW Press.

Greene, R. R. (2005b). Redefining social work for the new millennium: Setting a context. *Journal of Human Behavior and the Social Environment, 10,* 37–54.

Greene, R. R. (2007). *Social work practice: A risk and resilience perspective.* Belmont, CA: Thomson Brooks/Cole.

Greene, R. R. (2008a). *Human behavior theory and social work practice* (3rd ed.). New Brunswick, NJ: Aldine Transaction.

Greene, R. R. (2008b). *Social work with the aged and their families* (3rd ed.). New Brunswick, NJ: Aldine de Gruyter.

Greene, R. R. (2014). Resilience as effective functional capacity: An ecological stress model. *Journal of Human Behavior and the Social Environment, 24,* 937–950.

Greene, R. R., & Barnes, G. (1998). The ecological perspective and social work practice: Applying the ecological perspective. In R. R. Greene & M. Watkins (Eds.), *Serving diverse constituencies* (pp. 63–96). Hawthorne, NY: Aldine de Gruyter.

Greene, R. R., & Cohen, H. L. (2005). Social work with older adults and their families: Changing practice paradigms. *Families in Society, 86,* 367–373.

Greene, R. R., Galambos, C., Cohen, H., & Greene, N. (2016). *Social work with the aged and their families* (4th ed.). New Brunswick, NJ: Aldine Transaction.

Greene, R. R., & Kropf, N. P. (2014). *Caregiving and care sharing: A life course perspective.* Washington, DC: NASW Press.

Greene, R. R., & Kropf, N. P. (2017). From caregiving to caresharing. In *Encyclopedia of social work* [Online]. http://socialwork.oxfordre.com/view/10.1093/acrefore/9780199975839.001.0001/acrefore-9780199975839-e-1265?rskey=qLL7VZ&result=25

Greene, R. R., & Schriver, J. (2016). *Handbook of human behavior and the social environment: A practice-based approach.* New Brunswick, NJ: Aldine Transaction Press.

Greene, R. R., & Watkins, M. (1998). *Serving diverse constituencies: Applying the ecological perspective.* Hawthorne, NY: Aldine de Gruyter.

Greenfield, E. A. (2015, August 12). *Age-friendly community initiatives: Coming to a neighborhood near you?* Retrieved from http://blog.oup.com/2015/08/age-friendly-community-initiatives

Greenfield, E. A. (2016). Support from neighbors and aging in place: Can NORC programs make a difference? *Gerontologist, 56,* 651--659. doi:10.1093/geront/gnu162

Greenfield, E. A., & Fedor, J. P. (2015). Characterizing older adults' involvement in Naturally Occurring Retirement Community (NORC) supportive service programs. *Journal of Gerontological Social Work, 58,* 449–468. doi:10.1080/01634372.2015.1008168

Greenfield, E. A., Oberlink, M., Scharlach, A. E., Neal, M. B., & Stafford, P. B. (2015). Age-friendly community initiatives: Conceptual issues and key questions. *Gerontologist, 55,* 191–198.

Greenfield, E. A., Scharlach, A. E., & Davitt, J. K. (2016). Organizational characteristics and volunteering in age-friendly supportive service initiatives. *Nonprofit and Voluntary Sector Quarterly, 45,* 931–948.

Griffin, L. (2005). Friendship Club and the Chaplain's Lunch: Small-group activities for low functioning individuals. *Activities Directors' Quarterly for Alzheimer's and Other Dementia Patients, 6*(3), 4–8.

Gutheil, I. A., & Congress, E. (2000). Resiliency in older people: A paradigm for practice. In E. Norman (Ed.), *Resiliency enhancement: Putting the strengths perspective into social work practice* (pp. 40–54). New York: Columbia University Press.

Gutierrez, L. M., & Lewis, E. A. (1998). A feminist perspective on organizing with women of color. In F. G. Rivera & J. L. Erlich (Eds.), *Community organizing in a diverse society* (3rd ed., pp. 97–116). Boston: Allyn & Bacon.

Hagan, R., Manktelow, R., Taylor, B. J., & Mallett, J. (2014). Reducing loneliness amongst older people: A systematic search and narrative review. *Aging & Mental Health, 18,* 683–693.

Haight, J. M. (2003). Human error and the challenges of an aging workforce [Electronic version]. *Professional Safety, 48,* 18–24. Retrieved from http://www.asse.org

Hamel, G., & Välikangas, L. (2003). The quest for resilience. *Harvard Business Review, 81,* 52–63.

Hardcastle, D. A., Wenocur, S., & Powers, P. R. (2011). *Community practice: Theories and skills for social workers* (3rd ed.). New York: Oxford University Press.

Hareven, T. K. (1996). *Aging and generational relations over the life course: A historical and cross-cultural perspective.* Hawthorne, NY: Aldine de Gruyter.

Hareven, T. L. (1982). The life course and aging in historical perspective. In T. K. Hareven & K. J. Adams (Eds.), *Aging and life course transitions: An interdisciplinary perspective* (pp. 1–26). New York: Guilford Press.

Harrell, R. Lynott, J., & Guzman, S. (2014). *What is livable? Community preferences of older adults,* Washington, DC: AARP Public Policy Institute. Retrieved from https://www.aarp.org/ppi/issues/livable-communities/info-2015/what-is-livable-AARP-ppi-liv-com.html

Harrigan, M. P., & Farmer, R. L. (2000). The myths and facts of aging. In R. L. Schneider, N. P. Kropf, & A. J. Kisor (Eds.), *Gerontological social work: Knowledge, service settings, and special populations* (2nd ed., pp. 26–51). Belmont, CA: Brooks/Cole.

Hawley, D. R., & DeHaan, L. (1996). Towards a definition of family resilience: Integrating the life span. *Family Process, 35*, 283–298.

Hébert, R., Lévesque, L., Vézina, J., Lavoie, J. P., Ducharme, F., Gendron, C., et al. (2003). Efficacy of a psychoeducative group program for caregivers of demented persons living at home: A randomized controlled trial. *Journals of Gerontology, Series B: Psychological Sciences and Social Sciences, 58*(1), S58–S67.

HelpAge International. (2009). *Why it's time for a convention on the rights of older people.* London: HelpAge International. Retrieved from http://cotavic.org .au/wp-content/uploads/2013/02/Why-convention-older-people1.pdf

Hepworth, D. H., Rooney, R. H., & Larsen, J. A. (1997). *Direct social work practice.* Pacific Grove, CA: Brooks/Cole.

Hepworth, D. H., Rooney, R. H., Rooney, G. D., & Strom-Gottfried, K. (2013). *Direct social work practice: Theory and skills* (9th ed.). Belmont, CA: Brooks/ Cole.

Herr, S. S., & Weber, G. (1999). *Aging, rights, and quality of life.* Baltimore: Paul H. Brookes.

Hicks, M., & Lam, M. (1999). Decision-making within the social course of dementia: Accounts by Chinese-American caregivers. *Culture, Medicine & Psychiatry, 23*, 415–452.

Hinton, L., Guo, Z., & Hillygus, J. (2000). Working with culture: A qualitative analysis of barriers to the recruitment of Chinese-American family caregivers for dementia research. *Journal of Cross-Cultural Gerontology, 15*, 119–137.

Hodge, D. R. (2001). Spiritual assessment: A review of major qualitative methods and a new framework for assessing spirituality. *Social Work, 46*, 203–214.

Hodge, D. R., & Holtrop, C. (2002) Spiritual assessment: A review of complementary assessment models. In B. Hugen & T. L. Scales (Eds.), *Christianity and social work: Readings on the integration of Christian faith and social work practice* (2nd ed., pp. 167–192). Botsford, CT: NACSW Press.

Holland, L., & Courtney, R. (1998). Increasing cultural competence with the Latino community. *Journal of Community Health Nursing, 23*, 49–64.

Holstein, M. B., & Minkler, M. (2003). Self, society, and the "new" gerontology. *Gerontologist, 43*, 787–796.

Homan, M. S. (2016). *Promoting community change: Making it happen in the real world* (6th ed.). Boston: Cengage Learning.

Hoogenhout, E. M., de Groot, R. H., van der Elst, W., & Jolles, J. (2012). Effects of a comprehensive educational group intervention in older women with cognitive complaints: A randomized controlled trial. *Aging & Mental Health, 16*, 135–144.

Hooyman, N. R. (1996). Curriculum and teaching: Today and tomorrow. In Mandel School of Applied Social Sciences (Ed.), *White paper on social work education—Today and tomorrow* (pp. 11–24). Cleveland: Case Western Reserve University Press.

Hooyman, N., Hooyman, G., & Kethley, A. (1981, March). *The role of gerontological social work in interdisciplinary care.* Paper presented at the annual program meeting of the Council on Social Work Education, Louisville, KY.

Hornung, C., Eleazer, G., Strongers, H., Wieland, G., Eng, C., McCann, R., & Sapir, M. (1998). Ethnicity and decision-makers in a group of frail older people. *Journal of the American Geriatrics Society, 46*, 280–286.

Hornsby, E. (2006). *Using policy to drive organizational change.* Hoboken, NJ: Wiley.

Hubble, M. A., Duncan, B. L., & Miller, D. (Eds.). (1999). *The heart & soul of change: What works in therapy.* Washington, DC: American Psychological Association.

Hunt, C. K. (2003). Concepts in caregiver research. *Journal of Nursing Scholarship, 35*, 27–32.

Huntley, A. L., Mann, T., Huws, D., Paranjothy, S., & Purdy, S. (2013, June). Is case management effective in reducing risk of unplanned hospital admissions for older people? *Family Practice, 30*, 266–275.

Hutchison, E. D. (2013). *Essential of human behavior: Integrating person, environment and the life course.* Thousand Oaks, CA: Sage Publications.

Hutchison, E. D. (2015). *Dimensions of human behavior: The changing life course* (5th ed.). Thousand Oaks, CA: Sage Publications.

Hwang, K. (1999). Filial piety and loyalty: Two types of social identification in Confucianism. *Asian Journal of Social Psychology, 2*, 163–183.

Ife, J. (2008). *Human rights and social work: Towards rights-based practice.* Cambridge, England: Cambridge University Press.

Ihara, C. (2004). Are individual rights necessary? A Confucian perspective. In K. Shun & D. B. Wong (Eds.), *Confucian ethics: A comparative study of self, autonomy, and community* (pp. 11–30). New York: Cambridge University Press.

Institute of Medicine. (2001). *Crossing the quality chasm: A new health system for the 21st century.* Washington, DC: National Academy Press.

Institute of Medicine. (2011). *The health of lesbian, gay, bisexual, and transgender people: Building a foundation for better understanding.* Washington, DC: National Academies Press.

International Federation of Social Workers. (2012, February 20). *Ageing and older adults.* Retrieved from http://ifsw.org/policies/ageing-and-older-adults/

International Labour Organization, Office of the United Nations. (2015, July 15). Sixth Session of the Open-ended Working Group on Ageing Item 4: Existing international framework on the human rights of older persons and identification of existing gaps at the international level. Statement made by Mr. Vinicius Pinheiro retrieved from https://social.un.org/ageing-working-group/documents/sixth/ILOStatement.pdf 9/13/17

Ivery, J. M. (2014). The NORC supportive services model: The role of social capital in community aging initiatives. *Journal of Community Practice, 22*, 451–471.

Iwarsson, S. (2005). A long-term perspective on person–environment fit and ADL: Dependence among older Swedish adults. *Gerontologist, 45*, 327–336.

Janevic, M., & Connell, C. (2001). Racial, ethnic, and culture differences in the dementia caregiving experience: Recent findings. *Gerontologist, 41*, 334–347.

Janoff-Bulman, R., & Berger, A. R. (2000). The other side of trauma: Towards a psychology of appreciation. In J. H. Harvey & E. D. Miller (Eds.), *Loss and trauma: General and close relationship perspectives* (pp. 29–44). Philadelphia: Brunner-Routledge.

Jansson, B. S. (2014). *Becoming an effective policy advocate: From policy practice to social justice* (7th ed.). Pacific Grove, CA: Brooks/Cole.

Johnson, A. K. (1998). The revitalization of community practice: Characteristics, competencies, and curricula for community-based services. *Journal of Community Practice, 5*(3), 37–62.

Johnson, A. K. (1999). *The place of community in social work practice research: Conceptual and methodological developments.* Thousand Oaks, CA: Sage Publications.

Johnson, J. L., & Grant, G. (2005). *Community practice.* Boston: Pearson Education.

Johnson, L. C., & Yanca, S. J. (2007). *Social work practice: A generalist approach* (9th ed.). Boston: Pearson Education.

Joint Commission. (2010). *Advancing effective communication, cultural competence, and patient and family-centered care: A roadmap for hospitals.* Oakbrook Terrace, IL: Author.

Kadushin, A. (1992). *Supervision in social work* (3rd ed.). New York: Columbia University Press.

Kadushin, A., & Kadushin, G. (1997). *The social work interview: A guide for human services professionals.* New York: Columbia University Press.

Kahn, R. L. (1994). Opportunities, aspirations, and goodness of fit. In J. W. Riley, R. L. Kahn, & A. Foner (Eds.), *Age and structural lag: Society's failure to provide meaningful opportunities in work, family, and leisure* (pp. 37–56). New York: Wiley.

Kane, R. (1992). Case management: Ethical pitfalls on the road to high-quality managed care. In S. Rose (Ed.), *Case management and social work practice* (pp. 219–228). White Plains, NY: Longman.

Kane, R. A. (2006). A social worker's historical and future perspective on residential care. In B. Berkman & S. D'Ambruoso (Eds.), *Handbook of social work in health and aging* (pp. 591–600). New York: Oxford University Press.

Kaplan, C. P. (2000). A case study of resiliency enhancement interventions with an African American woman. In E. Norman (Ed.), *Resiliency enhancement: Putting the strengths perspective into social work practice* (pp. 55–69). New York: Columbia University Press.

Kapp, M. B. (1998). Forcing services on at-risk older adults: When doing good is not so good. *Social Work in Health Care, 13*, 1–13.

Karel, M., & Hinrichsen, G. (2000). Treatment of depression in late life: Psychotherapeutic interventions. *Clinical Psychology Review, 20*, 707–729.

Karger, H. J., & Stoesz, D. (2014). *American social welfare policy* (7th ed.). New York: Pearson.

Kaye, L. W. (2005). *Perspectives on productive aging: Social work with the new aged.* Washington, DC: NASW Press.

Kelley, S. J., & Whitley, D. (2003). Psychological distress and physical health problems in grandparents raising grandchildren: Development of an empirically based intervention model. In B. Hayslip & J. H. Patrick (Eds.), *Working with custodial grandparents* (pp. 127–144). New York: Springer.

Kelly, T. B. (2004). Mutual aid groups for older persons with a mental illness. *Journal of Gerontological Social Work, 44*(1–2), 111–126.

Kenyon, G. M., & Randall, W. (2001). Narrative gerontology: An overview. In G. Kenyon, P. Clark, & B. de Vries (Eds.), *Narrative gerontology* (pp. 3–18). New York: Springer.

Kimmel, D. C. (1978). Adult development and aging: A gay perspective. *Journal of Social Issues, 34*, 113–130.

Kirschner, J. D. (1986). Context and process: An ecological view of the interdependence of practice and research. *American Journal of Community Psychology, 14*, 581–589.

Kirst-Ashman, K. K. (2000). *Human behavior, communities, organizations, and groups in the macro social environment: An empowerment approach.* Belmont, CA: Wadsworth/Thomson Learning.

Kirst-Ashman, K., & Hull, G. H. (1999). *Understanding generalist practice* (2nd ed.). Chicago: Nelson-Hall.

Kitchener, K. S. (1984). Intuition, critical evaluation, and ethical principles: The foundation for ethical decisions in counseling psychology. *Counseling Psychologist, 12*, 43–55.

Kivnick, H. Q. (1993, Winter/Spring). Everyday mental health: A guide to assessing life strengths. *Generations, 17*, 13–20.

Kivnick, H. Q., & Murray, S. V. (1997). Vital involvement: An overlooked source of identity in frail elders. *Journal of Aging and Identity, 2*, 205–223.

Kivnick, H. Q., & Murray, S. V. (2001). Life strengths interview guide: Assessing elder clients' strengths. *Journal of Gerontological Social Work, 34*(4), 7–32.

Kiyak, H., & Hooyman, N. (1999). Aging in the twenty-first century. *Hallym International Journal of Aging, 1*, 56–66.

Klein, D. M., & White, J. M. (1996). *Family theories: An introduction.* Thousand Oaks, CA: Sage Publications.

Kleinman, A. M. (1978). Rethinking the social and cultural context of psychopathology and psychiatric care. In T. C. Manschreck & A. M. Klunman (Eds.), *Renewal in psychiatry: A critical rationale perspective* (pp. 97–138). New York: John Wiley & Sons.

Kleinman, A. M. (1980). *Patients and healers in the context of culture.* Berkeley: University of California Press.

Kleinman, A. M. (1992). Pain as a human experience: An introduction. In M. DelVecchio, P. E. Brodwin, B. Good, & A. Kleinman (Eds.), *Pain as a human experience: An anthropological perspective* (pp. 169–197). Berkeley: University of California Press.

Kline, M., Schonfeld, D. J., & Lichtenstein, R. (1995). Benefits and challenges of school-based crisis response teams. *Journal of School Health, 65*, 245–249.

Knight, B. (1999). The scientific basis for psychotherapeutic interventions with older adults: An overview. *JCLP/In Session, 55*, 927–934.

Kochera, A., Straight, A., & Guterbock, T. (2005). *Beyond 50.05: A report to the nation on livable communities—Creating environments for successful aging.* Washington, DC: AARP Public Policy Institute.

Kolomer, S. (2009). Grandparents raising grandchildren. In S. M. Cummings & N. P. Kropf (Eds.). *Handbook of psychosocial interventions with older adults: Evidence-based treatment* (pp. 321–344). New York: Routledge.

Konopka, G. (1983). *Social group work: A helping process* (3rd ed.). Englewood Cliffs, NJ: Prentice Hall.

Kottler, J. A. (2001). *Learning group leadership: An experiential approach.* Needham Heights, MA: Allyn & Bacon.

Kraft, M. E., & Furlong, S. R. (2015). *Public policy: Politics, analysis, and alternatives* (5th ed.). Thousand Oaks, CA: CQ Press.

Krause, N. (2004). Stressors arising in highly valued roles, meaning in life, and the physical health status of older adults. *Journals of Gerontology, Series B: Psychological Sciences and Social Sciences, 59*(5), S287–S297.

Kretzmann, J. P., & McKnight, J. L. (1993). *Building communities from the inside out: A path toward finding and mobilizing a community's assets.* Chicago: Assertive Community Treatment Association.

Kretzmann, J. P., & McKnight, J. L. (1997). *A guide to capacity inventories: Mobilizing the community skills of local residents.* Chicago: Assertive Community Treatment Association.

Kropf, N. P. (2006). Community caregiving partnerships promoting alliances to support care providers. *Journal of Human Behavior in the Social Environment, 14*(1/2), 327–340.

Kropf, N., & Cummings, S. (2017). *Evidence based treatment with older adults: Theory, practice, and research.* New York: Oxford University Press.

Kwak, J., & Haley, W. (2005). Current research findings on end-of-life decision making among racially or ethnically diverse groups. *Gerontologist, 45,* 634–641.

Laird, J. (1993). *Revisioning social work education: A social constructionist approach.* New York: Haworth Press.

Lawton, M. P. (1982). Competence, environmental press, and the adaptation of older people. In M. P. Lawton, P. G. Windley, & T. O. Byerts (Eds.), *Aging and the environment: Theoretical approaches* (pp. 33–59). New York: Springer.

Lawton, M. P. (1989). Behavior-relevant ecological factors. In K. W. Schaie & C. Schooler (Eds.), *Social structure and aging: Psychological processes* (pp. 57–78). Hillsdale, NJ: Lawrence Erlbaum.

Lawton, M. P., & Nahemow, L. (1973). Ecology and the aging process. In C. Eisdorfer & M. P. Lawton (Eds.), *The psychology of adult development and aging* (pp. 619–674). Washington, DC: American Psychological Association.

Lazarus, R. S., & Folkman, S. (1984). *Stress, appraisal, and coping.* New York: Springer.

Lee, Y., & Sung, K. (1998). Cultural influences on caregiving burden: Cases of Koreans and Americans. *International Journal of Aging & Human Development, 46,* 125–141.

Lemke, S., & Moos, R. H. (2002). Prognosis of older patients in mixed-age alcoholism treatment programs. *Journal of Substance Abuse Treatment, 22,* 33–43.

Lenze, E. J., Hickman, S., Hershey, T., Wendleton, L., Ly, K., Dixon, D., et al. (2014). Mindfulness-based stress reduction for older adults with worry symptoms and co-occurring cognitive dysfunction. *International Journal of Geriatric Psychiatry, 29*, 991–1000.

Leven, C. (2004). *Older workers: Opportunity at our doorstep.* Tokyo: Nikkei Senior Work-Life Forum.

Levy, C. S. (1973). The value base of social work. *Journal of Education for Social Work, 9*, 34–42.

Levy, C. S. (1984). Values and ethics. In S. Dillick (Ed.), *Value foundations of social work* (pp. 17–29). Detroit: Wayne State University, School of Social Work.

Lewis, J. S., & Harrell, E. B. (2002). Older adults. In R. R. Greene (Ed.), *Resiliency: An integrated approach to practice, policy, and research* (pp. 277–292). Washington, DC: NASW Press.

Lichtenberg, P. A. (Ed.). (2000). *Handbook of assessment in clinical gerontology.* New York: John Wiley.

Lin, Y., Dai, Y., & Hwang, S. (2003). Effect of reminiscence on the elderly population: A systematic review. *Public Health Nursing, 20*, 297–306.

Lindland, E., Fond, M., Haydon, A., & Kendall-Taylor, N. (2015). *Gauging aging: Mapping the gaps between expert and public understandings of aging in America.* Washington, DC: FrameWorks Institute.

Linzer, N. (2002). An ethical dilemma in home care. *Journal of Gerontological Social Work, 37*(2), 23–34.

Löfqvist, C., Granbom, M., Himmelsbach, I., Iwarsson, S., Oswald, F., & Haak, M. (2013). Voices on relocation and aging in place in very old age—A complex and ambivalent matter. *Gerontologist, 53*, 919–927.

Long, D. D., & Holle, M. C. (1997). *Macro systems in the social environment.* Itasca, IL: F. E. Peacock.

Longres, J. F. (1990). *Human behavior in the social environment.* Itasca, IL: F. E. Peacock.

Lopez, O. (2007). Self-care practices and Hispanic women with diabetes. In R. R. Greene (Ed.), *Contemporary issues of care* (pp. 183–200). New York: Haworth Press.

Lowy, L. (1982). Social group work with vulnerable older persons: A theoretical perspective. *Social Work with Groups, 5*, 21–32.

Lowy, L. (1991). *Social work with the aging: The challenge and promise of the later years.* New York: Harper & Row.

Lum, D. (1999). *Culturally competent practice.* Pacific Grove, CA: Brooks/Cole.

Luna, I., Ardon, E., Lim, Y., Cromwell, S., Phillips, L., & Russell, C. (1996). The relevance of familism in cross-cultural studies of family caregiving. *Western Journal of Nursing Research, 18*, 267–274.

Lustbader, W., & Williams, C. C. (2006). Culture change in long term care. In B. Berkman & S. D'Ambruoso (Eds.), *Handbook of social work in health and aging* (pp. 645–652). New York: Oxford University Press.

Luyas, G. T. (1990). *An explanatory model of diabetes.* New York: Sage Publications.

Lyons, K. S., & Zarit, S. H. (1999). Formal and informal support: The great divide. *International Journal of Geriatric Psychiatry, 14*, 183–196.

Macgowan, M. (1997). A measure of engagement for social group work: The group-work engagement measure. *Journal of Social Service Research, 23*, 17–37.

Macgowan, M. (2003). Increasing engagement in groups: A measurement-based approach. *Social Work with Groups, 26*, 5–28.

Magana, S. (2006). Older Latino family caregivers. In B. Burkman (Ed.), *Handbook of social work in health and aging* (pp. 327–380). New York: Oxford University Press.

Malekoff, A. (2004). Remembering with and without awareness through poetry to better understand aging and disability. *Journal of Gerontological Social Work, 44*(1–2), 255–264.

Marx, M., Cohen, M. J., Renaudat, K., Libin, A., & Thein, K. (2005). Technology-mediated versus face to-face intergenerational programming. *Journal of Intergenerational Relationships, 3*, 101–118.

Masten, A. (1994). Resilience in individual development: Successful adaptation despite risk and adversity. In M. C. Wang & E. W. Gordon (Eds.), *Educational resilience in inner-city America: Challenges and prospects* (pp. 3–25). Hillsdale, NJ: Lawrence Erlbaum.

McAdams, D. P., Diamond, A., Mansfield, E., & de St. Aubin, E. (1997). Stories of commitment: The psychosocial construction of generative lives. *Journal of Personality and Social Psychology, 72*, 678–694.

McCallion, P., Janicki, M. P., Grant-Griffin, L., & Kolomer, S. (2000). Grandparent caregivers II: Service needs and service provision issues. *Journal of Gerontological Social Work, 3*(3), 57–84.

McCarthy, J. (2005). Planning a future workforce: An Australian perspective. *New Review of Academic Librarianship, 11*, 41–56.

McInnis-Dittrich, K. (2014). *Social work with older adults: A biopsychosocial approach to assessment and intervention* (4th ed.). Boston: Pearson.

McNulty, R. H. (2005). *Beyond 50.05: A report to the nation on livable communities: Creating Environments for successful aging.* Retrieved from https://assets.aarp.org/rgcenter/il/beyond_50_communities.pdf

McNutt, J. G., & Hoefer, R. (2016). *Social welfare policy: Responding to a changing world.* Chicago: Lyceum Books.

McSweeney, J. C. (1990). *Making behavior changes after myocardial infarction: A naturalistic study* (Doctoral dissertation). Austin: University of Texas at Austin.

McSweeney, J. C., Alan, J. D., & Mayo, K. (1997). Exploring the use of explanatory models in nursing and research practice. *Image Journal of Nursing Scholarship, 29*, 243–248.

Merck & Co., Inc. (2005). *The Merck manual of geriatrics.* Retrieved from http://www.merckmanuals.com/professional/geriatrics

Merleen, R. (2006). Workforce crisis: Preparing for the coming IT crunch. *Computerworld, 40*, 34–35.

MetLife Mature Market Institute. (2010, September). *The MetLife report on aging in place 2.0: Rethinking solutions to the home care challenge.* Retrieved from https://www.metlife.com/assets/cao/mmi/publications/studies/2010/mmi-aging-place-study.pdf

MetLife Mature Market Institute. (2011, June). *The MetLife study of caregiving costs to working caregivers: Double jeopardy for baby boomers caring for their parents.* Retrieved from https://www.metlife.com/assets/cao/mmi/publications/studies/2011/Caregiving-Costs-to-Working-Caregivers.pdf

Meyer, C. (1973). Direct services in new and old contexts. In A. J. Kahn (Ed.), *Shaping the new social work* (pp. 26–54). New York: Columbia University Press.

Meyer, C. (1983). Selecting appropriate practice models. In A. Rosenblatt & D. Waldfogel (Eds.), *Handbook of clinical social work* (pp. 731–749). San Francisco: Jossey-Bass.

Miley, K. K., O'Melia, M., & DuBois, B. (2007). *Generalist social work practice: An empowering approach* (5th ed.). Boston: Pearson Education.

Mill, J. S. (1957). *Utilitarianism.* New York: Bobbs-Merrill. (Original work published 1863)

Miller, S. D., Duncan, B. L., & Hubble, M. A. (1997). *Escape from Babel: Toward a unifying language for psychotherapy practice.* New York: W. W. Norton.

Minkler, M., Glover Blackwell, A. G., Thompson, M., & Tamir, H. (2003) Community-based participatory research: Implications for public health funding. *American Journal of Publich Health, 93,* 1210–1213.

Moeller, J. R., Albanese, T. H., Garchar, K., Aultman, J. M., Radwant, S., & Frate, D. (2012). Functions and outcomes of a clinical medical ethics committee: A review of 100 consults. *HEC Forum, 24,* 99–114. doi:10.1007/s10730-011-9170-9

Molinari, V. (2002). Group therapy in long term care sites. *Clinical Gerontologist, 25*(1–2), 13–24.

Moody, H. R., & Sasser, J. R. (2015). *Aging: Concepts and controversies* (8th ed.). Thousand Oaks, CA: Sage Publications.

Moon, A., Lubben, J., & Villa, V. (1998). Awareness and utilization of community long-term care services by elderly Korean and non-Hispanic white Americans. *Gerontologist, 38,* 309–316.

Moore, R. P., Cagle, J. G., Croghan, C. F., & Smith, J. (2014). Working with LGBT older adults: An assessment of employee training practices, needs, and preferences of senior service organizations in Minnesota. *Journal of Gerontological Social Work, 57,* 322–332.

Morano, C. L., & King, D. (2005). Religiosity as a mediator of caregiver well-being: Does ethnicity make a difference? *Journal of Gerontological Social Work, 45*(1–2), 69–84.

Mosner, E., Spiezle, C., & Emerman, J. (2003). *The convergence of the aging workforce and accessible technology.* Redmond, WA: Microsoft Accessible Technology Group.

Moss, A. S., Reibel, D. K., Greeson, J. M., Thapar, A., Bubb, R., Salmon, J., & Newberg, A. B. (2015). An adapted mindfulness-based stress reduction program for elders in a continuing care retirement community: Quantitative and qualitative results from a pilot randomized controlled trial. *Journal of Applied Gerontology, 34*, 518–538.

Myers, L., Kropf, N. P., & Robinson, M. M. (2002). Grandparents raising grandchildren: Case management in a rural setting. *Journal of Human Behavior in the Social Environment, 5*, 53–71.

NAACP. (2016). *Criminal justice fact sheet.* Retrieved from http://www.naacp .org/criminal-justice-fact-sheet/

Naito-Chan, E., Damron-Rodriguez, J. A., & Simmons, W. J. (2004). Identifying competencies for geriatric social work practice. *Journal of Gerontological Social Work, 43*(4), 59–78.

Naleppa, M. J., & Hash, K. M. (2001). Home-based practice with older adults: Challenges and opportunities in the home environment. *Journal of Gerontological Social Work, 35*(1), 71–88.

Naleppa, M. J., & Reid, W. J. (2000). Integrating case management and brief-treatment strategies: A hospital-based geriatric program. *Social Work in Health Care, 31*(4), 1–23.

Naleppa, M. J., & Reid, W. J. (2003). *Gerontological social work: A task-centered approach.* New York: Columbia University Press.

National Aging in Place Council. (2015). *CAPS remodelers: Helping clients stay in the home they love.* Retrieved from http://www.ageinplace .org/Practical-Advice/Housing/article/CAPS-Remodelers-Helping-ClientsStay-in-the-Home-They-Love

National Alliance for Caregiving. (2015). *Caregiving in the U.S.—Executive summary.* Retrieved from http://www.caregiving.org/wp-content/ uploads/2015/05/2015_CaregivingintheUS_Executive-Summary-June-4_ WEB.pdf

National Association of Social Workers. (2008). *International policy on human rights.* Retrieved from http://www.naswdc.org/pressroom/events/911/ humanrights.asp

National Association of Social Workers. (2013). *NASW standards for social work case management.* Washington, DC: NASW Press.

National Association of Social Workers. (2015). *Standards and indicators for cultural competence in social work practice.* Washington, DC: Author. http://www .socialworkers.org/practice/standards/NASWculturalstandards.pdf

National Association of Social Workers. (2016a). *Civil rights.* Retrieved from http://www.socialworkers.org/advocacy/issues/civil_rights.asp

National Association of Social Workers. (2016b). *NASW standards and indicators for cultural competence in social work practice.* Washington, DC: Author.

National Association of Social Workers. (2017). *Code of ethics of the National Association of Social Workers.* Washington, DC: Author.

National Center for Cultural Competence. (2016). *Conceptual frameworks/models, guiding values and principles.* Retrieved from https://nccc.georgetown.edu/ foundations/framework.php

National Resource Center on LGBT Aging. (2016). *Housing/homelessness/long term care.* Retrieved from https://www.lgbtagingcenter.org/resources/ resources.cfm?s=15

Neimeyer, R. A. (Ed.). (2001). *Meaning reconstruction and the experience of loss.* Washington, DC: American Psychological Association.

Netting, F. E., Kettner, P. M., & McMurtry, S. L. (2011). *Social work macro practice* (5th ed.). Boston: Pearson Education.

Netting, F. E., & Williams, F. G. (1995). Integrating geriatric case management into primary care physician practices [Practice Forum]. *Health & Social Work, 20,* 152–155.

Network, G. R. (2004). *What is resiliency?* Retrieved from http://www.global resiliency.net/brochure.0604.pdf

Newman, B. M., & Newman, P. R. (2005). *Development through life: A psychosocial approach* (8th ed.). Pacific Grove, CA: Brooks/Cole.

Norman, E. (Ed.). (2000). *Resiliency enhancement: Putting the strengths perspective into social work practice.* New York: Columbia University Press.

Northen, H. (1982). *Clinical social work.* New York: Columbia University Press.

Norton, D. (1976). *Dual perspectives: The inclusion of ethnic minority content in social work curriculum.* New York: Council on Social Work Education.

Nowitz, L. (2005). Geriatric case management: Spiritual challenges. *Journal of Gerontological Social Work, 45*(1–2), 185–201.

Noziak, R. (1974). *Anarchy, state, and utopia.* New York: Basic Books.

NPR Staff. (2014, May 19). "Silver tsunami" and other terms that can irk the over-65 set. *NPR* Retrieved from http://www.npr.org/2014/05/19/313133555/ silver-tsunami-and-other-terms-that-can-irk-the-over-65-set

O'Fallon, L. R., Tyson, F. L., & Dearry, A. (Eds.). (2000). *Successful models of community-based participatory research: Final report.* Research Triangle Park, NC: National Institute of Environmental Health Sciences.

Officer, A., Schneider, M. L., Wu, D., Nash, P., Thiyagarajan, J. A., & Beard, J. P. (2016). Valuing older people: Time for a global campaign to combat ageism. *Bulletin of the World Health Organization, 94,* 710–710A. doi:http://dx.doi .org/10.2471/BLT.16.184960

Ogbu, J. U. (1981). Origins of human competence: A cultural–ecological perspective. *Child Development, 52,* 413–429.

Okayama, C. M., Furuto, S., & Edmondson, J. (2001). Components of cultural competence: Attitudes, knowledge, and skills. In R. Fong & S. Furuto (Eds.), *Culturally competent practice: Skills, interventions, and evaluations* (pp. 89–100). Boston: Allyn & Bacon.

Older Americans Act of 1965, P.L. 89-73, 79 Stat. 218 (July 14, 1965).

Osborne, T., & Furlong, D. (2009). *The human rights of older people in the United States and Canada.* Retrieved from http://www.ageuk.org.uk/documents/ en-gb/for-professionals/international/the_human_rights_of_older_ people_in_the_us_and_canada_2009_pro.pdf?dtrk=true

Osman, H., & Perlin, T. M. (1994). Patient self-determination and the artificial prolongation of life. *Health & Social Work, 19,* 245–252.

Pantoja, A., & Perry, W. (1998). Community development and restoration: A perspective and case study. In F. G. Rivera & J. L. Erlich (Eds.), *Community organizing in a diverse society* (pp. 220–242). Boston: Allyn & Bacon.

Park, C. L., & Folkman, S. (1997). The role of meaning in the context of stress and coping. *General Review of Psychology, 1*, 115–144.

Park, I., & Cho, L.-J. (1995). Confucianism and the Korean family. *Journal of Comparative Family Studies, 26*, 117–134.

Parmelee, P. A., & Lawton, M. P. (1990). The design of special environments for the aged. In J. E. Birren & K. W. Schaie (Eds.), *Handbook of the psychology of aging* (3rd ed., pp. 465–489). San Diego: Academic Press.

Patient Protection and Affordable Care Act, P.L. 111-148, §2702, 124 Stat. 119, 318–319 (2010).

Patterson, J. M., & Garwick, A. W. (1998). Theoretical linkages: Family meanings and sense of coherence. In H. I. McCubbin, E. A. Thompson, A. I. Thompson, & J. E. Fromer (Eds.), *Stress, coping and health in families: Sense of coherence and resiliency* (pp. 71–90). Thousand Oaks, CA: Sage Publications.

Pearlin, L. I., Aneshensel, C. S., & Leblanc, A. J. (1997). The forms and mechanisms of stress proliferation: The case of AIDS caregivers. *Journal of Health and Social Behavior, 38*, 223–236.

Peluso, P. R., Watts, R. E., & Parsons, M. (Eds.). (2013). *Changing aging, changing family therapy.* New York: Routledge.

Pethokoukis, J. M. (2006). The economy may face a shortage of qualified workers. *U.S. News & World Report, 140*(22), 46–47.

Pillari, V., & Newsome, M. (1998). *Human behavior in the social environment families, groups, organizations, and communities.* Pacific Grove, CA: Brooks/Cole.

Pincus, A., & Minahan, A. (1973). *Social work practice: Model and method.* Itasca, IL: E. Peacock.

Pinderhughes, E. (1983). Empowerment for our clients and for ourselves. *Social Casework, 64*, 331–338.

Pinderhughes, E. (1989). *Understanding race, ethnicity, and power: The key to efficacy in clinical practice.* New York: Free Press.

Pinquart, M., & Forstmeier, S. (2012). Effects of reminiscence interventions on psychosocial outcomes: A meta-analysis. *Aging & Mental Health, 16*, 541–558.

Pinquart, M., & Sorensen, S. (2003). Associations of stressors and uplifts of caregiving with caregiver burden and depressive mood: A meta-analysis. *Journals of Gerontology, Series B: Psychological Sciences, 58*(2), 112–128.

Pitt-Catsouphes, M., & Smyer, M. A. (2006a, February). *How old are today's older workers?* (Issue Brief No. 4). Chestnut Hill, MA: Center on Aging and Work at Boston College.

Pitt-Catsouphes, M., & Smyer, M. A. (2006b, March). *One size does not fit all: Workplace flexibility* (Issue Brief No. 5). Chestnut Hill, MA: Center on Aging and Work at Boston College.

Poinier, A. C., & Herman, C. J. (Eds.). (2014) *Healthy aging.* Retrieved from http://www.webmd.com/healthy-aging/tc/healthy-aging-topic-overview#1

Popple, P. R. (2013). Social services. In *Encyclopedia of social work* [Online]. Washington, DC, and New York: NASW Press and Oxford University Press.

Portz, J. D., Retrum, J., Wright, L., Boggs, J. M., Wilkins, S., Grimm, C., et al. (2014). Assessing capacity for providing culturally competent services to

LGBT older adults. *Journal of Gerontological Social Work, 57,* 305–321. doi:10 .1080/01634372.2013.857378

Preschl, B., Maercker, A., Wagner, B., Forstmeier, S., Baños, R. M., Alcañiz, M., et al. (2012). Life-review therapy with computer supplements for depression in the elderly: A randomized controlled trial. *Aging & Mental Health, 16,* 964–974.

President's Commission for the Study of Ethical Problems in Medicine and Biomedical and Behavioral Research. (1983a). *Deciding to forgo life-sustaining treatment: A report on the ethical, medical, and legal issues in treatment decisions.* Washington, DC: Author.

President's Commission for the Study of Ethical Problems in Medicine and Biomedical and Behavioral Research. (1983b). *Summing up: Final report on studies of the ethical and legal problems in medicine and biomedical and behavioral research.* Washington, DC: Author.

Price, E. L., Bereknyei, S., Kuby, A., Levinson, W., & Braddock, C. H. (2012). New elements for informed decision-making: A qualitative study of older adults' views. *Patient Education and Counseling, 86,* 335–341. doi:10.1016/ j.pec.2011.06.006

Pritchard, J. (2004). *Support groups for older people who have been abused.* London: Jessica Kinsley.

Public Health Agency of Canada. (2015). *Age-friendly communities evaluation guide: Using indicators to measure progress.* Ottawa: Author.

Pulley, M. L. (1997, November 4). Leading resilient organizations [Electronic version]. *Leadership in Action, 17,* 1–5. Retrieved from http://www.theicor. org/art/present/art/AROB00014.pdf

Putnam, R. D. (2000). *Bowling alone: The collapse and revival of American community.* New York: Simon & Schuster.

Rand Corporation. (2017). *Community resilience.* Retrieved from http://www .rand.org/topics/community-resilience.html

Randall, W. L. (1995). *The stories that we are: An essay on self-creation.* Toronto: University of Toronto Press.

Ranji, U., Beamesderfer, A., Kates, J., & Salganicoff, A. (2014, January). *Health and access to care and coverage for lesbian, gay, bisexual, and transgender individuals in the U.S* [Issue Brief]. Menlo Park, CA: Kaiser Family Foundation.

Rantz, M. (2016). Aging in place: Critical for seniors to remain independent. *Population Health News, 3*(6), 1.

Rantz, M., Skubic, M., Miller, S. J., Galambos, C., Alexander, G., Keller, J., & Popescu, M. (2013). Sensor technology to support aging in place. *Journal of the American Medical Director's Association, 14,* 386–391. doi:10.1016/j. jamda.2013.02.018

Rawls, J. (1971). *A theory of justice.* Cambridge, MA: Harvard University Press.

Reamer, F. G. (1987). Informed consent in social work. *Social Work, 32,* 425–429.

Reamer, F. G. (1990). *Ethical dilemmas in social service.* New York: Columbia University Press.

Reamer, F. G. (2001). *Tangled relationships: Managing boundary issues in the human services.* New York: Columbia University Press.

Redfield, R., Linton, R., & Herskovits, M. J. (1936). Memorandum of the study of acculturation. *American Anthropologist, 3*, 149–152.

Reed, B. G., Ortega, R. M., & Garvin, C. (2009). Small-group theory and social work. In R. R. Greene & N. P. Kropf (Eds.), *Human behavior theory: A diversity framework* (2nd ed., pp. 201–230). New Brunswick: Aldine Transaction.

Reeves, S. (2005, September 29). *An aging workforce's effect on U.S. employers.* Retrieved from http://www.forbes.com/2005/09/28/career-babyboomer-workcx_sr_0929bizbasics_print.html

Reichert, E. (2003). Human rights and social work through an international perspective. *Journal of Intergroup Relations, 30*(1), 76–83.

Reichert, E. (2007). Human rights: Challenges and promises. *Social Justice in Context, 2*, 11–24.

Reilly, S., Miranda-Castillo, C., Malouf, R., Hoe, J., Toot, S., Challis, D., & Orrell, M. (2015). Case management approaches to home support for people with dementia. *Cochrane Database of Systematic Reviews, 1.* doi:10.1002/14651858. CD008345.pub2

Reker, G. T. (1997). Personal meaning, optimism, and choice: Existential predictors of depression in community and institutional elderly. *Gerontologist, 37,* 709–716.

Rennemark, M., & Hagberg, B. (1997). Social network patterns among the elderly in relation to their perceived life history in an Eriksonian perspective. *Aging & Mental Health, 1*, 321–331.

Resnick, H., & Patti, R. J. (Eds.). (1980). *Changes from within: Humanizing social welfare organizations.* Philadelphia: Temple University Press.

Richardson, V. E., & Barusch, A. S. (2006). *Gerontological practice for the twenty-first century: A social work perspective.* New York: Columbia University Press.

Riley, J. (2007). Caregiving: A risk and resilience perspective. In R. R. Greene (Ed.), *Social work practice: A risk and resilience perspective* (pp. 239–262). Monterey, CA: Brooks/Cole.

Riley, M. W., Kahn, R. L., & Foner, A. (Eds.). (1994a). *Age and structural lag: Society's failure to provide meaningful opportunities in work, family, and leisure.* New York: Wiley.

Riley, M. W., Kahn, R. L., & Foner, A. (1994b). Introduction: The mismatch between people and structures. In M. W. Riley, R. L. Kahn, & A. Foner (Eds.), *Age and structural lag: Society's failure to provide meaningful opportunities in work, family, and leisure* (pp. 1–14). New York: Wiley.

Riley, M. W., & Riley, J. W. (1994). Structural lag: Past and future. In M. W. Riley, R. L. Kahn, & A. Foner (Eds.), *Age and structural lag: Society's failure to provide meaningful opportunities in work, family, and leisure* (pp. 15–36). New York: Wiley.

Rivera, F. G., & Erlich, J. L. (1998). *Community organizing in a diverse society* (3rd ed.). Boston: Allyn & Bacon.

Roberts, A. (2003). In the eye of the storm? Societal aging and the future of public-service reform. *Public Administration Review, 63*, 720–733.

Robinson, M. M., Kropf, N. P., & Myers, L. (2000). Grandparents raising grandchildren in rural communities. *Journal of Aging and Mental Health, 6*, 353–365.

Rogers, C. R., & Dymond, R. F. (1957). *Psychotherapy and personality change.* Chicago: University of Chicago Press.

Romo, R. D., Walhagen, M. I., & Smith, A. K. (2016). Viewing hospice decision making as a process. *American Journal of Hospice and Palliative Medicine, 33,* 503–510. doi:10.1177/1049909115569592

Ronch, J., & Goldfield, J. A. (Eds.). (2003). *Mental wellness in aging: Strengths-based approaches.* Baltimore: Health Professions Press.

Ronen, T., & Dowd, T. (1998). A constructive model for working with depressed elders. *Journal of Gerontological Social Work, 30*(3–4), 83–99.

Rose, S. M. (2000). Reflections on empowerment-based practice [Special section: Alternative Writing Formats]. *Social Work, 45,* 403–412.

Rosen, T., Macka, K. A., & Noonan, R. K. (2013). Slipping and tripping: Fall injuries in adults associated with rugs and carpets. *Journal of Injury and Violence Research, 5*(1), 61–69.

Rossi, P. H., Lipsey, M. H., & Freeman, H. E. (2004). *Evaluation: A systematic approach* (7th ed.). Newbury Park, CA: Sage Publications.

Rothman, J. (1994). *Practice with highly vulnerable clients: Case management and community-based service.* New York: Prentice-Hall.

Rothman, J., Erlich, J. L., & Tropman, J. E. (Eds.). (2001). *Strategies of community intervention.* Itasca, IL: F. E. Peacock.

Rowe, J. W., & Kahn, R. L. (1998). *Successful aging.* New York: Pantheon Books.

Rowles, G. (1993). Evolving images of place in aging and "aging in place." *Generations, 17,* 65–71.

Ruffin, L., & Kaye, L. W. (2006). Counseling services and support groups. In B. Berkman (Ed.), *Handbook of social work in health and aging* (pp. 529–538). New York: Oxford University Press.

Ruiz, G. (2006). Gray eminence. *Workforce Management, 85,* 32–36.

Rutter, M. (1987). Psychosocial resilience and protective mechanisms. *American Journal of Orthopsychiatry, 57,* 316–330.

Ryff, C. D., & Singer, B. (2002). From social structure to biology: Integrative science in pursuit of human health and well-being. In C. R. Snyder & S. J. Lopez (Eds.), *Handbook of positive psychology* (pp. 541–555). New York: Oxford University Press.

Saint Arnault, D. (2009). Cultural determinants of help seeking: A model for research and practice. *Research Theory Nursing Practice, 23,* 259–278.

Saleebey, D. (1997). *The strengths perspective in social work practice* (2nd ed.). New York: Longman.

Saleebey, D. (2002). *The strengths perspective in social work practice* (3rd ed.). Boston: Allyn & Bacon.

Saleebey, D. (2004). "The power of place": Another look at the environment. *Families in Society, 85,* 7–16.

Saleebey, D. (2012). *The strengths perspective in social work practice* (6th ed.). Boston: Pearson

Sarkisian, C., Steers, W. N., Hays, R. D., & Mangione, C. M. (2005). Development of the 12-item Expectations Regarding Aging Survey. *Gerontologist, 45,* 240–248.

Saul, J. (2003). Strengths-based approaches to trauma in the aging. In J. Ronch & J. A. Goldfield (Eds.), *Mental wellness in aging: Strengths-based approaches* (pp. 299–314). Baltimore: Health Professions Press.

Scharlach, A. E., Davitt, J. K., Lehning, A. J., Greenfield, E. A., & Graham, C. L. (2014). Does the village model help to foster age-friendly communities? *Journal of Aging and Social Policy, 26*(1–2), 181–196.

Scharlach, A. E., & Kaye, L. W. (Eds.). (1997). *Controversial issues in aging*. Boston: Allyn & Bacon.

Schneider, J. K., & Cook, J. H. (2005). Planning psychoeducational groups for older adults. *Journal of Gerontological Nursing, 31*, 33–38.

Schoenberg, N. E., Amey, C. H., & Coward, R. T. (1998). Stories of meaning: Lay perspectives on the origin and management of noninsulin dependent diabetes mellitus among older women in the United States. *Social Science and Medicine, 47*, 2113–2125.

Schoenberg, N. E., Coward, R. T., & Albrecht, S. L. (2001). Attitudes of older adults about community based services: Emergent themes from in-depth interviews. *Journal of Gerontological Social Work, 35*, 3–19.

Schon, D. A. (1983). *The reflective practitioner: How professionals think in action*. New York: Basic Books.

Schrader, C., & Britt, T. (2001). Case management issues in rural long-term care models. *Journal of Applied Gerontology, 20*, 458–470.

Scollan-Koliopoulos, M., O'Connell, K. A, & Walker, E. A. (2005). The first diabetes educator is the family: Using illness representation to recognize a multigenerational legacy of diabetes. *Clinical Nurse Specialist, 19*, 302–307.

Seeman, T., & Chen, X. (2002). Risk and protective factors for physical functioning in older adults with and without chronic conditions: MacArthur studies of successful aging. *Journals of Gerontology, Series B: Psychological Sciences and Social Sciences, 57*(3), S135–S144.

Seligman, M.E.P. (2002). Positive psychology, positive prevention, and positive therapy. In C. R. Snyder & S. J. Lopez (Eds.), *Handbook of positive psychology* (pp. 3–7). New York: Oxford University Press.

Senior Independence Act of 2006, H.R. 5293, 109th Cong. § 2 (2005–2006).

Shirey, M. R. (2006). Authentic leaders creating healthy work environments for nursing practice. *American Journal of Critical Care, 15*, 256–267.

Shulman, L. (2006). *The skills of helping individuals, families, groups, and communities* (5th ed.). Belmont, CA: Thomson Brooks/Cole.

Shulman, L. (2016). *The skills of helping individuals, families, groups, and communities* (8th ed.). Boston: Cengage Learning.

Sijuwade, P. O. (1995). Cross-cultural perspectives on elder abuse as a family dilemma. *Social Behavior and Personality, 23*, 247–252.

Simon, H. (1945). *Administrative behavior*. New York: Macmillan.

Skinner, J. (2002). Acculturation: Measures of ethnic accommodation to the dominant American culture. In J. H. Skinner, H. John, J. A. Teresi, D. Holmes, S. M. Stahl, & A. L. Stewart (Eds.), *Multicultural measurement in older populations* (pp. 37–51). New York: Springer.

Sleap, B. (2012, August 20). *Protecting the rights of older people: Ten reasons why we need to act.* Retrieved from http://www.helpage.org/blogs/bridget-sleap-24/protecting-the-rights-of-older-people-ten-reasons-why-we-need-to-act-450/

Solomon, B. B. (1976). *Black empowerment: Social work in oppressed communities.* New York: Columbia University Press.

Steen, J. A., & Mathieson, S. (2005). Human rights education: Is social work behind the curve? *Journal of Teaching in Social Work, 25*(3–4), 143–156.

Substance Abuse and Mental Health Services Administration. (2016). *Age- and gender-based populations.* Retrieved from https://www.samhsa.gov/specific-populations/age-gender-based

Sugar, J. A., Riekse, R. J., Holstege, H., & Faber, M. A. (2014). *Introduction to aging: A positive, interdisciplinary approach.* New York: Springer.

Sullivan, W. P., & Fisher, B. J. (1994). Intervening for success: Strengths-based case management and successful aging. *Journal of Gerontological Social Work, 22*(1–2), 61–73.

Sung, K. (1997). Filial piety in modern times: Timely adaptation and practice patterns. *Australasian Journal on Ageing, 17*(Suppl. 1), 88–92.

Tallman, K., & Bohart, A. C. (1999). The client as a common factor: Clients as self-healers. In M. A. Hubble, B. L. Duncan, & S. Miller (Eds.), *The heart & soul of change: What works in therapy* (pp. 91–131). Washington, DC: American Psychological Association.

Taylor, N. F. (2014, June 16). Tackling the challenges of the multigenerational workforce. *Business News Daily.* Retrieved from http://www.businessnews-daily.com/6609-multigenerational-workforce-challenges.html

Tennstedt, S. (1999, March). *Family caregiving in an aging society.* Paper presented at the U.S. Administration on Aging Symposium: Longevity in the New American Century, Baltimore.

Teri, L., Logsdon, R. G., Uomoto, J., & McCurry, S. M. (1997). Behavioral treatment of depression in dementia patients: A controlled clinical trial. *Journals of Gerontology, Series B: Psychological Sciences and Social Sciences, 52,* P159–P166.

Tervalon, M., & Murray-Garcia, J. (1998). Cultural humility versus cultural competence: A critical distinction in defining physician training outcomes in multicultural education. *Journal of Health Care for the Poor and Underserved, 9,* 117–125.

Theurer, K., Wister, A., Sixsmith, A., Chaudhury, H., & Lovegreen, L. (2012). The development and evaluation of mutual support groups in long-term care homes. *Journal of Applied Gerontology, 33,* 387–415. doi:10.1177/0733464812446866

Thoits, P. (1995). Stress, coping, and social support processes: Where are we? What next? *Journal of Health and Social Behavior, 36*(Suppl.), 53–79.

Thomas, M. (2011, May/June). Villages: Helping people age in place. *AARP: The Magazine.* Retrieved from http://www.aarp.org/home-garden/livable-communities/info-04-2011/villages-real-social-network.html

Thompson, C. A., Spilsbury, K., Hall, J., Birks, Y., Barnes, C., & Adamson, J. (2007). Systematic review of information and support interventions for caregivers of people with dementia. *BMC Geriatrics, 7*(1), 18.

Thompson, C. D., & Wiggins, M. F. (2002). *The human cost of food: Farm workers' lives, labor and advocacy.* Austin: University of Texas Press.

Thompson, N. (2005). Holding fast: The struggle to create resilient caregiving organizations [Book review]. *Community Care, 46,* 1562.

Tice, C. J., & Perkins, K. (1996). *Mental health issues and aging: Building on the strengths of older persons.* Pacific Grove, CA: Brooks/Cole.

Toseland, R. W. (1995). *Group work with the elderly and family caregivers.* New York: Springer.

Toseland, R. W., & Rizzo, V. M. (2004). What's different about working with older people in groups? *Journal of Gerontological Social Work, 44*(1–2), 5–23.

Toseland, R. W., & Smith, T. (2001). *Supporting caregivers through education and training* (Selected Issue Brief prepared for the U.S. Administration on Aging, National Family Caregiver Support Program). Washington, DC: U.S. Department of Health and Human Services.

Trader, H. P. (1977). Survival strategies for oppressed minorities. *Social Work, 22,* 10–13.

Tran, T. V., Ngo, D., & Conway, K. (2003). A cross-cultural measure of depressive symptoms among Vietnamese Americans [Instrument Development]. *Social Work Research, 27,* 56–64.

Tully, C. T. (1994). Epilogue: Power and the social work profession. In R. R. Greene (Ed.), *Human behavior a diversity framework* (pp. 235–244). Hawthorne, NY: Aldine de Gruyter.

United Nations. (1948). *The universal declaration of human rights.* Retrieved from http://www.un.org/en/documents/udhr/

United Nations. (1994). *Human rights and social work: A manual for schools of social work and the social work profession.* Geneva: United Nations Centre for Human Rights. Retrieved from http://www.ohchr.org/Documents/Publications/training1en.pdf

United Nations Human Rights Office of the High Commissioner. (1991). *United Nations principles for older persons.* Retrieved from http://www.ohchr.org/EN/ProfessionalInterest/Pages/OlderPersons.aspx

United Nations Human Rights Office of the High Commissioner. (2010). *Human rights of older persons.* Retrieved from http://www.ohchr.org/_layouts/15/WopiFrame.aspx?sourcedoc=/Documents/Issues/OlderPersons/OHCHR_Summary_SG_report_HR_olderpersons2011.doc&action=default&DefaultItemOpen=1

United Nations Human Rights Office of the High Commissioner. (2017, March 3). *International covenant on economic, social, and cultural rights.* Retrieved from http://www.ohchr.org/EN/ProfessionalInterest/Pages/CESCR.aspx

United Nations Population Fund & HelpAge International. (2012). *Ageing in the 21st century: Ten priority actions to maximise the opportunity of ageing populations.* Retrieved from http://www.helpage.org/resources/ageing-in-the-21st-century-a-celebration-and-a-challenge/

ageing-in-the-21st-century-ten-priority-actions-to-maximise-the-opportu-nity-of-ageing-populations/

Urban Institute. (2003, October 9). *Assessing the new federalism: Children in kinship care.* Retrieved from www.urban.org/url.cfm?ID=900661

U.S. Department of Health and Human Services, Agency for Healthcare Research and Quality. (2003). *The role of community-based participatory research: Creating partnerships, improving health* [AHRQ Publication No. 03-0037]. Rockville, MD: Author. Retrieved from https://archive.ahrq.gov/research/cbprrole .htm

U.S. Department of Health and Human Services, Office of Disease Prevention and Health Promotion. (2010). *Leading health indicators development and framework.* Retrieved from https://www.healthypeople .gov/2020/leading-health-indicators/Leading-Health-Indicators-Development-and-Framework

van Wormer, K., Besthorn, F. H., & Keefe, T. (2007). *Human behavior and the social environment, macro level: Groups, communities, and organizations.* New York: Oxford University Press.

Village to Village Network. (n.d.). *Village model.* Retrieved from http://www.vtvnetwork.org/content.aspx?page_id=22&club_id=691012&module_id=248578

Viney, L. L., Benjamin, Y. N., & Preston, C. (1988). Constructivist family therapy with the elderly. *Journal of Family Psychology, 2,* 241–258.

Volland, J., & Blockberger-Miller, S. (2015). Closing the transition gaps: The changing context of home healthcare coordination. *Home Healthcare Now, 33,* 199–205.

Vourlekis, B., & Greene, R. R. (1992). *Social work case management.* Hawthorne, NY: Aldine de Gruyter.

Vourlekis, B., & Simons, K. (2006). Nursing homes. In B. Berkman & S. D'Ambruoso (Eds.), *Handbook of social work in health and aging* (pp. 601–614). New York: Oxford University Press.

Waite, P. J., & Richardson, G. E. (2004). Determining the efficacy of resiliency training in the work site. *Journal of Allied Health, 33,* 178–183.

Walsh, F. (1998). *Strengthening family resilience.* New York: Guilford Press.

Warren, R. L. (1978). *The community in America* (3rd ed.). Chicago: Rand McNally.

Wartel, S. G. (2003). A strengths-based practice model: Psychology of mind and health realization. *Families in Society, 84,* 185–191.

Watari, K., & Gatz, M. (2004). Pathways to care for Alzheimer's disease among Korean Americans. *Cultural Diversity and Ethnic Minority Psychology, 10,* 23–38.

Webster, J. (2002). Reminiscence functions in adulthood: Age, race, and family dynamics correlates. In J. D. Webster & B. K. Haight (Eds.), *Critical advances in reminiscence work* (pp. 140–152). New York: Springer.

Weiss, B. D., Berman, E. A., Howe, C. L., & Fleming, R. B. (2012). Medical decision making for older adults without family. *Journal of the American Geriatrics Society, 60,* 2144–2150. doi:10:1111/j1532-5415.2012.04212x

Weisstub, D. N. (1990). *Enquiry on mental competency: Final report.* Toronto: Ontario Ministry of Health.

White House Conference on Aging. (2015, July 13). *Fact sheet: The White House Conference on Aging.* Retrieved from https://www.whitehouse.gov/the-press-office/2015/07/13/fact-sheet-white-house-conference-aging

Whitfield, K. E., & Baker, T. A. (Eds.). (2014). *Handbook of minority aging.* New York: Springer.

Whitley, D. M., Kelley, S. J., & Campos, P. (2013). Promoting family empowerment among African American grandmothers raising grandchildren. In B. Hayslip, Jr., & G. C. Smith (Eds.), *Resilient grandparent caregivers: A strengths-based perspective* (pp. 235–250). New York: Routledge.

Whitten, T. M., & Eyler, A. E. (Eds.). (2012). *Gay, lesbian, bisexual, & transgender aging.* Baltimore: Johns Hopkins University Press.

Wiles, J. L., Leibing, A., Guberman, N., Reeve, J., & Allen, R. S. (2012). The meaning of "aging in place" to older people. *Gerontologist, 52,* 357–366.

Willis, S. L. (1991). Cognition and everyday competence. In K. W. Schaie (Ed.), *Annual review of gerontology and geriatrics* (Vol. 11, pp. 80–109). New York: Springer.

Wilson, H. W. (2014). *Reference shelf: Aging in America.* Armenia, NY: Grey House.

Witkin, S. (1998). Human rights and social work. *Social Work, 43,* 197–201.

Wolf, R. S. (2001). Support groups for older victims of domestic violence. *Journal of Women and Aging, 13,* 71–83.

Woods, B., Spector, A. E., Jones, C. A., Orrell, M., & Davies, S. P. (2005). Reminiscence therapy for dementia. *Cochrane Database of Systematic Reviews, 2.* doi:10.1002/14651858.CD001120.pub 2

Work Group for Community Health and Development. (2016). *Building culturally competent organizations.* Lawrence: University of Kansas.

World Health Organization. (1946). *Constitution of the World Health Organization.* Geneva: Author.

World Health Organization. (2006). *Constitution of the World Health Organization.* Retrieved from http://www.who.int/governance/eb/who_constitution_en.pdf

World Health Organization. (2007). *Checklist of essential features of age friendly cities.* Geneva: Author. Retrieved from http://www.aarp.org/content/dam/aarp/home-and-family/livable-communities/2013-12/3-age-friendly-cities-checklist.pdf

World Health Organization. (2013). *Second WHO consultation on developing indicators for age-friendly cities.* Retrieved from http://www.who.int/kobe-centre/ageing/age_friendly_cities/ AFC_Mtg-2_Report_SEP2013_Quebec.pdf

World Health Organization. (2014). *"Ageing well" must be a global priority.* Geneva: Author. Retrieved from http://www.who.int/mediacentre/new/releases/2014/lancet-ageing-series/en/

World Health Organization. (2016a). *Gender, equity and human rights.* Geneva: Author. Retrieved from http://www.who.int/gender-equity-rights/understanding/human-rights-definition/en/

World Health Organization. (2016b). *The global strategy and action plan on ageing and health.* Geneva: Author. Retrieved from http://www.who.int/ageing/global-strategy/en/

World Health Organization. (2016c). *Health systems aligned to older popula-tions.* Geneva: Author. Retrieved from http://www.who.int/ageing/health-systems/en/

Wronka, J. M. (2008a). Human rights. In T. Mizrahi & L. E. Davis (Eds.-in-Chief), *Encyclopedia of social work* (20th ed., Vol. 2, pp. 425–429). Washington, DC, and New York: NASW Press and Oxford University Press.

Wronka, J. (2008b). *Human rights and social justice: Social action and service for the helping and health professions.* Thousand Oaks, CA: Sage Publications.

Wronka, J. (2016). *Creating a human rights culture.* Retrieved from http://www.humanrightsculture.org/Relevance.html

Yao, X. (2000). *An introduction to Confucianism.* Cambridge, England: Cambridge University Press.

Yeh, K., & Bedford, O. (2003). A test of the dual filial piety model. *Asian Journal of Social Psychology, 6,* 215–228.

You, E. C., Dunt, D. R., & Doyle, C. (2013). Case-managed community aged care: What is the evidence for effects on service use and costs? *Journal of Aging and Health, 25,* 1204–1242.

Youn, G., Knight, B., Jeong, H., & Benton, D. (1999). Differences in familism values and caregiving outcomes among Korean, Korean American, and white American dementia caregivers. *Psychology & Aging, 14,* 355–364.

Zastrow, C. (2001). *Social work with groups* (5th ed.). Pacific Grove, CA: Brooks/Cole.

Zastrow, C. H., & Kirst-Ashman, K. K. (2016). *Understanding human behavior and the social environment* (10th ed.). Boston, MA: Cengage Learning.

Index

A

AARP, 197, 219
abuse, 124–125
acculturation, 56
activities of daily living (ADLs), 112
activity groups, 154–155
Addams, Jane, 187
ADLs. *See* activities of daily living (ADLs)
Administration on Aging (AoA), 195
adult protective services, 124–125
advance directives, 39–40, 91
adversarial strategies, 176–177
advocacy
  case management and, 237–238
  in empowerment evaluation technique, 179
  human rights, 65–66
  political, 217–219
advocacy organizations, 220, 222–223
African Americans
  families, 9, 59
  oppression and, 62
age discrimination, 217–218
Age Discrimination in Employment Act, 70,
    168, 210
age-friendly communities, 170, 184–185, 192,
    196–198
  definitions, 186
  domains of living, 197
  principles for creating, 197–198
  social work and, 198–200

ageism
  behavioral interventions and, 128
  defined, 217
  effects of, 167
  explanation of, 4–5
  political advocacy and, 217–219
agency-based model, 187–188
aging
  assessment of, 111–112
  changing perceptions of, 167–168
  demographics, 17
  healthy aging, 75
  productive, 15–16
  stereotypes, 4–5
Aging Friendly Cities and Communities, 184
aging in community, 170
aging in place, 193–194
  advantages of, 194
  cultural values and, 195–196
  defined, 170
  familiarity and, 92–93
  need for policies and programs for, 217
  support for, 170–171
Aging in Place Initiative, 198
Aging in Place Survey, 195
aging process
  assessment of, 111–112
  changing perceptions of, 196
alliance networks, 234–235, 238
Alzheimer's Association, 125

Alzheimer's disease, 106, 114
American Perceptions of Aging in the 21st Century, 167
American Society on Aging, 220
Americans with Disabilities Act, 211
analytical reasoning, 18
appraisal, 115
Area Agency on Aging (AAA), 179–180, 188
Asian American families
    caregivers in, 58
    filial piety and, 58–59
assessment
    of ADLs, 112
    of aging process, 111–112
    biopsychosocial, 94–95, 112–114, 118
    capacity, 38–39
    of client resiliency, 115–116
    of client system, 107
    of cognitive functional capacity, 33
    community engagement, 189–193
    of competence, 93–94
    as competency in social work practice, 14
    cultural competence and, 47
    of depression, 113
    ecological perspective, 82–83
    of family and caregiver situation, 116–117
    geriatric, 107–108
    of group structure, 142
    group work and, 146–147
    home environment, 115
    integrating elements of into intervention plan, 122–123
    at macro level, 83
    of neurocognitive disorders, 113–114
    principles, 107–108
    sociocultural functioning, 114
    spiritual, 94–95, 112, 114
    strengths-based, 108–110
    teams, 107
assessment tools, 27–29
Association for Gerontology in Higher Education, 220
Atchley, R. C., 37
authenticity, 7, 105
authoritarian filial piety, 59
autonomy
    ethical practice and, 36–40
    guardianship and, 38
    informed consent and, 34, 37
    involving clients in care plans to promote, 37
    principles, 36–40

B
baby boomers
    education and diversity of, 193

family caregivers for, 92
    in workforce, 168
Baer, B., 76
Ban Ki-Moon, 72
Barnes, G., 82
Barusch, A. S., 37
Beard, John, 75
Beauchamp, T. L., 31
Beaulieu, E. M., 192
Bedford, O., 59
behavioral interventions, for negative behaviors, 128
behaviorally oriented filial piety, 59
belief systems
    cultural, 50
    family, 132
bereavement, 92
Berger, A. R., 115
best practices, 80, 166, 178
biculturalism, 56–57
biofeedback, 128
biological health, 94
biopsychosocial assessments, 16
biopsychosocial/spiritual functioning, 94–95, 112–114, 118
bisexuals. *See* lesbian, gay, bisexual, and transgender (LGBT) older adults
Board of Charities, 226
Bohart, A. C., 105
boundary violations, 36
Bowers, B. J., 229
Britt, T., 233
Bronfenbrenner, U., 93
Brueggemann, W. G., 218, 219
Brueggemann model, 219
Buckley, W., 88
Butler, Robert, 4, 126, 193

C
Callanan, P., 28
capacity assessments, 38–39
capacity building, 141
caregivers, 90–91
    Asian Americans as, 58
    assessment of, 116–117
    balancing needs of with person cared for, 37
    caregiver burden, 91, 117
    interventions for, 117–118, 133
    Latinos as, 57–58
    LGBT people as, 10
    rewards of caregiving, 133
    support groups for, 148
care plans, 117
    including all relevant parties in, 38
    involving clients in, 37

Carter, E. A., 86
case management
    advocacy role of, 237–238
    defined, 228–229
    framework for, 227
    geriatric, 227, 229–230
    network of alliances in, 234–235, 238
    overview of, 226–228
    relationship building in, 231–233
    resources and services as function of,
        231–233
    services delivery, 236–237
    services plan, 235–236
    skills for, 231–238
    strengths-based models for, 229–230
case studies. *see also* Stanley family case study
    constructing an intervention plan, 136–137
    custodial grandparents, 179–180
    empowerment group, 151
    group-work interventions, 160–161
    psychoeducational group, 153–154
    reminiscence group, 156–157
    resilience-enhancing model in action, 134
    support group, 149
Centers for Disease Control and Prevention
    (CDC), 125
Chapin, R., 229, 238
charity organization societies, 226
"Check for Safety: A Home Fall Prevention
    Checklist for Older Adults" (CDC), 231
Chinman, M., 178
Chipungu, S., 216
chronic diseases, developing strategies for
    reducing, 184
civil rights, 68. *See also* human rights
clinical trials, 159
closed systems, 166
Code of Ethics (NASW), 7, 26–27, 29–30
    on cultural competence, 168–169
    domains of health-responsive organizations,
        165
codes of ethics, 29–30
cognitive–behavioral approach, 128
cognitive capacity, 94
collaborative model, 188
collaborative strategies, 176
collective identity, 89
collective responsibilities, 72, 74
communication, patient-provider, 37
communities
    age-friendly, 184–185, 196–198
    for aging in place, 193–194
    assets of intergenerational, 172, 185
    as context for practice vs. target of practice,
        187

contributions of older adults, 184, 185
    development of (transformation of), 192
community assets and resources
    case management and, 233–235
    identifying, 189, 195, 200
community-based research, 200
community-based services, 194–196
community capacity, 189, 191, 197
community engagement assessment, 189–193
community organization, 219
Community Partnerships for Older Adults,
    198
community practice
    new approaches, 189–190
    role of social work in, 186–188
Community Practice Pilot Project (CPPP),
    189
Community & Regional Resilience Institute
    (CARRI), 191
Community Resilience System Initiative
    (CRSI), 191–192
competence
    assessing, 93–94
    legal competence, 33
    in oppressive environments, 56
    resilience as, 95–96
competency-based education
    aging-related competencies, 20
    explanation of, 19
conceptual thinking, 18
confidentiality, 36
conflict model, 188
confrontational strategies, 176–177
Confucian ethics, 58
Congress, E. P., 29, 34
Consolidated Omnibus Budget Reconciliation
    Act, 211
constructionist therapy, 129
consumer-directed care, 95–96
continuum of care
    adult protective services and, 124–125
    health education, 123–124
Corey, G., 28, 140
Corey, M. S., 28, 140
Council on Social Work Education (CSWE), 17
    Educational Policy and Accreditation
        Standards, 66
    on human rights education, 66
countertransference issues, between case
    worker and client, 233
Courtney, R., 50
Cox, C. B., 221
Cox, E. O., 150
Cress, C., 229
crisis competence, 56

critical evaluation model, 28
cross-cultural models
    acculturation, 56
    biculturalism, 56–57
    competence and, 56
    dual perspective, 55
    explanation of, 54–55
culturagram, 55
cultural competence
    explanation of, 46–47
    multicultural, 168–169
    preparation for, 47–48
cultural diversity
    defined, 46
    end-of-life decisions and, 91
    help-seeking and, 49–52
    and meaning of illness, 49–50
    relational worldview model, 51, 52
cultural humility, 11, 12
cultural influences, acknowledgment of, 48–49
cultural lag, 166–167
Cummings, S. M., 158
Cusicanqui, M., 145
custodial grandparents, 21–22, 61. *See also*
    Stanley family case study

D
Davis, C., 234
Davitt, J. K., 144
death. *See also* end-of-life care
    establishing a definition of, 6
    grief counseling, 129
"Decade of Healthy Aging," 76
decision making
    advance directives and, 39–40
    assessment model, 28–29
    autonomy and paternalism in, 36–40
    consultation with committees and teams, 35
    continuum of support for, 10
    critical evaluation model, 28
    end-of-life, 36, 91–92
    ethics and, 6, 27–28
    general model for, 35
    informed practice and, 30
    for long-term care, 233
    shared, 37
    thoroughness and, 34
DeCoster, V., 230
dementia
    intervention and, 114, 125
    liberty-limiting principles and, 32
demographics, 17
depression
    assessment of, 113
    intervention and, 125, 128

despair, 127
developmental unit, family as, 116
diabetics, 230
DiNitto, D. M., 214
DiNitto and Johnson Rational model, 214
discrimination
    age, 4, 13, 72, 74, 168, 217–218
    impact of, 11, 25
    against LGBT adults, 71, 203
    NASW *Code of Ethics* on, 169
    personal and institutional oppression, 60–61
    racial, 58
    women and, 8
    workplace, 73
disease self-management, 128
distal environments, 93
distorted thinking, cognitive interventions
    and, 128
diversity. *See also* cultural diversity
    and complexity of service needs, 3
    cross-cultural models and concepts, 54–55
    embracing, 8
    engaging, in social work practice, 11
Dolgoff, R., 27, 30, 35
domestic abuse, 125
do-no-harm principle, 41
dual perspective, 55

E
ecological perspective
    clinical application of, 84
    competence in handling environmental
        issues, 115
    explanation of, 20–21, 82–83
    life course and, 85–86
    multisystemic view, 83–85
    relatedness and, 87
    stress and adaptation and, 82–83, 86–87
ecological systems theory, 15
ecological systems thinking, 127–128
ecomap, 60, 87, 116
economic justice, 12, 13
Eden Alternative project, 173
education, competency-based, 19
ego strength, 94
emotionally oriented filial piety, 59
empathy, 7, 14, 53, 105, 133
Employee Retirement Income Security Act, 211
empowering evaluation, 177–179
empowerment groups, 150–151
end-of-life care, 6–7, 35, 36, 150
end-of-life decisions
    advance directives for, 39–40
    cultural diversity and, 59–60
    families and, 91–92

engagement, 103, 104
  practitioner-client relationship, 105–106
  in social work practice, 114
Enguidanos, S. M., 234
environmental issues, client competence and,
    115
environmental justice, 12, 13
environmental press competence model, 93–94
environments, characterizations of, 93
equifinality, 235
equity issues, in policy practice, 216–217
Erikson, Erik, 116, 126–127, 155
ethical practice
  assessment tools for, 27–29
  autonomy and, 36–40
  challenges facing, 30
  codes of ethics for, 26–27, 29–31
  decision making for, 27–28, 30, 34–35
  ETHIC five-step model, 29
  liberty-limiting principles for, 31–34
  principles of autonomy and paternalism for,
    36–40
  resources for, 27–34
ethical principles screen, 30, 32
ethical rules screen, 30, 31
ETHIC five-step model, 29
ethics
  Confucian, 58
  decision making and, 6
  demonstrating ethical behavior, 10–11
  historical overview, 5–7
  life-sustaining medical care and, 35
  values and, 7–8
ethics committees, 35
ethnic diversity, 3. *See also* diversity
evaluation of outcomes, 16–17
evidence-based practice, 125, 136
exclusionary language, 147
exercise programs, 154
exosystems, 83
Expanded Family Life Cycle, 86

F
facilitation, in empowerment evaluation
    technique, 178
fairness in practice, 216–217
fair treatment, 216
fall prevention, 231–232
families
  assessment of, 116–117
  belief systems of, 132
  changes in family structure, 9–10
  communication patterns of, 132
  diverse types of, 57
  expectations for care, 54

general systems theory and, 88
  immigrant, 55, 58, 59
  interdependence and, 57
  intervention, 131–132
  nuclear, 9–10
  organizational patterns of, 132
  as primary caregivers, 90–91
  resilience and, 89, 96
  roles within, 88
familism, 54, 57–58
family systems theory, 127–128
Family and Medical Leave Act, 211
family meanings, 90
family resilience, 132–133
family systems theory, 89–90
family transitions, 90
Family Unification Program, 220
Fast, B., 229, 238
Fetterman, D. M., 178
filial piety, 58–59
financial exploitation, 124
flexible work hours, 174–175
Flynn, D., 72
Flynn, J. P., 216
Food Stamp Program, 209
formative evaluation, 157, 158
Framington Heart Study, 95
Frankel, A. J., 238
Frankena, W., 217
Fraser, M. W., 96
Freud, Sigmund, 4, 126
full guardianship, 38
functional age, 107
functional-age assessment, 94–95, 112
functional-age model of intergenerational
    treatment, 131–132
  assessment using, 116
  explanation of, 89–90
Furlong, S. R., 212

G
Galambos, C., 36
Garwick, A. W., 90
gays. *See* lesbian, gay, bisexual, and
    transgender (LGBT) older adults
Gelman, S. R., 238
general systems theory, 88
genogram, 116
Genrich, S. J., 228
genuineness, 7, 105
geriatric assessment, 107–108
geriatric case management, 227, 229–230
geriatric case manager, 229
Geriatric Social Work Competency Scale, 17
geriatric social workers, 2

Germain, C. B., 87
Gero-Ed Center, 17
gerontological knowledge, 92–93
Gerontological Society of America, 220
gerontology and gerontologists, 1–2
Gerontology Education in Social Work
    Initiative programs, 17
Gibson, L., 39
Gitterman, A., 87
global meaning, 90
*Global Strategy and Action Plan on Ageing and
    Health,* 76
Goelitz, A., 150
goodness of fit, 83, 94
Gostin, L., 76
Graham, C. L., 144
Grand Challenges for Social Work initiative,
    72–79
Grandfamily Housing, 202
grandparents
    custodial, 21–22, 61, 117, 220–221
        (*see also* Stanley family case study)
    in households with grandchildren, 9
    raising grandchildren with disabilities, 145
GrandRallys, 221
Grant-Griffin, L., 145
Graybeal, C., 109
Gray Panthers, 188, 219
Green, J., 54
Greene, R. R., 82, 89, 98, 141, 206
Greenfield, E. A., 144
Green House project, 173
grief counseling, 129
group process evaluation, 157
group work
    activity groups, 154–155
    assessment process, 146–147
    benefits of, 141
    considerations for older group members,
        142
    duration and number of sessions, 145–146
    effectiveness of, 157–159
    importance of, 140, 159
    leadership dynamics, 144–145
    life review and reminiscence, 155–157
    meeting place considerations, 143–144
    membership composition, 145
    membership structure, 146
    multicultural, language use and, 147
    mutual aid and empowerment groups,
        150–151
    optimal size considerations, 145
    psychoeducational groups, 151–154
    relationship building in, 146–147

resilience-enhancing model approach,
    142–147
support groups, 148–149
types of groups, 147–155
Groupwork Engagement Measure (GEM), 158
guardianship, 36, 38–40

H
Hagberg, B., 127
Hardcastle, D. A., 187
harm principle, 31, 33
Harrell, E. B., 227
Harrell, R., 196
Harrington, D., 27
Hartford Partnership Program in Aging
    Education, 17
health care access, as human right, 74–75
health care systems, and "responsiveness,"
    76
health education, 123–124
Health Insurance Portability and
    Accountability Act, 211
Healthy aging, 75
Healthy People 2020, 184
Hébert, R., 152
helping process, 104
help-seeking behaviors, 8–9
help-seeking models
    function of, 49
    Kleinman's, 50–51
Hepworth, D. H., 110
Herr, S. S., 33
Hispanic households, 9
Hodge, D. R., 114
Hoefer, R., 216
Holland, L., 50
home-based services, 194–196
home environment
    assessment, 115
    fall prevention, 231–232
    modifications for aging in place, 195
    repairs and maintenance, 232
hostile environments, 56
Housing and Community Development Act, 210
human development theory (Erikson), 127, 155
human rights, 12, 13
    and civil rights compared, 68
    defined, 67–70
    Flynn model of, 72
    Grand Challenges for Social Work initiative,
        72–79
    health care and, 75–77
    indicators, 77
    older adults and, 70–78

universal human rights, 78
human rights treaties, 69–70

I

Ife, J., 66
illumination, in empowerment evaluation
      technique, 179
Imm, P., 178
immigrants
   dual perspective and, 55
   families of, 55, 58, 59
informed consent
   client confidentiality and, 36
   elements of, 33–34
   prior to interventions, 34
   to promote autonomy, 33–34, 37
informed practice, 30
inputs, 166
institutional abuse, 125
institutional oppression, 60–61
instruction directive, 39
intake interview, 8
integrity, 116, 127
integrity vs. despair stage of life, 127
intergenerational equity debate, 216–217
International Association of Gerontology and
      Geriatrics, 78
International Federation of Social Workers
      (IFSW), on human rights, 66
interventions
   caregiver, 117–118, 133
   cognitive–behavioral approach, 128
   as competency in social work practice, 15–16
   constructionist therapy, 129
   continuum of care and, 121–125
   ecological systems thinking, 127–128
   family resilience, 132–133
   functional-age model of intergenerational
         therapy, 116, 131–132
   grief counseling, 129
   group (See group work)
   informed consent and, 34
   life review, 126–127
   mental health care and, 125
   narrative gerontology, 129–130
   for organizational change, 176–177
   resilience-enhancing model, 130–131, 134
interviews
   of Alzheimer's patients, 106
   as assessment tool, 110
   in cognitive intervention process, 128
   cultural context, 53
   issues to cover in initial, 106–107
   preparation for initial, 105–106

strengths-based, 109–110
theory-based, 108

J

Jacobson, N., 228
Janicki, M. P., 145
Janoff-Bulman, R., 115
Jansson, B. S., 206, 207, 218
Johnson, A. K., 189
Johnson, J. H., 215
Johnson, L. C., 198

K

Kadushin, A., 53
Kapp, M. B., 33
Karger and Stoesz model, 212
Katz, L., 234
King, Martin Luther Jr., 68
Kitchener, K. S., 28
Kivnick, H. Q., 2
Kleinman, A. M., 50–51
knowledge, 82–86, 95–98
Kolomer, S., 145
Konopka, Gisela, 140
Kraft, M. E., 212
Kraft and Furlong model, 212
Kretzmann, J. P., 192
Kropf, N. P., 158, 237
Kuhn, Maggie, 188

L

language, exclusionary, 147
Larsen, J. A., 110
Latino families, caregivers in, 57–59
legal competence, 33
legal moralism principle, 31
Lehning, A. J., 144
lesbian, gay, bisexual, and transgender (LGBT)
      older adults
   challenges faced by, 8
   crisis competence and, 56
   cultural lag in serving needs of, 167
   culturally competent services for, 175, 195
   group work and, 141
Levy, C. S., 26
Lewis, J. S., 227
liberation, in empowerment evaluation
      technique, 179
liberty-limiting principles, 31–34
Lichtenberg, P. A., 107, 108
life events, appraisal of, 115, 116
life expectancy, 2–3
life review, 126–127, 155–157
life stage approach, 85

limited guardianship, 38
Linzer, N., 33
Livable Communities for All Ages, 198
Loewenberg, F. M., 27
loneliness, 141
longevity projections, 2–3
long-term care, 122
    activities to preserve cognitive functioning
        in, 154–155
    coordination of services, 233
Lowy, L., 140

M
Macgowan, M., 158
macro–social work practice, 218
macrosystems, 83
Madrid International Plan of Action on
    Ageing, 71, 72, 78
Magana, S., 57–58
Masten, A., 97
McCallion, P., 145
McGoldrick, M., 86
McKnight, J. L., 192
McNutt, J. G., 216
meaning making, 49, 115–116
meaning systems, 129
Medicaid, 195, 209–210
medical model, 189
Medicare, 195, 209, 216–217
mental health care
    evidence-based practice in geriatric, 125
    resources, 125
mental health problems, 125
mesosystems, 83
Mexican Americans, health beliefs and
    practices of, 50
microsystems, 83
Mill, J. S., 217
Minahan, A., 26
motor skills, 94
multicultural considerations, 147
*Multisectional Action for a Life Course Approach
    to Healthy Ageing*, 76
multisystemic approach, 83–85
Murray, S. V., 2
mutual aid groups, 150–151

N
Naleppa, M. J., 232
narrative gerontology, 53–54, 129–130
National Affordable Housing Act, 211
National Association of Social Workers
    (NASW)
    case management standards, 228
    Code of Ethics, 26–27, 29–30, 66

on human rights education, 66
    *Standards and Indicators for Cultural
        Competence in Social Work Practice*, 168, 169
National Commission for the Protection
    of Human Subjects of Biomedical and
    Behavioral Research, 6
National Council on Aging, 220
Native America households, 9
naturally occurring retirement communities
    (NORCs), 170, 173, 174, 185, 198–200
Neatherlin, J. S., 228
neglect, 124
negotiated risk concept, 37
networking, 207–208
neurocognitive disorders, assessment of,
    113–114
nonmaleficence, 41
nonpossessive warmth, 7, 105
NORCs. *See* naturally occurring retirement
    communities (NORCs)
normalizing, 129
Norton, D., 55
Nowitz, L., 234

O
Obama, Barack, 237
objective burden, 117
offense principle, 32
Older Americans Act, 206, 209
Older Women's League, 188, 219–220
Open-Ended Working Group on Ageing,
    71–72
open systems, 166
oppression, personal and institutional, 60–61
oral traditions, 127
organizations
    accessible technology and work flexibility,
        174–75
    age-friendly, 170–171, 178
    aging workforce in, 167–168
    analysis of, 175–176
    challenges faced by, 171
    characteristics of, 165–166
    culture of, 165–166, 172–173
    effectiveness of, 176–177
    evaluation methods, 177–179
    interdependent principles of, 172
    leadership in, 172
    missions and purposes of, 165
    multicultural competence and, 168–169
    overview of, 164–165
    resiliency principles for, 171–174
    structural and culture lag in, 166–167
    systems of support for older workers,
        173–174

outcome evaluation, 158
outputs, 166

P
Pacific Islanders, 9
Parsons, R. R., 150
Partnership to Improve Community Health, 184
paternalism principle, 31, 32–33, 36–40
Patient Protection and Affordable Care Act, 210, 237
Patterson, J. M., 90
peer evaluation, 157–158
personal environments, 93
personal oppression, 60–61
person guardianship, 38
person-in-environment perspective, 107, 194
    age integration and, 167
    explanation of, 82
physical environments, 93
physical neglect, 124
physical violence, 124
Piaget, Jean, 4
Pincus, A., 26
Pinderhughes, E., 53
policy analysis
    attention to well-being, 217
    community organization and, 219
    frameworks, 205–207, 212, 216
policy analysis models
    analysis of older adults' independent living options using, 213
    bounded rationality, 214
    DiNitto and Johnson Rational model, 214
    Karger and Stoesz model, 212
    Kraft and Furlong model, 212
policy development, fairness in practice and, 216–217
policy practice
    ageism and discrimination and, 217–218
    community resources and programs, 207–208
    engaging in, 13–14
    equity and fairness in, 216–217
    evaluation frameworks, 214–215
    explained, 206
    federal, state, and local policies, 208–211
    information gathering, 207–211
    Jansson's framework for, 206, 207
    political advocacy and, 217–219
political advocacy, 217–219
Portz, J. D., 175
positive psychology movement, 97
practice-informed research, 12–13
Practice Partnership Scale, 17

practitioner–client relationship, 105–106
President's Commission for the Study of Ethical Problems in Medicine, 6
Pritchard, J., 143
problem-based assessment, 109
problem-solving
    community practice and, 187, 192–193
    ethics and, 35
    strengthening client's abilities for, 135
process evaluation, 157
professional collaboration, 122, 123
program evaluation
    empowering evaluation approach, 177–179
    questions, 215
    steps, 214–215
Project Healthy Grandparents, 230
property guardianship, 38
proximal environments, 93
proxy directive, 39
psychoeducational groups, 151–154
psychological abuse, 124
psychological functioning assessment, 112–113

R
racial diversity, 3. *See also* diversity
Randall, W. L., 155, 156
randomized clinical trial, 159
reciprocal filial piety, 59
reciprocal roles, family and, 116
redistribution policies, 216
Reid, W. J., 232
relatedness, 87
relational worldview model, 51, 52
relationship building
    engagement as, 190–191
    group work and, 146–147
relativistic models, 94
relaxation training, 128
reminiscence, group work and, 155–157
Rennemark, M., 127
Research Agenda for Ageing in the 21st Century, 78
research-informed practice, 12–13
resilience
    assessment of, 115–116
    community, 191–192
    defining, 96–97
    faith and faith-based practices and, 133
resilience-enhancing model (REM)
    case study, 134
    explanation of, 97–98
    group work and, 142–147
    intervention strategies, 98, 130–131
    stress and, 87

resilience perspective, 95–98
"responsiveness" and health care systems, 76
rights, violation of, 125
risk and resilience theory, 95–97
Roberts, A., 166
Rooney, R. H., 110
Roosevelt, Eleanor, 67
ROPES, 109–110
Rossi, Lipsey, and Freeman model, 214–215
rule utilitarianism, 217

S
safety
    abuse and, 124–125
    fall prevention, 231–232
    home environment assessment, 115
    self-neglect and, 125
Saint Arnault, D., 51–52
Saleebey, Dennis, 81
Salmon, R., 145
SAMHSA mental health disorder resources, 125
Scharlach, A. E., 144
Schrader, C., 233
science, use of in social work practice, 18–19
Section 202 Supportive Housing for the Elderly, 220
self-awareness, 48
self-determination, 10, 36, 136
self-efficacy, 135
self-evaluations, 127
self-governance, 32, 33
self-help groups, 150
self-motivation, 135
self-neglect, 125
sensory-perceptual capacity, 94
services
    continuum of care and, 122, 123
    delivery of, 195
    home- and community-based, 194–196
services delivery systems
    changes in, 18, 236–237
    cost-effectiveness of, 236
    ethical considerations in, 35
    policy practice and, 13, 206
services plans
    case management and, 235–236
    client goals and, 117
settlement house movement, 187, 201
Simon, Herbert A., 214
situational meaning, 90

skill development, 141, 142–143
social action model, 187–188
social diversity, 169
social engagement, 141
social environments, 93
social justice, 12, 13
social network scale, 114
Social Security, 216–217
Social Security Act, 208
social support networks, 92
social system
    explained, 206
    family as, 116
social workers
    in change process, 188
    demographic imperative for, 2–3
    geriatric, 2
    personal biases of, 4, 8
    professional networks, 207–208
    social and political action and, 169
Social Work Leadership Institute, 17
social work practice
    competency-based education for, 19
    context of, 2
    cultural competence and, 47–48, 53–54
    within a cultural context, 53–54
    demographics and, 17
    elements of, 10–17
    engaging diversity and difference in, 11
    practice-informed research/research-informed practice, 12–13
    using science and technology in, 18–19
sociocultural changes, and gerontology, 2
sociocultural functioning, 112
socioeconomic status, sensitivity to, 147
spiritual functioning, 94–95, 112, 114
SSI, 210
Standards and Indicators for Cultural Competence in Social Work Practice (NASW), 168, 169
Stanley family case study
    assessment of family's functioning, 100–102
    constructing an intervention plan for, 136–137
    developing a relationship with, 117–118
    diversity within, 61–62
    ethical issues in, 40–41
    as example of custodial grandparenting, 21–22
    geographic and nonplace communities in, 201–202
    group-work interventions with, 160–161
    human rights protection, 78–79
    macro issues affecting, 220–221

organizational support for, 179–180
resources and advocacy for, 239
stereotyping, 4
Strengthening Aging and Gerontological
    Education in Social Work Initiative, 17
strengths-based approaches
    to geriatric case management, 229–230
    resilience-enhancing models, 130
strengths-based assessment, 108–110
strengths-based human behavior theory, 2
stress, ecological perspective on, 82
structural lag, 166
subjective burden, 117
summative evaluation, 158
Supplemental Nutrition Assistance Program
    (SNAP), 209
support groups, 148–149
suprapersonal environments, 93
systems, defined, 205–206

T
Tallman, K., 105
Tax Code Provisions Related to Older
    Americans, 210
technology
    in social work practice, 18–19
    support groups and, 148–149
theories, critique of, 98–99
theory-based interviews, 108
throughput step, 166
time line, 86, 115
Tonnies, Ferdinand, 186
Toseland, R. W., 154
training, in empowerment evaluation
    technique, 178
transference issues, between client and case
    worker, 233
transgender. *See* lesbian, gay, bisexual, and
    transgender (LGBT) older adults
transportation
    in age-friendly communities, 197
    to group meetings, 144
    services provision and, 237
"Treatment of Older Adults Evidence-Based
    Practice Kit," 125

U
United Nations Declaration of Human Rights,
    67
"United Nations Principles for Older
    Persons," 71, 73–74
United Nations Programme on Ageing, 78
Universal Declaration of Human Rights
    core ideas, 68
    older adults and, 67
    and relationship to the U.S. Constitution,
        68–69
    social, economic, and environment rights
        defined in, 66
U.S. Constitution, 68–69
utilitarianism, 217

V
values
    defined, 26
    ethics and, 7–8
Villages, 170, 173, 198, 199–200
violation of rights, 125
violence, 124

W
Walsh, F., 132
Wandersman, A., 178
Weber, G., 33
well-being, 217
women, marginalization of, 8
workforce, aging of, 167
World Health Organization (WHO)
    Aging Friendly Cities and Communities
        initiative, 184
    establishment of, 75
    on healthy communities, 164–165
    on preparing for increase in older adult
        populations, 77

Y
Yanca, S. J., 198
Yeh, K., 59

Z
Zastrow, C., 140, 157